CW00545554

Swansea & Gower
in
Victorian & Edwardian
Times

VOLUME ONE

Swansea & Gower in Victorian & Edwardian Times

VOLUME ONE

by

Derek Draisey

Draisey Publishing

DRAISEY PUBLISHING
73 Conway Road
Penlan
Swansea SA5 7AU

First published in 2011 by Draisey Publishing

Copyright © Derek Draisey 2011

All rights reserved. No part of this publication
may be reproduced, stored in a retrieval system,
or transmitted, in any form or by any means,
electronic, mechanical, photocopying recording
or otherwise, without the prior permission,
in writing, of the publisher.

ISBN 978-0-9546544-5-0

Set in Minion Pro by Logaston Press, HR3 6QH
and printed in Great Britain by
Bell & Bain Ltd., Glasgow

To my grandson, Joshua

Contents

Acknowledgements

My sincere thanks to the staff at Swansea Central Reference Library, the Penlan Library, the West Glamorgan Archive Service, the Swansea Museum, the University of Wales, Swansea, and the South Wales Miners' Library for their ready assistance; their courteous and dependable response to enquiries and the location of documents and images is commendable. In particular I would like to thank Kim Collis (Archives), Marylin Jones and Gwilym Game (both of Swansea Library) and Jodi Jones (Penlan Library) for their unstinting contributions towards making this publication possible. Special thanks are also due to the Gower Society for their plan of a farmhouse at Rhosili, the Oystermouth Historical Association for images, the South Wales Police Museum for their response to enquires, the Fairyhill Restaurant and Parc le Breos House for information on their respective buildings, and to all those who kindly responded to calls, or gave their permission to take photographs of their property.

Images in this work have been kindly provided by the City and County of Swansea: Swansea Museum Collection (10) and by the Oystermouth Historical Association (3). Apart from photographs taken by myself, almost all other images (47 in all) have been provided by the West Glamorgan Archive Service, which also provided tithe and O.S. maps, as well as several illustrations from their book entitled *Thomas Rothwell – Views of Swansea*.

Special thanks to Ron Shoesmith for the commendable way he has presented this work for publication, and to Andy Johnson of Logaston Press, for his unstinting assistance with the cover, printing and various other aspects of this work. Last, but by no means least, my thanks to Ann, my partner and constant support.

Derek Draisey

PROLOGUE

The Lordship of Gower and Kilvey

Barely 18 years old, Victoria succeeded to the throne on 20 June 1837. She died on 22 January 1901, and during her 63½-year reign Britain experienced a tremendous growth in its population and its prosperity, the growth due to the Industrial Revolution and an enormous expansion in trade. There were technological advances as well, creating an odd mix in which, for example, the age-old use of the horse and horse-drawn transport vied with steam-powered engines and an ever-expanding railway network; while at sea, multi-sail windjammers contested with steam-powered, iron ships. Queen Victoria's reign was certainly an era of change, a time when the old order of a Conservative society, with its privileged hierarchy, gave way to Liberalism and a progressively more modern way of life, one in which prosperous middle-class professionals and entrepreneurs played a leading role in shaping Britain for its 20th-century destiny.

The winds of change had a tremendous impact on Victoria's realm, and nowhere more so than in South Wales where, in the old Medieval Lordship of Gower and Kilvey, the Tawe Valley was scarred by industrialisation beyond all recognition. At the same time the trade in refined metals at Swansea grew to the extent that the town became known as Copperopolis and, later, it vied with Llanelly for the title of Tinopolis; moreover, the port's overseas exports eclipsed those even of Bristol.

The Victorians of the Lordship of Gower and Kilvey saw the implementation of democratic and local government reforms. They also witnessed the creation of poor law unions, local boards of health, public-funded education, as well as hospitals, a police force and a fire service. Innovations such as these – and many more – may have stemmed from industrialisation, but with industrial growth came a yearning for religion,

Queen Victoria – born in 1819 and trained expressively to be Queen of the U.K. of Great Britain and Ireland, she was shielded from undesirable influences in the hope of moulding her character along moral, conservative lines, but after her succession to the throne she immediately displayed a love of gaiety and festivity, whilst politically she leaned towards liberalism. Under the influence of her husband, Albert of Saxe-Coberg-Gotha, whom she married in 1840, she became a staunch conservative. She gave birth to nine children. After Albert's death in 1861, Victoria entered a period of mourning from which she never really withdrew. In 1876 she was crowned Empress of India. Her reign was the longest in English history. She became a living symbol of the age.

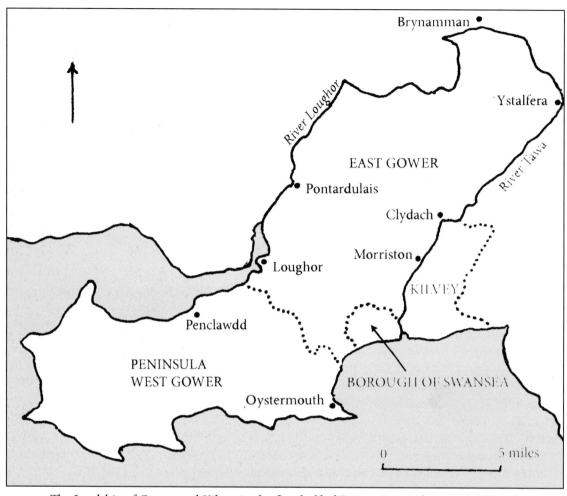

The Lordship of Gower and Kilvey in the first half of Queen Victoria's reign (1837-67), showing (1) the old pre-1835 Borough of Swansea, (2) Peninsula Gower, (3) East Gower and (4) the Lordship of Kilvey.

and it was the Nonconformist chapels that benefited most from the large numbers in search of spirituality.

The changes that took place in Swansea during the Victorian era were all too apparent, for not only did the town experience a tremendous expansion in its area, its housing and its public buildings, but it also saw the creation of several docks; moreover, the sheer volume of its maritime trade made the area closest to the waterfront a hive of commercial and industrial activity. Swansea was also in the forefront of political and local government reforms – but the changes that took place in other parts of the lordship were limited by comparison and they came late.

In the Tawe Valley and in the Lordship of Kilvey, for example, the population certainly increased as a result of migrant workers, giving rise to industrial villages in which workers and their families lived in close proximity to the ever-increasing number of collieries and metallurgical industries. Beginning with the Hafod on the west and St. Thomas on the east, these villages could be

2

found all the way up the Tawe Valley, as far as Ystalyfera (and beyond to Ystradgynlais and Abercraf). They also extended westwards along the River Twrch as far as Brynamman. Unlike Swansea, which was cosmopolitan in character, life in the industrial villages revolved mainly around work and the chapels. There were no theatres and no variety of shops; nor were there services such as mains sewage and a piped water supply.

There were similar pockets of industry with their attendant villages at Pontardulais, Penclawdd, Loughor, Fforestfach and elsewhere, and also places like Oystermouth, which benefited from oyster fishing, limestone quarrying, the Mumbles Railway (which brought in train-loads of day-trippers) and municipal reform – but in rural Peninsula Gower, and in the bleak uplands to the north of Swansea, the old world lingered longest.

Queen Victoria died on 22 January 1901, to be succeeded by her 59-year-old son, Edward, on the very day of her demise. During his 9¼-year reign as Edward VII, this once popular prince became an extremely popular king. Everything that may be regarded as Victorian reached its peak in Edward's reign, which also witnessed the growing strength of the Labour Party, the appearance of motor vehicles on the road, aeroplanes in the air and the prospect of pensions for those who had reached the end of their working life. Edward died on 6 May 1910, and within a few short years a whole way of life was shattered by the First World War, never to be revived when the guns fell silent – but the memory of the Victorian and Edwardian eras lingers on as a unique and colourful part of our heritage.

King Edward VII – born 1841, the eldest son of Albert and Victoria, he acquired the title Prince of Wales. In 1863 he married the Danish princess Alexandra. As his mother had by then retired from public life, it fell to Edward to perform the duties of royalty, with the result that he became much travelled and extremely popular. He became known as the Peacemaker; he introduced the Crown to all parts of the Empire, and the country profited from a marked degree of prestige abroad. He died aged 68 in May 1910.

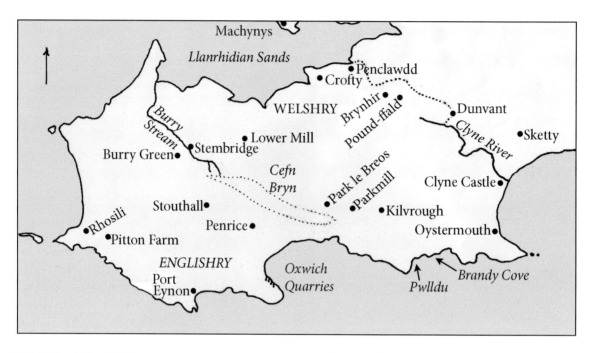

Machynys
Llanrhidian Sands
Penclawdd
Crofty
WELSHRY
Brynhir
Pound-ffald
Dunvant
Clyne River
Sketty
Burry Stream
Lower Mill
Burry Green
Stembridge
Cefn Bryn
Park le Breos
Parkmill
Clyne Castle
Stouthall
Kilvrough
Rhosili
Penrice
Oystermouth
Pitton Farm
ENGLISHRY
Oxwich Quarries
Brandy Cove
Port Eynon
Pwlldu

Above: *Places mentioned in the text relating to Peninsula / West Gower*

Left: *C.R.M. Talbot of Margam and Penrice (1803-90) – only son of Thomas Mansel Talbot. As lord of 13 manors, patron of six church livings and the biggest landowner in Glamorgan, C.R.M. was extremely rich, as well as being a cultured man with many talents. He was a collector and connoisseur of art and antiques, a lover of music, and had a keen interest in science, botany and photography. He was also keen on outdoor pursuits such as riding and shooting, often holding game-shoots on his Margam and Penrice estates.*

CHAPTER ONE

Peninsula Gower

Aristocratic Landowners

At the time of Victoria's coronation, Henry Somerset (1792-1853), 7th Duke of Beaufort, was Lord of Gower and Kilvey, a title that his forefathers had held for almost 350 years and which his descendants have continued to hold to the present day. During the Napoleonic Wars, Henry had served as an *aide-de-camp* to the Duke of Wellington; between 1813-32 he had been Tory MP for Monmouthshire. Throughout those early years, Henry had been renowned for his amorous escapades. Then, in 1835, he succeeded to his father's title and possessions, which he held for 18 years before dying of gout in 1853.

As Duke of Beaufort, Henry's main residence was at Badminton House in Gloucestershire, and only occasionally did he visit his Welsh lordship. The man responsible for safeguarding his interests in Gower and Kilvey was his agent who, prior to 1835, had been known as the Steward. It was the agent's responsibility to collect what was due to the Duke from his Gower and Kilvey estates, which included whatever was due from manorial rights in manors such as Pennard, Oystermouth and the southern half of Bishopston parish. The Duke also held a considerable amount of land in the eastern half of Peninsula Gower that was his personal property, from which he was entitled to rent from leases on land used for both agricultural and industrial purposes.

The Duke, however, was not the only aristocrat to hold land in Peninsula Gower. The Earl of Dunraven (in the Vale of Glamorgan) held several farms in the Burry Green area, amounting in total to around 160 acres; he also owned a few collieries in the vicinity of Swansea. The Earl of Dunraven was also lord of the tiny manor of Knelson, but the title had little to do with the ownership of land.

The Talbots of Margam and Penrice

Aristocrats, however, were not the only big landowners in Peninsula Gower. The local gentry were also landowners of note, the most notable of whom was Christopher Rice Mansel (C.R.M.) Talbot (1803-90) of Margam and Penrice. These two estates – Margam and Penrice – came into the possession of the Talbot family as a result of marriage, that of C.R.M.'s great-grandfather, John Ivory Talbot of Lacock Abbey, to Mary Mansel, to whom the estates had passed. C.R.M. inherited the estates when he became of age in 1824 – and they were large.

In 1873 the combined estate consisted of nearly 34,000 acres in the County of Glamorgan, which at the time provided C.R.M. with an annual rent of around £44,000. According to the tithe awards of the early 1840s, he held about 8,000 acres of enclosed land in the Gower Peninsula, and a great deal of common land as well. He was also lord of several manors: Oxwich, Penrice, Horton, Port Eynon, Nicholaston and Rhosili. C.R.M. had grown up at the family's principal seat, Penrice Castle, which his father had built between 1773 and 1779. Three years after succeeding to his inheritance C.R.M. commenced work on a new mansion at Margam, work that continued for a decade or more. Thereafter, Margam Castle became the family's principal residence, although Penrice continued in use as the census returns for 1841 record five servants in residence there.

Apart from being a wealthy landowner, C.R.M. was also a successful businessman and the creator of Port Talbot docks. His most profitable ventures were connected with railways, he being a major investor in the South Wales Railway, which in 1863 became the Great Western Railway. At the time of his death his railway investments were worth around £3 million. In political circles he was known as 'the wealthiest commoner'.

A committed Liberal, C.R.M. was elected MP for Glamorgan in 1830, and as such supported the Reform Bill of 1832, which transformed politics in both England and Wales. The Bill created new Parliamentary seats in that, formerly, there had been only one MP to represent Glamorganshire; now there were two. C.R.M. was re-elected to represent the 'senior' county constituency, which he

*Penrice Castle – a four-storey mansion (plus basement) that Thomas Mansel Talbot built in 1773-79. What is remarkable about this mansion is that most of the materials used in its construction came by sea to Oxwich, and were then hauled over the marshes along a track that had to be constantly repaired – for example, 400 tons of stone were delivered by this route in 1775; the following year 12 tons of slates. The mansion stood in extensive parkland, overlooked by the ruins of a medieval castle, which at the time served as an aviary.
There was an artificial lake and flower gardens nearby. The (lower) wing on the right was built by Emily Talbot in 1893-6. This wing was demolished in fairly recent times.*

Right: *Penrice Castle Gatehouse in 1854 – a folly described in 1798 as fictitious fragments of a modern ruin. The fictitious ruin is, of course, that which can now be seen from the South Gower Road, near the turn-off for Oxwich Bay.*

Below: *The* Lynx *at the South Dock – like many of the South Wales gentry, C.R.M. Talbot was a keen yachtsman, the owner of successive vessels in which he embarked on several trips to the Mediterranean. His most famous vessel was the* Lynx, *a paddle-steamer yacht with a crew of over 20, most of them Gower men. In 1869 the* Lynx *was the first vessel to pass through the newly-constructed Suez Canal.*

held for 53 years; thereafter he represented Mid-Glamorgan for approximately five years. He rarely spoke in the House of Commons, but his 60 years as an MP earned him the title of 'father of the House of Commons'.

C.R.M. had four children, one of whom, a son, died in 1878. When C.R.M. died in January 1890, the Margam and Penrice estates passed to his eldest daughter, Emily Charlotte (1840 – 1918), who was a spinster, aged 50 at the time. Emily has been described as a benevolent autocrat; this was no mean praise as most of the inhabitants in the western half of Peninsula Gower are likely to have been her tenants. She took a keen interest in local affairs, and would visit certain schools in a carriage drawn by two fine horses. In the autumn she resided for three months of the year at Penrice Castle, which she enlarged (1893-6). A prime example of her benevolence was her willingness to finance schooling in the parishes of Penrice, Oxwich and Port Eynon, thereby relieving her tenants of the burden of paying School Board rates.[1]

Emily died in 1918. The Margam and Penrice estates she bequeathed to her nephew and niece, the offspring of her younger sister, Bertha Isabella (d.1911) who had married John Fletcher of Soulton Hall, East Lothian. The nephew, Captain Andrew Talbot Fletcher, inherited the Margam estate, but in 1942 this was sold to D.M. (later Sir David) Evans-Bevan, owner of the Vale of Neath Brewery. The Penrice estate went to the niece, Evelyn Lady Blythswood, who married Archibald Douglas Campbell, 4th Baron Blythswood. Their daughter and heiress, Olive Douglas Campbell, inherited the Penrice estate, and she married the Hon Laurence Paul Metheun. In 1940 Olive changed her name to Olive Douglas Metheun-Campbell.

The Lucases of Stouthall

Another member of the Gower gentry was John Nicholas Lucas of Stouthall, otherwise referred to as 'the Colonel' due to his 40 years service in the Royal Glamorgan Militia. The Colonel's forefathers had been landowners since at least the 15th century. In his grandfather's day the Reynoldston part of the estate may have consisted of some 250 to 300 acres, with additional property further north. His grandfather had enlarged the family estate by marrying Hannah, sole heiress of the Nicholas estate of Garth, near Glais, but this was as nothing when compared with his father's acquisitions, the result of marriage to Catherine Powell, who had brought with her in marriage some 3,500 acres to the Lucas estate, the bulk of it in Carmarthenshire.

With this increased wealth the Colonel's parents had been able to build a new, three-storyed mansion at Stouthall. The Colonel took possession of the house on the death of his father in 1831. According to the census of 1841, he lived there with his second wife, his daughter, Mary Catherine

Left: *Stouthall, rear (southern) aspect – a three-storyed mansion built by John Lucas the Younger in 1787-90, complete with a secret door in the library shelves that enabled him – should he feel threatened – to pass from one room to another. John Lucas surrounded the house with 40 acres of parkland; he also built stables, devised a grotto, excavated an ice-house and erected the usual gentry 'folly', in his case a 'prehistoric' stone circle.*

Right: *Stouthall, front (northern) aspect – the small buildings on either side of the main entrance were offices added during the Second World War, when the house served as a hospital.*

(by his first wife), his unmarried sister, his wife's unmarried sister and five resident servants, and also five agricultural labourers. The Colonel appears to have been a retiring, unadventurous man – unlike his younger brother, Henry, who was quite the opposite.

On becoming of age in 1818, Henry had received a share of the family estate: from his father he had the Great House, Cheriton (which he dismantled) and Fairy Hill; from his mother he received part of her Carmarthenshire inheritance. Henry settled at Fairy Hill in the late 1820s, and it was there that his character first becomes apparent: outgoing and extravagant with a passion for breeding racehorses; he would often be seen exercising strings of horses over Cefn Bryn. Henry sold Fairy Hill to live the life of a country squire at his mother's old home, Taliaris, near Llandeilo. In c.1835 he appears to have built Uplands Villa. This house must have been impressive, but Henry's extravagant lifestyle and his losses in connection with horse racing were to cost him dearly. By the late 1840s he had to sell everything to pay off his debts. He then abandoned his wife and children.

In the meantime, the Colonel had come to terms with a problem. According to his father's will, the family estate was to pass to the heir of the eldest son; if the eldest son had no heir, then the estate was to pass to the heir of the younger son. The problem was that the eldest son – the Colonel – had only a daughter, whereas Henry had several children, some of them boys. If the estate passed

Left: *Fairy Hill, Reynoldston – the origin of this Georgian mansion is obscure, but in 1720 Richard Lucas brought his bride to this house, which was then known as Peartree. The name was changed to Fairy Hill by John Lucas in 1785. After John left to take up residence at Stouthall, Fairy Hill was leased several times, the most notable tenant being Lady Barham (1813-23), patron of no less than six Nonconformist chapels in Gower. After her Ladyship's death, Henry Lucas resided at Fairy Hill until he sold the property to finance his flamboyant lifestyle. In 1858 Starling Benson, a former mayor of Swansea, bought the mansion, which remained in the Benson family until its sale in 1922. After three more changes of ownership, Fairy Hill became the property of John and Midge Frayne, who did much to restore the house (which had become almost derelict) and converted it into a hotel. The present owners, Paul and Andrew, have kept up the good work, with the result that Fairy Hill is a now a stylish hotel and an award-winning restaurant; it is surrounded by 24 acres of peaceful parkland.*

Right: *Uplands Villa (1974) – built by Henry Lucas in c.1835, it stood a little to the west of what is now Cwmdonkin Drive. It is believed that the parkland that surrounded this house may have included part of what is now Cwmdonkin Park. The house later became Cleveland College and was demolished in 1980.*

to Henry's heir, then Henry – if he were a trustee during his eldest son's minority – might squander his son's inheritance.

No doubt legal advice was taken, and the upshot was that when the Colonel's daughter, Mary Catherine, married Edward Robert Wood in 1843, the Colonel took up residence at Brynfield, leaving his son-in-law to hang up his hat at Stouthall. The Colonel died at Brynfield in 1863. His son-in-law died in 1876; whereupon the Colonel's daughter, Mary Catherine Wood left Stouthall, accompanied by her four unmarried daughters. After that, Stouthall was let, usually in the summer months.

In 1870 the Lucas estate had been settled on Mary Wood's eldest daughter, Florentia, and she married William Crawshay of Cyfarthfa Castle. The couple never took up residence at Stouthall, and when Florentia died in 1919 the estate passed to her nephew (the son of one of her sisters). The following year Stouthall was sold by auction, along with a little over 1,000 acres, much of it bought by tenant farmers. The house became the property of the Morgan family and they rented it out as a school, a hospital, a maternity hospital, a convalescent home and, since 1974, it has been a field study centre for a London borough.

The Penrices of Kilvrough

Thomas Penrice (1789 – 1846) of Great Yarmouth was a captain the 16th Lancers when, in September 1819, he visited Swansea. It is possible that while he was in town someone passed remarks about his name, pointing out that there had been a Penrice family in Gower in times past, a family that had held sway over a great deal of land for at least 250 years; that is, until the mid-15th century when the property had passed by marriage to the Mansel family.

Two months after Thomas Penrice's arrival in Swansea, the mansion and 320-acre estate of Kilvrough were up for sale, the owner of which, Mary Dawkin (Madame de Choiseul by marriage)[2] was the last of a line that had held Kilvrough for over 250 years. The Dawkins' long association with Kilvrough may not have been of interest to Thomas Penrice, but it appears that he was interested in restoring his family connection with Gower. He bought Kilvrough in 1820, and then, over a period of time, he enlarged his estate to around 3,000 acres. In 1829 he became Major-commandant of

Left: *Kilvrough Manor 1870 – the service area at the rear of the mansion dates back to 1741, whereas the castellated extension seen here was built by William Dawkin prior to his death in 1774. In the south-eastern corner of the surrounding parkland there is a dingle in which stands a folly – a small round tower with ruinous battlements.*

the local militia, the Swansea and Fairwood Corps of Yeoman Cavalry. Two years later he led a detachment of 30 troopers to Merthyr where serious rioting had broken out. On the outskirts of the troubled town, he and his men were surrounded by 'a vast number of armed rioters' and disarmed. The incident led to the disbanding of the yeomanry a few months later.

According to the 1841 census, Thomas Penrice lived at Kilvrough with his nephew and five servants; there were also three agricultural labourers at Kilvrough Lodge. Thomas never married. When he died in 1846 his estate passed to his

Left: Thomas Penrice II of Kilvrough – second son of John Penrice of Great Yarmouth. When his uncle, Thomas Penrice I, died in 1846, he succeeded to Kilvrough manor; thereafter he was a well respected member of the Gower gentry, one who took an interest in both his tenants and his estate.

(Swansea Museum)

Park Mill c.1900 – note the absence of the wall that now adjoins the modern A4118. In the middle distance is Parkmill School, built in 1876 by Thomas Penrice II of Kilvrough, who also contributed to its upkeep. Beyond the school is the Gower Inn, built in 1824 by Thomas's uncle and predecessor, Major Thomas Penrice.

nephew, Thomas Penrice II (1820-97), second son of his elder brother. Thomas Penrice II was a far more colourful character, one who, in later years, was easily identified by his bushy, grey beard. In his 50 years as the squire of Kilvrough, Thomas II not only enlarged the estate to some 5,500 acres, he also made changes in both its management and its farming methods, so that it became one of the most productive estates in South Wales.[3]

Thomas II married Louisa Howman in 1852, by whom he had two daughters. In 1879 the eldest daughter, Louisa Jane, married Admiral Algernon McLennan Lyons, a naval officer with an impressive service record. In 1896 Thomas gave his consent for golf to be played on the burrows at Pennard, thereby establishing one of the earliest golf clubs in the lordship. The following year Thomas died; the estate passed to his eldest daughter and, by marriage, to her husband, Admiral Lyons. After the Admiral's death in 1908 the situation at Kilvrough deteriorated: crippling death duties and the First World War resulted in part of the estate being auctioned in 1919, and the remainder in 1920. The mansion is today owned by the Oxford Education Committee.

The Vivians of Clyne Castle

In 1790 Richard Phillips of Carmarthen bought 27 acres in Clyne Valley where he built a house called Woodlands. When Richard died in 1798 the property passed to a relative, and was then sold to Colonel (later General) George Warde, originally of Kent, an industrialist with coal interests on both sides of the Loughor estuary. George not only increased the estate to 330 acres, he rebuilt the house over a period of time to resemble a fortress, parts of which have remained virtually unchanged to the present day. This new residence he called Woodlands Castle. Ongoing costs relating to this house, coupled with his failing business interests, put George in debt, so much so that when he died in 1830, his son and heir could not afford to live at Woodlands Castle.

In 1834 the property was purchased by Jenkin Davies Berrington, a Swansea solicitor. Jenkin had married Charlotte, sister of Benjamin Hall of Llanover, a major industrialist and the MP after

William Graham Vivian (1827-1912) second son of John Henry Vivian, founder of the Hafod Copperworks. There is evidence to suggest that, had he taken control of the Hafod Works, Graham would have been an intolerant master. He was extremely rich, appears to have been something of a conservationist, and is said to have been eccentric, in part because he never owned a motor car nor had a telephone installed at his Clyne Castle residence, even though he could well afford both. He was a JP, sheriff of Glamorgan in 1868, and held responsible positions in several civil and commercial institutions. He was also on good terms with many of the highest dignitaries in the land, including King Edward VII.

Clyne Castle: part of this fine building was built as far back as 1800, when the approach drive was – and still is – via Mill Lane. What is seen here is mainly the work of Graham Vivian from 1860 onwards. Following the death of Admiral Algernon Walker-Heneage-Vivian in 1952, the Clyne estate was sold off in parcels. The castle and 76 acres of land were bought by the Swansea Borough Council. A few months later the castle was sold to the University Collage of Swansea, who converted it for use as a men's hall of residence, which they renamed Neuadd Gilbertson (Gilbertson's Hall) after the first president of the college, Frank Gilbertson. In 1954, the Swansea Borough Council opened to the public the remaining 52 acres of parkland, which they named Clyne Park. There is much in this beautifully kept park to remind visitors of the wealth and privileges of Graham Vivian.

whom Big Ben is named. Yet despite his wife's wealth and well-to-do connections, Jenkin found it difficult to maintain Woodlands Castle. So he demolished part of it containing 16 rooms. In 1857 the house passed to his son, Arthur, but he could not afford to live there. So the property was put up for sale.

In 1860 (or soon after) ownership of Woodlands Castle, along with 97 acres of surrounding land, passed into the hands of 33-year-old William Graham Vivian of Singleton Abbey, although he does not appear to have taken up residence there until *c.*1864. As a member of the Vivian family, Graham was a shareholder in Vivian & Sons, proprietors of the Hafod Copperworks. The day-to-day running of this huge copper-smelting concern was in the hands of Graham's elder brother, Henry Hussey, but Graham was, or was to become, a wealthy businessman in his own right. His huge investments in railways were extremely profitable, as were his investments in property in London and the south of England. At the time of his death in 1912, Graham's estate is said to have been worth £1½ million, about two-thirds of which had nothing to do with his share in Vivian & Sons.

During his 52-year ownership of the castle – which prior to 1870 he had renamed Clyne Castle – Graham made many alterations to it, extending it to the extent that he had in total more than 50 rooms at his disposal. Graham spoke several languages and travelled extensively, often returning with crates full of artistic treasures with which he adorned Clyne Castle, making it one of the most sumptuous residences in the land. The parkland surrounding the castle was also filled with exotic plants and trees from many parts of the world. Numerous dignitaries either visited or stayed at the castle, among them the Prince and Princess of Wales, the PM, Lord Palmerston, and many high-ranking aristocrats.

Graham made several purchases in the area surrounding Clyne Castle, including that of Clyne Farm, with the result that almost everyone between the Mayals and Blackpilll became his tenants, whereas in the village of Blackpill – which included property in Mill Lane as well as terraced houses along the Mumbles Road – the villagers were almost entirely dependant upon Graham for employment, either as servants or as estate workers: gardeners, woodmen, coachmen, masons, carpenters and game-keepers to look after the red deer that roamed in Clyne woods. In his later years Graham was the acknowledged 'Squire of Clyne', a title that may have prompted him to build, in 1907, Clyne Chapel of Ease, which is where he and his two successors were interred, and where he and his Anglican tenants worshipped.

Clyne Lodge – built in c.1860, it stands at the Mumbles Road entrance to Clyne Gardens. Clyne Chapel is on the opposite side of the lane.

At the time of his death in 1912, Graham's estate amounted to some 2,600 acres, which included property in both Gower and the south of England. He also owned a property at 7 Belgrave Square, in the then fashionable part of London. Graham never married, and his Clyne Castle estate plus his investments passed to his appointed successor, his unmarried sister, Dulcie Charlotte, who held it until her death in 1921, after which it passed to his nephew, Algernon Walker-Heneage, third son of his married sister, Henrietta. A distinguished admiral of First World War fame, Algernon, (who added Vivian to his surname in pursuance of a clause in Graham Vivian's will) held the estate until his death in 1952. Crippling death duties then led to the break up of the Clyne estate.

Park le Breos

This had once been a hunting preserve of the de Breos lords of Gower. It was dis-parked after their days, and according to a survey of 1650 Park le Breos consisted of around 500 acres 'divided into 3 partes which are farmed out', the farms being named as Longoaks, Park y Price (Park le Breos) and Llethrid. The woods, however, were protected by a tenancy agreement, which stipulated that the tenants were 'not to cutt down or tapp any oake, ash or elme'.

The estate of Park le Breos remained in the hands of the lords of Gower until the mid-19th century when – for reasons unknown – it appears to have been purchased by John Henry Vivian (1785-1855), managing-partner of the Hafod Copperworks. It was certainly part of a larger estate belonging to John Henry's eldest son and successor, Henry Hussey. In 1867 Henry Hussey had his estate valued in order to use it as security for a £25,000 loan. The estate included Park le Breos, Fairwood Lodge and Brinwhillach near Morriston. The valuation report stated that Park le Breos farm consisted of a house of 'moderate and first class character, being built of stone, [with a] slate roof'. The other farms – Longoaks and Llethrid – were in need of repair, but they

Park le Breos House – it is difficult to pinpoint exactly when and by whom this imposing residence was built. The house was certainly in existence by 1894-8. A house with similar proportions to the one seen here also appears on the 1877 O.S. map. It therefore seems likely that the property was built by Henry Hussey Vivian, possibly as a country retreat. In the time of Graham Vivian and Admiral Algernon Walker-Heneage-Vivian it was used as a hunting lodge in connection with the organized shoots that took place on the estate. The last shoot took place in the summer of 1938.
Following the death of Admiral Walker-Heneage-Vivian in 1952, the house was bought by Thomas and Gladys Edwards for use, initially, as a trekking centre. It is due to their dedication – and that of their present-day descendants – that the house has survived in such good order.
In more recent times the house was converted into a guest-house, one with a difference in that not only does it offer a wide range of amenities, but the house has retained its old-world charm; you sense it the moment you step inside the door. This is an ideal base from which visitors can explore the Gower Peninsula on foot, horseback, or by car.

nevertheless brought in rent, whereas the woods, which included 'thriving plantations of young oak', were valued at £6,000. It was stated that some wood was 'used as pit props or for making pyroligueous acid'.

In 1893 several royal commissioners conducted an inquiry into 'the conditions under which land in Wales and Monmouthshire is held'. The commissioners' remarks about Park le Breos farm suggest that it was a model farm at that time, one that Henry Hussey Vivian was evidently proud of. The farm was unique in that it used horse-drawn trams to convey food to its prize cattle, sheep, horses and pigs. Henry Hussey died in 1894 and his second son, John Aubrey, not only inherited Park le Breos, but apparently made use of it as his first residence. John Aubrey also had a survey carried out on the estate, one in which Park le Breos farm is described as a 'dwelling house and cottages in' his (John's) occupation, which included 'stables, coach-house and a garden'. After John died in 1898 the estate passed to his elder brother, Ernest Ambrose, and then to his uncle, Graham Vivian of Clyne Castle, who gifted it to his nephew and appointed heir, Admiral Algernon Walker-Heneage. In both Graham's day and the admiral's, Park le Breos was renowned for the organized shoots that were laid on for some of the highest dignitaries in the land.

After the admiral's death in 1952 the farms within the Park le Breos estate were sold, the woods went to the Forestry Commission and Park le Breos House, plus 70 acres, were bought by Thomas and Gladys Edwards for use, initially, as a trekking centre and for market gardening. The property has subsequently been converted into a guest-house and managed by the same family to the present day.

Fairwood Lodge

When Henry Hussey Vivian had his Gower estate surveyed in 1867, Fairwood Lodge was listed as one of the properties. There had been a Killay Lodge here, occupied by John Nicholas Lucas (the Colonel) until he took possession of his Stouthall inheritance in 1831. Soon after the Colonel's departure, Killay Lodge would appear to have been demolished, as it states in papers relating to Henry Hussey's survey that, prior to 1838, Mary Tottenham had built Fairwood Lodge on the same site. The survey describes Fairwood Lodge as a 'superior cottage with farm buildings adjoining'. What happened to the property after 1867 is difficult to establish. Presumably it remained a Vivian possession, which they leased until such time as it was earmarked as the site of Fairwood Hospital. The old lodge no longer exists.

Farmers

There were, of course, other great landowners in Peninsula Gower, such as Sir Digby Thomas Aubrey who, in 1843, held an 853-acre estate in the parish of Llanmadoc, but what the gentry families mentioned in the previous sections had in common was that they all resided in, or had close connections with, Peninsula Gower. They also appear to have been philanthropists, upholding the traditional roles of benevolent landlords and guardians of the poor. These gentry landlords employed agents to manage their estates. Between 1756 and 1887, for example, the Talbots employed members of the same family to manage their estates. These agents were responsible for the households at both Margam and Penrice, for paying wages, collecting rents and dealing with a host of other issues, including the keeping of accounts.

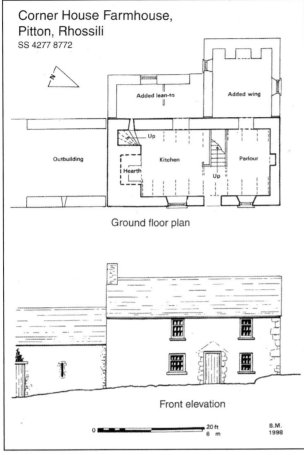

Corner House Farmhouse,
Pitton, Rhossili
SS 4277 8772

Added lean-to

Added wing

Outbuilding

Up

Kitchen

Parlour

Hearth

Up

Ground floor plan

Front elevation

0   20 ft
           6 m

B.M.
1998

Corner House Farmhouse, Pitton, Rhosili. A typical Gower farmhouse situated on the South Gower Road at a junction where the lane leads to Mewslade. The 18th century saw the introduction of what in Victorian times became typical Gower farmhouses and cottages, their design and appearance being peculiar to the area. Buildings such as these had a doorway placed centrally between two ground-floor windows; directly above there were two or three first-floor windows. What made these buildings distinctive was that one end had the appearance of an extension without windows. The reason for this odd appearance was that in one ground-floor room – the kitchen – there was an exceptionally large fireplace. The kitchen doubled as the main living room, whereas another room at the opposite end of the building served as a parlour (or an additional bedroom in the case of a cottage), having a much smaller fireplace on the end wall. Between the two ground-floor rooms was a staircase, which faced the front door. Some farmhouses had a back door, leading from the kitchen, but in their original state the type of building described here had no windows on the back wall. Sometimes additional buildings – such as stables or lean-tos – were added to the end walls, thereby taking advantage of the heat generated by the fires.

As with all early farms and cottages the walls were thick, and even at the close of Victoria's reign thatch was the predominant form of roofing. Coal from the Welshry was used for heating and cooking. Water was stored in a huge earthenware jar known as a cloam; it was kept in the porch or near the front door. Note

what appears to be a windowless extension on the southern end (left-hand side) of the building. Note also that the parlour chimney at the opposite end of the building has been removed.

(Plan by kind permission of Bernard Morris from *Old Gower Farmhouses and their Families* published by the Gower Society)

A ramshackle house, Parkmill, 1865

Lesser gentry, whose wealth was not dependent on the ownership of land, were to be found at Fairy Hill, Brynfield and Fairwood Lodge. There were also many farmers who managed their own properties, but the majority of agricultural land – some 90% of it – was held by leaseholders, tenants of the big land-owning aristocratic and gentry families. These tenant farmers invariably held their farms on annual tenancies. Those with the smaller holdings often had to struggle to make a living, the more so from 1870 onwards, when the soil suffered from exceptionally cold and wet weather, the animals from disease such as liver rot, the farms from a shortage of labour, and the farming industry from competition as more and more cheap foodstuffs came from outside the lordship.

Farm Labourers

In an age in which everything had to be done by hand, or with the aid of horses, farmers could not manage their farms without labourers to do much of the heavy work for them. In Peninsula Gower labourers were far more numerous than farmers, and yet the evidence concerning a labourer's lot is relatively sparse. Even their wages are difficult to determine, in part because wages varied according to the means of the employer. The Penrice and Margam estate papers, for example, record payments in 1825 to one William Morgan that amount to 12s. (60p. in today's currency) for a six-day working week. It may be presumed that the wages paid by struggling tenant farmers was considerably less – less than roughly 8s. (40p.) a week, which is what William Morgan earned prior to his massive 1825 pay rise.[4]

In the latter part of Victoria's reign, the situation differs in that extensive information on what life was like for farm labourers can be found in a report by a Royal Commission, one that inquired 'into the conditions and circumstances under which land in Wales and Monmouthshire is held, occupied and cultivated'. The commissioners were anxious to interview farm labourers, although they knew the chances of one appearing before them were remote. Yet when the commissioners met at the King Arthur on 26 May 1893 they were surprised to find that a labourer had presented himself at the hotel to answer their questions. The man was, in fact, the only one of his class in South Wales to do so. His name was David Williams; he was of Burry Green, formerly of Cheriton.

When asked about the nature of his work, David said he could plough, thatch, plant hedges – in short he could attend to 'anything on the farm'. The one thing he could not do was milk a cow because, as he said, 'it is not a common thing in Gower for a man to milk'. He would not divulge what he earned, but stated that the usual farm labourer's weekly wage was 'from 9s. (45p.) to 10s. for men on the employer's finding and 15s. on their own finding'.

As to accommodation, David stated that some labourers' cottages were in good repair, others were not, and the rent ranged from £2 to as much as £7 per annum. At Cheriton he had lived in a cottage which, he maintained, 'many of our farmers or our

David Williams's Burry Green cottage – originally a two up, two down, the cottage was renovated in the 1970s and an extension added to the rear. The interior still has some of its original features, making it one of Gower's little-known historical gems.

employers … would not like to put their animals in'. The roof had leaked, the windows were small; it had consisted of two rooms, one up and one down, the downstairs room having an earthen floor and an open grate, the fuel being coal. In these cramped conditions he had lived for two years with his wife and three young children, a situation made worse when one or other of his two eldest daughters (who were both out in service) were ill and had to come home. The only good thing about the property was that the rent had been only £2 per annum and the garden had amounted to over a quarter of an acre.

David maintained that his situation had since improved in that, for the last nine years, he had worked for a Mrs. Gordon of Tyle Farm, Burry Green, a tenant farmer of the Penrice estate. Not only did he now work for a good employer, but he lived in a two-bedroomed cottage (which still exists). He still worked from 6 a.m. to 6 p.m. in winter and summer, with time off for breakfast and dinner, but he stated that the labourer's lot had definitely improved over the past 20 years due, in his opinion, to a dramatic fall in the price of bread and the fact that food was generally cheaper. He and his family lived on plenty of potatoes and bacon; meat was a Sunday treat. They drank a great deal of tea. As to milk, the commissioners were horrified to hear him declare that he and others of his class rarely made use of it.

On a more general note, David maintained that most labourers could barely make ends meet. Some kept poultry or bees and grew their own vegetables, while he himself kept a pig. When asked about the drift of farm labourers to the collieries and to the towns, David replied that many had gone in the past, but fewer did so in recent years because colliers' wages were not much better than those of farm labourers.

If David had any complaints, it was that (1) not many employers provided free beer at harvest time, and (2) he deplored the practice whereby landowners let cottages to their tenant farmers who, in turn, sub-let the cottages to farm labourers. In David's opinion the landowners should be the ones to let; that way, if a labourer lost his employment with a tenant farmer, he would not lose his cottage as well; moreover, the landowner would be more likely to keep the cottage in a good repair.

Several farmers who were present agreed with much of what David had said, but tenant farmers, they pointed out, were suffering as a result of cheaper foodstuffs being shipped in from abroad, as a result of which many farmers were worse off than the labourers they employed. Interestingly, the farmers made reference to labourers who lived on their farms, how they fed them with bread and cheese for breakfast, bacon and potatoes for dinner, and often provided them with soup in the evening. Coffee, they said, was more frequently drunk than tea.

Domestic Service

Domestic servant c.1880 – few domestics in Peninsula Gower would have been issued clothes such as these – which were a mark of servitude. Most domestics would have carried out their duties in whatever clothes their parents had given them, or what they made themselves.

Women were also employed as agricultural labourers, as evidenced by the census returns from 1841 onwards. Many were employed as dairymaids, but the vast majority of working women – about 50% of them – were in service, residing in the homes of farmers, clergymen and others of moderate means, or, if they were lucky, in a gentry household where they were likely to receive better treatment and accommodation. Information on domestic servants in Peninsula Gower is, unfortunately, difficult to find, but in other parts of rural Wales domestic service was regarded as a degrading form of employment.

Forced to leave home rather than be a burden to their parents, girls often found employment in service by word of mouth, but in many parts of Wales women of all ages went to local hiring fairs – which were held twice a year – where they lined up on either side of a highway or byway to be scrutinized by those in need of servants. In a novel published in 1860[5] the character, Huw Huws, described what went on at a fair in no uncertain terms, saying he 'could see a line of girls of all ages … hard work had deformed their bodies, bent their shoulders, wrinkled their hands … men and women walked around this gathering with a critical look of slave purchasers, questioning them in such a way as to show they had … nothing to expect bar hard, physical labour … "If reform is needed in the case of the slaves in America", said Huw Huws to himself, "it is certainly needed in the case of the women of rural Wales".

What lay in store for these unfortunate women was that, in return for a 12-hour day, usually

20

with only one day off a month, they received full board and a wage of perhaps £3 a year. No doubt many employers were kindly, but talking down to servants and robbing them of their dignity would have been common; moreover, there are recorded instances in which domestics were beaten and the feeble-minded deprived of their wages. Even in wealthy households, domestics might not be paid for years, as happened at Fairy Hill where, in 1855, it was said 'servants not settled with for ten years'. It is hardly surprising, therefore, that domestics frequently moved on in the hope of finding more tolerable employment elsewhere. However, before taking up service they entered into a verbal contract with their employers that was legally binding. If they then 'deserted their service', they risked one to three months imprisonment. Similar rules applied to seasonal farm labourers.

For many women, marriage was a means of escape from such a poorly-paid, often lonely occupation, although even then poverty and drudgery remained their inescapable shadow, with frequent pregnancies adding to their never-ending workload. However – as shall be seen – many women in Peninsula Gower engaged in other forms of employment, which, although physically demanding and sometimes dangerous, were preferable to service because they could earn without leaving home to be subservient to someone outside the family circle.

The Agriculture Divide

Peninsula Gower may be divided into two parts according the fertility of the soil. The dividing line between the two parts extended from Oystermouth to Llanrhidian. South and west of the divide the soil overlays Carboniferous Limestone for the most part, much of it freely drained and,

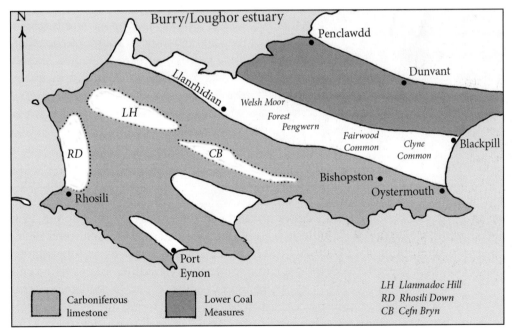

The agricultural divide in Peninsula Gower – the band of millstone grit between the carboniferous limestone areas and lower coal measures also served as a cultural divide in Victorian times between Englishry and Welshry.

therefore, ideal for both cultivation and rearing livestock. Most of the farms here were of the 'mixed' variety, rarely large, but having the advantage of common grazing rights on the poorer soils of Cefn Bryn, Rhosili Down and Llanmadoc Hill. Exceptions were to be found in the coastal area between Rhosili and Port Eynon, where the fertility of the soil combined with relatively frost-free conditions to encourage predominantly arable farming. In the parish of Bishopston the picture is somewhat different in that its close proximity to Swansea had encouraged a number of small farms to concentrate on growing fresh vegetables for an ever-increasing urban population.

North of the divide were the commons of Clyne, Fairwood, Pengwern and Forest, and also Welsh Moor, which overlay Millstone Grit, and which were suitable only for rough grazing. Beyond that lay the wet and woody ground of the Coal Measures, suitable mainly for rearing livestock and growing oats.

With the exception of horticulture in the Bishopston area, the farming pattern outlined above had probably been in existence for centuries with the soil dictating the terms. It was said, however, that agriculture in Gower was still quite primitive at the beginning of the 19th century. Oxen, for example, were still used to draw wooden ploughs, but farming methods did improve, despite depressions and outbreaks of disease among livestock.

The Cultural Divide

The agricultural divide also served as a boundary between two cultural groups. To the south and west of the divide lay the Englishry, where English Law and the English language had prevailed for centuries. In Victorian times it was believed that many of the people here were 'the successors of a colony of Flemings', originating from what is now Holland, but the records provide no evidence in support of such a claim. The privileged minority who originally held the manorial rights within the various manors were by and large French, or of French origin. The peasants, on the other hand – those who worked hard to earn a living as small-time farmers, labourers and village craftsmen – were neither French nor Flemings in origin. If language is anything to go by, they came from the West Country, from Somerset and North Devon. It was claimed that these peasants rarely intermarried with the Welsh; some commentators went so far as to say they mistrusted, even hated their Welsh neighbours. So where exactly did their Welsh neighbours live?

The answer is twofold. On the other side of the agricultural divide lay the Welshry, where Welsh was the mother tongue, and where medieval Welsh Law had probably prevailed until the mid-16th century. At the beginning of Victoria's reign, the people here were regarded as bilingual; some may have been monoglot Welsh. That Welsh was the first language for many in these parts is borne out by the fact that, in 1846-7, lessons in three Sunday schools in this area were in Welsh, and four others were bilingual. Coal mining – and to a lesser extent the metallurgical industry at Penclawdd – encouraged migrant workers to settle in the Welshry. Prior to, and during the early part of Victoria's reign, the majority of these migrant workers were Welsh-speaking; they came from Carmarthenshire and from other Welsh-speaking areas in South Wales. In the closing decades of the 19th century an increasing number of English-speaking workers were drawn to the area, many of them from English Gower, or from the West of England, Cornwall in particular. This influx of English-speaking workers contributed to the decline of the Welsh language in the Welshry.

That said, there were many within the Englishry who bore identifiable Welsh surnames, such as Williams (meaning *William's son*) or Beynon (from *ab Eynon*, meaning *son of Einion*). These people were obviously of Welsh origin; they were by and large the successors of the native

Welsh who had occupied the land before the arrival of West Country settlers. There were certainly Welshmen living in the Englishry as far back as the 14th century, as the records testify, but in Victorian times most of these people spoke no Welsh; they spoke the language of the Englishry.

The language – or rather the English dialect – that prevailed within the Englishry had been brought there by settlers from North Devon and Somerset probably in the 12th century, but centuries of isolation had resulted in a dialect that was peculiar to Gower – peculiar in that many of the words used had fallen out of use in the West Country, while other words were a corruption of Welsh. There would have been nothing unusual for anyone speaking the Gower dialect to have had an English surname such as Gamman or Rowe; nor would it have been odd for anyone with a Welsh surname to speak in exactly the same way. Evidently there had been a fusion of cultures within the Englishry. This fusion is evident in Welsh place-names, in dedications to Welsh saints, in festivities such as the Mapsant, and in marriage customs.

When couples married they had a choice of wedding ceremonies, depending on what they could afford, ranging from a simple civil marriage in a registry office (introduced in 1836) to something as extravagant as a gentry wedding, involving horse-drawn carriages, a sumptuous wedding breakfast for a restricted group of guests and a grand dinner for the locals. Bidding (known locally as *beading*) weddings were no doubt popular among the peasantry; they were certainly popular in Welsh districts throughout Wales, and yet the last recorded bidding wedding to take place in the peninsula was at Llandewi – in English Gower – on 6 February 1906. Both bride and groom had English names.

The folk-singer, Phil Tanner of *Llangenny* (Llangennith) had been a bidder. As such it often fell to him to bid everyone in the neighbourhood to a wedding. And they would come, bringing with them gifts and money that would enable the happy couple to set up home. After a church ceremony, Phil would head the procession, playing his fiddle, and at the bride's home he would not only entertain, but he took on the role of *maître d'*.

The Welsh Costume

There is no evidence that, in Victorian times, working men in the Lordship of Gower and Kilvey wore clothes that were significantly different from what was worn by others of their class throughout England and Wales, corduroy trousers and flannel shirts being more or less universal. There is, however, some evidence that men in rural areas were inclined to be a little outdated in their attire. For example, in 1861 two travellers[6] recorded what they observed about people on their way to Swansea Market. 'The men [they wrote] wear low-crowned hats, and are for the most part clothed in coats and vests of deep blue cloth, homespun and with brass buttons, have knee-breeches of corduroy, and [are] very partial to showy silk neckcloths'. No mention is made of footwear, but it can be assumed the men wore clogs.

The majority of Gower women wore clothes that were not only peculiar to Wales, they were also distinctive to the locality in which they lived. In 1851, for example, it was stated that women within the Englishry wore 'what was called a whittle, made of fine wool, and dyed scarlet; it is nearly a yard square, with a fringe at [the] bottom called ddrums. It is thrown across the shoulders, and fastened with a pin or brooch'. Scarlet, incidentally, was a dye extracted from cockles and was, therefore, a colour favoured by women in the coastal areas of South Wales. The whittle was also favoured by South Walian women; it provided a unique way of carrying a child, at the same time leaving the right arm free to attend to chores.

Women in local 'Costume'.

Top left: *A Langland woman selling laverbread.*   Top centre: *A Sketty woman selling gooseberries.*
Top Right: *A Swansea woman with apples for sale.*   Bottom left: *A Penclawdd cockle-woman, her tub empty.*
Bottom right: *A Gower milkmaid in traditional dress – milking was women's work; it was not a common thing in Gower for a man to milk.*

Far more detailed information is available with regard to the women of Penclawdd, who lived within the Welshry and who attracted the attention of commentators from far and wide. However, to obtain a clear picture of what these commentators said, it is necessary to consider what Gower women wore, both in the Englishry and the Welshry, starting from the feet upwards.

The majority of Gower women in Victorian times went about their business barefooted. And to keep their legs warm they wore sole-less woollen stockings, often with loops that were put over their big toes to prevent the stocking from rising above their ankles. The stockings were concealed to some extent by a long flannel petticoat, the top of half of which was usually hidden by an upper garment variously termed a dress, jacket, blouse or bedgown (*betgwn*). Shawls varied in size from the whittle referred to above, to something as small as a 'turnover'.

Bonnets with frills (*goffers*) were popular at the beginning of Victoria's reign, but by the end of the century they were worn only by older women, the younger ones having abandoned them. Tall beaver hats were rare; what was universally worn in Gower was a black or yellow Welsh straw hat, the crown flat, the brim wider at the front than at the back. In windy weather the straw hat could be held in place by a strip of cloth tied under the chin. The Welsh hat was practical in that women on both sides of the divide carried heavy burdens on their heads, using a wad of cloth known as a *dorch*, which cushioned the weight of pitchers, pails and baskets.

In her *Glimpses of Welsh Life and Character*, published in 1893, Marie Trevelyan maintained that cocklewomen wore

> short [bed] gowns of red and black flannel, which are turned up in front and pinned close under the waist at the back … [they] display neat short petticoats of Welsh flannel [which were invariably scarlet or crimson in colour]; aprons in front. On their heads they wear small Welsh hats, suitable for bearing the weight of the cockle pails. A thick pad, known as a dorch, protects both the hat and the head from heavy pails. They come slightly forward over the forehead and receded to the back of the head where they are turned up and curved.

Marie Trevelyan also referred to 'aprons of Welsh flannel, which are large and comfortable [which invariably had a checked pattern]'. She also mentioned 'shawls called turnovers, folded cornerwise and pinned rather low under the chin'.

Generally speaking, there was little difference in the costumes worn by women on both sides of the cultural divide, except perhaps in the choice of colours and patterns. These costumes continued to be worn throughout Victoria's reign, but by 1893 Marie Trevelyan maintained that 'Welsh flannel dresses [bedgowns] are still much worn, though they are being rapidly superseded by woollen and cotton fabrics of English manufacture'. Yet despite what Marie said, the costume lingered in some areas for many years to come, particularly in Penclawdd where the women were no doubt influenced by their fame and the sale of cockles.

Prodigious Talkers

The two travellers[6] referred to above had something personal to say with regard to their observations. 'The Welsh are', they said, 'among themselves and in their own tongue, prodigious talkers. Here, on the road, even if you are familiar with the language, you would have very great difficulty in making out what is said, for the conversation is so animated, and so many speak at once, that in the hum of voices the connection of the discourse is lost'.

Village Craftsmen

Farming was not the only occupation available to Gowerians. The farming industry and everyday living could not have functioned without the services provided by village craftsmen. The folk-singer, Phil Tanner (d.1921) could remember blacksmith shops in most of the parishes of West Gower, the blacksmiths wearing their customary aprons of sheepskin, the fleece closest to their bodies. He could recall wheelwrights, shopkeepers and joiners who not only made the coffins, but doubled as undertakers as well; also butchers who, in late Victorian times, took their meat by trap to Swansea Market, and stayed there until long after midnight when all their meat had been sold.

Mills

Lower Mill, Llanrhidian still stands, but in a dilapidated state; behind it is a millpond. The earliest reference to this mill is 1375. The one seen here is a rebuild, which according to a date plaque had been undertaken in 1803 for William Evans; it continued to function until c.1850, after which the records are silent. Lower Mill is worth a visit as the narrow lanes in this part of the Llanrhidian provide insights into what the village may have been like in the 19th century.

A total of 23 water-powered mills are known to have been active in Peninsula Gower during Victoria's reign, though not all of them at the same time. Nineteen were grist (corn-grinding) mills, one of which (Stembridge) was later converted into a woollen mill. The mills were for the most part owned by the big landowners and leased to millers who, after paying rent, expected to make a profit from what they charged for their services. All the mills were situated close to a stream, from which water was channelled into a mill pond, or leet, to ensure an adequate depth of water to activate a water wheel, which in turn got the mill-stones working.

There have been five woollen mills in the peninsula in the period covered by this work, all of them in the northern part of the Englishry. These mills were all family businesses, and four of them were worked at various times by members of the Tanner family. The largest mill was Stembridge, situated on the Burry Stream at Grid Reference 407 920. Stembridge had been a grist mill until the 1880s. In 1899 Isaac Tanner took charge of it and built a two-storey factory alongside it. In this factory Isaac placed his loom, as well as equipment for carding, spinning and dyeing. For 25 years the factory made cloth for suits, overcoats and ladies wear; also shawls and blankets.

Park Mill in 1865 – the best-known grist mill is Park Mill, one of the oldest in Gower, the earliest reference to it being 1428. The two buildings seen here are now part of the Gower Heritage Centre, complete with leet, waterwheel and millstones. It is well worth a visit.

Park Mill 1900-20 – the repeal of the Corn Laws in 1842 led to the closure of many grist mills in Victorian times. Those that continued to function in the 20th century often owed their survival to enterprising mill owners, who turned to milling animal feed, or converted to sawing timber. Park Mill became a grist-cum-sawmill in the mid-19th century, and continued as such until fairly recently, being sold in 1989.

By 1901 only seven grist and three woollen mills were still functioning. The defunct grist mills had suffered as a result of the agricultural depression, which had been brought about by cheap, foreign grain shipped into Swansea. The loss of two woollen mills, on the other hand, had nothing to do with the depression – they had both belonged to the Tanner family in the years before they built their enlarged factory at Stembridge. Perhaps the Tanners' good fortune had something to do with a trend whereby people preferred to buy factory-produced woollens rather than make their woollies at home.

Laverbread

Today laverbread is associated with cockles, but in times past it was produced by peasants on the south side of Peninsula Gower. The reason for the southerly location is that the purplish laver weed from which it is made is to be found mainly on limestone rocks at low tide, being most abundant in autumn. Transforming the streamers into laverbread requires repeated washes to remove sand and grit, boiling the streamers for several hours until they become a sticky, blackish pulp, then chopping the pulp before finally binding it with oatmeal.

How far back the weed has been harvested is unknown, but it would appear to have been processed by peasants in the 18th century. Once the South Gower Road had been improved by the Swansea Turnpike trust it became easier for peasant women to take their produce to Swansea Market. In the late 19th century its commercial potential led to the establishment of family laverbread 'factories', such as the one recorded at Newton, Oystermouth, in 1881. Today little, if any, laverbread comes from Gower, the weed now being harvested in coastal areas between Anglesey and Scotland. Fried in bacon fat and served with cockles – you will either love it or loathe it.

Oyster Fishing

Oyster fishing along the South Gower coast probably dates back over 2,000 years, as oyster shells have been found at several prehistoric sites within the lordship. An oyster-fishing industry must have been well established by the 17th century because, in 1684, it was said that 'Oystermouth could boast the best beds of oysters in Britain'. Some 220 years later it becomes apparent there were two oyster-fishing fleets, one at Oystermouth, the other at Port Eynon (*Partennan* in the Gower dialect). The fishing vessels used at that time were heavy rowing boats with single sails. Women often launched and rowed these boats, leaving the men on each vessel to concentrate on working a heavy dredge, one that was towed and comprised mainly of a metre-long iron blade (*sword*) for scraping the seabed. Attached to the blade was a net for catching oysters disturbed by the dredging.

More will be said of the Oystermouth fleet in a subsequent publication. As to Port Eynon, it was stated in 1851 that the village was 'celebrated far and wide for its fine oysters and lobsters'.

An oyster-dredging skiff in sail – in the 1850s rowing boats were superseded by decked cutters, which the locals called skiffs. These skiffs could be up to 40 foot in length; they each had a single 40-foot mast, carrying four triangular sails. The advantages of these crafts were that (1) they did away with rowing and (2) they could tow two dredges. They also required a smaller crew of three at Oystermouth, four at Port Eynon.

The oyster bed worked by the Port Eynon fishermen was known as *Bantam*, or *Bantum*. It was situated on the seaward side of the notorious Helwick Shoal – a lengthy, underwater sandbank stretching westwards from Port Eynon Point. As dredging was undertaken mainly during the winter months, the fishermen met at dawn to decide by majority vote whether it would be calm enough to dredge that day, a custom known as 'making almanacks'. Then the fishermen would be away, sailing towards Rhosili until such time as they turned around and dredged the *Bantam* bed. Navigation to avoid known hazards was achieved by observing various landmarks. When the fleet returned to Port Eynon, each crew placed their catch in their own 'perch' – an underwater area marked out by stones – where successive catches would remain until they were taken to Swansea for dispatch to big cities such as Bristol and Liverpool. If the oysters were small, they would be placed further out in stone-marked areas called 'plantations' where they were left to grow.

The fishermen came not only from Port Eynon, but from neighbouring parishes as well. Theirs was a hard and dangerous occupation. The weather might turn from fair to foul; worse, they might become shrouded in thick fog. It was said in situations such as these the church bells would be rung, and lamps placed in the windows of cottages on the quay. Even so, all told nine fishermen are known to have lost their lives in four separate instances over a period of about 70 years.

In the 1860s there were repeated complaints about the dwindling number of oysters. Consequently, the fleet became progressively smaller until, in 1879, the last catch of oysters was landed on the quay. There is little to remind us of Port Eynon's involvement in oyster dredging, except the quay which the fishermen made use of – but for those with a sharp eye the stones that marked out the 'perches' are still discernible at low tide from Salthouse. There is also the shipwright's workshop that stood on the quay, now someone's home. There is, however, a more obvious reminder of the past, one that had a close connection with the oyster fishermen. The oyster season is often said to have been from September to May, but the fishermen were most active in December, January and February. Outside that period most fishermen found employment in another industry, one that had connections with the sea and has left its mark all over the high ground of Port Eynon Point.

Limestone Quarrying

Patches of limestone rubble are the tell-tale signs of limestone quarrying. They can be found all along the south coast, from Oystermouth to Rhosili, and to a lesser extent on the north-west coast as well – anywhere in fact where limestone outcrops near a sandy foreshore from which it was shipped to either Swansea or North Devon. Limestone quarrying also took place in less accessible places for local consumption, the evidence being ruinous kilns where limestone was once calcined (burnt) to a powder for fertilizing fields and for whitewashing buildings.

How far back limestone quarrying goes is unknown, but in a survey of 1650 there is a reference to the tenants of Pennard having the right to 'all manner of quarries and stones, a right which they had enjoyed since time out of mind'. During Victoria's reign the three most important limestone ports were Oxwich, Pwlldu and Oystermouth. At Oxwich the quarries were situated on the north side of Oxwich Point, just beyond Oxwich Church. Steps take walkers on a detour around the quarries that are now concealed by trees, hidden reminders of a once-thriving industry, one in which limestone was taken to the beach and loaded onto ships. A description of how that was achieved is to be found in Walter Davies's *General View of the Agriculture and Domestic Economy of South Wales*, published in 1814. The information in this publication was provided by the Revd. John

Collins who, as rector of Oxwich, would have witnessed the local quarrymen in action; he wrote:

> A great trade is carried on along the coast of Gower … several hundred cargoes being shipped off for the coast of Devon … during the summer. The vessels employed in this trade are from thirty to eighty tons burden. The people of the country get a good livelihood by this means; the men dig the stones both winter and summer, and as the vessels trade only in summer, they get together several cargoes by the commencement of the trade; the men break the stones, after blasting the rock, to a size easy to be lifted up; the women then, having a horse, and a little staked car made for the purpose, convey the stones to the shipping place within low-water mark; and at high water the vessels are moored alongside the heaps, which are known by poles being fixed in them, and there wait till the tide begins to ebb, when they are thrown into the vessels (by means of a temporary stage) by men and women, who receive a good hire from the captains, with an allowance for beer. The stones are sold by the quarrymen at the rate of 1s. (5d.) per ton, or so much the cargo ….

Oxwich Quarries – part of a painting dated c.1780, showing two ships near the quarries on the headland at Oxwich. Once the tide receded, ships such as these would settle on the sand and be loaded with between 30 and 80 tons of limestone. The white building is the old rectory, which had disappeared by the time of Victoria's coronation; to the right, almost hidden by trees, is Oxwich Church. On the far right and barely discernable is the new rectory, now the Oxwich Bay Hotel.

(West Glamorgan Archive Service)

As stated above, the vessels came only in summer, and did so rather than risk winter storms. Quarrying, however, went on all year round as there was no oyster fishing at Oxwich. The quarrymen, therefore, made use of the winter to stockpile the results of their work on the beach, the stones piled into elongated heaps, roughly the length of a ship. The 'staked cars' used by the women were horse-drawn sledges, comprising mainly of two long poles. When it came to loading ships the women raised the stones to the men on the 'temporary stages', and the men threw the stones into the ships. It has to be said those Oxwich women must have been as hardy as the men, and no doubt drank as heartily when a ship's captain provided an 'allowance for beer'.

At the beginning of Victoria's reign the ships used in the limestone trade were by no means insignificant, but two-masted pollaccas, each with a crew of three men and a boy. The pollaccas were gradually superseded by fast schooners, each of which could make several trips a week, so that as many as 30 vessels might be seen in Oxwich Bay on a fine day, either loading or waiting to load. The Limestone shipped from Oxwich would have been around 10,000 tons in 1861. It is, therefore, surprising to find that, according to the census taken that same year, there were only 13 quarrymen in the parish – five of them members of the Grove family – while three others saw themselves as limestone diggers.

At Pwlldu (*pooldy* in the Gower dialect) the evidence for quarrying and dispatch by sea is all too obvious. Near the foreshore there are the huge mounds of stone that have been rubbed smooth by the action of the sea. The quarries are not so obvious, but on the open headland to the west are the slides, which the quarrymen used to convey large stones to the beach. The slides are close together; they have the appearance of huge furrows. Not so obvious are the private residences of Beaufort House and Ship Cottage. These residences were once public houses named the Beaufort Arms and the Ship Inn respectively. There were apparently three other public houses in the lower valley. A total of five inns in such a remote place is testimony to the tremendous thirst of the quarrymen and their wives.

Pwlldu – on the headland to the far left are the furrows used by quarrymen to convey limestone to the beach. The quarries are above and to the right of the furrows.
The whitish strip beyond the man is a ridge of limestone pebbles;
they are said to amount to 250,000 tons,[7] equivalent to upwards of 3,000 eighty-ton shiploads.
The stones are probably waste, being too small for sale to the ship captains who beached here.

So why then was so much limestone quarried in Gower? The answer is that limestone had many uses. It could be burnt (calcined) to become a powdery substance for controlling the acidity in fields, both arable and pasture, something that had to be done repeatedly as lime would be washed away by heavy rain. The peasants made use of lime to whitewash their homes; builders used it to make mortar. There was also a big demand for limestone in the heavily industrialized Lower Swansea Valley, and in Victorian times it was used for road making and repair. However, at Oxwich and Pwlldu the limestone was shipped to North Devon where it was burnt in kilns for farming purposes. The trade at both these ports was badly affected by the agricultural depression of 1879-96. By the end of Victoria's reign limestone quarrying at these ports had ceased.

Lime kilns

Gower farmers also burnt lime, and did so in kilns on their property; hence the reason why the remains of small kilns are found in remote places that have little or no contact with the sea. Larger and better-built kilns were sited beside roads (as is the one near Kilvrough) which suggest they produced lime for sale. A total of around 150 kiln sites have been located in the peninsula, almost all of them in the Englishry, which corresponds with those parts of the peninsula where the soil overlays Carboniferous Limestone. The majority of these kilns – which were known as 'perpetual kilns' – were built during Victoria's reign. The 'farm' kilns went out of use towards the end of Victoria's reign, whereas some of the 'commercial' kilns remained in use into the 20th century.

Limekiln near Kilvrough – perpetual limekilns were made primarily of limestone blocks. The bowl at the top of a kiln was lined with fire bricks, which is where layers of limestone and culm (coal dust) were placed and the coal ignited. The arched recess at the front was where burnt lime and ash were raked into containers. It was important that the burnt lime was not exposed to rain (hence the archway) as water generated heat and cart loads of burnt lime could re-ignite.

Lead Mining in the Bishopston Valley

Mining was not to be found within the Englishry, except that is, for the extraction of iron-ore at Mumbles (which will be dealt with in a subsequent publication) and for a short-lived lead-mining venture at Brandy Cove. The All Slade Mine at Brandy Cove had been worked intermittently since the 18th century, and in 1849 a decision was taken to re-open a mine in the same locality. A shaft was sunk near Hareslade farm. It is unlikely that more than a dozen men were employed in the venture, and it appears that little more than 50 tons of ore was sold. A severe storm in January 1853 caused sufficient damage to bring about the closure of the All Slade Mine. The storm also put an end to the new Long Ash Mine, which was situated higher up the valley.

Farms and Farming in the Welshry

The biggest landowners in the Welshry were all non-resident and their property dispersed and, therefore, difficult to locate. In the parish of Llanrhidian those same landowners were Nathaniel Cameron (723 acres), Thomas Penrice of Kilvrough (487 acres) and C.R.M. Talbot of Margam and Penrice (346 acres). All three men, along with the lesser landowners in Llanrhidian, leased their lands to tenant farmers and to those who mined coal. The poor nature of the soil meant that farmers were primarily involved in animal husbandry. The number of cattle and sheep – even horses – was such that whenever an animal strayed it was taken to the Pound-ffald at Three Crosses, where the owner was expected to pay for its release. There was, however, 'some corn ground' yielding wheat and oats, but in Victorian times corn gave way to root vegetables for the ever-increasing industrialized population.

Brynhir House (now Tanglewood) commands a fine view over the Loughor Estuary. With a drive curving round to the front porch, Brynhir was a two-storyed house with servants' quarters above; it also had a fine coach house close by. The property is over 150 years old, and owes its survival to the dedicated work of the present owners, Mr. and Mrs. Thomas. At one time the house was linked with Pencaerfenni, a 40-acre farm with several farm buildings. After the Second World War the latter farmhouse and its attendant buildings were modified for use as the Pencaerfenni Motel. (By kind permission of B. and S. Thomas of Tanglewood)

There were no castles in the Welshry; nor were there any great houses, though there had been one at Gelli-hir, near Three Crosses, until it was destroyed by fire during the winter of 1787-8. The most notable buildings belonged to prosperous farming families, such as Brynhir on the high ground between Penclawdd and Three Crosses, which in 1847 belonged to Philip Evans. Brynhir farm first appears in the records in the 17th century, and in Philip's day comprised of 131 acres. Also in Philip's possession – which he purchased in 1847 – was the 40-acres lowland farm of Pencaerfenni, first mentioned in the 16th century. Philip would appear to have been prosperous – prosperous enough to build himself an imposing residence near Brynhir farm, which he named Brynhir House. This new property put Philip in the category of minor gentry, for not only was it impressive by local standards, but in later life he was in a position to lease Pencaerfenni to one John Hopkins. Of course, one wonders where Philip got his money from because, in 1850, he was able to contribute £400 towards the rebuilding of the nearby chapel of ease *Llan-yr-newydd*.

Cockle Gathering

Penclawdd cockle-women

Left: *the tall 'beaver' hat worn by the older woman was not common to Gower, being both costly and impractical for carrying heavy pails, etc. It was, therefore, worn only on special occasions.*

Below: *The cockle-women are seen here sifting cockles from their shells in 1854. The women were noted for their black-and-white checked aprons and their plaid shawls. None of them have Welsh straw hats, but the tall woman appears to be wearing a padded cap that would enable her to carry a heavy pail upon her head. The remaining women are all wearing turnovers; two of them appear to have padded caps as well.*

Limestone quarrying and oyster fishing were not available as alternative forms of employment to farming in the Welshry, but other occupations there were, one of them in the cockle industry. Cockle gathering can be traced back at least 2,000 years as cockleshells have been found at several prehistoric sites. In the Victorian era cockle gathering was an occupation exclusively for women, children and donkeys, the men being employed in other industries such as coal mining. In his *History of West Gower*, published in 1885, the Revd. J.D. Davies stated there were 'cockle fisheries at Penclawdd, and near Llanelly, in which some five hundred families found employment, and the cockles and mussels taken are valued at £15,000 a year'. Two years later an Inspector of Fisheries maintained that cockle gathering was 'wholly carried out by women; they work as far as Pembrey and that the cockles are also pickled in jars'. It was later stated in 1909-10 that 250 people were employed in cockle gathering at Penclawdd.

When out on the Llanrhidian Sands the cockle-women took with them their donkeys, the number of which has gone unrecorded, but Penclawdd was probably renowned for the constant braying of those hardy beasts, and to a lesser extent so was every village in the peninsula, the donkey being the peasant's beast of burden.

Twice a week the women set out with their donkeys from various points between Wernffrwd and Penclawdd, following the retreating tide closely till they reached the cockle bed of their choosing. There they engaged in back-breaking work, gathering cockles and loading them into sacks or buckets. The work had to be done quickly; there was no time to dawdle on their return.

Penclawdd cockle-women with their donkeys on their way to market in 1903.
Note the various ways they transported their cockles.

The incoming tide could come in, filling the gullies, faster than they could walk. On the sea front the cockles were 'boiled in rude fireplaces built of turf and stones', the walls semi-circular, perhaps a metre high, with iron bars across the top on which a boiler would be placed. Then they were 'sifted from their shells over a table, and afterwards well washed at a spring to cleanse them from the sand'.

Come Saturday morning the women set out to sell their wares, some traversing the marsh to Loughor, others taking the byways into English Gower. By far the majority walked nine miles to Swansea. At Olchfa they washed their feet, then put on their boots to walk into town. Many women sold their cockles at Swansea Market; others may have sold them in the streets. The journey to Swansea eased with the coming of the railway. From December 1867 onwards the women could board a train that took them through Gowerton, Dunvant and Clyne Valley, after which the train skirted Swansea Bay to arrive at Victoria Station (opposite York Place Baptist Church). The railway expanded distribution to places far and wide. It also encouraged some women to alight at Victoria Station, make a short journey to High Street Station, then board a train to Morriston.

Fishing

Fishing in one form or another was carried out in all parts of Peninsula Gower. In the Burry/Loughor estuary fishing from small boats, or with the use of nets, provided full-time employment for seven men in 1841. There are also a number of old documents that refer to individuals and small groups obtaining permission to fish and raise weirs on the south side of the estuary. The weirs were no more than nets, which were suspended on short posts in such a way as to trap fish when the tide receded. Yet another occupation connected with the estuary – if only for one man – was that of ferrying passengers from Penclawdd to Machynys, south of Llanelly. The Penclawdd ferry had been in operation during the 18th century, but it appears to have been discontinued during the early part of Victoria's reign.

Coal Mining – Clyne Valley

Besides farming, one of the principal occupations for men in the Welshry was coal mining, which took place in three main areas. The first of these areas to be considered is Clyne Valley, which extends inland to the edge of Fairwood Common. Collieries were established on both sides of the Clyne River, which to some extent formed Peninsula Gower's eastern boundary. However, due to their close proximity, collieries on both banks will be dealt with in this section of the work.

The earliest reference to coal mining in the valley is in a document dated 1319, which refers to 'sea coal at Blackpill in the Clyne Valley'. Thereafter, no records exist for the next 300 years, but from the 17th century onwards there are a growing number of documents relating to mining in Clyne Valley. The physical evidence is in the form of numerous 'bell pits', so named because the excavation resembled the shape of a bell. Coal from these pits was taken by packhorse to Blackpill where a quay definitely existed in 1795, and had probably been in existence as far back as c.1580, if not earlier. From the quay, ships took the coal to Swansea and places further afield.

Advances in mining techniques led to John Morris (I) of Clasemont opening the Ynys Colliery in c.1800 (on the east side of the river, near today's adventure playground), which involved digging a tunnel, or level, into sloping terrain and following a coal seam underground.

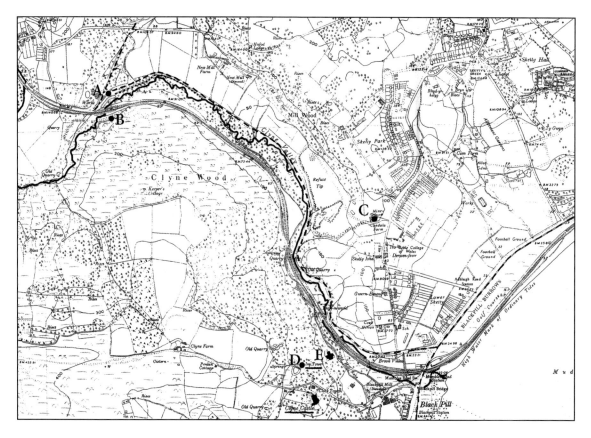

Clyne Valley – much of it is now a country park. The Clyne River (overlaid with a continuous black line) once served as part of the eastern boundary of the Gower Poor Law Union and the Gower Rural District (Union and R.D. By.). The black dots follow the line of a surface canal, one that emerges from the Rhyd-y-defaid Boat Level; this surface canal channelled excess water into the river.

The Oystermouth Tramroad branch line (overlaid with black dashes) is now a riverside trackway, providing an easy walk, but beyond a large pool the track becomes waterlogged; it leads to the Rhyd-y-defaid (A) and Clyne Wood (B) colliery sites.

Near the top left-hand corner is another tramroad (overlaid with black dots and dashes) connected with the Commercial Colliery (the site of which is just beyond the top edge of the map). The line of the latter tramroad survives as an embankment leading to what was once the main line railway.

Later tramroads laid in connection with Clyne Valley Colliery (C) terminated at the Mumbles Road Station near the shoreline (written in italics).

The Ivy Tower (D) was originally a chimney stack connected with the Clyne Valley Arsenic Works (E), the site of which is in the valley and marked 'Hay Sheds' on some early maps. From the works a buried flue ran all the way up the steep, wooded slope to the west to connect with the Ivy Tower chimney stack, which, sited high up on the hill, made it possible for the wind to disperse the fumes at a much higher altitude.

(West Glamorgan Archive Service)

A bell pit – after digging down some five to ten feet to reach a coal seam, miners had then to work outwards, removing coal until such time as it become unsafe to continue, at which point the pit would have been abandoned and a new one dug elsewhere. Bell pits were an advance on 'scrapes' that simply removed coal from where it outcropped near the surface. The obvious progression from these early excavations was to tunnel into the hillside and follow a coal seam underground, thereby creating a mine known as a 'level'.

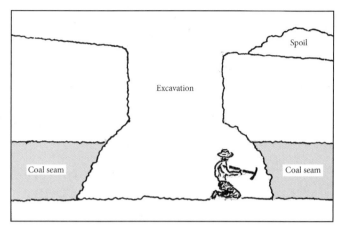

Six years later a branch line of the Oystermouth Tramroad (built 1804-6 and later known as the Mumbles Railway) enabled John Morris (I) to convey coal from Ynys to the Strand, Swansea, in horse-drawn trams. The colliery proved less than successful because the coal seams in the valley were subject to faults; that is, the miners reached a point where the seam came to an abrupt end, the ground in front of them (including the coal seam) having dropped (or risen) a considerable distance, at which point the colliery's days were numbered.

In *c.*1838 John Morris II started work on the Rhyd-y-defaid Boat Level, which was situated higher up on the east side of the valley. This level was unique in that coal was conveyed to the surface by an underground canal, a lengthy waterway which can still be traced today. The branch tramroad that had serviced Ynys is likely to have been extended to some point on this waterway, so that coal could be loaded into horse-drawn trams and taken to Swansea, although there is no evidence to support this hypothesis. John Morris II surrendered the lease connected with this level in 1847.

The next level of note was the Rhyd-y-defaid (No.1) Colliery, also located on the east bank, a little to the west of the Boat Level mentioned above. Opened in 1856, Rhyd-y-defaid was certainly serviced by an extension of the branch tramroad, as there is both documentary and physical evidence to prove that this was so; moreover, in 1872 the then proprietor, Philip Richard II, was using steam

Steam-powered engine for hauling trams, dated 1897. When this photograph was taken in the 1970s the engine lay abandoned in the woods south-west of The Railway Inn, Killay, in the vicinity of Clyne Wood Colliery, which closed in 1885.

locomotives on this line until a high court ruling put a stop to locomotives travelling alongside a public highway, in this case Mumbles Road. The colliery closed in 1895.

The first colliery of note on the west bank was Clyne Wood, opened in 1867 on a site only a few hundred metres to the south of Rhyd-y-defaid. This colliery was also serviced by an extension of the branch tramroad. Clyne Wood closed in 1885 and (following the closure of Rhyd-y-defaid in 1895) the tram-road fell into disuse. There was, however, a main line railway (not a tramroad) on the west bank, one that opened for goods – mainly coal – in 1866, and for passengers in December the following year. The line (now a cycle path) came down the valley from Killay, crossed the Mumbles Road by way of an iron bridge and continued to Swansea at the top of an embankment (now the promenade).

In 1899 Philip Richard (II) opened the Commercial Colliery (alias Rhyd-y-defaid No.2) on the east bank, well to the north of his Rhyd-y-defaid Colliery mentioned above. To connect

Sleepers, Clyne Valley – tramroad sleepers in the vicinity of what was once the Mumbles Road (passenger railway) Station.

his Commercial Colliery with the main-line railway to Swansea he laid a short tramroad on top of an embankment (which still exists). Both the Commercial and its raised tramroad closed in 1908 when the coal seam was found to suddenly drop to a great depth.

The last and largest colliery to open in the period covered by this work was known as Clyne Valley. Opened in 1903, Clyne Valley Colliery was situated on the east bank, in the lower part of the valley. To facilitate the conveyance of coal from this colliery, the lower part of the branch tramroad was brought back into service; it terminated at sidings connected to the main-line railway at Mumbles Road Station. That station was not the one situated on the south side of the present-day car park at the bottom of Derwen Fawr Road – that was the passenger station – but the station on the seaward side of the Mumbles Road. In its heyday Clyne Valley Colliery employed around 300 men. The colliery closed in 1915.

Another industry in the valley was brick-making, the kilns sited near the larger collieries. Using clay taken from the mines, brick-making was a profitable sideline for colliery owners. In the early 1830s a small iron works was built near Rhyd-y-defaid (No.1) Colliery, the iron-ore coming from the coal measures in the locality. A great deal of money was expended in the belief that mining would be profitable, but the ore – which could only be obtained by shifting huge quantities of shale and clay – proved to be of poor quality. The works closed after c.1850 and its buildings now lie buried under an early 20th-century coal tip.

An arsenic works stood only a few hundred metres to the north of Clyne Castle. Established between 1825 and 1837, the Clyne Wood Arsenic Works had a short existence, closing in 1841. It was re-opened by Henry Kingscole of Devon in 1844-5. By 1852 it was worked by John Jennings & Co., but closed again c.1860. The first closure may have been due to its location. It stood beside an old canal of 1799-1803, which suggests that coal may have been brought to the site by boat from a level upstream, whereas the copper-ore (from which arsenic was extracted) was offloaded at Blackpill Quay, then taken by cart to the works. Its final closure may have had something to do with the fact that Graham Vivian had bought Clyne Castle. It is probable that the new owner also bought the works and promptly closed it down.

Ivy Tower above Clyne Valley – the most prominent remains of the Clyne Wood Arsenic Works is a chimney stack, which was sited high up on the steep hillside above the works. Sometime after 1864, Graham Vivian of Clyne Castle leased Clyne Wood from the Duke of Beaufort and converted the lower part of this stack into a pavilion, adding to it a castellated parapet, door, window and an internal staircase. The pavilion become known as Ivy Tower.

There were colliery undertakings in the valley above Killay Railway Station as well. In the Victorian era the most important were Wernfawr No.1 (on the edge of Fairwood Common, near a marsh called Ddol) and Wernfawr No.2 (behind and to the north of the houses at Upper Killay). What all these collieries in Clyne Valley had in common was that, with the exception of Upper Killay, they did not lead to the establishment of villages in the valley. People simply walked miles to get to work from places as far afield as Oystermouth. Today, old tramroad sleepers, the remains of canals, and an abandoned steam-powered engine, all bear testimony to the coal mining activity that went on in this now tranquil, wooded valley.

Coal Mining in Llanrhidian Parish

The second coal mining area to be considered lies within Llanrhidian, or at least that part of the parish that is within the Welshry and within sight of the Burry/Loughor Estuary. Mining in this particular area appears to have begun with scrapes and bell pits in the late Tudor period. As in Clyne Valley, these early mining ventures were carried out in the summer when the ground was not so wet; they were concentrated on the high ground to the south of Llanmorlais. Local farmers, who used farm labourers to mine and stockpile coal in the summer months, often initiated mining operations in this area.

In the 17th and 18th centuries, larger landowners and industrialists were keen to exploit coal wherever it could be worked close to the estuary so that it could be shipped to places such as Devon, Cornwall, Ireland, France and to places around the Gower coast for domestic use, lime burning and forges. Loading ships with coal was made possible by the fact that the Loughor River flowed close to the present-day high-water mark, and continued to do so until silting in the late 19th century caused the river to move towards its present course further north.

A total of four shipping places have been located in Llanrhidian. All four had ceased to function by c.1820, but three of them – Salthouse Pill, Penclawdd and Abercedi (to the east of Penclawdd) – were back in use before c.1859. Of these, Penclawdd is by far the more interesting. There had been a jetty at Penclawdd in 1757 and a dock was constructed in c.1800-10 in connection with a nearby copperworks. The dock probably ceased to function when the copperworks closed down, but by c.1840 the dock was again in use and for a while it prospered. Its best year was the financial one for 1860-61, when 214 vessels left with cargoes – mainly of coal – for destinations within the U.K., and a further 20 vessels sailed for foreign ports. Trade declined after the arrival of the railway in 1866 and, unable to compete with this new form of transport, the dock closed in c.1875.

Eighteenth-century colliers in Llanrhidian worked coal by tunnelling into a hillside and following a coal seam as far as it was practical, or until they reached a fault, beyond which the seam would have dropped (or risen) due to a disturbance that occurred thousands of years ago. This

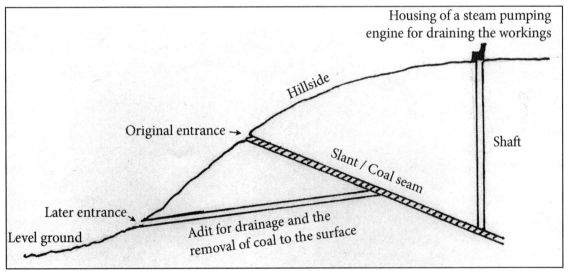

Mining tunnels – a mining level would be referred to as a slant when it followed a coal seam to the 'dip' meaning downhill and this type of working required a drainage tunnel known as an 'adit' to discharge the water at a point lower than the original entrance to the mine, but if this was not practical, then a shaft had to be sunk and a steam-powered pumping engine installed to de-water the workings. An adit could also be used as a downhill route for conveying coal to the surface. Another method of working coal was by way of a tunnel called a 'drift', which did not follow a coal seam from the surface, but was driven through strata, usually downhill, until a seam was reached well below the surface.

form of mining created a 'level'. If the level followed a seam to the 'rise' – meaning uphill – then drainage was straightforward, relying on gravity to rid the level of water. A gradual slope to the entrance also made moving coal less fatiguing for the men who wheel-barrowed coal to the surface on planks. The bulk of the coal would then be taken by packhorse (and later in the century by horse-drawn waggons running on wooden or iron rails) to the shipping places mentioned above, smaller quantities being distributed for local consumption. The work-forces at these early collieries would have been small compared with the undertakings of Victorian times; moreover, collieries in the area were often short-lived due to faults and flooding.

By the early 19th century, vertical shafts were taking colliers to coal seams well below the surface, particularly in the low-lying areas that bordered the Burry/Loughor Estuary. In some of the coastal collieries the colliers worked seams that were beneath the estuary, which must have been unnerving for newcomers, as the ebb and flow of tidal water was audible to those underground. Later collieries, particularly those further east, were subject not only to faults and flooding, but to fire-damp (gas) explosions as well.

As to the colliers in Llanrhidian, most appear to have resided in the farms and cottages in the vicinity of the mines. A few of these scattered hamlets grew to become villages. Crofty, for example, had originally been a meadow, or croft, enclosed by two lanes, which later became known as Forge Lane and Church Lane. By 1869 the hamlet consisted of several collier cottages on the periphery of the croft, and also a farm that eventually became the Crofty Inn. Twenty years later the layout (of the older part) of the village was very much as it is today – minus the mini-market.

Coal mining in Llanrhidian declined from *c.*1800 onwards, but after 1830 the industry began its ascendancy to the boom years of the Victorian era. One of the most productive collieries of the boom period was Penclawdd on the high ground above the village. Opened in 1834, Penclawdd Colliery was taken over by Starling Benson and his partner, Hart Logan, in *c.*1839, and they laid a tramroad from the colliery to Penclawdd Dock. Part of this tramroad – the part laid on the hillside – was a self-acting incline-plane. For traction, the waggons on the incline relied on gravity in that, linked by a chain, loaded trams pulled empty trams in the opposite direction. Penclawdd Colliery remained productive under successive ownerships until *c.*1887.

Copperworks Archway – this is all that remains of the Penclawdd Copperworks. A date plaque reads: L.P.C.Co. rebuilt 1848. The initials stand for Low's Patent Copperworks Company. The archway now serves as a lockup or garage.

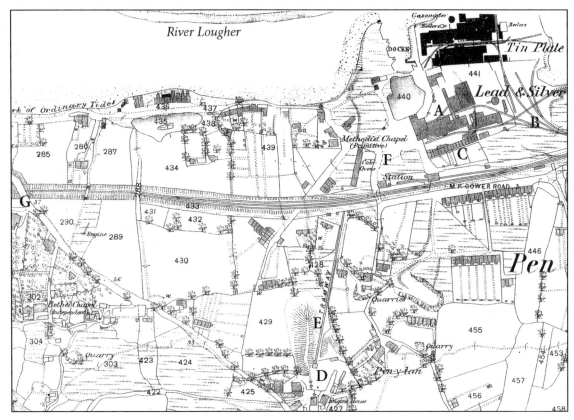

Ordnance Survey of Penclawdd 1879 showing the Tin Plate Works, part of which occupied the site of the old copperworks slag tip. Below this is the Lead and Silver Works, part of which (A) had formerly been the copperworks and (B) the tramways used by both the copper works and the tin-plate works. The 'Barracks' (C) originally provided accommodation for key workers. In 1881 the 'Barracks' provided accommodation for 68 people living in 17 separate dwellings. The Dock was prone to silting; hence the pond marked '440'. Sluice gates were periodically opened to allow water from the pond to flush sediment from the Dock. Note how close the river is to the shore line. Penclawdd Colliery is shown at (D) and its 'incline' tramway at (E). The railway station is at (F) – part of the platform survives as a low wall in front of the supermarket. On the far left is the road bridge (G, which survives) over the railway line to Llanmorlais.

(West Glamorgan Archive Service)

Penclawdd and its Metal Works

In the 18th century Penclawdd appears to have been little more than a handful of scattered mining hamlets. Its status began to change towards the end of the century with the establishment of several small works, all of them sited in close proximity to an inlet that had previously been used for shipping coal. The change in status began with the establishment of a small brassworks in the early 1770s. This was followed in the 1780s by a small leadworks. A copperworks appears to have been in operation there by *c*.1788, its output consisting – among other things – of copper rods and bronze *manilas*, which were used to purchase slaves from tribal leaders in

*Penclawdd Copperworks and Tinplate Works in c.1896, the year before the tinplate
works was demolished. The copperworks barracks can be seen to the left
of what appears to be the largest chimney, whereas the roof of
the smelting house is immediately to its rear.
Beyond those two buildings is the tinplate works with its several chimneys.
In the foreground is the railway station, and the railway line that
ran on the seaward side of the modern B4295.*

West Africa. In c.1800 the copperworks came under the management of John Vivian, who later founded the Hafod Copperworks. Production appears to have ceased shortly after John Vivian's departure because, in 1823, it was said that the copperworks there had been 'discontinued for many years'.

The copperworks re-opened in 1848 under the ownership of Low's Patent Copper Co., and from 1852 it appears to have undergone several changes in ownership. It was converted to a lead and silver works in c.1870 and closed in 1884. At no time during its 100 years existence did the works have a large workforce. Large scale employment came later when, in 1872, the Penclawdd Tinplate Works was established to the east of the dock. The tinplate works had a workforce of up to 600, which undoubtedly led to the expansion of the village. All was not well, however, as strikes and depressions led to several closures, on one occasion for a period of two years. The tinplate works closed for the last time in 1895; most of its buildings were demolished two years later. As to the tinplate men, many would have no doubt found employment in the new works and mines that had sprung up around Gowerton.

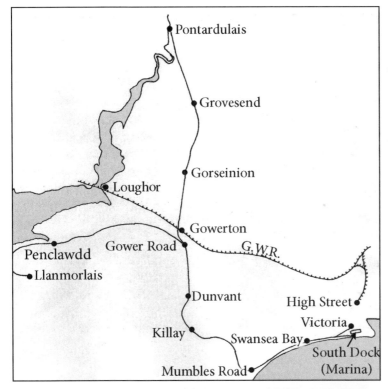

Pontardulais to Swansea Railway – laid by the Llanelly Railway and Dock Company in 1863-66 to convey coal to Swansea's South Dock (now the Marina); at a later stage there was an extension to the North Dock (alongside the Strand). The passenger service came into operation when Victoria Station opened in December 1867. At a later date there was a rail connection (up the Strand) with the GWR's High Street Station.

The Railway Inn, Upper Killay – stand pretty much as it did when built in 1864. This is a good starting point for an easy walk down Clyne Valley, as this small-roomed inn has retained much of its old world charm. It also provides genuine hospitality and welcome refreshment on the return journey. The beer here is local, supplied by the Swansea Brewing Co., whose premises are at The Joiners, Bishopston.

The Coming of the Railway

In April 1863 the Llanelly Railway & Dock Co. commenced work on its 12½-mile Pontardulais to Swansea line. Single-track throughout, except at stations, the line was intended to facilitate the transportation of coal from Pontardulais and places *en route* to Swansea's South Dock (now the

Bridge below The Railway Inn, Killay – this once carried local traffic over the LNWR line. A short distance below this point (where the river passes beneath the now tarmacked railway route) is an area of woodland in which are the remains of surface installations connected with the Clyne Wood and Rhyd-y-defaid (No.1) collieries, as well as the entrance to the earlier Rhyd-y-defaid Boat Level of John Morris II. Also in this same area is a tramway embankment from the Commercial Colliery and an old steam-powered engine for hauling trams.

Victoria Station, Swansea – there were several railway stations in Swansea in late Victorian and Edwardian times. Victoria Station was situated on the south side of Victoria Road, opposite York Place Baptist church. Opened for passengers on 14 December 1867, the station proved to be a busy one after the line had been taken over by the London and North Western Railway in 1873, as trains were arriving here daily from as far afield as Shrewsbury. The original station had been little more than a shack, but in 1882 the LNWR built the glass-roofed structure seen here.
Although bomb-damaged in the Second World War, the station survived until its closure in 1964.

Marina) where it would be loaded onto ships. After a descent through Clyne Valley the last part of the journey entailed crossing the Mumbles Road by way of an iron bridge, then skirting Swansea Bay on top of an embankment (the promenade). For almost three years gangs of navigators (navvies) – both Welsh and Irish – worked on the line, though not without incident. In May 1865 *The Swansea and Glamorgan Herald* reported an affray at the Gower Road (Gowerton) Junction between the two ethnic groups. The main line, along with a branch line from Gower Road (Gowerton) to Penclawdd, opened for the transportation of coal in January 1866.

Providing a passenger service on the line was also envisaged by the LR & D Co., but due to problems at Swansea's Victoria Station (Victoria Road, on the open ground opposite York Place Baptist Church) the service was delayed until December 1867. Six years later the company sold out to the London and North Western Railway Co., with the result that passenger trains from as far away as Shrewsbury travelled on the line daily.

The branch line from Gower Road (Gowerton) to Penclawdd was extended to Llanmorlais in 1877, and this acted as an incentive for more and more pits to be opened in the Llanmorlais area, many of which had their own tramroads linked to the new railway sidings. Consequently, coal mining in Llanrhidian prospered during the 1880s, so much so that many miners formed syndicates to work their own pits; moreover, at the opposite end of the parish the railway led to the creation of a new mining community.

Dunvant

At the beginning of Victoria's reign Dunvant consisted of scattered farms on either side of a wooded gorge, in which stood a solitary forge known as the Smith's Shop. No turnpike road ran through Dunvant; it was a place to be avoided for fear of footpads. It was also a place where three parishes met, the boundary being a brook known as *Y Dwfnant*, which flowed down a valley to the north-east of Killan-fawr farm to where Ebenezer Chapel now stands, at which point the brook turned southwards to join the Clyne River. Dunvant, then, was a backwater, but its peaceful surroundings were destined to change when, in 1863, work started on the railway.

Even before the line opened in January 1866 the Dunvant Gap – or gorge – and the surrounding hills became a hive of coal mining activity. One of the first collieries to open was the Voylart, its location to the south of what is now the main road to Three Crosses. It is believed that one owner of the Voylart, Edward Evans, built Company Row on Dunvant Road for his workers. The colliery closed in 1877 due to flooding. Another large colliery was Killan-Penclawdd, near Killan-fach farm, which opened before 1866 and closed in 1892. This was superseded in 1899 by a far more productive colliery known as Killan-Penlan, situated near Killan-fawr farm, which remained in use until flooding brought about its closure in 1924. A mile-long tramroad from these two collieries ran down the valley to the north-west of what is now Dunvant Square. Initially, the trams were horse-drawn; the horses were later replaced by steam locomotives.

East of the Square was the railway and Dunvant Railway Station. There were a number of sidings on either side of the railway line, both to the north and to the south of the station. East of the line there were several collieries, all of them levels into Graig-y-Bwldan, all of them benefiting from their close proximity to the railway sidings. One of the earliest of these collieries was the Dunvant, its location immediately east of the station. When exactly this level opened in the 1860s is unknown. It is marked 'disused' on the O.S. map of 1878, but between 1883 and 1905 it was worked by Philip

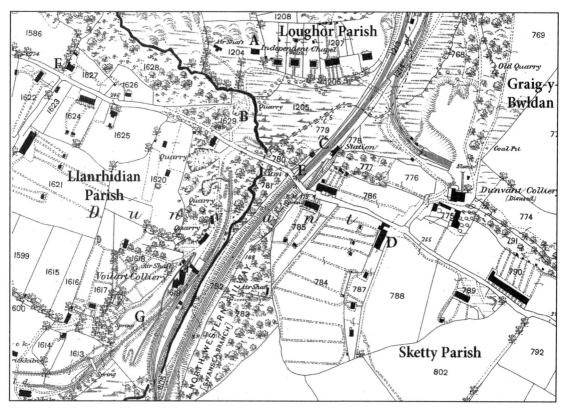

Above: Dunvant as depicted on the O.S. map of 1878. The brook known as Y Dwfnant (overlaid with dark ink) served as a boundary between Llanrhidian Higher, Loughor and Swansea (later Sketty) parishes. Noteworthy features are (A) Ebenezer Chapel, (B) site of today's Dunvant Square, (C) the railway station, (D) Hywel's Row, (E) the road bridge over the railway line, (F) site of today's Foundout P.H., and (G) tramroad from the vicinity of Three Crosses.

(West Glamorgan Archive Service)

Left: Ebenezer Chapel – there was no place to worship in the village until 1873 when the Nonconformists (or rather the Independents, later to be known as Congregationalists) built Yr Ysgoldy (The School-room). Sunday services were also held there, the services being bilingual. Yr Ysgoldy soon proved to be too small. So in 1881-2 a new chapel was built alongside the schoolroom (which later became the Vestry); it was called Y Capel Haiarn (The Iron Chapel), it being made of corrugated iron sheets. The present stone building – Ebenezer – was built in 1893. As with other chapels in the Welshry, Ebenezer was keen to promote its own choirs, one of which, the Dunvant Excelsior Male Voice Choir, first won recognition in 1901.

Richard II, a coal master who has already been mentioned as one who worked two collieries in Clyne Valley. In later years the workforce of this colliery numbered 75 men. The year after he abandoned the Dunvant, Philip Richard opened the Dunvant-Penlan only a short distance to the north of Dunvant Railway Station. This later level into Graid-y-Bwldan also had a workforce of around 75 men. It closed in 1916 due to flooding.

Most of the early collieries had closed before the end of Victoria's reign, but their closure is unlikely to have resulted in Dunvant becoming a depressed area, as larger later collieries had workforces numbered in their hundreds – Killan-Penlan, for example, had a workforce of 403 in 1913. Brickworks, quarries and an iron foundry provided employment for many more. Yet despite the availability of work, the village did not expand into a township such as Morriston. Around 50 homes can be identified on the O.S. map of 1878. By 1916 the number had increased to around 250. Clearly, many of those who worked in and around Dunvant were either lodgers, or came from outside the village. An hour's walk to work in all weathers would not have been unusual.

As to the village itself, there were a few short terraces, but the majority of houses were detached and scattered over the hillsides on both sides of *Y Dwfnant*. Many of the houses were situated on the Llanrhidian Higher side of the brook. Others were sited on the slopes of Brynaeron and were, therefore, in the parish of Loughor. The remainder straddled Dunvant Road (east of the brook) and were, therefore, in Swansea (later Sketty) parish.

Communications by Road

Roads throughout South Wales had long been in a deplorable state when, in 1764, Parliament passed an Act that would remedy the situation. The Act permitted the formation of trusts in which landowners and industrialists invested money to improve and repair the main highways in their areas, and to erect barriers for the collection of tolls. By the early 19th century the through routes in the Lordship of Gower had been greatly improved by the Swansea and the Wych Tree trusts, but in Peninsula Gower there were still 'long lines of barren, desolate, uninhabited tracks', their surfaces broken by potholes and outcrops of rock. So bad were these tracks that wheeled vehicles were virtually unknown. To get about Gowerians either walked or rode; if they had to move heavy goods they used donkeys, or horse-drawn slide-cars – which were sledge-like, consisting of two long poles – and the later, wheeled variety known as truckle-cars. Truckle-cars continued to be used in some localities right up to the close of Victoria's reign.

By 1843, conditions had improved in that the Swansea Trust had four turnpike roads in Peninsula Gower, all of which were part of a network radiating from Swansea. The most southerly of these highways was the one from Swansea to Oystermouth, completed in 1826. Further north was

A slide-car – its wheeled successor was known as a truckle-car.

49

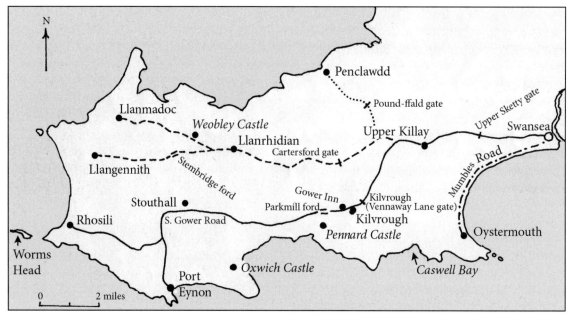

Turnpike roads into Peninsula Gower

the main route into Gower (now the A4118). It ran through Sketty, Upper Killay and continued westwards, following a route that is now referred to as the South Gower Road. At the edge of Fairwood Common a third turnpike forked right for Llanrhidian and Llanmadoc (now the North Gower Road). The fourth turnpike left Fairwood Common in the direction of Three Crosses and Penclawdd (there was no turnpike road through Dunvant at that time, nor was there one on the line of the modern B4295). All four highways had tollgates or chains at strategic points, where tolls were levied on all vehicles and animals that passed through the barriers; there were no easy detours.

The turnpike roads in South Wales may have made travel easier, but the tolls alienated farmers, who often found themselves paying tolls several times on their way to market; the same applied to those who transported bulk commodities such as limestone and coal. By 1839 the grievance of paying tolls exploded into outright violence when farmers in West Wales began destroying the hated tollgates and attendant tollhouses. Disguised and sometimes attired in women's clothes, the activists were referred to as Rebecca and her Daughters; their lawless activities became known as the Rebecca Riots.

Rebecca was most active in the summer of 1843, so much so that *The Cambrian* newspaper reported on Saturday 22 July that an artillery detachment was on its way to Carmarthen, and that 'two hundred of the 75th [Regiment of Foot had] arrived in Swansea last night by the *Bristol* steamer'. *The Cambrian* also reported an attack on the Pound-ffald tollgate near Three Crosses:

> On Friday night last [14 July], or rather early on Saturday morning … a number of persons (some say about sixty, and others represent them as being many more) who had their faces blackened, and were otherwise disguised, amidst the firing of guns, entirely destroyed the gate posts, and all the 'appurtenances thereto pertaining', excepting the toll-house, which they had ascertained belonged – not to the Trust … but to Mr. Eaton, a farmer, residing near the gates

50

Tollgate at Upper Sketty Cross in the late 19th century – the tollgate at the Pound-ffald, Three Crosses, may have been similar to this one, as both were built by the Swansea Turnpike Trust. Pedestrians could pass through without cost, but a charge was placed on all animals, animal-drawn vehicles and hand carts.

… A portion of wall along the road-side was [also] pulled down. They sent the toll-collector to the house, and threatened to shoot him if he had the presumption to peep out either through the door or window. Mr. Eaton, the owner of the toll-house approached them, but he was soon compelled to retreat having been assailed by a volley of stones, pieces of gate, etc. It was reported that they had contemplated the destruction of another gate in the neighbourhood, but as dawn was approaching they abandoned their design.

The occasion prompted the authorities to assign constables to guard eight tollgates in the outlying parts of the lordship. Two of these gates were in Peninsula Gower – Cartersford on the North Gower Road, and Kilvrough on the South Gower Road (at the corner of Vennaway Lane). No further attacks occurred in Peninsula Gower, but several attacks took place in the more northerly part of the lordship in the months that ensued.

Some five weeks after the attack on the Pound-ffald gate, the authorities decided that Rebecca was no longer a threat and withdrew the constables from their gate-guarding duties. The question then was who should pay the police for guarding the Cartersford and Kilvrough gates? The government declared that the cost should be borne by the parishioners of Ilston and Pennard, but the local magistrates considered that to be unfair. One magistrate, who was also a turnpike trustee, went to great lengths to explain why the charge for guarding the two gates was so unjust. The magistrate, Major Thomas Penrice of Kilvrough, pointed out that the rioting had been confined to 'the Welsh district', whereas the Cartersford and Kilvrough gates were sited in that part of Gower where, he maintained, the people 'are all English'.

The major may have failed to get the government to change its mind about who should pay for the policing, but some good was to come of Rebecca's activities. The Pound-ffald gate, for example, was removed altogether, as were several other gates in the more northerly part of the lordship. More important still, the Rebecca Riots led to the phasing out of the hated tollgate system – but that will be dealt with in a subsequent publication.

Carriers

Road improvement continued to the extent that, by the 1870s, horse-drawn carriages and farm wagons were a common sight in Peninsula Gower. In the same decade at least one horse-drawn carrier service came into existence. Soon there were carriers operating from such places as

Top: *The Favourite Ready – a horse-drawn carrier at Llanmadoc c.1905. The service ran from Llanmadoc via Llanrhidian and Killay to Swansea.*

Left: *Gower Express – a horse-drawn carrier, which ran between Llanrhidian and Killay, its probable destination being Swansea.*

Right: *Pioneer motor bus 1912 – similar to (if not the same as) the one bought by J. Grove three years earlier (see p.54). As advertised on the side, this one operated from Penmaen and Parkmill.*

Dennis motor bus 1910 – initially, the Taylor brothers operated buses of this type from Rhosili and Llangennith. By 1914 they had six Dennis buses at their disposal. Roof racks were used for conveying passengers and produce to market, and for carrying all sorts of purchases made at Swansea on the return.

Llangennith and Llanmadoc on the north side of the peninsula, and from Rhosili and Port Eynon on the south side. The services provided by the carriers were as follows: to take passengers to Swansea or Swansea Market, and to purchase or pick up all manner of things for those who could not afford a day out.

A carrier had to set out early, around 4.30 a.m., as the journey to Swansea could take five hours or more. When confronted by a steep hill, such as the one out of Port Eynon, or the one at Stembridge, the passengers were obliged to get out and walk, or help push the carriage up the gradient, or prevent it from careering out of control on a downward slope. There were also streams to ford, as at Stembridge and Parkmill. The passengers had the option of passing over a stream by way of a nearby wooden footbridge (the one that survives at Parkmill is late and made of concrete), whereas the carriage had to be hauled across the stream with the aid of ropes; this could be hard work if a stream was in flood. Then there were additional passengers to be picked up along the way, or requests for the carrier to perform a service for those who could not afford to spend a Saturday in town.

When the carrier arrived at Swansea around 10.30 a.m., he parked his carriage near the market and, while his passengers dispersed to sell their produce on stalls or in the streets, he had other things to attend to: money had to be paid into a bank; medicine, clothes and household requirements had to purchased – it was all part of the service, for which he made a charge. Then, when the stall-holding passengers had finished trading around 5.30 p.m., the carrier set off on the return journey. Hills and fords had again to be negotiated; passengers would alight here and there, and purchases had to be delivered; and most time-consuming of all, halts took place at public houses such as the Gower Inn and the Greyhound, Oldwalls. Somewhat inebriated, the carrier was unlikely to arrive home until well after midnight.

Despite an extremely long and tiring day, the carriers must have considered their Saturday services to be a profitable once-a-week sideline. This is evident by the recollections of the folk-singer, Phil Tanner, who could recall the names of at least nine carriers operating at the turn of the century. So good was the carrier business that several enterprising carriers invested in motor buses. Opinion differs as to who was the first to use a motor bus, but it would appear that J. Grove of Swansea started a service between the Ship Hotel, Port Eynon, and Swansea Market in 1909, using a Pioneer motor bus. In March the following year, George Taylor began operating from Rhosili, using a Dennis motor bus. Others soon followed George's example, but none were as enterprising as George and his brother Rowland. In 1912, when they had several buses in service, the brothers registered under the company name of 'Vanguard', later changed to 'Gower Vanguard'. By 1914 the brothers had six Dennis buses at their disposal. For Gower the writing was on the wall: centuries of isolation were about to end.

Tourism

As far back as the 1780s Swansea aspired to become a fashionable seaside resort, offering visitors the opportunity to drink and bathe in seawater, which was believed to be beneficial to health at that time. For several decades Swansea prospered as 'the Brighton of Wales', but by the beginning of Victoria's reign the town's charm had been blighted by industrialization and its attendant slums. Yet despite these setbacks, efforts to attract visitors to the town persisted, more so after 1850 when the first train arrived at High Street Station. Guide books relating to Swansea and the surrounding area had been periodically published since 1802. *The Swansea Guide 1851*, by John Lewis, is a good example of how visitors were lured to the Gower Peninsula. After informing the visitor of what the town had to offer, the guidebook directs them to the Mumbles area.

> A mile beyond Langland is the beautiful bay of Caswell, famed for its pellucid streams and the beauty and number of its shells. Caswell has often been compared to Lulworth Cove, Dorestshire, and is formed by two projecting rocks, and an opening descent from the hills conducts you to the shore…The violence of the sea has produced wonderful excavations of various shapes…some assuming the appearance of temples, with mighty gothic arches; and others of subterranean passages.

The author may have allowed his imagination to run wild here, but no fault can be found with his final statement that 'Caswell is one of the most attractive spots in the neighbourhood'. And so to *Pwldie* and the 'dilapidated ruin' of Pennard Castle. At later stages in the book the author mentions several other castles, but omits to say that in his day two of those castles were still lived in – *Webley*, which was occupied by a farming family until *c.*1900, and *Oxwich* by the Bevan family until the early 1950s.

> At Park Mill is a well-conducted house called the Gower Inn, which is situated in a fine sporting country and affords a very convenient resting-place for excursionists to Cefn Bryn, one of the highest mountains in Wales [a slight exaggeration there] from the summit of which a magnificent view of the surrounding country may be obtained, embracing several counties. [The author goes on to describe] King Arthur's Stone … as the remains of druidical superstition.
> At Rhossily Village, Worm's Head [according to the author] is so called because the sailors used to think it resembled a worm creeping with its head erect. [After a brief description of the island the author ends with] Having now arrived at what has often been described as 'one of the ends of the earth', – Tourist! in this appropriate spot, we must depart!

Top: *Oxwich Castle – built in the early 16th century, the 'farmhouse' block (roofed) was occupied by the Bevan family before 1694. The Bevans were tenant farmers, paying rent to first the Mansels, then the Talbots of Margam and Penrice. The Bevans were in occupation right through to the early 1950s, when they moved to a modern farmhouse nearby. The castle is now in the care of CADW.*

Middle: *The Gower Inn 1900-20 – built by Major Thomas Penrice in 1824, the Gower Inn was described in* The Cambrian *newspaper that same year as a new spacious, well-furnished public house, with stables, coach house, piggery and large garden. Situated on the main turnpike road through South Gower, the inn served as a hostelry for early tourists; it was also frequented by locals en route to and from Swansea. Today the Gower Inn offers welcome refreshment, particularly when homeward bound after a long walk or a day on the beach.*

Bottom: *Worms Head Cottage c.1920 – built in c.1880, this is probably Gower's first purpose-built accommodation for tourists.*

How many middle-class tourists were lured into Peninsula Gower at that time is unknown – presumably not many, but Mumbles seems to have been receiving some visitors as far back as *c.*1800 if hotels such as the New Mermaid are anything to go by. The parish of Oystermouth, however, was soon to be overwhelmed by day trippers when the Oystermouth Railway's horse-drawn passenger service was revived in 1860. *The Cambrian* newspaper described the majority of day trippers as of 'the rougher class'.

Further west, it was recorded in 1847 that at Penmaen a private school was 'discontinued for three months during the summer, [the mistress] being then occupied by lodgers, who resort to the neighbourhood for the purpose of sea-bathing'. Tourism beyond Penmaen does not appear to have been taken seriously until the late 1860s, when middle-class families began to arrive in horse-drawn vehicles at Easter and in July and August. No doubt local innkeepers were only too willing to provide accommodation, spartan though it may have been, but more suitable accommodation became available when, in 1870, a William Tucker built the King Arthur Hotel at exactly half its present size (the other, matching half being built 19 years later). Others were soon to provide accommodation of a different sort. When Colonel Wood died in 1876, his wife and daughters left Stouthall for good, and from then on the house was let to well-to-do families, usually in the summer months. A few years later, in *c.*1880, the Worms Head Cottage was built to provide holiday accommodation for less discerning families. Bicycles first appeared on the road in the 1890s. They became popular in the Edwardian era (1901-10), but so too did the motor car. That is when the tourist invasion of Gower began in earnest.

British Singer c.1900 – a three-wheeled motor vehicle, one of the earliest to be seen locally. It is seen here somewhere between Blackpill and West Cross.

Communications by Sea

Bounded for the most part by water, it is hardly surprising that Peninsula Gower had strong links with ships, fishing and maritime trade. The coastline on the south and west has several bays that, at high tide, permitted ships to sail in close to the shore, there to rest on the sand when the tide receded. On the north-east the River Loughor hugged the coastline, allowing vessels to get in close to shipping places until silting caused the river to flow further north. The coastal waters around the peninsula were, therefore, part of a world-wide highway that enabled men to travel and trade far more effectively than on land, particularly when it involved the transportation of bulk goods such as coal, limestone and ores.

Mention has already been made of building material shipped into Oxwich Bay for the construction of Penrice Castle, but other commodities were imported beside slates and stones. Coal, for example, was required in the Englishry for domestic use, forges and limestone burning, and it all

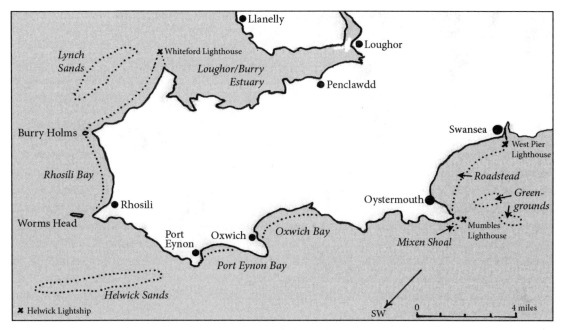

Gower and Swansea Bay coastal waters – the dotted lines indicate the low water line on the larger beaches, and also the offshore sandbanks that were hazardous to shipping.

had to be shipped to places such as Oystermouth, Oxwich, Port Eynon and Rhosili; even Cheriton had its coal by the boat-load. Cloams (water storage jars) were shipped from Devon. Timber for use at Penclawdd came from as far away as Canada. Livestock, on the other hand, could be shipped from any of the bays on the south coast.

Ships involved in localized trade within the U.K. were referred to as coasters. They were relatively small vessels that sailed around the British and Irish coastlines, similar in some respect to the way heavy lorries travel up and down modern motorways, albeit at a different pace. Other ships either arrived with cargoes from abroad, or departed with freight destined for foreign ports. The Crown demanded a levy on certain commodities, and it was the responsibility of H.M. Customs and Excise officers to collect what was due. At one time customs officers also had to combat smuggling, but this latter duty passed to a new formation in 1809, that of the Prevention Water Guard, which 13 years later became H.M. Coastguard. With a look-out post and a detachment of armed men stationed at both Oystermouth and Port Eynon the Water/Coastguard must have been an effective deterrent because, by the time of Victoria's coronation, smuggling appears to have died out. The prime concern of the coastguards then had more to do with the perils of the sea.

Wrecks in the Victorian Era

For centuries 'wrecking' – searching the shoreline for wreckage – must have been a rewarding pursuit for Gowerians. At times a stretch of coastline might be littered with the wreckage of a ship that had been smashed to pieces by a combination of gale force winds, breakers and jagged rocks; even a partially damaged ship might be stranded on a beach, abandoned by its crew while breakers swept over its decks. Wrecks, however, were not necessarily the result of inshore disasters. Severe storms could drive

The Mumbles Roadstead – the western half of Swansea Bay provided a safe haven for ships in bad weather, the Mumbles Headland sheltering them from fierce south-westerly winds. Note the beach, how it slopes inland almost to the road at Southend; that was before the sea wall was built c.1892-3. The reclaimed land behind the wall is now occupied by housing, open-air leisure and car-parking facilities, and also Verdi's Restaurant.

a vessel miles off course, as happened to many a ship coming in from the Atlantic with the intention of either navigating the English Channel, or heading northwards through the Irish Sea.

The majority of ships that ended up wrecked, stranded or damaged on the Gower and Swansea Bay coastlines were the result of fog or tempest in the Bristol Channel, one of the most treacherous stretches of water in the western hemisphere. Over 200 ships became casualties on these coastlines in Victorian times, which is unsurprising as the Bristol Channel was also one of the busiest waterways in the world. A fair number of wrecks had been *en route* to, or departing from, Swansea or Neath. Others had been heading for one of the few places on the South Wales coast that offered shelter from fierce south-westerly winds. That safe anchorage was known as the Mumbles Road, or Roadstead; it was the name given to the curve of Swansea Bay between Mumbles Head and West Cross. The Roadstead was where upwards of 100 ships could sit out a storm, protected by the Mumbles Head.

The Roadstead was well known to mariners, and to enable them to find it at night or in foggy conditions a lighthouse had been erected on the outer island of Mumbles Head in 1794. Initially, light had been provided by two braziers, one positioned above the other, but by 1798 the braziers had been replaced by oil lamps and reflectors. The light was an aid to navigation; it signalled safe anchorage. Yet the Roadstead could be a dangerous place if the wind suddenly backed to south-east, as it did on occasion, sometimes with disastrous consequences. On the night of 27 February 1856 a south-westerly gale suddenly shifted to south-east. The wind increased, sending waves directly at the ships at anchor in the Roadstead. Eight vessels simply sank, nine parted their cables and were

Sailing ships in the Roadstead – ships often sheltered in the Roadstead whilst waiting their turn to enter Swansea Harbour. Note the stony foreshore. Many of these stones may have been dumped there as unwanted ballast.

driven onto the beach; a further five were damaged. When the storm abated the shoreline was strewn with wreckage. In all some 70 ships were sunk, wrecked or beached as a result of sheltering in the Roadstead, which constituted around one-third of the total number of vessels that came to grief on the Gower and Swansea Bay coastlines.

To the west there were other dangers. If a ship came in too close to the South Gower coastline, it risked being grounded on a sandbank. The Mixon Shoal to the south-west of Mumbles Head proved to be the undoing of no less than 15 vessels. Once stranded on the Mixon a ship was likely to be battered by wind and waves until it broke up. On four separate occasions entire crews perished in the dark, despite the close proximity of the lighthouse. A bell-buoy placed near the Mixon in 1852 failed to put an end to the sandbank's claim to notoriety. On the other side of the lighthouse the two sandbanks known as the Greengrounds were responsible for the sinking of a further seven ships, all of which had drifted there after parting their cables in the Roadstead.

Several miles to the west the Helwick Sands presented another danger, extending as they did from a position south-west of Port Eynon Point to a position south-west of Worms Head. The Helwick was responsible for the loss of some nine ships, many of which ended up as wreckage around the coast of West Gower. A Trinity House lightship was anchored near the western end of the Helwich in 1846. It proved to be a welcome aid to navigation, but it failed to end the notoriety of the Helwick Sands.

Closer inshore were rocks backed by 60-metre high cliffs. Nigh on 50 ships came to grief on the rocks along the South Gower coast. Yet dangerous and despairing though those rock may appear to be, for many desperate mariners they provided a means of escape from relentless waves and pounding surf. This was certainly the case in 1875 when, in the teeth of a fierce gale, the Russian barque *Jenny* grounded on the rocks below Pilton. The crew managed to crawl along the bowsprit and drop down onto the rocks, leaving the *Jenny* to be smashed to pieces by a cruel sea.

Wide sandy bays could often be more dangerous than rocks. A ship might run aground, but its position from the shoreline could prove too far for exhausted survivors to reach safely. If the

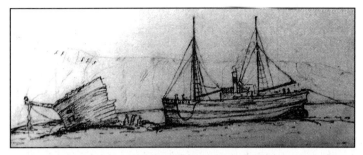

Top: *The wrecked* Helvetia *and the salvage vessel* Cambria – *a sketch by Lady Caroline Wilkinson dated 27 January 1888. There were no lives lost as a result of the* Helvetia's *misfortunes. However, when an unsuccessful attempt was made to salvage the ship by the salvage vessel* Cambria, *in the course of operations it lost its anchor. Two months later, six men tried to recover the anchor using a rowing boat. The sheer weight of the anchor and its chain caused the boat to capsize. Only one man made it to the beach.*

(Swansea Museum)

Bottom: *The remains of the* Helvetia – *they have protruded from the sands at Rhosili for 120 years, a gaunt reminder of how this part of the coastline could be a graveyard for shipping.*

survivors took to a longboat, they might easily be swamped. If they attempted to swim, they were just as likely to be submerged by one breaker after another until, gasping, they swallowed more water than air. Their only hope was to cling onto the rigging, hoping that relief would come soon. That relief sometimes took the form of a life-line launched from the shore. In the early part of Victoria's reign heavy mortars were used to throw a line into the rigging of a stranded ship. Later, the cumbersome mortars were replaced by far more effective rockets. Both mortars and rockets were in the care of the coastguard. When called out the coastguard personnel were aided by local volunteers who, together, formed Life Saving Apparatus (L.S.A.) Companies. There were L.S.A. Companies at Rhosili, Oxwich and elsewhere.

No less than 15 ships went aground in Port Eynon Bay, and a similar number were beached at Rhosili. There are no remains of wrecked Victorian ships at Port Eynon today, but Rhosili Bay still has the remains of three wrecks to remind us of how dangerous that part of the coast could be. Today, anyone enjoying the scenery around Rhosili is unlikely to miss the gaunt timber remains of the *Helvetia*. In 1887 this Norwegian barque suffered a series of misfortunes. Firstly, having failed to receive the assistance of a pilot boat at the Roadstead, it was driven westwards by a south-easterly gale until it struck the Helwick Sands. The *Helvetia* was then blown around Worms Head into Rhosili Bay, where she anchored in the shelter of the headland. The Rhosili L.S.A. Company managed to get a line aboard. One man was brought ashore with the aid of a breeches buoy; the rest of the crew came ashore in a boat. All seemed satisfactory until the wind shifted again, this time blowing from the west, causing the *Helvetia* to drag her anchor. It then became a matter of abandoning ship. By the following morning the *Helvetia* had come to rest where part of her wooden bows still protrude from the sand. Her 500-ton cargo of timber was discharged onto the beach, where some of it was appropriated by the locals, and the remainder bought by Swansea timber merchants.

Engines of the City of Bristol –
*as seen by Lady C. Wilkinson
during an exceptionally low
tide on 18 September1887.*
(Swansea Museum)

Closer to the headland and, therefore, less conspicuous, lie the remains of the Danish barque *Vennerne*, which became stranded in 1894 under similar circumstances to the *Helvetia*. The crew of seven, along with the captain's wife and child, made it ashore in a boat. There were no lives lost. However, the remains of a third wreck are associated with a considerable loss of life. Only occasionally, during exceptionally low spring tides, are the engines of the wrecked *City of Bristol* ever seen; they lie in the northern half of Rhosili Bay. This wooden paddle-steamer was bound for Bristol, having left Waterford in Ireland in December 1840, carrying a crew of 22, seven passengers, a cargo of provisions, and 280 pigs. When the wind veered south-east the captain decided to shelter in the lee of Worms Head. The *City of Bristol* then ran aground and was soon at the mercy of wind, waves and blinding rain. People were swept overboard, the ship began to break up; a total of 27 people drowned. Only two crewmen survived.

On Gower's north coast lay the Burry/Loughor Estuary, where ships threaded their way through several channels to reach shipping places such as Penclawdd, Loughor and Llanelly. There were no doubt many hazards relating to the channels, but the most hazardous place – if wrecks are anything to go by – was the mouth of the estuary in the vicinity of Whitford Point. More than 30 ships are known to have been wrecked, stranded or damaged in this area in Victorian times. Five of them ran into trouble on the Lynch, a sandbank to the west of Whitford Point. Most of the remaining ships ended up as wrecks on the coastline between Burry Holms and Llanmadoc. The worst disaster occurred in January 1868 when 19 vessels left Llanelly with no more than a breeze to accompany them. The vessels had for several days been prevented from leaving Llanelly by bad weather. When they set sail on a calm afternoon, no one had any reason to believe they would encounter troubled waters, but no sooner had they passed the lighthouse near Whitford Point than they saw a fearful swell before them, one that had followed in the wake of the bad weather. Some ships were damaged in the swell, but made headway. Eleven others ended up as wrecks on the coastline between Rhosili Bay and Llanmadoc. In the weeks that followed, many bodies were washed ashore. At one point it was believed that some 50 souls had perished in the tragedy, but an inquest set the number at 18.

The dangerous waters in the vicinity of Whitford Point had long been recognized, which was why in 1840 a lightship had been positioned to the north of Burry Holms. The lightship was replaced in 1844-5 by a lighthouse on wooden piles. This lighthouse was several times damaged by passing ships and was in turn replaced by a cast-iron lighthouse in 1865. Manned by one man, this last lighthouse remained in use until after the First World War.

The naming of the Wolverhampton, *1866 – the cost of this lifeboat was covered by donations from the people of Wolverhampton. Consequently, they had a ceremony before sending the lifeboat to Swansea by rail, the GWR providing the service free of charge. The* Wolverhampton *was stationed at Mumbles for more than 16 years, its crew of 13 almost entirely oyster fishermen. Its most famous – and tragic – launching took place in January 1883, when the German barque* Admiral Prinz Albert *was driven onto the outer island off Mumbles Head. Pounded by 15 to 20-foot waves, the lifeboat capsized on three occasions. Four crewmen lost their lives, leaving four widows and 19 orphans. The dead were honoured for their courage and self-sacrifice, as were the Ace sisters who bravely plucked one crewman from the waves that crashed against jagged rocks.*

The appalling loss of life around the Gower coast as a result of shipwreck undoubtedly prompted calls for lifeboats. The first lifeboat was stationed at Mumbles in 1835. That is not to say there were no boats available prior to that date. There were boats in every seaside village; there were men able and willing to man those boats as well – but the lifeboat stationed at Mumbles was different in that it was specially built for the purpose; it also served as a rallying point for volunteer crewmen. The boat – a small sailing boat – was transferred to Swansea Harbour in 1841. It returned to Mumbles a few years later, where successive lifeboats have been stationed till the present day. A second lifeboat station was established in 1852 on the lightship to the north of Burry Holms. Eleven years later the lifeboat was transferred to a new station at Pembrey. A third lifeboat station was established at Port Eynon in 1884. This station closed in 1916 after its lifeboat capsized twice near Pennard with the tragic loss of three crewmen.

Seventeen ships were either damaged or lost as result of collision, seven of them in Swansea Bay. A similar number came to grief as a result of thick fog, and to counter this menace, fog signals were in use at Mumbles lighthouse and on the Helwick lightship. Other ships sank in deep water a mile or more from shore, and did so for a variety of reasons that are beyond the scope of this work.

Wrecks in the Edwardian Era

The Leonora, *1913 – although outside the period covered by this work, the photograph illustrates the point that no part of the Gower coastline could be regarded as a safe landfall. After colliding with a tug, the damaged ketch* Leonora *was abandoned by its crew and allowed to drift onto the rocks at Rotherslade. There she remained, her sails in shreds, until she broke up in the face of gale force winds.*

Only nine ships came to grief around the Gower and Swansea Bay coastlines in the Edwardian era (1901-10), a mercifully small number when compared with an average of more than three ships each year during Victoria's reign. No doubt lighthouses and other warning systems played their part, as did the fact that, by then, wooden sailing-ships had by and large been superseded by iron steamships that could battle against wind and waves far more effectively than sail. All this may have been to the benefit of shipping in general, but lifeboats were still basically small sailing ships, with oars that enabled the crew to get in close to someone in distress. The dangers faced by crewmen were, therefore, as unrelenting as they always had been. This was made evident in 1903, when the Mumbles lifeboat *James Stephens* went to the aid of a steamer that had gone aground near the harbour entrance at Port Talbot. So severe were the wind and waves that the lifeboat capsized and six crewmen perished in a merciless sea.

Ship-building

There were shipwrights based at shipping places such as Oystermouth and Port Eynon. These shipwrights undoubtedly made a living out of repairing damaged boats and oyster skiffs, and may also have occasionally been involved in boat-building ventures. There was certainly small-scale ship-building activity in the parish of Llanrhidian as early as the late 17th century. This activity was still taking place in the decades prior to Victoria's coronation. In 1828, for example, a John Bennet rebuilt the single-masted sloop *Lark*, which had originally been built at Oxwich. The following year Howell John built the two-masted, 79-ton schooner *Friends*. Howell's yard was near Tabernacle Chapel, Penclawdd, and in the course of ten years he built at least six vessels, the last and largest being the 110-ton schooner *William and Mary*, which he built in 1838. A small amount of shipbuilding activity also took place at Oystermouth, but that will be dealt with in a later chapter.

The Church of England; the Anglican or Established Church

According to the *Religious Census* of 1851, there were 17 ecclesiastical parishes in Peninsula Gower, all of them within the Deanery of Gower and were, therefore, subject to the Bishop of St. David's. All the parishes, save one, had a parish church. The one exception was the tiny parish of Knelston, where

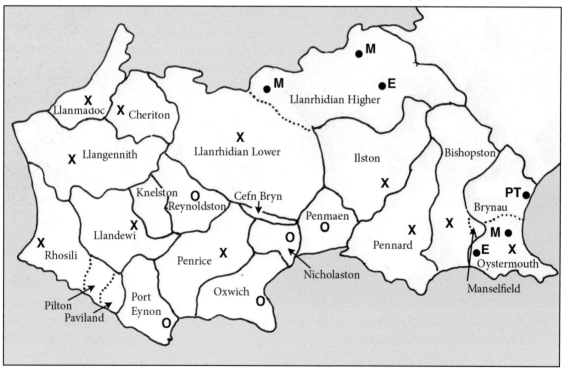

*The 17 parishes in Peninsula Gower – parish churches with military-type towers are marked with an **X** ; the five without towers with an **O**. The two chapels of ease are marked with an **E**; the three mission halls with an **M**; and the one private chapel with **PT**.*
Cefn Bryn belonged to no particular parish, but was common pasture for Gower farmers.

the Church of St. Taurin had become defunct in the 17th century. In 1851 the parish of Knelston was served by the vicar of Llandewi. Another deviation from the norm was that the exceptionally large parish of Llanrhidian was split into two parts – Llanrhidian Lower with the parish church in the village of Llanrhidian, and Llanrhidian Higher in which stood Llan-yr-newydd, a chapel of

Left: Llan-y-newydd – *a chapel of ease, rebuilt in 1850 on the site of much older building.*
The ancient spelling of Glynynewr *first appears in a document dated 1535. Fifty-two years later the people of Llanrhidian Higher were 'exempted from attending services' at the parish church at Llanrhidian. The exemption saved them a long walk, one that would have been dangerous in wet weather when the River Morlais was in flood.*

Right: *The Tower of Llanrhidian Church – today twelve churches in Peninsula Gower still have towers, one of the most impressive being the one attached to the church at Llanrhidian.*
At one time St. Cattwg's at Port Eynon also had a tower, which was demolished when the nave was enlarged in 1860-1. Most towers date back to the troubled times of the 13th century, when churches served as places of refuge and defence against marauding Welshmen. Although embattled, the top of the tower at Llanrhidian would have been concealed by hourds – protruding wooden structures from which crossbowmen would have shot at the attacking Welsh.

St. Cattwg's, Cheriton, differs from other Peninsula Gower churches in that its tower occupies a fairly central position in a building that is roughly cruciform in shape. The church was probably erected in its entirety in the early 14th century and may, therefore, be the last of the towered churches to be built.

ease built near Penclawdd. The vicar of Llanrhidian maintained that he preached 'alternatively at Llanrhidian and Penclawdd' and that his services were 'partially in English and Welsh', the Welsh part of the service being 'performed by the curate' of Llan-yr-newydd. All other churches in Peninsula Gower had their services in English only.

Nine churches were dedicated to Welsh saints – St. Illtyd's, Oxwich, being one of them – whereas Llan-yr-newydd (meaning The New Church) was dedicated to a Breton named St. Gwynour. A further seven churches were Norman/English dedications, such as St. Mary's, Rhosili. All the churches stood in an east-west alignment. They each comprised of a nave where the congregation gathered, entry into which was by way of a porch that was usually attached to the south wall. Almost all the churches had an extension on the eastern end of the nave known as the chancel, which is where the local clergyman conducted services.

At the beginning of Victoria's reign all the churches were old, the fabric of some dating back to the 12th century. All these buildings were, or were to become, desperately in need of restoration. Among the first to be restored were St. Mary's, Pennard, (1847), St. Illtyd's, Ilston, (1847) and St. Teilo's, Bishopston, (1851), all of them through the generosity of Thomas Penrice II of Kilvrough. Llan-yr-newydd, on the other hand, was so dilapidated that it had to be demolished and completely

St. Nicholas's, Nicholaston – as a memorial to her father, Olive Talbot undertook an almost complete rebuild of this church in High Church fashion, and did so in 1892-4 at her sole expense. With its lavish use of oak, teak, alabaster and coloured marble St. Nicholas's was described after its completion as the most elaborately treated ecclesiastical building in Wales. By that time there were five churches in Peninsula Gower with bell-cotes or bell-gables instead of towers.
St. Nicholas's, Nicholaston, and St. John the Baptist's, Penmaen, were originally built in the 14th century when the threat posed by Welsh insurgents was regarded as past. Both churches were completely rebuilt in Victorian times, the latter in 1854-5. Other churches included in this group are St. George's ,Reynoldston, and Llan-yr-newydd, Llanrhidian Higher, both of which were rebuilt from the foundations up, the former in 1866-7, the latter in 1850. St. Cattwg's Port Eynon also fell within this group when its tower was demolished in 1860.

rebuilt. The work, which was completed in 1850, was largely financed by a local landowner, Philip Evans of Brynhir, who recovered his outlay through the parish rate.

The churches at Penmaen (1855), Llanrhidian (1858) and Oystermouth (1860) were all restored in the space of six years, the work of all three being supervised by the same architect. At Llanrhidian – where the church bears the distinction of being dedicated to two saints: Rhidian and Illtyd – the restoration was restricted to rebuilding the nave and the porch. In the case of St. John's, Penmaen, an almost entire rebuild destroyed the earlier fabric. All Saints, Oystermouth, was spared a similar fate by the intervention of the antiquarian, George Grant Francis.

The 1860s witnessed the restoration of St. Cattwg's, Port Eynon (1861), St. Madoc's, Llanmadoc (1866), and St. George's, Reynoldston (1867), the last named undergoing an entire rebuild from the foundations up. In the next decade it was the turn of St. Cadoc's, Cheriton (1875), and St. David's, Llandewi (1876). Restoration at Llanmadoc and Cheriton was undertaken by the rector, the Revd. R.D. Davies, who used his inheritance to finance the work. The entire cost of restoring Llandewi was defrayed by C.R.M. Talbot of Margam and Penrice, whose daughter Emily was largely responsible for financing further renovation in 1905. The generosity of the Talbot family was second to none. Apart from Llandewi, (1876) C.R.M. Talbot had been almost entirely responsible for the cost of renovation at Port Eynon (1861) and had made substantial contributions to work carried out elsewhere. His daughter Emily bore the entire cost of restoring both St. Illtyd's Oxwich (1892) and St. Andrew's, Penrice (1894), and also contributed huge sums of money towards the renovation of the churches at Rhosili (1891), Llanrhidian (1901) and Llandewi (1905), whereas her sister, Olive, paid for the lavish rebuild of St. Nicholas's, Nicholaston (1894). Another church to be restored in this period was that of St. Cenydd's, Llangennith, the work being completed in 1884.

Many of the churches were held by rectors – clergymen who were entitled to pocket the tithes. Most rectors held the living of more than one church (plural livings) and employed a curate to officiate at one of the churches in their care. A few churches were held by vicars – clergymen who were appointed by whoever held the right of patronage to a particular church, which meant that the patron pocketed the tithes. For example, the Wardens and Fellows of All Souls College, Oxford, were once the patrons of St. Cenydd's, Llangennith, and St. Mary's, Pennard, and it was, therefore, the Wardens and Fellows who pocketed the tithes. In 1838 Thomas Penrice of Kilvrough acquired the right of patronage to both churches from All Souls College. Other laymen held rights of patronage to the churches at Oystermouth and Llanrhidian. In the case of Llandewi the right of patronage was held by the Bishop of St. David's until, in 1881-2, it was acquired by C.R.M. Talbot of Margam and Penrice.

Churches with the largest Sunday morning congregations were Oystermouth (300), Bishopston (250) and Llan-yr-newydd (230). Llanrhidian did not have a morning service, but its afternoon congregation was between 200 and 300. The smallest Sunday morning congregation was at Nicholaston (30), whereas Penmaen, Reynoldston, Llandewi and Rhosili all had congregations of around 40. The census also records the number of scholars who attended Sunday school, their number varying from nought at Nicholaston to 100 at Oystermouth.

Anglo-Catholics

The clergy were, of course, ordained by bishops of the Established Church, and the services that were conducted by these clergymen were basically the same in all Anglican churches. However, in 1833, several men connected with the University of Oxford called for changes to be made within the Church of England. The Oxford Movement, as it became known, called for a revival of Catholic ceremonial and a return to symbolic architecture. From about 1840 onwards many Anglican clergymen embraced the Oxford Movement; they became known either as High Churchmen or as Anglo-Catholics.

The movement had no impact on Peninsula Gower until 1860, when the Revd. R.D. Davies became rector of Llanmadoc. The Revd. Davies is perhaps the most colourful of the Victorian

Above: *St. Madoc's, Llanmadoc – probably the smallest of the Peninsula Gower churches. The extensive renovation of 1865 included lowering the tower to its present position.*

Left: *The Revd. R.D. Davies – rector of Llanmadoc and Cheriton, a High Churchman who might easily have been mistaken for a Catholic priest.* (Swansea Museum)

clergymen. A local man, born at Oxwich in 1831, he was ordained in 1856; that same year he became curate to Llanmadoc. Then, in 1860, he was appointed to the living of Llanmadoc. A staunch High Churchman, the Revd. Davies soon made changes to the services in which music had a prominent part. He heard confessions, he dressed like a Catholic priest, and in 1865 he had the church renovated without destroying too much of its ancient character. In 1867 he was appointed rector of Cheriton, and ten years later he renovated that church as well, using his inheritance to fund the work. Loved and respected, the Revd. Davies died in 1911. He is remembered most for his invaluable *History of West Gower*, which he published in four volumes between 1877 and 1894.

The Nonconformists

Nonconformists were Christians who refused to conform to the established practices of the Anglican Church. There were several denominations in Peninsula Gower. The Baptists and the Independents had originated from would-be reformers in Elizabethan times, who, as Puritans, eventually broke away from the Anglican Church. The Methodists also originated from within the Established Church. They first made their appearance as revivalists in the 1730s – their purpose, to counter the sleepy, intellectual aspect of the Established Church by appealing to the emotions of sinners. Their open-air meetings led to mass conversions and to the establishment of religious societies, the members of which met in farms and cottages to enhance their spiritual growth. So successful were the revivalists that many of the older Nonconformist denominations adopted the Methodists' approach to conversion and worship.

In South Wales there were initially two forms of Methodism. In the Welsh-speaking areas the fiery preacher Howell Harris established societies that were eventually to become known as Calvinistic Methodists. In the English-speaking districts, John Wesley and others founded societies that later became known as the Wesleyan Methodists. Neither Harris nor Wesley wanted their

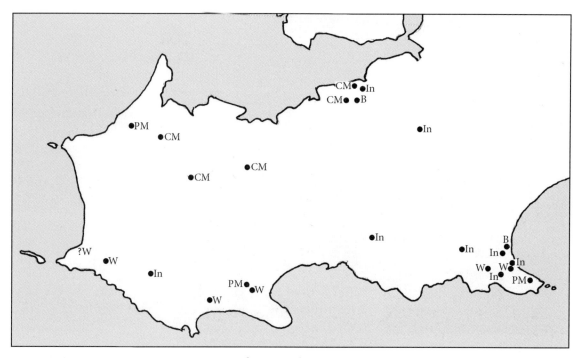

Nonconformist Chapels in 1851

In	*Independent (8)*	B	*Baptist (2)*	PM	*Primitive Methodist (3)*
CM	*Calvinistic Methodist (5)*	W	*Wesleyan Methodist (6)*		

societies to break away from the Established Church, but in a church that was unwilling to change, schism was inevitable. The Wesleyian Methodists broke away in 1795; the Calvinistic Methodists did the same 16 years later. The two groups, therefore, became Nonconformists.

The older Nonconformists had flourished for a while in the days of Oliver Cromwell, but shortly after the restoration of the monarchy in 1660, laws were passed that were intended to suppress Nonconformist gatherings. The situation eased when, in 1672, the Nonconformist (or Dissenters as they were then called) were permitted to worship in private residences, providing those residences were licenced for the purpose. In 1689 a further concession permitted them to build their own chapels. A hundred years were to pass before the Nonconformists in Peninsula Gower took advantage of this concession, and the first to do so were the Independents within the Welshry – they built Capel y Crwys, Three Crosses, in 1788. A further 20 years were to pass before chapel-building began in earnest.

Six chapels were built by the English aristocrat, Lady Barham, all of them for the Calvinistic Methodist cause. These early chapels were built to serve rural areas and were, therefore, small and basic in their design. At the time of the religious census of 1851 there were five Calvinistic Methodist chapels, all of them situated on the north side of the peninsula; they were Ebenezer, Oldwalls (1813); Bethesda, Burry Green (1814); Trinity, Cheriton (1816); Tabernacle, Penclawdd (1836); and Penuel Y Rallt, Wernffrwd (1844, now a private residence). The congregations of these chapels varied in number from 60 to 160. Their best-known minister was William Griffiths (the Apostle of Gower)

Top: *Ebenezer, Oldwalls – built in 1813 by the Wesleyan Methodists and then abandoned when their cause failed in this area. The original chapel was taken over by William Griffith on behalf of the Calvinistic Methodists in 1823. In 1851 Ebenezer had an average Sunday evening attendance of 160. What is seen here is a rebuild of 1852.*

Middle: *Bethesda, Burry Green – built in 1814 by Lady Barham on behalf of the Calvinistic Methodist cause, the chapel is a typical rural foundation – small and basic in its design. In 1851 it had an average Sunday evening congregation of around 140.*

Bottom: *Trinity, Cheriton – one of the six Lady Barham foundations. Built in 1816 and used as a schoolroom as well as for services, it was described as a small building, long, low and thatched. Trinity was renovated in 1867, its thatched roof replaced by slate. Its average Sunday morning service in 1851 was said to have been 130 plus 60 scholars.*

Tabernacle, Norton – founded by the Independents in 1831, it was abandoned when, in c.1870, the congregation moved to its present location opposite Oystermouth Police Station. The original chapel shown here is now a private residence.

who began preaching locally in 1816. At the time of the religious census of 1851, he had charge of both Bethesda, Burry Green and Ebenezer, Oldwalls.

The Baptists had only two chapels in Peninsula Gower in 1851 – Mount Hermon, Penclawdd (1807, now defunct) and Bethany, West Cross (1851). The average Sunday evening attendance ranged from 30-40 at Mount Hermon to around 100 at Bethany. When Bethany became too small, a new chapel was built (1867) close to the earlier one, which became a schoolroom. One of the best known Baptist ministers was Joseph Harris (Gomer) who came to Penclawdd in *c.*1803 and later founded the chapel of Mount Hermon. Joseph Harris is remembered as the creator of *Seren Gomer*, a successful religious periodical.

The Independents, on the other hand, had eight chapels in 1851, all of them, save one, situated in the eastern half of the peninsula; they were Capel y Crwys, Three Crosses (1788); Providence, Bishopston (1807, no longer a place of worship); Bethel, Penclawdd (1818); Paraclete, Newton (1818); Immanuel, Pilton Green (1821, now a private residence); Mount Pisgah, Parkmill (1822); Tabernacle, Norton (1831, now a private residence); and Mount Zion, Oystermouth (1851). Four of these chapels (those built between 1818 and 1822) were originally Lady Barham foundations, but due to a disagreement with her ladyship, the four chapels abandoned their allegiance to the Calvinistic Methodist cause and became Independent instead. Five Independent chapels had quite large congregations, the largest being Capel y Crwys, Three Crosses (building enlarged 1831), which had a general congregation of around 5-600. The minister, John Evans, also had charge of Bethel, Penclawdd, which had a Sunday evening congregation of around 300.

The Wesleyan Methodists differed from the Calvinists in that they owed their existence to John Wesley, who had visited the English-speaking parts of Peninsula Gower on five separate occasions between 1764-71. Consequently, the six Wesleyan chapels recorded in the 1851 census were all situated along the south coast and were, therefore, in the heart of the Englishry. None of these chapels had Biblical names; they were situated at Oxwich (1808, now defunct); Horton (1813); Oystermouth (the Dunns, 1814); Murton Green (1831); Lower Pitton (1833, now a private residence); and Rhosili (1835). However, the last named has never been located and is considered to be a mistaken entry. Wesleyan chapels were described in 1851 as 'built in … dog-kennel fashion' presumably because the main entrance was at one end of the building. The Wesleyan congregations varied between 50 (the Dunns, Oystermouth) and 140 (Horton).

A related denomination was the Primitive Methodists, otherwise known by the derogatory name of 'Ranters'. The Primitive Methodists had been expelled from the Wesleyan cause because

Top: *The Old Chapel, Lower Pitton – the original Wesleyan chapel of 1833. It stands within the hamlet of Lower Pitton, on the lane to Mewslade, and is now a private residence called The Old Chapel. In 1851 this chapel had a congregation of around 100. In 1847 an ex-farmer was also using this building as a private school.*

Bottom: *Wesleyan chapel, Pitton – this later chapel at Pitton was built in 1887 on a windswept site that had previously been used for winnowing corn. It replaced the chapel at Lower Pitton.*

they refused to abide by certain rules. Their fiery preachers first appeared in the Lordship of Gower in the early 1830s and by *c*.1838 they had established chapels at Llanmadoc and Oxwich. Eight years later they built their third chapel at Southend, Oystermouth. The congregations at these chapels were relatively small, the largest being Oxwich, which numbered around 160.

In total, the religious census of 1851 recorded 24 chapels in Peninsula Gower, a quarter of which were situated in the Welshry of Llanrhidian Higher; six others were in Oystermouth parish. Although the census is too vague to provide overall attendance figures for both Anglicans and Nonconformists, it is nevertheless possible to make approximations. In the Welshry, for example, the Nonconformists would appear to have outnumbered the Anglicans by 5 to 1; in Oystermouth parish the figure was about 3 to 1. In all other parishes taken as whole the Anglicans appear to have had a slight numerical advantage over the Nonconformists.

Tithes Wars

For centuries the Anglican Church had claimed 10% of the annual produce of the land for the support of its clergy, although, as stated above, tithes (tenths) were often paid to laymen who held the right of patronage to some churches. For the most part the tithes were paid in kind – in corn, livestock, eggs, wool and the like, but by the early 19th century payments in kind were no longer practical in a society where money was the means of exchange. So in 1836 Parliament passed an Act whereby the payment of tithes would be in money, the amount levied on each landowner, or leaseholder, being dependent on the average price over the preceding seven years of wheat, barley and oats.

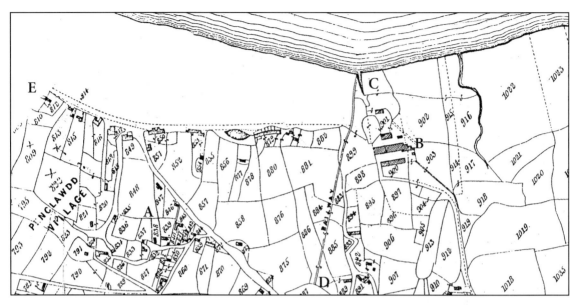

*Tithe map, Penclawdd – in 1847 the village (A) was centred on the hillside behind the Royal Oak;
additional buildings lined the foreshore to the west. There were few buildings in what is today
regarded as the centre of the village, other than the old copperworks (B) and the copperworks'
barracks. Penclawdd Dock (C) is shown as a narrow inlet, perhaps because it was of little interest to
the map makers. A railway – part of it an incline – extends inland to what was then
Penclawdd Colliery (D). Note there was no road leading to what is now Gowerton.
The only roads – or tracks – shown are the three leading south towards Three Crosses,
and also the one leading westwards to Crofty (E).*

(West Glamorgan Archive Service)

The change-over required the production of detailed maps of every parish in the realm,
each map showing and numbering every productive field within the parish bounds. In the case of
Peninsula Gower the tithe maps were published between 1841 and 1848. These maps have proved
invaluable to historians, as they show not only fields, but tracks, farms and villages. They are, in
fact, the earliest detailed maps of the peninsula. What is equally valuable to the historian is the
tithe assessment schedules, which record who owned the land, and who held it by lease. The data in
the assessment schedules make it possible to calculate exactly how much acreage each landowner
possessed. With regard to detail there is nothing to compare with the tithe maps of the 1840s until
the appearance of O.S. maps of *c.*1878.

However desirable payments in money were to the Anglican clergy, the tithes were resented
by both Nonconformists and by those who had no religious convictions. What the situation may
have been locally is not known, but in mid-Victorian Wales the Nonconformists outnumbered the
Anglicans, whereas the uncommitted amounted to approximately half the population. It is hardly
surprising, therefore, that there was opposition to the clergy's right to tithes. Yet the tithe-rent
charge continued to be upheld until 1878, when the price of cereal word-wide began to fall. The
falling price reduced the value of the tithes, which in turn reduced the clergy's income. The price fall
also affected the farmer's income, and pretty soon the payments of many farmers fell into arrears.

This put the Anglican clergy in a difficult position: if they took steps to distrain (confiscate) the farmers goods for non-payment, they risked alienating the local population. The Church, on the other hand, faced growing opposition from both the Nonconformists and the nationalists, who had the support of many Liberal MPs. For several years this tithe war, as it was known, was non-violent, but when, from 1886 onwards, attempts were made to distrain farmers, the campaigners in North Wales became involved in violent scuffles with the police. The violence led to a government inquiry, the outcome of which was the Tithe Act of 1891. The Act did not put an end to the payment of tithes, it simply passed the buck on to the landowners, who became responsible for the payments and who recouped their outlay by way of rent. The Act did, however, put an end to the violence. Several minor tithe wars flared up intermittently until Parliament finally abolished the tithe-rent charge in 1936.

Population Statistics

The first ten-yearly census, which took place in 1801, recorded a population in Peninsula Gower of 5,153. Fifty years later, the census for 1851 showed that the population had increased to 8,506. Thereafter, despite depopulation in the western half of the peninsula, the overall population continued to rise, reaching 11,727 in 1901 (the year of Victoria's death), and 14,498 in 1911.

Between 1801 and 1851 there had been 'blips' when the population of several parishes declined in one decade only to rise again in the next. In most cases the blips were quite small, but between 1801 and 1811 the population of Pennard fell by 47 (from 314 persons to 267), and did so for no apparent reason; thereafter it rose slightly during the following three decades. However, in the early part of Victoria's reign the population of several parishes went into long-term decline. In Port Eynon, for example, the depopulation began between 1831 and 1841. In Pennard, Ilston and Llangennith it commenced some ten years later. In four other parishes (Penrice, Oxwich, Knelston, and Llanmadoc) the depopulation took place from c.1851 onwards. In Pennard the decline was ascribed to emigration; in Llangennith it was attributed to 'emigration and the removal of families to Swansea'.

Irrespective of where these people went the reasons for their removal were poor wages and a lack of employment opportunities. Indeed, agriculture, oyster fishing and limestone quarrying all slumped in the latter part of Victoria's reign. Depopulation, then, was the result of migration to urban and industrialized areas, to Swansea in particular, where the call of the sea combined with the prospect of promotion, even to that of ship's master. Emigration, on the other hand, was made easier by the growing number of steamships, providing a voyage that was much less demanding than on windjammers. In the 1850s the destination of many was Australia; in the 1860s it was the U.S.A.

In five parishes the population rose steadily between 1801 and 1851. In Rhosili the rise was attributed to an 'extension of the limestone trade', which may have been the reason for a similar rise in Llanmadoc (after 1851 this parish went into long-term decline). In Bishopston the population rose from 303 in 1801 to peak at 513 in 1851. The population then declined in the following decade; thereafter it rose steadily to peak again at 893 in 1911. The latter increase may be attributed to some extent to the oyster fishing boom in the third quarter of the 19th century, but more so to employment opportunities in market gardening, the produce of which was destined for ever-expanding urban areas such as Swansea.

In the coal mining parish of Llanrhidian the population rose (except for one very small blip) from 1,275 in 1801 to peak at 3,700 in 1881. The most dramatic increase in this period took place in the decade 1871-81 when the population rose by 1,549 persons. This rise may be attributed to the opening of the Penclawdd Tin-plate Works, to the extension of the railway to Llanmorlais, and to a boom in coal mining. After 1881 the population fell to 3,560 in the next ten years, and remained virtually unchanged until 1901. Thereafter the population rose to 4,433 in the years leading up to 1911.

In Oystermouth parish, the population in 1801 had stood at 715 persons. Thereafter the population rose continuously throughout both the Victorian and Edwardian eras to an unprecedented 6,571 persons in 1911 (this included what was then the two civil parishes of Oystermouth and Brynau). The most dramatic increase occurred in the decade between 1861 and 1871, when the population rose from 2,460 to 3,574 – an increase of 1,114 persons. The decade coincides with a period in which oyster fishing boomed. More important still, the Oystermouth Railway passenger service (discontinued in 1826) was revived in 1860, and this service had a tremendous impact on Oystermouth parish, for not only did the railway encourage both workers and professionals to live in Mumbles and commute to Swansea, but it also brought in huge numbers of day-trippers during the summer months; this in turn encouraged the settlement of entrepreneurs to cater for the seasonal influx.

The Church's Response to a Rising Population

In most parishes in Peninsula Gower the Established Church ministered to a dwindling population and had, therefore, no need to increase the number or size of its churches. In two parishes, however, the Church of England did provide additional places of worship. In Llanrhidian Higher the Church erected *St. David's* mission at Wernffrwd (on the edge of the marsh) in 1898. Twelve years later the Church established at Penclawdd a second mission, using a hall that had originally been built by the Primitive Methodists. In Oystermouth, St. Peter's chapel of ease was built at Newton in 1903-4; this was followed by the erection of a tin mission at Norton in 1908. Clyne Chapel was also erected about this time (1907), but as this was built by Graham Vivian of Clyne Castle for his own use and that of his tenants it cannot be regarded as a place of worship established by the Church of England.

St. David's Mission, Wernffrwd – an Anglican foundation, built on the edge of marsh in 1898 to accommodate the growing coal mining community in and around Llanmorlais.

The Chapel's Response to a Rising Population

The Nonconformists – unlike the Anglicans – were not confined to parishes, but formed gathered churches in which members came from as far away as they were prepared to travel. Nonconformist chapels were, therefore, built according to how successful their ministry was in a particular area.

Top: *Carmel, Cilibion – built in 1885, primarily as a school, the building also served as a daughter chapel of Capel y Crwys, Three Crosses; as such it accommodated a mining community centred on Mynydd Bach y Cocs.*

Bottom: *Defunct chapel, Penclawdd – originally built by the Primitive Methodists sometime after the census of 1851, it was taken over as a mission hall by the Church of England in 1910. The porch bears a date of AD1915, which probably relates to the building of the porch and to extensions added to the hall.*

The Independents, for example, having built Capel y Crwys, Three Crosses, in 1788 and witnessing a growing membership elsewhere, established daughter (or branch) chapels at Penclawdd (Bethel) in 1839, Cilibion (Carmel) in 1885 and Upper Killay in 1911. Likewise, the Calvinistic Methodists, having built Tabernacle, Penclawdd, in 1836, went on to establish daughter chapels at Wernffrwd (Penuel) in 1844 and Crofty (Zoar) in 1884.

At times the membership of a 'gathered church' could grow rapidly whenever a fiery preacher appeared on the scene. Numbers could also increase rapidly as a result of local and national revivals. The 1859 revival, for example, had started in America two years earlier. When it reached South Wales, its effect in Peninsula Gower led to a flurry of chapel building and renovation between 1861 and 1870. No less than six new chapels were built in this decade, while four older chapels were either renovated or enlarged, and the Mumbles Methodist chapel was completely rebuilt on the site of an earlier place of worship.

There were other revivals, the most notable occurring in 1904-5. It is, therefore, not surprising to find that the 24 chapels recorded in 1851 had increased to 32 by the time of the religious census of 1911. These figures suggest an additional eight chapels came into existence in the 60 years after 1851, but this is not the true picture. The Baptists, for example, lost Mount Hermon, Penclawdd (defunct), but established four other chapels elsewhere, resulting in an overall gain of three places of worship. Unsurprisingly, the unlocated Wesleyan Methodist chapel that was supposed to have existed at Rhosili does not appear in the census of 1911; nor does their chapel in Cock Street, Llangennith

Denomination	Public places of worship	
	in 1851	in 1911
Total Anglican	17	21
Independent	8	9
Calvanistic Methodist	5	7
Wesleyan Methodist	6	8
Primitive Methodist	3	0
Baptist	2	5
Christadelphian	0	1
Salvation Army	0	1
Plymouth Brethren	0	1
Total Nonconformist	24	32

(1862), as their cause there was short-lived (the building is now a private residence). What is most surprising is that the Primitive Methodists did not survive the Victorian era; their three chapels eventually became defunct and were, therefore, lost; lost, too, was their post-1851 chapel at Penclawdd. The picture is complicated still further by the fact that Oystermouth's close proximity to Swansea made it susceptible to new influences. Mount Zion in the Dunns, for example, had been an Independent foundation in 1851, but in

Left: *Capel y Crwys, Three Crosses – the original building of 1788 was the first chapel to be erected in Peninsula Gower. It was an Independent foundation. The chapel seen here is an entire rebuild of 1877, its style common to Welsh-speaking industrialized areas. The style may be described as an imposing frontage, the main entrance flanked by large, usually round-headed windows and other eye-catching features.*

Left: *Tabernacle, Penclawdd – the Calvinistic Methodists built their original chapel on the seafront at Penclawdd in 1836. The Tabernacle shown here is an entire rebuild of 1911, its location close to the chapel it replaced. Its Gothic style makes it appear more like a church than a chapel.*

Below: *Mumbles 1868 – the chapel towards the right of this picture is the second Wesleyan chapel to have been built on the corner of Dunns Lane. The first chapel had been erected in 1814 and that depicted below in 1861 to accommodate a growing congregation. The congregation evidently continued to grow because, in 1877-8, this chapel was demolished to make way for the Mumbles Methodist chapel that can be seen today. Oystermouth Castle appears on the skyline of the photograph. The wall on the right-hand side of the road overlooks the beach, which became reclaimed land after the Mumbles Railway was extended (on an embankment) from the Dunns to Southend in 1892-3.*

(Swansea Museum)

Oystermouth pre-1877 – the second Wesleyan chapel of 1861-77 and the houses to the left, as seen from that part of the beach known as Horsepool. Had they survived, the above buildings would now be obscured by shops, tennis court, bowling green and Devon Place.
The Promenade (formerly the route of the Mumbles Railway) and the sea wall on which it stands also fronts the modern-day buildings and leisure facilities listed above.

Right: *The Mumbles Methodist chapel – built in 1877-8 and extensively renovated in recent years, this building still holds services for a Methodist congregation. It also houses a café and a Tourist Information Centre.*

c.1870 its congregation became Christadelphian instead. The Salvation Army also established a presence in Oystermouth from *c*.1875 onwards, whereas in 1881 the Plymouth Brethren (of West Country origin) made use of the old Primitive Methodist's hall at Southend until such time as their Castleton Gospel Hall was built in 1902-3.

Increasing the number of chapels was not the only Nonconformist response to the spiritual requirements of the late Victorian and Edwardian eras. All the early chapels that were to survive until 1911 were either renovated or enlarged, or were completely rebuilt, either on the same site or on a nearby plot. Some of the rebuilt chapels in Llanrhidian Higher were not only large – far larger than those in rural areas – but they reflected the wealth and piety of the times. Capel y Crwys. Three Crosses, for example, was completely rebuilt on an adjacent plot in 1877. The resulting edifice reflected the wealth generated by industrialization. The same may be said of Bethel, Penclawdd, rebuilt by the Independents in 1910, and Tabernacle, Penclawdd, rebuilt by the Calvinistic Methodists in 1911.

A similar development took place in Oystermouth parish. It began when the Wesleyans built a large and impressive chapel at the bottom of Dunns Lane in 1861, which they rebuilt again in 1878. Further inland the Independents built Tabernacle (near the Police Station) in 1870 to replace a smaller place of worship in Norton (now a private residence). Some ten years later they rebuilt Paraclete Newton. Later still, the Mumbles' Baptists erected a new building near Underhill Park in 1910, its style more that of a church.

Sunday Schools

In the *Report of the Commission of Enquiry into the state of Education in Wales*, published in 1847, the government-appointed commissioners and their assistants made it plain that schools fell into two main categories – Sunday schools and (week)day schools. The first Sunday school in Peninsula Gower was set up by the Anglicans at Oystermouth in 1805. By 1847 the number had increased to the extent that the report listed 30 such schools, and referred to two others elsewhere in the text (at Knelston and at Llangennith) – 32 in total. Generally speaking, Sunday schools taught pupils to read the Scriptures. In Nonconformist Sunday schools there was a mixture of worship and discussion as well, whereas in Anglican Sunday schools it was important that pupils learned the Church catechism. Lessons usually lasted two to three hours; they took place in churches, chapels, farmhouses (4), cottages (3) and day school-rooms.

Fourteen Sunday schools were held 'in connection with' the Established Church; there was usually one such school in each parish. Sixteen Sunday schools 'were in connection with' the Nonconformists, nine of them located in the parish of Llanrhidian. The Independents kept eight such schools, the Calvinistic Methodists five, the Wesleyans three and the Baptists one. There was, however, one Sunday school unconnected with any denomination. This last school, which was held in a cottage in Nicholaston, was supported by a local landowner, William Voss.

In the Englishry, lessons were in English. In the Welshry, lessons at three schools were in Welsh – Berthllwyd, Three Crosses and Penclawdd (all of them Independent). Four other schools (three of them Independent) were bilingual – Killay (or rather Upper Killay in Bishopston parish), Tycoch (a farmhouse in Llanrhidian parish), Wimblewood (also a farm in the same parish), and Mount Hermon (a Baptist Church in Llanrhidian parish). What is noteworthy about Nonconformist Sunday schools is that a significant number of adults attended them as well as children.

The cost of these schools was usually covered by subscriptions and collections from the better-off. Instruction was usually provided by unpaid lay volunteers, 182 of them in all. At three Anglican and three Nonconformist schools instruction was provided by either clergymen or ministers. However, the Sunday schools that had the most to offer were under the patronage of the Talbots of Margam and Penrice. The school at Middleton, Rhosili, for example, had one paid teacher, as did the one at Reynoldston, whereas Oxwich had two paid teachers and Penrice three. The last named was the only Sunday school to have writing included in the curriculum.

Only two Sunday schools were actually visited by assistants, both of them 'in connection with' the Nonconformists (Penclawdd Calvinistic Methodist and Three Crosses Independent). In the assistants' opinion the children at both these schools were very ignorant when it came to answering questions of a religious nature. It has been suggested that the commissioners and their assistants were prejudiced against the Nonconformists, who were themselves suspicious of the government's motives for conducting the enquiry. However, whatever the shortcomings of Sunday schools in general, they did give children from poor families the opportunity to have at least a rudimentary education. In Peninsula Gower over 1,500 children benefited from this form of education in 1847.

Church Day Schools

In the report the visiting assistants referred to day schools in which instruction was in accordance with the teachings of the Established Church. In Peninsula Gower there were 14 such schools, all of which owed their existence to the generosity of patrons and regular subscribers, and also to the weekly 'school pence' which parents had to provide for each child. Thirteen of these schools were founded between 1805 and 1846. The one exception was the Village School, Bishopston, which had been founded as far back as 1728, if not earlier. In the report of 1847 the Village School was described as follows:

> The school-room, which is close to the village, is large and open-roofed [meaning the rafters were not hidden by a ceiling]; it abuts the churchyard wall … and is repaired by a parochial rate … The furniture consists of two rude planks nailed on piles driven into the floor, glazed with age, soiled with ink, and cut all over with names, which served the purpose of desks. The benches were equally rude and in bad repair.

Little is known of what went on at the Village School, it being closed on the day the visiting assistant called. Ordinarily a schedule should have been filled in, one that would have provided the assistant with all the relevant information, but the schedule was incomplete, presumably because there was no one there to provide detailed information. However, an entry concerning this school stated that 'the Church Catechism is taught in it', but it can be assumed that – like most other day schools – the 22 children in attendance would have been taught to read the Scriptures; a reference to 'ink' suggests they may have been taught to write as well.

The number of children registered at Church day schools varied between 12 at Mrs. Clement's (1831) in Knelston parish and 80 at Mr. Philip's (1834) in Llangennith parish. In most schools the children's behaviour was described as 'orderly'. Reading was taught at all Church schools, and all bar two (Mrs. Clement's and Mrs. Gronow's) gave instruction in writing as well (with chalk, on slates or on paper). Only half the schools provided instruction in all the 3Rs. At five schools the visiting

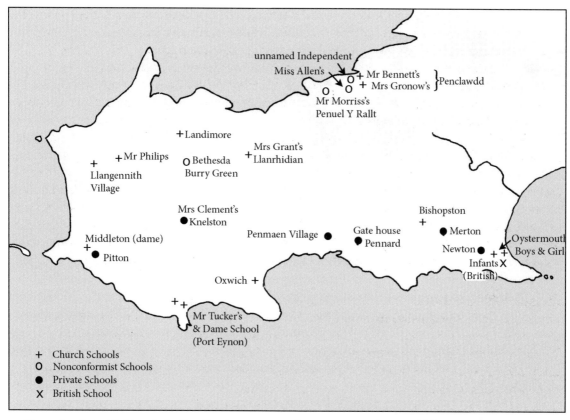

Day schools in 1847 – their distribution suggests that most parishes could boast at least one such school. The schools, however, were not so evenly distributed as they may seem. Most private schools, which were all small, are presumed to have closed when the master or mistress could no longer teach, leaving the parishes in which they had been situated without a school.

assistants were critical of the way questions on religious matters were answered. In fact, it would appear that the assistants were more interested in the children's response to such questions than they were in the children's ability to read and write. Consequently, the children at some schools were described as 'ignorant', although at one of these schools at least their 'ignorance' was attributed to irregular attendance, the parents unable at times to afford the weekly 'school pence'.

The report stated that at Bishopston the master (who was also the village tailor) 'did not speak English at all correctly'. This sort of criticism was levelled at the masters and mistresses of most Peninsula Gower schools, both in the Welshry, and in the Englishry where the local dialect was broad. The master at the Village School (1844), Llangennith, was described as 'ignorant [and] not properly educated for his business', he being formerly a joiner. A mistress at Penclawdd, Mrs. Gronow, had formerly been a servant, but she was described as 'intelligent', and the 28 children in her charge were 'very orderly ... far from being ignorant, especially of the Scriptures'. Only the master at the Village School (1845), Llanrhidian, had any formal training, and his 22 children were 'orderly, but very ignorant' (due to irregular attendance). The lowest paid teacher was Mrs. Gronow, who provided 'instruction in reading' only, for which she received £7 per annum from 'school pence'. The best paid teacher was the mistress at Oxwich Village School, who had 43 children on her books, for which she was paid £30 per annum and had a house and garden rent-free.

In all these one-room day schools, children of all ages received instruction in English only, although at two schools at Penclawdd (Mr. Bennett's and Mrs. Gronow's) Welsh was 'spoken in explanation of English books'. In at least five schools the master or mistress appointed older children to be monitors, their task being to supervise younger children, thereby leaving the master or mistress free to concentrate on the class in general. The monitorial system had first been promoted in England by one Joseph Lancaster, and had since been adopted by two nationwide school societies as a means of maintaining order in school-rooms.

Four schools were under the patronage of the Talbots of Margam and Penrice. At Port Eynon, C.R.M. Talbot had given land for the erection of what had become Mr. Tucker's School (1840), and had since contributed towards the master's salary. Mr. Tucker, a former joiner, taught 42 children, eight of whom were monitors. He taught the 3Rs, as well as English Grammar and Etymology (the study of the origins and historical development of words). Yet despite the extended curriculum the visiting assistant was unimpressed by the children's answers to questions relating to fundamental beliefs.

Three schools were under the patronage of Miss Talbot (presumably one of C.R.M.'s sisters), who visited them on a regular basis. One school stood alongside Mr. Tucker's Port Eynon school-room. This was a dame school (1838) with 22 pupils on its books. The school at Oxwich (1813) had 43 pupils, four of them monitors, and was assessed as an 'efficient school'. The school at Middleton, Rhosili (1833) also met the approval of the visiting assistant, who maintained 'there are very many schools less efficient than this … The children read pretty well, were well versed in the Catechism, and gave ready answers on religious subjects'.

Surprisingly, at the time of the report, none of the day schools associated with the Church had taken advantage of government funding. In 1833 the government had introduced funding for use by the 'National Society for Promoting the Education of the Poor in the Principles of the Established Church'. This funding was only available to Church schools if they met certain criteria. Presumably most Church schools in Peninsula Gower did not meet the criteria, perhaps because many of them were too poor. As to the schools under the Talbots' patronage, it may be that they preferred not to have government inspectors intruding into what they considered to be their domain. The Village School, Bishopston, was the first to receive government funding. In 1850 the Village School agreed to be open to the … inspector of schools, and by doing so became a National School in receipt of grant-aid.

Other Day Schools

The Nonconformists in the peninsula had only four day schools in 1847, three of which were connected with the Calvinistic Methodist cause. It may be that the Nonconformists preferred to make use of Sunday schools, rather than day schools, but in this they may also have been influenced by a lack of financial support. The Calvinistic Methodist school (1819) in the care of Miss Evans, for example, was the only one to be supported by subscriptions and donations; it was held in the vestry at Bethesda, Burry Green. The other two schools connected with this denomination were Miss Allen's (1827), Penclawdd, and Mr. Morris's (1845), which was held in the chapel of Penuel Y Rallt. Both these schools were entirely dependent on 'school pence' for their survival. Miss Allen had 16 pupils on her books, described as 'orderly, moderately well informed on religious subjects, and read pretty well', for which she was paid £16 per annum out of 'school pence'. Mr. Morris, on the other hand, had only eight children, who were described as 'disorderly and ignorant', for which he was paid £5 per annum out of 'school pence'. It was recorded that at Mr. Morris's school 'Welsh was spoken in explanation of English books'. The school held at Bethesda, Burry Green was closed on the day the visiting assistant called, but according to a schedule filled in by the minister's wife there were 15 children on its books.

The report refers to 'another day-school, usually kept in the Village of Penclawdd, but closed on the day' the visiting assistant called. In another part of the report the school is listed under the name of the Revd. W. Williams, which means that it was held in connection with the Independents. The Revd. Williams was apparently unwilling to co-operate with the assistant, for not only was the school closed, but no one was available to fill in a schedule.

Also referred to in the report were five private schools unconnected with any denomination. These schools had been set up by enterprising individuals who wished to make a living out of teaching children. Schooling took place in the homes of the self-appointed masters or mistresses. The schools were, therefore, all quite small. At Gatehouse (1846), Pennard, for example, a mistress had only six children in her charge, for which she was received 16s. per annum from 'school pence'. At Pitton (1842), on the other hand, an ex-farmer had 18 children on his books, for which he received £20 per annum again from 'school pence'.

The most interesting school in this group was Newton, Oystermouth, founded in 1807 by a 'Purser's steward in the Navy'. In the space of 40 years this former sailor 'had taught almost all the parish, and had then with him the grandsons of former pupils, [but] at the time [of the assistant's visit the] school was upon decline'. The reason for this, according to the master, was that 'the farms in the parish were much more subdivided than formerly'. The parents who could afford to 'send their children to his school had [therefore] diminished in number'. Schooling was held in a house that 'was neat and clean, and of the size of a farm-house'. Aged 77, the master was described as 'hale and sharp … His wife helped him to teach the little ones', and for these services they received an annual income of £18. The school was closed the day the assistant called, but according to a schedule that had been filled in, 30 children attended this school.

The last school to be considered is the Infant School (1813), Oystermouth, which was not connected with any denomination and promoted by one Henry Bath, a Swansea shipowner. What is noteworthy about this school is that the building – which was held in trust – had then recently been built (on the site of today's library) with a grant of £30. Presumably the grant-aid came from the British and Foreign School Society, which, in simplified terms, supported schools that did not teach a catechism. There were 55 children on the books, five of them monitors, for which the mistress received £28 and had a house and garden rent-free and free coal.

Comments on two parishes

It may reasonably be assumed that the enquiry of 1847 would have been seen by middle-class Welsh society as a necessary step to improving education in Wales, but when the results of the enquiry were published they caused uproar because the commissioners and their assistants had seen fit to criticize both the Welsh language and the morals of the Welsh people, and of Welsh women in particular. Consequently, the report was referred to as 'the betrayal of the Blue Book'.

No inflammatory remarks were made about Gowerians because they were mostly either English-speaking or bilingual. With regard to Oystermouth, it was said:

> This is an important and growing parish. Iron mines have been discovered in it, and are being worked. It is likely to be comprised in the improvements of Swansea Harbour. From these causes the population may be expected to increase rapidly. Wages are good, and the people very well off; if otherwise, it was owing to intemperance and carelessness. [To this may be added the remark] that this is a parish in which no Welsh is spoken.

It was also stated that, in the parish of Bishopston:

> the labouring population are employed either in agriculture or oyster-dredging, and earn on an average two shillings per diem [day]. There are no large proprietors resident. Many children are attending no school. There is little distress except what results from drunkenness, which is a very prevalent vice.

The Demon Drink

Roughly 100 licensed houses are known to have existed in Peninsula Gower throughout, or during some part of the Victorian and Edwardian eras. Some licensed premises were old – the Beaufort Arms, Kittle, may have existed as far back as 1460. Others, such as the Gower Inn (1824), were hostelries. Similar though later establishments such as the King Arthur were built (1870) as hotels. The best licensed hotels were to be found in Oystermouth parish, the Langland Bay (a converted villa, licensed in 1863), the Mermaid (rebuilt in 1898) and the purpose-built Rotherslade (1899) among them. The overwhelming majority of licensed premises, however, were cottage inns in which usually one room was set aside for the benefit of customers.

Licenses – which were required by law from 1753 onwards – were for either 'beer-houses or ale-houses', the former for the sale of beer and cider only, the latter for wines and spirits in addition to various brews. To obtain a license a would-be licensee had to approach a magistrate, provide sureties and agree not to:

The King Arthur Hotel, Reynoldston – only the right-hand side of this hotel was built in 1870; the matching left-hand side followed when the building was enlarged in 1889. Apart from its hotel facilities – which include a landscaped garden and a lily pond – the King Arthur offers welcome refreshment for tourists on a fine summer's day.

dilute or adulterate [any beer, ale, or liquor, and not use] any pots or other measures that are not of full size, [nor] permit drunkenness or tippling, nor get drunk in his house; [nor] knowingly suffer any gaming with cards, draughts, dice, bagatelle, or any other sedentary game, [nor] knowingly permit or suffer any bull, bear, or badger baiting, [or] cock-fighting, [nor] permit or suffer men or women of notoriously bad fame, or dissolute girls and boys to assemble … in his house, [nor] suffer any drinking … during the usual hours of divine service on Sundays, [nor] keep open house … during the late hours of the night, or early in the morning for any other purpose than the reception of travellers.

Running a beer-house was often a side-line for enterprising farmers, many of whom brewed their own beer from the barley they grew. A fair number of licensees were former mariners, or mariners who wished to provide for their wives during their absence, the more so should they

Langland Bay Hotel, c.1900 – built as a summer retreat soon after 1856 by Henry Crawshay, third son of William Crawshay of Cyfarthfa Castle. The property was bought by a syndicate in 1887. It was then converted and extended to become the 50-roomed Langland Bay Hotel, which opened in 1889. Its days as a grand hotel, however, were short-lived and the property changed hands again. Then in 1922 the main block of this mock-Gothic pile was taken over by the Working-men's Club and Institute Union, under whose management it proved far more of a success.
The coach-house and outbuildings on the far left became a non-residential public house known as the Langland Bay Hotel, and continued as such until shortly before its demolition in 1989.

(Mary Lewis)

The Bishopston Valley Hotel – originally the Cross Inn, it was given its present name in 1877. Its unusual appearance is the result of an entire rebuild towards the end of the 19th century. The Valley Hotel is one of those places where locals have a wealth of information to share.

fail to return. In fact it was not unusual for the licensees of larger establishments to be engaged in alternative forms of employment – as oyster skiff owners, butchers, horse carriers and a miscellany of other occupations – leaving their wives to manage their licensed premises.

Almost half of all licensed establishments were within Oystermouth parish because it was a populous parish; it was favoured by well-to-do visitors, and after the revival of the Mumbles Railway in 1860 it became frequented by thousands of day trippers, many of whom came to drink, and did so to the extent that, in 1866, a visitor remarked that 'drunkenness seems to be the bane of this village, vacancy of mind being the consequence'.

Further north the coal mining part of Llanrhidian parish had more than 15 public houses, almost all of them beer-houses catering for mainly colliers and tin-plate men as well as those engaged in agriculture. Only Knelston, Penmaen and Penrice appear to have had no public houses. All other parishes had at least one licensed premises, more usually three or four, whereas Bishopston had at least eight.

So why was beer drinking so popular, and drunkenness so prevalent in Victorian and Edwardian times? The principal reason for this state of affairs was the Beer House Act of 1830, which permitted anyone to sell beer on payment of a two-guinea (£2.10) license. This Act, coupled with the removal of duty on beer, led to the establishment of thousands of new beer-houses, or beer-shops as they were called. Beer, or course, was safer to drink than water, and by late Victorian times it was cheaper at 3d. (approximately 1p.) a quart than either tea or coffee.

At the beginning of Victoria's reign most licensees brewed their own beer, having a small brewery attached, or close to their premises. These licensees, or victuallers, made use of malt provided by the half dozen or so malthouses that were dotted about the peninsula. Some of this do-it-yourself brewing activity ceased with the establishment of the Reynoldston Brewery in *c.*1870, which was sited on the periphery of the lower green (the premises served as a craft shop in fairly recent times). The Reynoldston Brewery was taken over by the Old Swansea Brewery in 1900 and, under new management, it continued brewing until the 1930s. Other breweries also made inroads into the peninsula in that, from *c.*1880 onwards, a growing number of public houses were taken over by town-based breweries, among them Fultons of Swansea, the Swansea United Brewery and Buckleys of Llanelly.

The New Inn, Park Mill – now a private residence, the two storeyed building with steps extending into the road was a beer-house for about 100 years until its closure in c.1906. Its appearance – five windows and a door on the front wall – was typical of 19th-century Gower public houses. All that is missing from this particular house is a porch and a board bearing the name 'The New Inn'.

One can image a few locals drinking in a small, grotty room in a cottage inn, the floor strewn with straw, the wooden casks in full view. The customers might be farm labourers, or colliers who had recently finished their shift. In larger premises such as the Greyhound, Oldwalls, the customers were often travellers returning from Swansea in carriers' carts, and who sat warming themselves around a blazing fire. Scenes such as these were common in rural Gower, and although the scenes would have been more lively at weddings and funerals, there was nothing to compare with the 'ungodly gatherings … for drinking and dancing' that usually accompanied the annual 'Mapsant' [the feast of St. Cenydd], or the agricultural fairs that were held at Penrice, Kittle, Reynoldston and Llanrhidian. These communal events attracted both itinerant traders and wandering minstrels. Amid the booths men gathered round to witness, after placing their bets, cock-fighting (abolished in 1849), or prize fights in which men battered and bruised each other with their bare fists.

Not everyone approved of the revelry at these communal events, nor the drunkenness that followed in the wake of trains arriving at Mumbles. The Nonconformists had long been opposed to drink; moreover, there had been a temperance movement in Wales in the years leading up to Victoria's coronation. The movement's campaigning in the 1860s and '70s eventually led to the Welsh Sunday Closing Act of 1881. The Act, however, created a situation in Oystermouth parish that was the opposite to what had been intended. A clause in the Act stipulated that victuallers could, on Sundays, serve *bona fide* travellers who had journeyed three miles or more and were in need of refreshment; that meant anyone travelling from Swansea, even on the railway, could, once they reached the three-mile limit at West Cross, claim to be a *bona fide* traveller. So, from the Current Tree (now the West Cross Hotel) onwards, the seafront – which already had a fair number of licensed premises – became the location for several additional beer-houses, as did some of the side streets leading inland. Most of the Oystermouth public houses catered for the 'lower classes [and] drunkenness became scandalously prevalent, especially among young girls, who seemed to cause most of the fights'.

A train on the Mumbles Railway – steam driven and very crowded. So popular was this railway that passengers were prepared to travel in carriages that resembled cattle trucks.

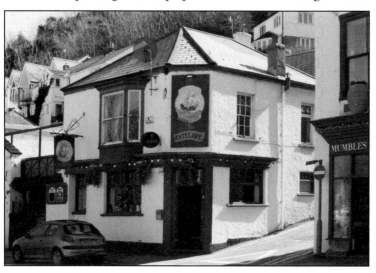

The Antelope Inn, Mumbles – originally the Oystermouth Castle Hotel, it was renamed the Antelope in c.1870. Its notoriety as a disorderly house almost brought about its closure in the Edwardian era. Its survival has ensured a glimpse of what a small-roomed Victorian public house looked like.

Temperance campaigners pressurized the police, the magistrates and Parliament to close down disorderly houses and those in a dilapidated state. Parliament's eventual response was to pass the Compensation Act of 1904, whereby licensees and breweries were compensated for the closure of their premises. By 1910 five beer-houses in Oystermouth had closed under the terms of this Act; more were to close in the years following King Edward's death.

Meanwhile, in the peninsula a similar number of beer-houses closed under the terms of the same Act, but many more had closed their doors at an earlier date, most of them for reasons unknown. Some closures were probably due to depopulation, or in certain areas to a decline in limestone quarrying or coal mining, whereas others are known to have been the result of pressure from the local population. However, most of the licensed premises that survived beyond the Edwardian era are still with us today.

Rural petty crime

In Victorian and Edwardian times Wales was not regarded as a land bedevilled by serious crime, but one plagued by innumerable petty offences. Those accused of serious crimes such as murder and arson were prosecuted by the Crown, whereas those suspected of less serious offences, such as petty theft, poaching and common assault, were prosecuted by those who considered themselves the victims. With regard to serious crimes, only a small number of indicted persons were tried by jury in the two higher courts – the Quarter Sessions and the Assizes. In the lower courts – the Petty Sessions, which dealt with the overwhelming majority of court proceedings – cases were heard by local magistrates, who were empowered to pass judgement on a wide range of petty offences. It was the Petty Sessions that the people of Peninsula Gower were most familiar with, for this lower court dealt with the most common infringements of the law.

However, the low number of reported crimes and court proceedings, coupled with half-empty gaols, led many to believe that Wales was pretty much 'a country without crime'. What criminals there were, were said to have been outsiders – vagrants, foreign workers, sailors and the like. Unfortunately, the truth was that the Welsh were generally unwilling to take those who had wronged them to court. They preferred to confront those they suspected of wrong-doing and demand either the return of stolen goods, or, if the offence had been against their person, to press for some form of reparation or an apology. This course of action had its roots in Medieval Welsh law, but in Victorian times it was preferred because it saved the time and expense of court proceedings.

It was also wrongly believed that crime levels were lower in the countryside than in towns and industrialized areas, and that the most obvious failing of the Welsh peasantry was the promiscuity among women (not men!). The truth was that excessive drink was a much more obvious problem, particularly on festive occasions and at weekends. That was when young farm labourers and servants became drunk, boisterous and unruly to the extent that they shouted abuse, vandalized property and fell to fighting among themselves and with youths from neighbouring villages. With regard to petty theft, the most common items taken were milk after surreptitiously miking someone's cow, vegetables and underwood from someone's land, and clothes from someone's line or hedge – none of which was worth the bother of taking someone to court.

Some crimes such as bestiality were seen as 'common rural offences', whereas incest, although frowned upon, would have been concealed by a veil of secrecy. Poaching was another common countryside offence, and in some parts of Wales it led to violent clashes between poachers and bailiffs. In Peninsula Gower poaching appears to have been limited mainly to pheasants, partridges, rabbits and trout. Domestic servants, usually female, were often suspected of, or caught stealing from their employers, but if the items taken were not costly, such as bedding or plates, the employer would no doubt have ended the episode with a dismissal, thereby adding to the incalculable list of unrecorded crime. Only one other offence needs be mentioned as being applicable to Peninsula

Gower – wrecking. Although Gowerians regarded it as their right, wrecking – laying claim to anything found on the shore – was an offence, one that might be overlooked when it was flotsam, but when it came to the fittings and cargoes of wrecked ships, Gowerians often risked prosecution for what was really another form of theft.

The theft of farm animals (which was a serious offence), fowl and quantities of grain could, of course, amount to considerable loss, as could burglary, arson and malicious damage, in which case the victim had to weigh up his losses against the cost of legal proceedings. He also had to consider intimidation and malicious acts of revenge by the perpetrator, or the perpetrator's friends and family.

In a bid to encourage legal proceedings, the Gower United Association for the Prosecution of Felons had been established in 1810. The association was comprised mainly of farmers and landowners, its membership never exceeding 62. The association kept a record of income and expenditure, and among the entries are payments to parish constables

> for executing a warrant [1shilling]; for conveying a prisoner to Cardiff [£1 5s. 0d. – obviously to be tried in a higher court; and for' bringing robbers to Swansea [£8 – presumably robbers who had departed from the peninsula].

There were also rewards recorded, each entry amounting to several pounds. Throughout its 82-year existence the association did not encourage prosecutions beyond those pursued by its members.

To go through the process of law usually meant calling upon a magistrate to issue a warrant. The victim had then to find a parish constable to execute the warrant, and he expected a small fee for his trouble. Parish constables were elected yearly from among the ratepayers. They were unsalaried and unqualified for the appointment, and probably loathed what they had to do to the extent that, had they the means, they would pay someone to do the job for them. Their task was one that could easily make them unpopular. If they were diligent, they risked being vilified, threatened. physically abused, or becoming the target of a vindictive campaign. If they were less than diligent, they risked admonishment from the magistrate.

After an arrest had been made, the next stage was a preliminary hearing, one in which both the victim and the accused appeared before a magistrate. Both parties were given every opportunity to come to an out-of-court settlement. A settlement at this point was certainly in the interest of the victim, for if he wished to proceed, there were several things to be considered. It would be his responsibility to provide evidence and secure the support of witnesses. That witnesses might not want to get involved is supported by Glamorgan's first chief constable, who complained in 1842 of 'a species of clanship [which] renders the Welshman particularly averse to give evidence against a neighbour'. The victim also had to pay a clerk to prepare the necessary paperwork. As few could afford the added expense of an attorney, it would, in the final analysis, fall to the victim to present his case in open court.

There were other, less obvious considerations. Had the accused moved on, or fled after committing an offence, then his return under escort – either by a parish constable from a distant location, or by a professional policeman – had to be paid for. If, on the other hand, the offence was a serious one, and the accused had to be tried in a higher court, then the cost of a police escort had likewise to be borne by the victim. In short, expenses could prove costly, and that at a time when court proceedings had barely begun.

Magistrates

Justices of the Peace (magistrates) first appeared in Gower as a result of what became known as the Act of Union. By this Act of 1536 the 'Laws and Justice to be ministered in Wales [were to be] in like form as it is in this [the English] realm'. At the time of Victoria's coronation some JPs were clergymen and, as time went by, more middle-class professionals and businessmen were to join them, but throughout Victoria's reign the majority of magistrates were landowning gentlemen and gentry such as Thomas Penrice of Kilvrough. As landowners these men already occupied a position of importance within Glamorgan. They were rich, they were influential and they had authority over their tenants. As magistrates these same men also administered the law, acted as arbitrators in disputes, issued beer-house licenses, called out the military when necessary, appointed Poor Law guardians and were, therefore, a controlling influence in many areas of county administration, and continued to exercise that influence until the creation of the Glamorgan County Council in 1889.

Prior to 1889, civil matters relating to the administration of Glamorgan were decided upon by magistrates at the Court of Quarter Sessions. In criminal proceedings held in the same court, magistrates presided, but the verdict rested with juries. There were no juries at the Petty Sessions. In these lower courts, magistrates dispensed summary justice in that they both presided and reached a verdict. At one time the Petty Sessions were held in country mansions and public houses, but by Victorian times hearings relating to rural Gower were held at the (old) Guildhall, Swansea.

Two or more magistrates (the bench) presided over the Petty Sessions at Swansea. At one time Petty Sessions were held monthly, or when necessary, but as the number of cases increased, so the frequency with which the court met became fortnightly, weekly and finally daily. The magistrates dealt with matters relating to Poor Law, vagrancy, breaches of the peace, petty theft, common assault, trespass and poaching. More serious offences, or those involving persistent offenders, were transferred to the higher courts, either the Quarter Sessions or the Assizes.

The punishment for theft was severe. In the higher Court of Assize held at Swansea, *The Cambrian* reported, in July 1847, that:

> John Downing, 25, labourer was sentenced for having … broken and entered the dwelling house of Daniel Owen of Oystermouth, and stealing some wearing apparel. He was also charged with stealing a pair of sheets belonging to John Rowe of Swansea. The prisoner pleaded guilty to both charges, and was sentenced to 12 months imprisonment for the first offence, and six months for the second.

Fines for common assault could amount to more than a man's weekly wage. An example of this appeared in *The Cambrian* on 24 September 1842, which reported that at the Petty Sessions held at Swansea:

> Mary Williams of Gower, single woman, and Mary Bennett, wife of William Bennett of Gower, labourer, were severely convicted … in the penalties of 15s. 6d. and 11s. 6d. each, including costs, for assaulting Eleanor Williams, wife of John Williams of Gower, blacksmith, and in default of immediate payment they were … to be committed to the House of Correction at Swansea for one calendar month. Their fines were paid [by whom is not stated] and they were, therefore, discharged.

Vagrants were considered to be a burden to the ratepayers. They were blamed for all sorts of things, and they were dealt with harshly. In 1844

Ellen Burnett was brought before the Rev. Dr. Hewson [the magistrate] charged under the following circumstances. The Rev. Samuel Davies, of Oystermouth … said, 'Yesterday evening … I was called to the house by Mrs. Davies, who informed me that there was a woman at the door begging. … I went to the front-door, where I saw … Ellen Burnett … from Cowbridge. She complained of being very ill, and said that she had a cancer in her breast. Her right breast was bound up with wrappers and cloths. She said she had a ticket for the Swansea Infirmary, and that it was necessary she should have a guinea on going in … and begged me to give her something. I asked her to show me the cancer. … She came into the hall and sat down. My cook came there, and the prisoner … drew down part of the gown and I saw her breast. I then put my hand on her breast, to feel for the cancer, and she called out that I hurt her. I then, accompanied by my servant, Thomas Davies, went with the prisoner towards the house of police-constable Jenkins. I told the prisoner that she had been deceiving me … and she admitted that she had. She went on her knees and begged I would not punish her. When we arrived near the Briney-inn [now the Woodman] the prisoner ran from us, and went, as fast as she could towards the Mayalls. Thomas Davies and myself pursued and overtook her. I seized her cloak and arm, and Thomas Davies also seized her. She struggled with us, and often fell down, dragging myself and Davies with her. She endeavoured to lay hold of a stone … but I prevented her … She cried out that I hurt her, and she kicked me on my chin and on my breast. I afterwards delivered the prisoner to Morgan, one of the [parish?] constables of Oystermouth'. The prisoner … was committed to the House of Correction for two months, for vagrancy, and soliciting charitable contributions under false pretences.

In 1860 about half of those who appeared before magistrates at Petty Sessions were discharged, often with a warning 'to be of good behaviour', which today would be regarded as probation. Again in 1860 about two-thirds of those who were awarded sentences were fined, sometimes with costs added. The fines could be heavy – 5s. for being drunk and disorderly amounted to half of a farm-labourer's weekly wage. Such sentences might be pronounced '5s. or ten days'. If the offender could not pay immediately, which was often the case, then he spent ten days in jail. Custodial sentences in 1860 were awarded to less than one-in-ten of those punished, rising to about one-in-five 30 years later. Sentences of more than six months were rare, 14 days or less being the norm. Public whipping, though rare, might be awarded to some offenders, usually juveniles, but after 1862 this form of punishment was carried out within prison walls.

Other courts

Apart from the Petty Sessions and higher courts, there were the manorial courts, some of which had been in existence since the 12th century. In Peninsula Gower the leet was first and foremost a civil court, one that was primarily concerned with matters pertaining to agriculture. Leet courts were usually held twice yearly in public houses to ensure harmony among those who held land, whether as freeholders, or leaseholders. It was from among those who attended these courts that many of the parish constables were appointed, as well as ale-tasters to monitor the quality of local brews, pound-keepers to take responsibility for impounded animals, and haywards to seize stray animals and safeguard common land. Few leet courts survived the Victorian era. The leet held at the

Gower Inn in 1870 – which was probably connected with the manor of Pennard – did not survive, nor did the one that met at Oxwich Board School in 1884, but the one at Oystermouth still met at the Marine Hotel in the Edwardian era, and the one held at the Bishopston Valley Hotel continued, albeit as a fraternity, until the 1920s.

The Police

The first professional police force in the Lordship of Gower and Kilvey was the one established by the Municipal Borough of Swansea in 1836, which consisted of one inspector and six constables. Forces were also established at Cardiff and Neath at roughly the same time, but in the rural areas outside the boroughs there were no professional policemen until the creation of the Glamorganshire Constabulary in August 1841. The man chosen to be the county's first Chief Constable was Charles Fredrick Napier, a captain in a rifle brigade. Some critics claimed that Captain Napier got the appointment because of his connections in high places, but the fact that, prior to his appointment, he had spent a month travelling about the county on horseback, getting to know it well, must have been considered in his favour. He was awarded a salary of £300 a year and £150 for his horse and other expenses.

Captain Napier immediately set his plans in motion. He divided the county into four districts – Merthyr, Newbridge, Ogmore and Swansea – each of which was placed under the command of a superintendent. The Swansea District embraced that part of the county west of the River Afan.

A Glamorganshire constable, 1841 – his uniform consisted of a stovepipe hat, a pilot-blue, swallow-tailed coat with the letter 'G' (for Glamorgan) and his number on the collar. His trousers were navy blue in winter, white in summer. He was issued with a new uniform each year, and was expected to wear it at all times, except when in bed. The reason for this is that he was expected to devote himself to duty every day of the year. There was no such thing as leave or rest days until 1860 when he was awarded one week's annual leave and a few hours off for special reasons. His first pair of Wellington boots – which were issued – were a source of discomfort. In 1842 the issue was replaced by a weekly boot allowance of 6d.

Each constable was issued with a cape, but permitted to carry an umbrella. Attached to his belt was a scabbard for carrying a cutlass. His truncheon was decorated with a royal coat-of-arms and the words Glamorganshire Constabulary. Other equipment included handcuffs, a Bull's Eye lantern and a rattle for raising the alarm, all of which were attached to his belt. He also had permission to wear, if he so wished, a four-inch leather collar (stock) with spikes to prevent an assailant from garrotting him with a piece of string from behind.

The Swansea superintendent was to be based at Neath and have two sergeants and four constables under his command.

Captain Napier had no trouble appointing four superintendents, but experienced difficulty when it came to recruiting 34 men aged 18 to 27 and no less than 5 feet 9 inches tall. Married men he would accept, providing they had no more than two children at the time of their appointment. For approximately three months the men were billeted in part of the Bridgend workhouse, where they were trained and issued with uniforms and equipment. On 27 November 1841 the men, including the sergeants, were sent out – not to purpose-built stations, but to localities in which each and every one of them had to find their own lodgings. In the Swansea District a sergeant established himself at Loughor. A constable was sent to Pontardawe and another to Ystalyfera. No one was sent into Peninsula Gower.

Parish constables continued to serve their communities in the manner they were accustomed to, but an Act of 1842 directed them to assist professional policemen whenever they were called upon to do so. The parish constables were unpaid except for the relatively small fees they charged for certain services. The professional policemen were paid according to their rank. Initially, a second-class constable received 18s. a week, a first-class constable 20s. and a sergeant 22s., the money coming from additional parish rates. There were, however, circumstances in which parish ratepayers could find themselves paying an additional levy, as the ratepayers of Pennard and Ilston discovered when, in 1843, parish policemen stood guard on two tollgates following Rebecca's attack on the Pound-ffald gate.

Captain Napier was answerable to a police committee of magistrates. At the Court of Quarter Sessions (held four times a year) the Glamorganshire magistrates dealt with county administration and finance, and continued to do so until 1889 when an elected county council took over their responsibilities. In July 1847 *The Cambrian* reported that the magistrates at one Quarter Session had considered whether 'to provide or erect a police station or strong house at Oystermouth'. The term 'police station' is misleading in that what was intended was to station one policeman in the parish. The intention was apparently realized because, in May the following year, *The Cambrian* reported that the magistrates had considered moving 'Sergeant Jenkins [from the station at] Blackpill to the Cross Inn, Sketty'.

Some 19 years later, in January 1867, *The Cambrian* devoted almost a whole page to the business of county policing. The information was provided by a journalist who had been present at a Quarter Session in which a full bench of 23 magistrates were present. The journalist reported that Captain Napier had at his disposal 133 policemen, their ranks ranging from 'Superintendents (4) ... to Second-class Constables (57) [and] 22 constables maintained at the expense of private companies'. The strength of the Swansea District stood at one superintendent and 27 policemen, plus an inspector, a rank that had been added to the force the previous year.

Where all the Swansea District policemen were stationed is difficult to determine, but their presence in Peninsula Gower was almost negligible. In 'the 16 [most westerly Gower] parishes there was only one policemen, [and he] was stationed at Penrice'. One magistrate, Thomas Penrice of Kilvrough, insisted that an additional 'police constable should be stationed at Park Mill [on the ground that it] was a very disorderly locality, [owing to] the very large number of cases which came before the bench'. The root of the problem would appear to have been the Gower Inn. The reasons for this deduction are that (1) another magistrate said the locals were 'generally very orderly', (2) a second magistrate stated that 'a great number of persons from the surrounding localities resorted there', and (3) a third magistrate maintained that while 'some few persons did drive down on Sundays, he did not think they were of such character as to require the special attention of a policeman'.

Left: *The old police station – Park Mill was denied a police station when Thomas Penrice pressed for one in 1867, but in c.1920 the village was afforded the protection of a resident constable. The characters of an older generation may remember this station well.*
Right: *The Old Police Station, Oystermouth – built like a fortress in 1871-2, this former police station in Myrtle Terrace still has its original heavy, studded-oak front door and windows protected by iron bars. There are also a number of strategically-placed, narrow slits (originally unglazed) in the walls. The purpose of these slits (along with the recesses in the inside walls) must surely have been for defence in that they enabled the police to aim firearms at would-be attackers without exposing themselves as easy targets. This station is now split between two private residences.*

The third magistrate also suggested that, in the event of trouble, 'there was a Swansea [District] policeman stationed at Cross Inn [Sketty] – not very far away – and another at Mumbles'. Yet another magistrate declared 'there were no fewer than five policemen stationed not more than five miles away'. Thomas Penrice had, however, already 'written to the Chief Constable on the matter', only to be told that no policemen could be spared 'from either of the places in the district where they were at present stationed – the Mumbles and Penclawdd – as they were both fully occupied'. What can be deduced from all this is that in 1867 there were only three policemen in the whole of Peninsula Gower, and that they were stationed at Penrice, Penclawdd and the Mumbles.

Captain Napier died of T.B. in mid-January 1867, having served as a very capable Chief Constable for 25 years. Later that same year there were several articles in *The Cambrian* relating to proposals for the construction of police stations with lock-ups at several locations within the Lordship of Gower, including one at Oystermouth. These stations were not intended to be built as homes for individual policemen to work from, but as bases from which several policemen could work. No progress appears to have been made at Oystermouth until 1870, when plans were finalized and the land on which the station would be built was leased from the Swansea ship-owner, Henry Bath, who resided at nearby Rosehill, a mansion that later became St. Ann's Hotel. The station would appear to have been built between April 1871 and April 1872. There is little in the records about this particular police station other than, for a short while, it was where the bodies of seamen, washed up on the beach, were placed until they were taken away for burial; moreover, it was reported in *The Cambrian* that, in *c.*1893, the station was manned by a sergeant and two constables. The station probably continued in use until after the Edwardian era.

The Military

Gowerians could, if they so wished, enlist in the regular army with the nearest unit, the Welch Regiment, based at Cardiff. Those who did not enlist were liable to serve in the Royal Glamorgan Light Infantry Militia. This militia was a part-time battalion, which, based at Cardiff, comprised of 22 officers and 830 men in 1862. Glamorganshire men were, prior to c.1860, enrolled by compulsory ballot (the names drawn from a hat) for a period of three years, but they could avoid this early form of national/territorial service provided they paid a fine, or found a substitute to take their place. The minimum requirement for militiamen was that they did one month's annual training (in May - June). When embodied (mustered) the militiamen could serve in defence of the realm, or in aid of the civil powers, and could be sent to any part of the U.K., but they could not be sent abroad except on a voluntary basis. After c.1860 the compulsory ballot was replaced by voluntary service for a period of six years. In 1881 the R.G.L.I. Militia became the Third (Militia) Battalion of the Welch Regiment; as such it became a T.A. battalion in 1908.

Between 1794 and 1815, when Britain was at war with France, numerous volunteer units were raised for the duration of hostilities, the best known locally being the Sea Fencibles (1798-1813). There can be no doubt that large numbers of men joined these volunteer units in order to avoid the compulsory ballot, and the reason they did so was because all they were required to do as volunteers was train for short periods. Shortly after Napoleon's defeat at Waterloo in 1815, all the Glamorganshire volunteer units were disbanded – all, that is, except the four troops of Gentlemen and Yeoman Cavalry.

There were several reasons for the yeoman cavalry's continued existence: the men were regarded as dependable gentlemen and yeoman farmers, who provided their own horses and paid for their own uniforms; moreover, they were mobile and they cost the government virtually nothing. Throughout their 33-years existence (1798-1831) the three troops that formed the Swansea and Fairwood Yeoman Cavalry Corps were several times deployed against rioters, both in the Swansea and Merthyr areas. The last deployment took place in 1831, when volunteer cavalrymen from Peninsula Gower suffered humiliation in what became known as the Merthyr Rising. At the time the whole of industrial South Wales was in a state of agitation due to a depression, the hated truck system and the imminent reforms that were expected to change people's lives. The rising was an unprecedented incident in British history, one in which thousands of workers took over Merthyr, and for several days a red flag fluttered in the face of authority.

The trouble began on 1 June 1831, when angry colliers and ironworkers destroyed a court house at Merthyr. The following day workers took over the town and besieged local magistrates in the Castle Hotel. In total around 500 soldiers were hastily dispatched from Brecon, Swansea and the Cardiff area. A fierce struggle took place in Merthyr's streets. Twenty rioters were shot dead. A detachment of Cardiff Yeoman Cavalry was ambushed in a ravine, the troopers showered with missiles.

Meanwhile, on 4 June, and only two miles to the west of Merthyr, a detachment of the Swansea and Fairwood Yeoman Cavalry also ran into trouble. Led by Major Thomas Penrice of Kilvrough, the detachment – more than 30 troopers strong – had been advancing along a road flanked by 'cinder tips', when Major Penrice and a fellow officer rode ahead to be 'surprised under a mask of friendship by a body of the mob' and quickly disarmed. To their rear, the troopers were hemmed in by thousands of armed insurgents, who had been hiding among the cinder tips. The troopers were likewise disarmed and, with their officers, forced to retire towards Neath.

Despite this humiliating incident, Major Penrice and his troopers rearmed and, joined by other troopers from Swansea and Gower, took a circuitous route to Merthyr, arriving there early on 6 June. Later that morning they took part in a magnificent and bloodless rout of thousands of insurgents, a rout that put an end to the uprising. Two days later the corps was ordered to return to Gower in haste, as trouble was fermenting among the colliers at Clydach and in the Cwm Tawe Valley. The corps remained in the Swansea Valley until 10 June when the threat of disorder was deemed to have passed. The troopers were then dismissed. However, the disarming of Major Penrice's advance detachment sparked off an inquiry. Although favourably inclined towards the major and his men, the inquiry did not stop those who were opposed to the existence of yeoman cavalry from having their way. Consequently, the seven troops of cavalry that existed in Glamorgan at that time were all disbanded.[8]

There were no mounted volunteer units in Glamorgan for 69 years. Then, in December 1899, when the British Army suffered a serious reverse against the Boers in South Africa, the government called for the formation of mounted infantry to counter the enemy's mobile, hard-hitting form of warfare. Within two months 120 volunteers had been recruited to become the Fourth Glamorgan Company of the First Battalion Imperial Yeomanry. The company served in South Africa in 1900-1, but as this unit has no obvious connection with Gower the details of its arduous campaigning are beyond the scope of this work. For similar reasons nothing need be said of the Glamorgan Imperial Yeomanry Regiment, which replaced the Glamorgan Company in 1902; nor the regiment's absorption into the newly-formed Territorial Army in 1908.

Glamorgan Rifle Volunteers at Hythe in 1859 – some of the men have uniforms, which they purchased themselves. Notice how the uniforms resemble those worn by American infantrymen during the Civil War period.

However, there were infantry and artillery units formed during Victoria's reign that did have an unquestionable connection with Gower. In 1859, when the government became alarmed by the military activity of Napoleon III of France, the call went out for the formation of volunteer units. In Glamorgan C.R.M. Talbot was the Lord Lieutenant and, therefore, responsible for military matters within the county. In May he appealed for volunteers to serve in defence of the county, and immediately began recruiting men for the First Corps of Glamorgan Rifle Volunteers, which he largely financed. No doubt many who volunteered for service in this corps were tenants from his Margam and Penrice estates. Two other influential Gowerians followed his example – Lewis Llewelyn Dillwyn, an industrialist and MP for Swansea District, created the Third Corps. His elder brother, John Dillwyn Llewelyn of Penllergaer, formed the Fifth Corps. Men from Peninsula Gower would have served in any of these three corps. In 1870 *The Cambrian* reported that the combined strength of the Third and Fifth Corps stood at 531 men, 53 of them marksmen. That same year the French army – considered to be the best in Europe – was defeated by the Prussians and Napoleon III was taken prisoner. Even with the threat passed, the three corps continued to parade and practice for war until 1878, by which time the Fifth had been absorbed into the Third. The latter corps still existed in 1893, and nine years later one of its companies became a mobile unit equipped with bicycles.

The Mumbles Battery

There had been a battery on Mumbles Hill during the Napoleonic Wars. That battery had long been removed when, in the 1850s, attention was drawn to the fact that both Swansea Harbour and the Mumbles Roadstead had no defence against hostile ships. Then, in the summer of 1859, the

Gunnery drill at the Mumbles Battery, c.1880 - built 1859-60 in front of the lighthouse on the outer of the Mumbles Islands, the purpose of this fort was to protect both the Roadstead and Swansea Harbour from hostile ships. The fort was in fact a 5-gun tower with three guns mounted behind a parapet, and two guns mounted in the vaulted chamber at a lower level.
The men manning the gun are militiamen from the First (Swansea) Corps, Glamorgan Artillery Volunteers, founded by George Grant Francis in 1859. (Swansea Museum)

government agreed to the erection of a battery on the Lighthouse Island off Mumbles Head. Work started on a 5-gun tower in July that year.

In the meantime, George Grant Francis of Swansea – who had been largely responsible for pressurizing the government into agreeing to the battery – was offered command of what became the First (Swansea) Corps of Glamorgan Artillery Volunteers. The men had to purchase their own uniforms, the government provided the armaments – swords, rifles and two 18-pounder field guns that were kept at Swansea.

Work on the Mumbles Battery was completed in May 1861. The following month five 68-pounders arrived by sea from Woolwich. It took a further two months to get these guns in position. When a salvo was fired for the first time these powerful guns shattered every pane of glass in the lighthouse; thereafter the guns were fired individually. At a later date some – if not all – of these guns were replaced by 80-pounders, the barrels of each weighing five tons.

The battery was initially designed to accommodate 21 men under the command of a staff sergeant. Presumably this would have been the required strength to man the guns had the threat of invasion ever materialized. The census returns for 1881 record six men and two women at the Mumbles Battery; by 1891 the figures had dropped to two men and two women. Presumably the figures represent the minimum requirement to both guard and keep the battery operational. However, in the latter part of Victoria's reign the guns had become increasingly outdated and, in 1899, the 80-pounders were removed and buried in the sand at low tide. The gun tower was then adapted as a platform for two quick-firing guns. When exactly the QF guns were installed is unknown, but they were said to have been in place by 1914; they remained in service until 1942.[9]

Parishes and the Beginning of Local Government

Parishes began taking shape in Peninsula Gower in the 12th century. In many cases the parish boundaries were also those of manors such as Oystermouth and Port Eynon. Some parishes originated as a grouping of several small manors. The parish of Llandewi, for example, comprised of the manors of Scurlage, Henllys and the tiny ecclesiastical manor of Llandewi itself. By the time of Victoria's coronation the Peninsula Gower parishes had long been established. However, changes did occur in c.1881 when the parish of Rhosili was enlarged by the addition of the hamlet of Paviland (which had been a detached part of Penmaen parish) and the hamlet of Pilton (which had been a part of Penrice parish). Further east the parish of Bishopston was also enlarged by the addition of Manselfield (which had been a detached part of Nicholaston parish). No further changes occurred until 1924, when the civil parish of Llanrhidian Higher became a separate ecclesiastical parish with Llan-yr-newydd as the parish church.

Throughout the Middle Ages the parish had been a locality in which all residents were obliged to worship in the parish church, but in the time of Henry VIII the parish took on a civil function as well. In 1536 Henry VIII dissolved the monasteries, which for centuries had provided food and shelter for the poorest elements in society – the paupers – with the result that there was nowhere for the destitute to go. This soon developed into a situation that the authorities could not ignore.

In 1563 an Act was passed whereby the poor became the responsibility of the parish. Necessary funding was to be met by those parishioners who were assessed as having sufficient means to contribute to a 'poor rate' – they were to become the first ratepayers – whereas farm labourers and other low earners were exempt from paying rates. Collection and administration of the rates became the responsibility of prominent ratepayers, whose meetings became known as the Vestry. The system underwent modification from time to time until, in 1601, an Act was passed that made further changes unnecessary for some 230 years. No doubt the Poor Law Act of 1601 was deemed an effective way of dealing with paupers. It cost the authorities nothing, as the government had offloaded the problem onto the parish. Many ratepayers may have found their poor law responsibilities onerous; others would have seen the system as a means whereby they had a say in the affairs of their community.

In time other responsibilities fell on the parish. Roads, for example, were in such a deplorable state that the parish was made responsible for their upkeep. This was never a successful method of dealing with poor roads; hence the introduction of the turnpike/tollgate system in 1764, which, despite the resentment it caused, did lead to a definite improvement in the main highways. The parish, however, continued to be responsible for minor roads until such time as they were taken over by the County Roads Board.

In carrying out their duties the ratepayers worked within the bounds of an ecclesiastical parish, in which case the parish became a civil parish as well. There were, however, some ecclesiastical parishes that were too extensive for ratepayers to operate within the limits of their meagre resources. In Peninsula Gower the ecclesiastical parish of Llanrhidian fell into this category and was, therefore, split into two civil parishes – Llanrhidian Higher and Llanrhidian Lower. It was in industrialized civil parishes such as Llanrhidian Higher that the system of poor relief became strained to the point that it had to be changed.

The Poor Law Union

The Poor Law may have been adequate for orphans, the aged, the sick and the handicapped in rural parishes, but the Industrial Revolution led to large numbers of urban poor. Dependence on coal mining alone led to many families becoming destitute because the breadwinner had been killed or injured in a mining accident, which were daily occurrences. Some would have become blind or rheumatic due to the dark, damp conditions in which they worked. Others would have been rendered unable to work as a result of inhaling too much dust. At times, large numbers of colliers would be laid off due to a slump in the market. It is hardly surprising, therefore, that coal mining areas such as Llanrhidian Higher could not cope with the ever-increasing number of destitute people. The old system of poor relief had, therefore, to be changed.

In 1832 the government set up a Royal Commission to inquire into the shortcomings of the existing system, and to make recommendations for a more effective way of dealing with paupers. The commissioners' report led to The Poor Law Amendment Act of 1834, which in turn resulted in the grouping of civil parishes to form Poor Law Unions. How this translated within the Lordship of Gower and Kilvey was that in 1836 all the civil parishes – save Loughor and Llansamlet – were grouped together to form the Swansea Union. The money raised from the ratepayers in these parishes was pooled, and the administration of the Swansea Union was entrusted to a Board of Guardians, elected yearly by and from among the ratepayers themselves.

Almost from its inception the Swansea Union found itself caught up in differences of opinion, the main bone of contention being that the guardians representing the Peninsula Gower parishes repeatedly accused their counterparts at Swansea of being wasteful with ratepayers' money, whereas those at Swansea saw their Gower counterparts as being mean and obstructive.

What is it? Viewed from the South Gower Road, this large white building has the appearance of a former country mansion. It was the Penmaen Workhouse; it is now the Three Cliffs Care Home. It commands a magnificent view of Three Cliffs Bay.

The wrangling led to the break up of the Swansea Union in 1857 with the Peninsula Gower parishes forming a separate Gower Union.

A site for a new workhouse was acquired at Penmaen, on the lower slopes of Cefn Bryn. Built in 1861-2, the Penmaen Workhouse was designed to accommodate 50 inmates in several wards, and to provide accommodation for the master and the matron. The workhouse also had a dining hall, a clerk's office and a boardroom for 30 guardians. Outside was a stone-breaking yard, and at a slightly later date the guardians acquired a field for the inmates to use as a garden. A new wing was added to the main building in 1939.

Schooling between 1847 and 1870

The 1847 report is an invaluable work, but what happened to the day schools for the lower classes during the 23 years that followed is, in most cases, difficult to determine as only snippets of information have survived. Presumably some of the private schools closed when the master or mistress could no longer teach, leaving the parishes in which they had been situated without a school. In the populous Oystermouth parish the situation differed in that there is evidence of a growing number of small, private day schools to cater for those who could afford tuition

Church School, Dunns Lane – Oystermouth Church School had a history for moving. In 1847 the Village School for boys was described as a slovenly unsystematic school of the old sort. In 1856 this school (along with the girls) became a National School and moved into a building on Mumbles Road (directly below All Saints Church). Twelve years later the school moved to a new building (later to become the Mumbles Motorboat and Fishing Club). In 1907 the school moved again, to new premises in Dunns Lane. The photograph that is shown here is undated. The school remained in use until 1984.

Park Mill (Church) School – there had been a school established at Park Mill in 1872.
The school seen here was built by Thomas Penrice (II) of Kilvrough at a cost of £2,500,
which made it the most ornate in Peninsula Gower. When it opened its doors in July 1876
it did so to accommodate 48 children from the parishes of Pennard and Ilston.
Thomas not only provided accommodation for resident teachers (at the rear of
this building), he also contributed to the school's upkeep, while Mrs. Penrice
visited the school regularly. The building is now home to the
West Glamorgan Guide Activity Centre.

fees. Thistleboon School, for example, (which was not mentioned in the 1847 report) had been a private school in Oystermouth parish for children from well-to-do families since before *c.*1840, so well-to-do in fact that some of the children were attended by servants. After 1847 more schools for the privileged came into existence, among them Mrs. Bush's ladies seminary, Miss Thomas's seminary, Habbakuk's school for ladies, and Miss Champion's girl school, all of them in Oystermouth parish.

With regard to the lower classes, the majority of children whose parents wanted them educated, and who could afford the school pence, attended day schools that taught the Church catechism. There were 14 of them in Peninsula Gower in 1847. Bishopston was the first Church school to become a National school, and did so in 1850. Others were to follow suit. Oystermouth, for example (which presumably was an amalgamation of the boys and girls schools of 1847), became a National school in 1856. In addition, other Church schools came into existence, one of them at Newton, Oystermouth, which opened in 1863 (the building became the Old School House Restaurant). Penmaen and Park Mill came later, their doors opening in *c.*1873 and 1876 respectively.

Oystermouth Infants (on the site of today's library) had already become a British school by the time of the 1847 report, and remained so until c.1880. Other schools were to follow Oystermouth Infants' example, and these schools, together with some National schools, received funding for both building and running costs, in return for which they were expected to comply with the standards set by the societies and, to ensure those standards were adhered to, their doors were 'open to the … inspector of schools'.

The Education Act of 1870

Despite the improved standards introduced by the National and British societies in both England and Wales, schooling for the lower classes remained a hotchpotch affair. Standards varied, and in some localities schools were either inadequate or non-existent. What was required was a comprehensive network of elementary schools, which would 'fill the gaps' where schools did not exist. For decades there had been calls for the government to intervene, but nothing was done because the Anglicans and the Nonconformists were unwilling to compromise over religious instruction.

Then, in 1870, Parliament passed its first Education Act, which permitted the establishment of locally elected School Boards with power to build elementary schools for the lower classes in areas where they were needed. The Act did not do away with existing schools, nor the grants to cover the running costs of National and British schools (providing they were efficient), but it discontinued the capital grants for building new schools. School Boards, however, could obtain government loans for building through the Public Works Loan Board, loans that were to be repaid out of a local rate. None of the new Board schools were to be denominational, and if there was to be any religious education at all, it was for the Board of ratepayers to decide. The Board was also empowered to pay the school pence in cases where the parents could not afford the outlay, even if the children were attending existing National or British schools.

The Education Act of 1870 was in fact a compromise, one that satisfied neither the Anglicans, nor the Nonconformists. The Anglican Church, for example, refused to surrender its right to teach the Church catechism. Consequently, it was denied capital grants for building new schools (which became a grievance), although it continued to receive funding to cover the running costs of its existing schools. The Nonconformists, on the other hand, were willing to have their schools become non-sectarian Board schools, which meant their schools continued to receive funding for both running costs and erecting new school buildings. Their willingness to comply with the non-sectarian rules can be explained by the fact that they were able to provide their children with religious instruction of their choosing in their Sunday schools. Their grievance was that no non-sectarian Board schools were to be built in areas where there were well-established Church schools. Consequently, in these areas their children had to attend a Church school where they were obliged to learn the Church catechism. The most famous example of this state of affairs is to be found in North Wales, where the future Prime Minister, David Lloyd George, had to learn the Church catechism even though he came from a Nonconformist family.

Despite its shortcomings, the Education Act of 1870 was unique in one area. It created a precedent in that women could at last have a public voice; as ratepayers, propertied women could be elected to sit on a School Board. Unfortunately, many years were to pass before propertied women were elected to School Boards in appreciable numbers.

Board Schools

Top: *Oystermouth Board School – the original school building of 1877-8 still retains its distinctive Victorian appearance, despite being partially surrounded by later buildings. Although situated in a populous district, the dressed-stone walls and brick dressing around the windows and doors of this particular building were common features of rural Board schools. In May 1878 the Board advertised in* The Cambrian *for two mistresses – one to take charge of the infants, the other the girls.*

Bottom: *Oxwich School – built as a Board school in 1884 to replace the earlier National school. What was unusual about this, and the school at Port Eynon, was that despite being Board schools, Miss Emily Talbot paid virtually all the expenses relating to these two establishments, thereby relieving her tenants in the parishes of Penrice, Oxwich and Port Eynon of School Board rates.*

Miss Talbot visited the schools regularly. She also managed the two schools more or less as she saw fit, which the Board members representing the three parishes were quite happy to permit as it was not their money she was using. In many respects she emulated what an earlier Miss Talbot had been doing in 1847. The building is now part of the Oxwich Bay Hotel.

One of the first parishes to respond to the Education Act of 1870 would appear to have been Llanrhidian Higher. *The Cambrian* in November 1872 reported:

> The Clerk of the Guardians of the Gower [Poor Law] Union gave notice [that he had] received a requisition in writing, signed by 50 ratepayers of the … parish of Llanrhidian Higher, requesting him to call a meeting … for the purpose of passing a resolution … that a School Board should be formed for the parish … to be held at the School-room Penclawdd.

When formed, the School Board took over the existing school-room at Penclawdd. In 1875 the school was transferred to a new and spacious premises at the opposite end of the village (a little to the south-west of the railway bridge behind the Royal Oak). As a result of this move, attendance more than trebled in less than 12 months. In 1877-8 the new school was altered and enlarged, and today it is almost hidden by later additions and extensions.

By 1876 it had been established that all children in Board School catchment areas should receive elementary education. Unfortunately not everyone agreed. In 1878 *The Cambrian* reported that:

> Thomas Thomas was charged by one of the officers of the Llanrhidian Higher School Board with neglecting to send his children to school. The case was adjourned for a week, the officer not having produced his by-laws before the court.

In 1862 regulations were introduced whereby head teachers were obliged to keep school log books. The books were used to record attendance levels, reasons for closures such as an outbreak of measles, and a wide range of noteworthy events in the life of a school. Log books that have survived for schools in the West Glamorgan area are kept at the County Hall Archives; they are an excellent source of information for those who wish to research a school in their locality.

Most of what has been written about schooling in the Victorian and Edwardian eras relates to Board schools, although National and British schools continued to function in some areas. The information comes from a variety of sources; personal reminiscences, school log books and official documentation being the main ones. Legislation, for example, set the elementary school leaving age at ten in 1880. Further legislation in 1893 raised the age to 11, and to 12 in 1899. The boys were noted for their knickerbockers – longish trousers, which below the knees were tucked into stockings. The girls were noted for their ankle-length dresses and white, often starched pinafores. Both sexes wore leather, laced boots, although clogs may still have been worn by some.

Children as young as five often had to walk distances of up to two or three miles to get to school. Those at Llangennith, for example, had to walk to Llanmadoc, no doubt traversing Llanmadoc Hill to get there. They made the journey in all sorts of weather; in winter they carried lanterns in the grey light of dawn. Until 1906, when school meals were introduced, they would have taken with them a canister of milk or cold tea, and a packed lunch of cheese or dripping sandwiches. On Monday morning they also took with them the school pence (abolished in 1891).

If their attendance was anything other than regular the locally appointed truant officer, the wipper-in, came a-calling. School log books show that attendance might be good at the beginning of each week, but would diminish towards Friday. Sickness, of course, was grounds for absence, and schools were invariably shut when contagious diseases appeared in the district, but it would also appear to have been accepted by head teachers that children would be absent as a result of bad weather, or during times of hay-making, potato planting or some other agricultural necessity. Even the collection of seaweed after a heavy storm could result in poor attendance. Shipwrecks in the neighbourhood were always a temptation for boys.

The school day began when a bell rang, signalling the children 'to form orderly lines in pairs' in an open space outside the main building. The children then marched into their classrooms where a teacher called the register, the children responding with 'Yes, Sir,' or 'Yes, Miss,' to establish their presence. This sequence of events would be repeated after the dinner break. An inspection of hands for cleanliness followed the morning sequence. There were periodic inspections of the hair for lice, and periodic medical inspections from 1907 onwards. Discipline was strict, often enforced by a slap, knuckles ground into the head, a ruler across the knuckles, a cane or some other instrument to inflict pain. That is not to say all teachers resorted to such measures. According to the reminiscences of one man, a school mistress at Penclawdd used to tie disobedient pupils to her apron string, compelling them to follow her wherever she went.

The majority of schools consisted of two classes – infants and mixed – whereas Oystermouth Board School had three classes – infants, girls and boys. Classes could amount to 50 pupils or more. In cold or wet weather the classroom would be heated by coal or wood-burning stoves. Teaching focused on the 3Rs, and much of the time would be spent learning things by heart, or by writing specific lines repeatedly. A child would begin to form letters in sand, progressing to scratching on slates before finally using pen, ink and paper. Drills, either outdoors or in the classroom, were an important part of elementary education, being necessary for discipline as much as anything else.

Religious education, on the other hand, was tricky in that it was left to the parents to decide whether their children should receive scripture lessons, and the teachers were to avoid getting involved in anything to do with denominational differences. Even the inspectors of schools were not 'to enquire into any religious subjects [nor were they] to examine any scholar … in religious knowledge' – a far cry from the inquiries made by the commissioner's assistants of 1847. However, one of the shortcomings of late Victorian education was that girls were singled out for subjects that were intended to make them good domestic servants and housewives. It was in accordance with the view that a woman's place was in the home.

Ink-monitors – those appointed to mix ink-powder with water and deposit it in the inkwells – were in a position of some responsibility. Even more responsible were the monitors, otherwise referred to as pupil-teachers. These were promising young pupils, aged 13 and above, who were persuaded to stay on at school as unpaid assistant teachers. Most children, certainly the boys, left school before they were 13 to take up work, whereas the pupil-teachers, if they remained at school until they were 18, were likely to go to college to train as professional teachers.

Not all parishes were to have their own Board schools. The National school at Penmaen, for example, which was established before 1873, was still a National school in 1906. Other parishes such as Llangennith, Llanmadoc and Cheriton banded together for the purpose of establishing a Board school at Llanmadoc (now defunct). Likewise, the parishes of Reynoldston, Llandewi and Knelston combined in 1874 to establish a School Board, which, that same year, arranged for lessons to be held in the local Baptist chapel. A new Board school at Knelston opened in c.1878. Conversely, in Llanrhidian Higher there were three Board schools – Penclawdd (1872), Three Crosses (1875, opposite the chapel) and Llanmorlais (1893, then known as Cwmcynor, the name was changed to Llanmorlais in 1897).

Some schools, such as Penclawdd, were the result of a Board taking over an existing school. Others, such as Oystermouth, were new buildings on the day they opened their doors. Board schools were a fine example of a democratic system in which communities provided their children with elementary schools, but all that was to change in 1903 after Parliament had legislated for the abolition of School Boards the previous year. The Board schools in Peninsula Gower then passed into the hands of the Glamorgan County Council, at which point they became County schools.

The Welsh language

The Education Act of 1870 has been blamed for the decline in the Welsh language – all lessons being in English – but the die had been cast when, in 1861, the allocation of grant aid became linked with annual tests in reading and arithmetic in English. In the Englishry of Peninsula Gower there was no Welsh language to be lost, but lessons by professional teachers may have had a diminishing effect on the local, West Country dialect. It also has to be borne in mind that in the Welshry day-schools lessons were in English in 1847, and no doubt earlier. In Welsh-speaking areas outside Peninsula Gower Welsh was the medium used in the Sunday schools. In the Peninsula Welshry only Nonconformist Sunday schools provided lessons either in Welsh or were bilingual. It can, therefore, be said that the Act of 1870 was not in itself responsible for the decline in Welsh; rather it was a late development in an education system that originated several decades earlier.

The census for 1891 (the first to record languages) states that in Peninsula Gower 857 persons over the age of two spoke Welsh only, and a further 1,849 were bilingual, which means that a total of 2,706 people in the Peninsula spoke Welsh – almost 24% of the population. Twenty years later the 1911 census is not so clear cut, but approximately 140 people over the age of three were monoglot Welsh, and a further 3,580 or so were bilingual. When combined these figures show there were more Welsh speakers in Peninsula Gower (approximately 25% of the population) than 20 years earlier. It can be assumed that the increase was due to immigration, probably into the coal mining areas, but also into Oystermouth Urban District where over 400 Welsh speakers resided.

Gower Rural Sanitary Authority

The year 1872 saw the establishment of the Gower Rural Sanitary Authority, which came into being when the Board of Guardians at Penmaen Workhouse elected, from amongst their number, a committee to oversee the authority's activities. A Dr. Ellis was appointed as the first Medical Officer of Health, and a Mr. Rosser became Inspector of Nuisances. Between them, these two salaried officers were responsible for ensuring that wells and springs were not contaminated as a result of farming, fisheries or burials, as well as night soil (human excrement) which had to be removed from cesspits and privies. Overcrowding in cottages was another matter the officers dealt with, as was drainage and matters connected with keeping pigs.

The remoteness of Peninsula Gower spared Gowerians from the worst outbreaks of contagious diseases. Nevertheless, outbreaks did occur, as in September 1877 when *The Cambrian* reported that Port Eynon School had closed due to an outbreak of typhoid fever. The worst affected area was Overton where 18 people contracted the disease. 'In the house of Mr. S. Bevan seven persons were said to have been lying severely afflicted with this disastrous disease'. In Horton there had been one fatality.

Typhoid – meaning typhus-like – was usually the result of a human 'carrier' contaminating food with bacteria, or contamination by flies that had been in contact with a carrier's excrement. Once the food had been swallowed, the bacteria then lodged in the intestines, where they multiplied and invaded the blood stream. The fever began with malaise, headache, body pains and loss of appetite. After a week or so the abdomen became bloated and covered with a rash. There were many complications and no vaccine until after the Boer War, but good nursing was essential if more than a 10% mortality rate was to be avoided. The final outcome at Overton, Port Eynon and Horton was not reported by *The Cambrian*.

The death toll from contagious diseases, often the result of filth and lack of sanitation, was unbelievably high in Victorian Wales, especially in seafaring towns and industrialized areas; hence the creation of sanitary authorities. Funding for these authorities came from a parish rate. In Peninsula Gower, one third of the funding came from the populous parish of Oystermouth – but the bulk of Oystermouth's contribution was soon to be lost when the southern half of the parish became a separate sanitary authority.

Oystermouth Urban Sanitary Authority

Migration from the country to wherever there were employment opportunities not only increased the size of long established boroughs such as Swansea, but it also created new urban areas. Sanitary arrangements in these new, often sprawling urban areas were virtually nonexistent. Piles of refuse, overflowing cesspits, contaminated water and the filthy living arrangements of some families presented serious health hazards, a breeding ground for all sorts of epidemics. Oystermouth – which by late Victorian times consisted of several expanding hamlets that were destined to become contiguous – was already a populous area when, in 1875, Parliament passed an Act that permitted populous localities to set up their own urban sanitary authority.

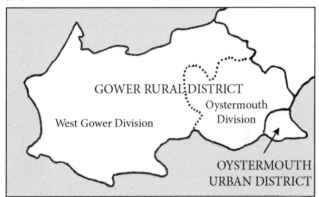

Gower's rural and urban districts – the dividing line between the two districts is shown by an unbroken line. The dividing line between Gower's two county constituencies is shown by dots.

That same year (1875) the people of Oystermouth – with the exception of those in the northern half of the parish, which became a separate civil parish known as Brynau and included Blackpill, the Mayals and Clyne Moor – took advantage of the Act by electing 12 prominent men to form the Oystermouth Urban Sanitary Authority. As with the earlier Gower Rural Sanitary Authority, from which it became divorced, the Oystermouth Authority appointed a Medical Officer of Health and an Inspector of Nuisances. It also appointed a Rate Collector. Where exactly the new authority was based initially is difficult to determine, but from *c.*1880 it occupied the old British school in Dunn's Lane (on the site of today's library), which presumably became vacant with the establishment of the Oystermouth Board school in 1878.

One of the first acts of the new authority was to address the water shortage problem. People living within the southern half of the parish relied on water butts and wells. There were virtually no springs or streams because that part of Oystermouth was 'on dry rock, covered over in parts by a light layer of glacial drift'. The authority sank five new wells between Southend and Newton. These wells did not solve the water shortage problem and within a few years a private enterprise, the Oystermouth Waterworks Co. Ltd., devised a scheme for pumping water from a spring at

Caswell. Work began in 1881 when a powerful steam-pump was installed at the spring. A 5-inch water main conveyed the spring water to a reservoir at Newton, and from there it was piped by gravity to places within the authority's domain, and to part of Bishopston parish as well, but still the water supply to Oystermouth, particularly in the dry season, was never enough to meet the requirements of a growing population. At times the water supply was available for only two hours a day. The problem was not resolved until Oystermouth's water supply was linked with Swansea's Cray Reservoir in the 1920s.

The authority's attempts to deal with sewage and refuse collection were in some respects equally disappointing, as were its efforts in tackling the problem of limestone dust from the roads. Yet despite these early problems the situation at Oystermouth gradually improved; moreover, the authority took on other responsibilities, providing, for example, street lighting (the gas supplied by a private company), fire-fighting equipment and, in the 1880s, it put an end to burials in overcrowded church and chapel yards by opening up a communal cemetery at Callencroft. In 1887 the authority became involved in developing amenities for the benefit of tourists and, from then on, it was only a matter of time before it took on a role equivalent to that of a town council.

Glamorgan County Council

In the 350 years leading up to 1889, county administration and finance had been in the hands of JPs. The deliberation and decision-making were carried out by a full bench of county magistrates at the Court of Quarter Sessions, which assembled four times a year. Although undemocratic by today's standards, this system of county administration worked satisfactorily. The problem was that, by late Victorian times, ratepayers were receiving demand notes from several quarters – from Poor Law guardians, highway boards, sanitary authorities, school boards, and many other bodies. What was needed was a single, central authority to 'consolidate all the rates and have one demand note, and then distribute the proceeds among such other authorities as have the power to call for contributions'.

In August 1888 Queen Victoria put her signature to 'An Act to Amend the Laws Relating to Local Government in England and Wales'. The act stipulated that 'a council shall be established in every administrative county. [Each council would] be entrusted with the management of the administrative and financial business of that county [and would] consist of the chairman, aldermen and councillors'. The council, however, was to have no control over Poor Law, public health or education. These omissions were due to anticipated opposition to getting the intended bill through Parliament. Education came under county council control in 1903, whereas the Poor Law remained in force until 1930.

A few months after the Act had been passed several Gowerians began presenting themselves as candidates for either the West Gower Division or the Oystermouth Division (Bishopston, Pennard, Ilston and Oystermouth). Candidates were mostly businessmen, the one exception being Thomas Penrice II, landowner and a JP with 40 years experience in county administration.

Polling took place on Thursday 17 January 1889. In the Oystermouth Division (or ward) polling took place in Oystermouth Board school and at the Gower Inn. In the Gower Division there were polling stations at schools in Penclawdd and Reynoldston. Thomas Penrice of Kilvrough won the Oystermouth Division with 284 votes, which gave him a majority of 40 over his closest rival. The Gower Division was won by Mr. Frank Cory Yeo, a colliery proprietor, whose 478 votes gave him a majority of 150 over his only opponent.

In all 88 councillors were elected, most of whom were to serve for a period of three years. At their first meeting, held at the Gwyn Hall, Neath, on 31 January 1889, the councillors elected from amongst their number 22 aldermen, 'and the vacancies so created' among the representatives were 'to be filled up by by-elections'. As their first Chairman the councillors chose Henry Hussey Vivian, managing-partner of the Hafod Copperworks, who had won the Tyrdeunaw Division to the north of Swansea. At their second meeting at Pontypridd on 1 April 1889 the council established committees to deal with finance, local government, roads and bridges, and several other important matters. The role of magistrates in local affairs was to all intents and purposes at an end, although JPs such as Thomas Penrice continued to have a role in county affairs.

District Councils

The Local Government Act of 1894 led to the formation of elected district councils, both rural and urban, to replace the existing sanitary authorities. The Act stipulated that, in the case of rural districts, each parish should be represented by one or more councillors, depending on how populous the parish might be. The new councils were to consist of a chairman and at least five councillors, who not only inherited the functions of a sanitary authority, but were responsible for such matters as local planning and development. The councillors also doubled as Poor Law guardians, although matters pertaining to the poor remained a separate function, its funding still dependent on Poor Law parish rates.

In Peninsula Gower, the Oystermouth Urban Sanitary Authority was superseded by the Oystermouth Urban District Council. Oystermouth continued to have its own elected council until 1918, when the area voted to be incorporated into the Swansea County Borough. The Gower Rural Sanitary Authority was superseded by the Gower Rural District Council. Both urban and rural district councils were dependent of the county council for such things as policing, highways and (after 1902) education. An example of the relationship between the different councils can be illustrated by what took place in 1902. In that year the Gower Rural District Council asked the Glamorgan County Council to contribute to the cost of widening the north and south Gower roads, the total cost of which was estimated at £4,000.

Political Representation

Since c.1540 Glamorganshire had been represented in Parliament by two MPs – one for the county, and one to represent the eight ancient boroughs within its bounds. Peninsula Gower was part of the county constituency, and the only rural Gowerians entitled to vote were adult males who held freehold property with a yearly value of 40s. or more. In the county constituency roughly half the voters were farmers, about a quarter were big landowners; the rest were clergymen and other professional men.

The MPs who represented both the county and the boroughs of Glamorgan in the early 19th century fell into three categories – Tories, Whigs and Independents. The Tories (forerunners of the Conservatives) had originated in the late 17th century as a royalist bloc, supporting royal prerogative, the supremacy of the Established Church, and landed interests such as the Corn Laws that kept the price of corn high. In a word the Tories were reactionary – opposed to change – although they were responsible for some notable reforms. The Whigs (forerunners of the Liberals) also originated in the late 17th century, and did so in opposition to the royalist bloc, supporting parliamentary prerogative, tolerance towards Nonconformists and the promotion of free trade, which put them in opposition to the Corn Laws. The Independents, by contrast, supported or opposed the two main parties according to their conscience.

Despite these fundamental differences, the Tory and Whig MPs at Westminster had a great deal in common. They were all rich and influential men, and they often defected, singly or in groups, from one party to the other over issues that had nothing to do with fundamental differences. In Glamorganshire the most obvious difference between MPs was whether they were great landowners, or big industrialists. The landowners, be they Tories or Whigs, were concerned with landed interests and, therefore, supported the Corn Laws. The industrialists were not simply Whigs; some were Radicals who supported reform and upheld the view that the wages of industrial workers could not be kept down while food prices – bread in particular – remained high.

In 1830 the Whigs won a general election after a long period of Tory rule, and did so on a platform of reform. In Glamorgan, C.R.M. Talbot of Margam and Penrice won the county constituency, which must have pleased Gowerians as he had strong connections with Gower, he being the biggest landowner in the peninsula and the owner of Penrice Castle. C.R.M. Talbot was to represent the county until 1885; thereafter he represented Mid-Glamorgan until his death in 1890. His 60 years as an MP earned him the title of 'father of the House of Commons'. His repeated victories at the polls may have been due to the fact that he was a political oddity in that he was a Whig and, therefore, in favour of moderate reform, yet as a landowner – the biggest in Glamorgan – he was against repeal of the Corn Laws, which must have pleased the farmers.

C.R.M. Talbot of Margam and Penrice – a Whig, though not a Radical, his political career started when he won the Glamorgan County Constituency in 1830. He continued to represent the county until 1885; thereafter he represented Mid-Glamorgan until his death in 1890. His aversion to Toryism probably influenced his decision to refuse a peerage in later life.

C.R.M. Talbot rarely spoke in the House of Commons, but he did vote for notable reforms. The Whig Government's Reform Bill of 1832 extended the county franchise to include copyholders, leaseholders and tenants-at-will of land above a specified value. As a result, the number of adult males entitled to vote throughout the realm rose from 1 in 8 to 1 in 5. The Bill also raised the number of Glamorgan MPs from two to five – two to represent the county. Consequently, voters in county elections had two votes – one for the senior constituency and one for the junior. In the 1832 elections C.R.M. won the senior constituency unopposed. The junior county seat was taken, also unopposed, by a fellow Whig, Lewis Weston Dillwyn, who was trustee of the Penllergaer estate on behalf of his eldest son. So Glamorganshire was represented at Westminster by two men from the Lordship of Gower and Kilvey.

Lewis Weston Dillwyn – (1778-1855) born at Ipswich, the son of a wealthy American Quaker of Welsh extraction, Lewis settled in Swansea in 1803 as the manager of the Cambrian Pottery. He was of Whig principles and (like his father) in favour of the immediate abolition of slavery, but he was no radical. Lewis was the author of several books, kept extensive diaries, a magistrate for many years, was high sheriff of Glamorgan in 1818, an alderman and elected mayor of Swansea in 1839. He was elected to represent the junior county constituency in 1832. Re-elected in 1835, he lost his seat to a Conservative in the elections of 1837.

The Whig Government did not repeal the Corn Laws, but it did enact several important reforms such as the abolition of slavery (1834) and the Poor Law Amendment Act of 1834, whereby groups of parishes united to form Poor Law Unions. In 1835 the Whigs passed the Municipal Corporation Act, which changed the way towns and cities were administrated (which will be dealt with in a later volume). The Municipal Corporation Act was the last big reform because, in 1835, the Whigs lost a general election to the Conservatives. In Glamorgan both C.R.M. Talbot and L.W. Dillwyn held onto their seats, but two years later Lewis lost his junior constituency to a Conservative.

Control at Westminster changed hands several times during the next 20 years, whereas in Glamorgan C.R.M. continued to hold his seat for the Whigs and two big landowners based near Cardiff held the junior constituency in succession for the Tories. It was during this time that the Tories became increasingly referred to as Conservatives. The Whigs also found themselves increasingly referred to as Liberals, which to some extent was due to Radical industrialists becoming the dominant element in the party. However, rather than pursue what may be regarded as a difficult subject, the political aspect of this work will be dealt with piecemeal in later volumes.

Epilogue

There would appear, at first hand, to be little in Peninsula Gower to serve as reminders of the Victorian and Edwardian eras. The distinct West Country dialect of the Englishry has gone; gone too is Welsh as the first language in what was once the Welshry. Yet there is much that is very English about the landscape and place-names of south Gower, as indeed there is a distinctly Welsh aspect about north Gower.

Incredible though it may seem, there is virtually nothing to serve as reminders of the coal industry that had such a long and overwhelming impact on the former Welshry and Clyne Valley – almost everything has been removed, grassed over or hidden by trees – nor are there any obvious signs of oyster fishing along the south coast. The limestone industry came to an end 100 years ago, time enough for the quarries at Oxwich to be masked by trees, but the industry has left reminders in the form of kilns, widespread patches of rubble and the mounds of sea-washed stones at Pwlldu. Most grist mills are either gone, or have been converted into private dwellings; only Park Mill and the one at Llanrhidian survive as reminders of the need to grind corn. The cockle industry, on the other hand, has survived, but apart from a modern cockle factory at Wernffrwd, there are only thin patches of cockleshells to remind us of the hard-working Penclawdd cocklewomen and their donkeys. Farming, of course, has also survived, the fields, hedgerows and dry-stone walls testifying to its continued existence – but gone are the farm labourers and domestic servants whose services were indispensable; they have been replaced by farm machinery and electrical appliances.

The signs of former occupations may be sparse, but of old buildings there are aplenty, though few have retained the appearance or use that the Victorians and Edwardians would have been familiar with. Castles that once reminded the Victorians and Edwardians of manorial lords who lived by the sword are still to be seen at Oystermouth, Pennard, Penrice, Oxwich and Weobley, the last two occupied by farming families throughout the Victorian era. The later residences of a less-violent gentry are likewise still standing at Clyne, Kilvrough, Stouthall, and Brynhir, but only Penrice remains occupied by a landowning family. Also still standing and serving a variety of uses are the residences of more industrious families, such as the Bensons of Fairy Hill and the Vivians who built an imposing hunting lodge at Park le Breos. Farms and cottages have, on the other hand, been modernized and extended to the extent that it requires local knowledge to identify houses that are more than 100 years old, and Gowerians are very knowledgeable about such matters.

Almost all the churches and chapels in Peninsula Gower were renovated, rebuilt or erected as new in the Victorian and Edwardian eras. The churches have all survived, and many are open to visitors who take the trouble to obtain a key. What the explorer will discover inside many of these churches – such as those at Llangennith and Oxwich – are small, white-walled interiors that give a sense of how things once were. Chapels, on the other hand, are not usually open to those who simply want to view. Some chapels that were in use in the period covered by this work have fallen to decay, several have been converted into private dwellings, and a few survive as communal venues that have nothing to do with worship. Many gravestones, of course, have been lost through neglect, whereas those that survive may have weathered with age, but they are still perfect reminders of people who have passed on.

Many rural beer-houses and the classy hotels that flourished in Oystermouth parish are either gone, or have been converted into private residences. Few of those that have survived have retained

The Mumbles Pier – built in 1898, the lighthouse in 1784, the battery in 1861 and the lifeboat station are all reminders of the past. Today there is no railway to bring thousands of day-trippers, but the Pier and its surroundings still offer a variety of attractions, to say nothing of fresh air and extensive views.

much of their 19th-century appearance, the Railway Inn, Killay, being the most notable exception. The railway line that ran from Swansea to Pontardulais can still be traced for much of its course, being preserved as a tarmaced cycle track and footpath. The route of the Mumbles Railway is also preserved as a cycle-footpath, and although virtually nothing remains of the line itself, there is still its ultimate destination, the Pier, completed in 1898. The Pier attracted thousands of Edwardian tourists, offering music, dancing, vending machines and paddle steamer trips to several places across the Channel, to say nothing of a beach and a scramble to the lighthouse and the battery. There is still something very Victorian and Edwardian about Southend and the buildings that lie between the 'Hill' and the shoreline. There is something far older, too, for lining the higher part of Village Lane are the surviving cottages of fishermen.

Oystermouth – or rather Mumbles as it is known today – is an attraction that is quite distinct from the more westerly parts of the peninsula, and for this reason it deserves to be dealt with in more detail in a later volume. Suffice to say there are many easily recognized Victorian houses in the Mumbles, but surviving mansions that once belonged to the rich are not so easily identified. There were once many fine houses along the coastal fringe between a house known as Llwynderw in West Cross, and what was once St. Ann's Hotel (originally a house called Rosehill); Norton House (formerly Norton Hall) is one fine house that has retained much of its original appearance. On Newton Road there is the British Legion Club, once a mansion occupied successively by several rich and influential families. More fine houses stood in the vicinity of Underhill Park. Langland and Caswell also attracted the very rich, particularly when it came to establishing summer residences. The great landowner, John Dillwyn Llewelyn of Penllergaer, acquired and enlarged Caswell Cottage, which stood on what is now Caswell car park. Although this mansion was demolished in the 1960s, the coach-house connected with it now serves as a Countryside Centre. Several prominent industrialists had residences in the Rotherslade-Langland Bay area, what became the Langland Bay Hotel being the only one to survive.

Old coach house, Caswell – like Caswell Cottage (a marine villa occupying a site in the nearby Caswell car park) this former coach house belonged to John Dillwyn Llewelyn of Penllergaer. Caswell Cottage was demolished in fairly recent times. The coach house survives as a Countryside Centre; it provides information on wildlife and walks in the wooded Caswell Valley.

In the 72 years that spanned the Victorian and Edwardian eras the people of Peninsula Gower did not – with the exception of Rebecca's attack of the Poundffald tollgate – experience the often violent unrest that periodically swept through South Wales, both in the rural west and in the industrialized valleys to the east. That peace still reigns in spite of the summer tourist invasions that take place on occasions when the sun shines. Also unchanged is that Gowerians still see themselves as a community apart, one in which almost everyone knows pretty much what is going on elsewhere in the peninsula, whereas Swansea people are often unaware of what is going on in their own street. Gowerians may no longer work near the coast, or take to the sea in ships as their predecessors did, but they can still look seawards and, on a bad day, envisage the hazards that sailors once had to contend with. The Peninsula Gower of yore may have been somewhat 'messy', the byways muddy, the houses and yards often ramshackled, the ground strewn with coal, cockleshells, limestone rubble and pigs' muck, but the landscape was still one of outstanding natural beauty. In short, Peninsula Gower is a truly fascinating place to visit and explore, the more so when you have the knowledge to link the past with what you see.

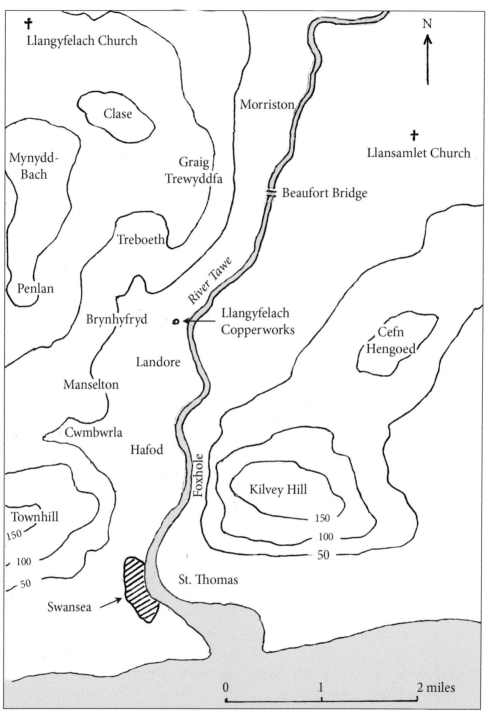

Lower Swansea Valley – showing (by contours in metres) the high ground on either side of the River Tawe, which, at high tide, had sufficient depth for ships to travel as far inland as the Beaufort Bridge below Morriston.

CHAPTER TWO

The Lower Swansea Valley (L.S.V.) 1837–67

Beyond Peninsula Gower lay the other half of the Lordship of Gower (between the Loughor and Tawe rivers), commonly referred to as East Gower; east of the Tawe lay the manor of Kilvey. East Gower will be dealt with in a subsequent publication. What will be dealt with in this chapter is the Lower Tawe Valley (including the manor of Kilvey), which strictly speaking stretched from the Swansea foreshore all the way up to Clydach and Glais. However, the part of the valley that will be considered in this chapter is the area that lay outside the old Medieval Borough of Swansea and extended inland to Ynysforgan (above Morriston) on the west bank, and Upper Forest on the east. This small area – commonly known as the Lower Swansea Valley – was one that, in Victorian times, became heavily industrialized to the extent that, scarred and stripped of vegetation, it was referred to in 1850 as the 'bad-lands' of South Wales.

The people in the Lower Swansea Valley were, for the most part, either immigrants, or the descendants of immigrants who had been drawn to the area in search of work, either in the numerous mines, or in the many and varied metal works that sprang up on both sides of the river. The people here were overwhelmingly Welsh-speaking, living in communities in which the workplace and the chapel were dominant, and where Welsh culture and a way of life was as unique as any in the coal mining valleys further east. The mines have long been abandoned, the derelict furnaces swept away, and the 'bad lands' have become green again, but what the people here produced by sheer sweat and toil made Swansea a leading coal port, and then, in succession, the Copperopolis and, later, the Tinopolis of the World; they also made the town renowned for the production of spelter and steel.

Peninsula Gower may be seen for what it is, a place of natural beauty with reminders here and there of a rich and varied history, whereas in the Lower Swansea Valley almost all that it once was has passed away, but in every street where there are old houses, in places where shopping complexes now sprawl, the past may not be so obvious, but these places have a past, they still have a story to tell, one that should not be forgotten.

Early coal mining in the Lower Tawe/Swansea Valley

In the Victorian era Swansea was one of the busiest ports in the U.K. This was due to the tremendous amount of industrial activity that took place in the Swansea Valley, and the basis of that activity was coal. To appreciate the enormity of this activity it is necessary to consider developments in the centuries preceding Victoria's coronation. The metallurgical industry, for example, had its origin in the 18th century, but Swansea had been a leading coal port in the 17th century – the third largest in the U.K. after Newcastle and Sunderland. So why, then, was Swansea Valley coal in such demand?

The answer is that, in the 16th century there had been a growing shortage of fuel – wood in particular – both in the U.K. and abroad, but coal was of no worth unless it could be easily worked and transported a short distance to where it could be loaded onto ships (hence the designation 'sea coals'). There were several places in South Wales where coal could be mined in close proximity to the sea, but Swansea had an advantage – the River Tawe, which at high tide was navigable as far inland as the Beaufort Bridge below Morriston. Miners had, therefore, only to locate a coal seam in the high ground overlooking the navigable part of the river; and once a tunnel had been driven into the hillside the coal could then be wheel-barrowed to the surface and taken a relatively short distance by packhorses to the riverside. The ease with which this could be achieved, coupled with low wages, made Swansea Valley coal relatively cheap.

The earliest reference to coal mining in the Lower Swansea Valley (abbreviated L.S.V. from hereon) relates to the Lordship of Kilvey and dates to the 14th century, but the records provide nothing specific about the west bank (apart from vague mineral leases) until 1563, when a royal commission reported that coal was being worked in the Cwmfelin-Cwmbwrla area. As to what part of the river the coal was taken, the Swansea Corporation records for 1585 refer to riverside plots called 'coal places' that later evidence confirms were located on the Strand.

In the 17th and 18th centuries, the search for coal spread northwards, as far north as the high ground above Morriston. Throughout these centuries mining remained in the hands of local landowners, the most prominent of whom were the Prices, Popkins, Mansels and the C.R. Joneses. Successive dukes of Beaufort, on the other hand, did not mine coal, but sold mineral leases to those who wished to mine coal beneath their Trewyddfa and Kilvey manors. Haulage was contracted out, usually to farmers, who used strings of packhorses to convey coal to the navigable part of the river. The hauliers made use of coal roads, which were basically unsurfaced tracks cut into the hillsides. These coal roads terminated at quays fronted with baulks of timber that were formed on the riverside, either at Landore, or at Swansea, where some 'coal places' were partially excavated to create indentations in the riverbank that were large enough for a single ship to berth and be loaded with coal.

In the early 18th century the demand for coal led to the sinking of vertical shafts to reach coal seams that were below those worked by levels. It has been estimated that, in the early 18th century, coal production in the L.S.V. amounted to around 30,000 tons annually. By the end of the century, production had risen to at least ten times that figure. The increase was due mainly to the establishment of a new industry. In the 1680s large reserves of copper-ore had been discovered in Cornwall. Coal was required to smelt that ore (by repeated roastings), and the nearest coalfield was in South Wales. The fact that it required three tons of coal to smelt one ton of copper-ore meant that it made sense to ship the ore, rather than the coal.

The attraction of coal in close proximity to a navigable river led to the first Swansea Valley smelter – the Llangyfelach Copperworks – being set up at Landore in 1717. The location of this new works was near St. Paul's Church, on the steep slope at the eastern end of Cwm Level Road. The site was chosen because an old leet from the nearby and fast-flowing Nant Rhyd-y-Filais would provide the necessary water power to operate bellows and machinery. Although an 18th century drawing shows the works to have been quite large, its workforce in 1717 was 40 men and two boys. However, a further ten smelter works were established in the Swansea Valley in the 130 years leading up to

The Strand in 1748 – prior to the construction of the New Cut and the North Dock in 1844-52, the lowest part of the Tawe flowed further west than it does today. It ran alongside the Strand, through what is now the Parc Tawe complex. The river was in fact the 'Harbour' – all the way up to the Beafort Bridge below Morriston. Ships had only to sail into the harbour and, when the tide receded, rest upon the mud while their cargoes were unloaded and their holds filled with outgoing freight. By 1748 a number of recesses had been cut into the riverbank adjoining the Strand and, being timber-lined, they served as docks, sufficient to accommodate the small sailing ships of the day.

(West Glamorgan Archive Service)

Victoria's coronation, all of them sited on the lowland that bordered the River Tawe. The copper smelters had a voracious appetite for coal, which was good for the coal producers; better still, the ore-bearing ships left with return cargoes of coal, which in turn provided fuel for pumping water from the Cornish copper mines.

The increasing demand for coal led to many changes within the industry, one of the most notable being that mining operations became less the prerogative of local landowners and more that of industrialists – the copper smelters in particular – who took out mineral leases that permitted them to mine and sell coal. Both landowners and industrialists endeavoured to increase productivity and speed up the conveyance of coal to both the copperworks and the riverside quays. It was, however, the industrialists – who invariable came from outside Wales – who had the capital for large-scale investment. Some of these newcomers were to settle locally and become the founders of dynasties, which in the Victorian era were among the leading industrialists of the day. To obtain a clearer understanding of the coal and copper industries in Victorian times it will be helpful to consider the leading industrial dynasties in some detail.

The Morrises

The earliest and one of the best known industrialists to be involved in both copper smelting and coal mining was a Shropshire man by the name of Robert Morris. In 1724 Robert came to Swansea to manage the Llangyfelach Copperworks (built in 1717). Two years later, when the owner of the works was declared bankrupt, Robert took on the role of receiver; as such he succeeded in winning the financial backing of several English industrialists, thereby creating a partnership in which he, as a junior partner, dealt with the daily running of Lockwood, Morris & Co. For coal the company relied on a local landowner, Thomas Popkins, whose insufficient deliveries of 'muck and dirty coal' drove Robert to distraction. Robert knew that for the company to survive it would have to secure its own coal supply. And to that end he took out a lease on the Trewyddfa Colliery at Tre-boeth in 1728. Two year later he secured an ore-supply from Cornwall by outbidding rival companies.

Under Robert's management the company prospered. The Llangyfelach Works had been designed as (1) a smelter for refining copper-ore and (2) rolling-mills for producing mainly domestic utensils and, to a lesser extent, copper rods for use as barter in the slave trade. Business must have been good because, in 1732–5, he built the Lower Forest Coppermills up river to serve as a forge, or battery mill, for the production of large bowl-like vessels that had a variety of commercial uses. The site was chosen because water from the Tawe could be diverted to provide the necessary power for operating bellows and machinery.

In 1735 Robert took over the Cambrian Copperworks. Built in 1720, and therefore the second copperworks to be established in the L.S.V., the Cambrian was situated on the Upper Strand at Swansea. For 15 years it had suffered long periods of inactivity for want of coal and copper-ore. Then Robert took it over for ten years, using it for smelting ore; thereafter he may have used it as copper rolling-mills until 1764.

Robert's quest to keep his copperworks supplied with fuel led to Lockwood, Morris and Co. becoming one of the largest coal producers in the Lordship of Gower. From 1732 onwards he was mining coal in the Pencaerfenni area. In 1733 he took out a lease on a 'coal place' on the Strand. In the same decade he must have improved at least some of his coal roads to the extent that he used coal carts drawn by bullocks to convey coal to the Strand, much to the annoyance of Swansea residents who complained about the noise. The use of carts, however, caught on as each cart carried eight times as much coal as a packhorse.

In c.1746-8 Robert erected his second smelter, the Forest Copperworks, near the Beaufort Bridge, Morriston; at the same time he had the (original) three-arched Beaufort Bridge built to connect his new smelter with his Lower Forest Coppermills on the east side of the river. Coal for the smelting works came from high up on Graig Trewyddfa, for which he acquired a lease in 1746. The coal was conveyed down a cart road that later became Clyndu Street, Morriston. This new complex at Forest led to the closure of the old Llangyfelach Copperworks in 1749.

When Robert died in 1768 he was succeeded by his second son, John (later Sir John Morris) who was aged 23 at the time. John certainly had his father's business acumen; he was also both a remarkable builder and an innovator. More than that, he was fortunate in that, in the years leading up to his father's death, the company had been producing copper sheets (sheaves). These sheets were used to sheathe the wooden-hulled ships of the East India Company, thereby protecting the hulls from shipworms. Huge quantities of copper bolts were also required to fix the sheets to the thick wooden hulls. It was business such as this that provided John with capital for investment.

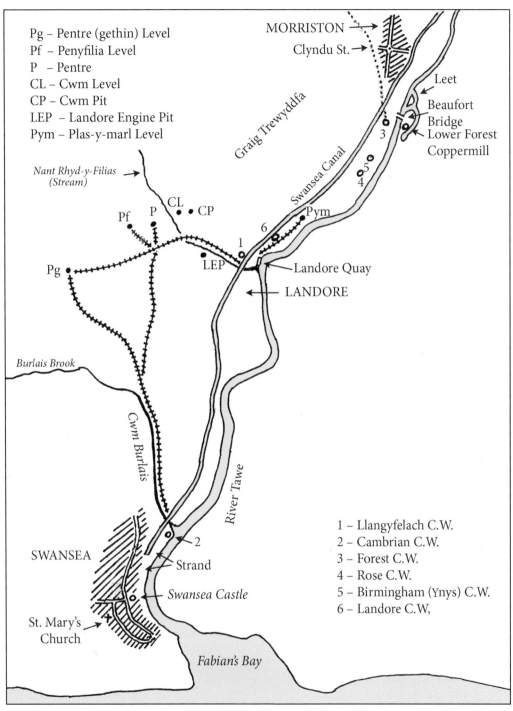

Pg – Pentre (gethin) Level
Pf – Penyfilia Level
P – Pentre
CL – Cwm Level
CP – Cwm Pit
LEP – Landore Engine Pit
Pym – Plas-y-marl Level

MORRISTON

Clyndu St.

Leet

Beaufort
Bridge
Lower Forest
Coppermill

Gráig Trewyddfa

Nant Rhyd-y-Filias
(Stream)

Swansea Canal

3

5
4

CL
Pf   P   CP

Pym

6
1
LEP

Landore Quay

LANDORE

Pg

Burlais Brook

Cwm Burlais

River Tawe

2

SWANSEA

Strand

Swansea Castle

St. Mary's
Church

Fabian's Bay

1 – Llangyfelach C.W.
2 – Cambrian C.W.
3 – Forest C.W.
4 – Rose C.W.
5 – Birmingham (Ynys) C.W.
6 – Landore C.W,

The West Bank – showing six early copperworks, and also the collieries mentioned in the text, which are only a few of the numerous workings that existed in fairly close proximity to the navigable part of the river.

Forest Copperworks 1791 – on the far right of various smelting halls is a building that may have been either a works office, or an assay office for testing the quality of copper-ore.
The Beaufort Bridge further to the right was built to communicate with the Lower Forest Rolling-mills on the east bank. In 1968 the bridge was demolished, being replaced by an iron bridge that, although closed to traffic, still stands as a reference to where exactly the copperworks stood in relation to what is now the top end of Beaufort Road. Several rowing boats are depicted, two of them alongside a quay where there is a crane for unloading copper-ore.
It is likely that these boats were used to bring ore from sailing ships that were too big to sail right up to the quay. The works were converted into a spelter (zinc) works by Vivian & Sons in 1868, and finally closed in 1926.

(West Glamorgan Archive Service)

A new pit, the Plas-y-Marl Level, had been opened during the 1760s, the coal being taken to the riverside at Landore for export. In 1769–71 John speeded up conveyance from this level by laying a waggonway to the riverside. This waggonway – one of the first recorded on the west bank – consisted of narrow-gauge oak rails, the upper surface shod with iron to reduce wear and tear. The main advantage of a waggonway was that the wheels of horse or ox-drawn waggons encountered far less friction on rails than on badly-pitted coal roads. Waggons, therefore, travelled faster and they carried more coal. Other coal producers on the west bank were soon following John's example, with the result that waggonways became a feature of the landscape – but John went one step further in 1776 when he ordered 100 tons of cast iron tram plates that appear to have been a local invention. Yet another innovation was the construction in 1772-4 of the valley's first stone quay at Landore, which reputedly still stands.

Landore Quay c.1792 – drawing by J.C. Ibbotson. Above the stone quay is a tipping staithe and coal chute for loading coal (in this instance) into a lighter. The coal had evidently been brought to the quay in waggons drawn by oxen (one oxen is leaving with an empty waggon). A man can be seen tipping the contents of a waggon into the chute. Below the staithe are packhorse laden with bags of coal – to what end is unclear. Two of the hauliers are women. Upriver is the newly-built Landore Copperworks, and on the hilltop to the left stands what was then a block of flats known as Morris Castle.

One of John's most outstanding innovations was the construction of the Clyndu underground canal in the 1770s, which brought coal from deep within Craig Trewyddfa directly to the Forest Copperworks. The canal was over 1,000 metres long, its entrance at today's roundabout at the southern end of Martin Street, Morriston. It was said that 'boats went up the level to the face of the coal where the waggons were tipped into them – each boat could hold 2 waggons full – or 4 tons.'

John made a seemingly surprising move when he encouraged other copper magnates to establish new works on the Tawe. The first of these works, the Rose Copperworks, was established at Plas-y-Marl in c.1780; the second, the Birmingham (alias the Ynys) Copperworks, was founded in 1791, its location also at Plas-y-Marl. Owned by Birmingham-based companies, the new works were not in competition with Lockwood, Morris & Co. because they produced goods for a different kind of market. However, the new works needed huge quantities of coal and John, of course, was in a position to supply them. The coal came from deep within Graig Trewyddfa and, for conveyance purposes, he constructed a mile-long surface canal (the Lockwood, Morris & Co. Canal) in *c*.1787-91. This surface canal was an extension of the Clyndu underground canal. It supplied coal to the new copperworks, then continued on to Landore – and for good reason.

In *c*.1793 production commenced at John's new Landore Copperworks, its location near a sharp bend in the Tawe, a little to the north-east of what is now St. Paul's Church. This new works had its own tidal dock for unloading copper-ore. The accompanying stamping and rolling-mills were built on the site of the old Llangyfelach Copperworks, thereby making use of the old works' leet to operate bellows and machinery. The same year as the new works went into production, John sold his Forest Copperworks and the Lower Forest Coppermills to the Bristol Brass Wire Co. He continued to supply both Forest works with coal.

In 1788 John took out a lease on the Pentre (gethin) Level, its location a little to the north of St. John's Road, Manselton. This level had belonged to the coal-producing landowner, Gruffudd Price, and although the colliery was 'nearly exhausted in the upper range of working' (meaning the 5-foot coal seam presumably) John managed to increase production by working the lower coal seams as well. In 1791 a tourist, E.D. Clarke, visited this colliery, describing it in a manner that gives insight into the hellish environment endured by colliers.

The entrance is vaulted, and perfectly level, and continues so for about one hundred yards, when our guides made us turn off to the right, to a sort of staircase, which they call the horse road. By this we descended to a depth of eighty fathoms (about 480 feet) and came to a spacious area, where the miners were sending up the coal in baskets through a shaft, to the vaulted level we had quitted. It is there put into carts, with friction wheels (run on waggon-ways) and drawn by oxen to the mouth of the mine.

It is pleasing to see (by candle light) the ease and quickness with which these amazing works are carried on. If a stranger beholds the dark passage by which the horses descend, who bring the coal from the place where it is dug to the shaft, he would be astonished, and unable to conceive how these animals can be taught to practise, without stumbling ... what he with care and attention would find it difficult to perform. Proceeding onwards we came to some miners, who were engaged in blowing up part of the rock with gun powder, in order to make the communication from one part of the mine to another. Still further onward, about half a mile from the entrance, we came to the cutters [coal face workers] ... a troop of miserable black devils, working away their very lives amidst sulphur, smoke and darkness.

As you creep among these regions of darkness the guide who precedes you, calls out, every now and then desiring you to stand close. This happens when a load of coal is coming along the passage [in a waggon], which is heard at a distance, and if you stand close to the side, you are sure to be safe. The [waggon] wheels are placed on the iron bars, which they receive in a groove, and these bars being continued parallel to each other, they serve both as a guide to the carts [waggons] and by lessoning the friction, greatly diminish the weight of the load. [These iron bars may have been similar to the ones John ordered in 1776.] As soon therefore as the guide gives warning that a load is coming, you know by your distance from the parallel bars, how near the load will approach you.

It is curious to see one of these carts pass. They are drawn by horses, and if they are empty, the driver lays along in them, seizing his beast by the tail, which serves him as a rein to guide the animal round the different turnings and windings in the passages. It is really astonishing to see the horses perform their work. They move securely along, enveloped by total darkness, never either striking their heads against the roof, or mistaking the road they are to go, or falling among the number of uneven places they meet with. Among others, an old blind horse, who had been fifteen years a servant in the mine, passed by us. Our guide assured us, that he was so well acquainted with his work, that if left to himself, he would find his way through all the mazes of the mine.

A horse-drawn waggon about to exit a mining level. Hauliers (drivers) were usually boys aged between 14 and 17. The haulier seen here is guiding his horse by the tail, which, according to the records, was the practice when a waggon was empty. Note the walls – the first 100 metres of many Swansea Valley levels were vaulted with stones. The first waggons had run on wooden – later iron-shod – rails. From c.1800 onwards wooden rails were gradually replaced by L-shaped, cast-iron tramplates, the toes pointing outwards. Consequently, the terms waggons and waggonways were gradually replaced by trams and tramroads. By the time of Victoria's coronation, tramplates were in the process of being replaced by edge rails, similar to those used by modern railways.

A waggonway led south from the Pentre(gethin) Level towards the Strand, Swansea (a small portion of this line led down what is now the upper part of Brondeg Road). In 1790 John obtained a lease from the Swansea Corporation that permitted him to extend this waggonway down through the Cwm Burlais to coal places on the Strand, which he leased from the Corporation in 1793. At about the same time he laid another waggonway from Pentre(gethin), along Penfilia Road, through Brynhyfryd, to what was then his new Landore Copperworks. It is interesting to note that, like

Penfilia Road, many roads in the L.S.V. originated as horse-drawn waggonways. In late Victorian times houses were built on either side of these thoroughfares.

Due to a court action that had nothing to do with him, John could no longer work the Pentre(gethin) Level after 1795, but he still had several other collieries in operation, and in 1797 he took over the Penyfilia Level (a little to the northwest of Brynhyfryd Square, on the north side of the 'incline') with its attendant waggonway. There were many collieries and waggonways in and around Brynhyfryd at that time. In fact, the whole area between Pentregethin Road and Morriston was riddled with the collieries of smaller coal producers, each with relatively short coal roads or waggonways to either the navigable part of the Tawe, or to what was then the newly-constructed Swansea Canal. How so many coal producers managed to operate in the same area may be explained by the fact that they worked different coal seams, each of which were located at varying depths below ground.

Cwm Burlais c.1900 – originating to the east of Cockett Church, the Burlais Brook flowed close to the old Gorse Road, as far as Cwmbwrla, and from there it continued on down to the steep-sided ravine of Cwm Burlais before finally discharging into the Tawe. For much of its course the brook is now culverted, whereas the bottom of the ravine (seen here) is now Cwm Road. The cwm channelled coal supplies to coal places on the Strand. In the early days of mining, a coal road ran down the cwm; from the late 18th century onwards it became a route for John Morris's waggonway. The brook itself provided water-power for grist mills and for several industrial enterprises, among them the Cambrian Copperworks and the Cambrian Pottery.

Hafod Bridge – as viewed from the north. The smaller, left-hand archway was for the horse-drawn trams of John Morris (1790) and later Messrs Richard & Glasbrook (1848). The larger archway spanned the roadway (as it does today). A third, right-hand archway (now blocked up) permitted the Burlais Brook (now culverted) to flow towards the Tawe.

The bridge was widened in the 1870s to allow passenger street trams to pass over the bridge. The join between the original bridge and what was later built alongside it can be seen from beneath the larger archway.

If John was an industrious innovator, he was also an innovative builder. Soon after his father's death in 1768, he built, for his colliers, Morris Castle, one of the earliest block of flats in the U.K. In 1779 he laid the foundations of Morriston (Morris's Town) for both colliers and copperworkers in his employ. For himself he built the Palladian-style mansion of Clasemont in *c.*1770–5, its location on the site of the present-day D.V.L.A. above Morriston. He also built several marine villas in the Sketty area, some of which he rented out. When he died in 1819 he did so at his London residence in Hans Place. Like his father before him, he was buried at St. John's (later St. Matthew's) Church, Swansea.

SOUTH-EAST VIEW of *CLASMONT,* the Seat of J. MORRIS, Esq.

Clasemont – a Georgian mansion built by John Morris (1) in c.1770. The site is now dominated by the D.V.L.A. The Wychtree Bridge (built 1778–80) seen here was superseded in 1959 by its modern replacement. Morriston now occupies the area between these two sites, but when this drawing was published in 1791 the earliest phase of this township must have been sited beyond the left-hand edge of this picture; either that, or the artist deliberately left it out.

(West Glamorgan Archive Service)

129

The Swansea Canal

By 1794 the mile-long Lockwood, Morris Canal had passed into the hands of the Duke of Beaufort. It was an acquisition that proved rewarding for the Duke because, that same year, Parliament passed an Act that permitted the construction of the Swansea Canal. The Lockwood, Morris Canal – renamed the Trewyddfa Canal – was incorporated into the Swansea Canal, and for that purpose it was both widened and deepened. Any barges passing through the Trewyddfa section of the Swansea Canal had to pay a separate toll to the Duke himself.

Built in 1794–8 to convey bulk commodities from the interior to Swansea Harbour, the Swansea Canal extended 16¼ miles inland. From the Strand the canal passed through Landore, Morriston and Clydach to reach its furthest point inland near the Lamb and Flag, Ystradgynlais. This was a remarkable feat of engineering, as there were no less than 36 locks that enabled barges to ascend almost 400 feet from the canal's lowest point on the Strand. There were also many aqueducts to carry the waterway over tributaries such as the Clydach, the largest and most impressive aqueduct being the one at Ystalyfera.

In the L.S.V. the Swansea Canal followed a course from the Strand, between the railway lines and the river, to the large roundabout near Morfa Stadium. Beyond the roundabout the canal followed a similar course to the northbound carriageway of the Landore bypass, as far north as the roundabout at the foot of Cwm Level Road. Thereafter, the route roughly followed today's Plasmarl and Morriston bypasses, then continued on up the valley. Most waggonways from collieries terminated at wharves on the canal, the coal taken by barge to either the harbour or the copper smelters.

The Swansea Canal was undoubtedly a success, opening up as it did the upper Valley as far north as Ystradgynlais, but from *c.*1850 onwards it began losing trade to the new railway companies. In 1872 it was taken over by the Great Western Railway. Within 20 years of the take-over, all long-distance traffic on the canal had ceased. Thereafter the canal served only local requirements until its demise in the 1930s. Thirty years later much of the canal was filled in, but some sections survive, and one section between Clydach and Pontardawe still holds water.

Swansea Canal – in this mid-19th century print of the Landore (Railway) Viaduct viewed from the south; the Swansea Canal is depicted as relatively wide at this point. Note the barge being towed by a horse on the towpath. In recent times the route taken by the canal has become the northbound carriageway of the present-day Landore bypass (part of the Cross Valley Link), which passes through what is now the central gap in the viaduct's supports. The houses on the left line the old Neath Road. The open space to the right of the canal is now the site of the southbound carriageway and the Morfa sports complex.

(Swansea Museum)

Landore (Railway) Viaduct 2009 – its appearance in this photograph is noticeably different from that in the 19th century print (opposite). The earlier structure was mostly timber-built, the work carried out by Isambard Kingdom Brunel in 1847–50. The first major change to its appearance occurred in 1888–9 when the timber elements were replaced with new masonry piers and steel girders; also the eastern part was converted into an embankment. The changes carried out in 1978–9 involved the removal of one of Brunel's five masonry piers to make way for the south-bound carriageway of the Landore bypass.

A Swansea Canal bridge – sited at the bottom/eastern end of Morfydd Street, Morriston. The bridge was built when the Swansea Canal was driven through this part of the township in 1794–8.

Lockwood & Co. and the Penyvilia Vein Co.

When Thomas Lockwood entered into partnership with Robert Morris, he left the day-to-day running of the business to his junior partner, while he continued to live in London. His son, also Thomas, married Robert's daughter, Bridget. Later – possibly after the death of Robert in 1768 – Thomas the Younger moved to the Swansea Valley. Then, for reasons unknown, he and his brother-in-law, John Morris, ended their long-standing partnership in 1800, although the two families continued to have a healthy business relationship.

The end of the partnership led to the creation of three new mining concerns, and the first to be considered is Lockwood & Co. Thomas Lockwood and his associates appear to have ended up with most of the assets that had belonged to the Lockwood, Morris partnership. The new company had control of the Landore Copperworks, which it sold to The Bristol Co. in c.1808; it also had possession of several of the more important collieries. Lockwood & Co. certainly had the Penyfilia Level (above Brynhyfryd Square) from which it continued to work the 5-foot coal seam. There were two other seams at a much greater depth – the 6-foot and the 3-foot – and to work these lower seams the company sank the new Pentre Pit in c.1807 (not to be confused with the old Pentre(gethin) Level). It should be noted that because of their close proximity the names Penyfilia and Pentre are often interchangeable. For example, in 1799 the Revd. J. Evans visited the Penyfilia Level, but he referred to it as 'at Pentre', which was the name of the estate on which it was situated. Several years after his visit the Revd. Evans wrote:

> The largest colliery is at Pentre, the property of Mr. Morris of Clasemont [this was before the Lockwood, Morris partnership was dissolved]. The whole hill is full of coal, and is obtained by what miners term audits, i.e, horizontal shafts driven into the hill, which form levels for draining the work as well as ways for the delivery of the coal. There are within, some vertical shafts, beneath these levels, and whimsies [i.e., a capstan or windlass, for raising coal by the weight of water, which descending in one bucket draws up another filled with coal] have given way to ... the improved steam engine of Bolton and Watt. One of the audits, which we traced about a mile in length, admits low waggons, holding a chaldron each, which running on an iron railway, one horse with ease delivers at the [Landore] quay.

Pentre Pit in the 1920s – it stood a little to the north of Brynhyfryd Square, in the angle formed by Llangyfelach Road and Cwm Level Road. The tall building on the right, with a chimney at one end, was the engine house containing the engine that operated the dual pumping-winding gears. To the left a stone pier supported the pulley over the colliery shaft. Pentre yielded coal for more than 180 years. It would appear to have been in use before 1748; it closed due to flooding in 1926.

Due to a financial reconstruction the assets of Lockwood & Co. were divided with the creation of a new company in 1806 – the Penyvilia Vein Co. – in which Thomas Lockwood was one of several partners. The purpose of the new company was to supply coal to the riverside copperworks. Lockwood & Co., on the other hand, worked the new Pentre Pit, coal from which was destined for export.

The Penyvilia Vein Co. had control of pits situated on the heights of Graig Trewyddfa. From these pits the company converted the upper part of the old Clyndu cart road into a waggonway – or rather a tramroad as it would then have been called – one that veered off down what is now Pentremalwod Road to supply the riverside copperworks. From its Penyfilia Level and its Cwm Level (situated near the sharp bend in Cwm Level Road) the company laid another tramroad in *c.*1813 on the line of present-day Dinas Street, Landore, to supply the same copperworks.

In the meantime, Lockwood & Co. concentrated on getting coal from its new Pentre Pit to Swansea for export, and for that purpose it laid a tramroad along what is now Eaton Road. This tramroad connected with the old Cwm Burlais line laid by John Morris in 1790. Thus coal from Pentre Pit reached wharves on the Strand.

John Morris II (1775-1855)

The third mining concern to be considered belonged to the Morrises, later to become the Landore Colliery Co. Following the break-up of the Lockwood, Morris partnership, John Morris appears to have withdrawn from business in favour of his son, also named John (and also to be knighted). What exactly the Morrises got out of the dissolved partnership is unclear, but their aim was to mine coal for export. In 1803 John II began work on the Cwm Pit (the site now occupied by St. Peter's Catholic Church, Landore). In *c.*1805 he re-laid the old tramroad connecting this pit with the Swansea Canal so that coal could be taken to wharves at Swansea.

At a slightly later date John II laid a spur to link up with Lockwood's Eaton Road–Cwm Burlais tramroad. Today, Eaton Road is an unusually wide road, and the reason for this is that its top end had once been a marshalling yard for the waggons of both Lockwood & Co. and John Morris II. Loaded waggons of both companies were assembled there for delivery to the Strand.

John II obviously prospered, whereas his father's former business partner failed, for in *c.*1829 he took over the Pentre Pit (which Lockwood & Co. had abandoned in *c.*1811) and also the Penyfilia Level from The Penyvilia Vein Co., which made him the largest coal producer on the west bank.

One of the characteristics of mining on the west bank was the frequency with which mines changed hands. Often a change of ownership took place because the original owner went bust, or because he could not raise the money required for investment. Then someone, or perhaps a consortium, would step in and either buy the original owner out, or buy sufficient shares to gain a controlling interest in the business. Changes such as these happened all the time; it happened in 1837-8 when the Penyvilia Vein Co. was taken over by a consortium of copper magnates and its assets became the property of the Swansea Coal Co.

John II held his own for a while, but times were changing. The coal reserves in close proximity to the river were near exhaustion. A tremendous amount of investment was needed to develop pits further afield. The only company with capital for that kind of investment was the Swansea Coal Co., and in 1843 John II was obliged to sell off much of his assets to the new company. Pentre Pit he held onto for a while longer, but even that went to the Swansea Coal Co. in the early 1850s.

The Townsend-Smith Dynasty of the East Side

There is plenty of evidence to show that coal mining on the East Side was in existence as early as the 14th century, and no doubt earlier, but development did not begin in earnest until after 1600. By the early 18th century the Mansels of Margam and Penrice were in possession of the Briton Ferry estate, which included a large part of the parish of Llansamlet. This, their Llansamlet Coalfield, the Mansels worked successfully, shipping the coal from a quay at Foxhole. It has been estimated that in a good year the Mansels' undertakings yielded around 15,000 tons of coal per annum, which made the Llansamlet Coalfield the most productive in Wales at that time. In a bid to create a market closer to home they leased a six-acre plot to a Bristol concern for the purpose of erecting what became known as the White Rock Copperworks; they even invested £1,000 in the project. In return the copperworks proprietors were to use only Mansels' coal.

White Rock Copperworks in the 1950s – in the following decade the site was cleared, but some masonry has been preserved, such as the eastern wall of the smelting house (the Great Workhouse), which today is hidden in the wooded area to the east of the White Rock Dock (seen here as an inlet alongside the river). The most prominent remains are those of a ramp on which an incline railway took waste to a secondary slag-tip on the slopes of Kilvey Hill (the position of the ramp is a little beyond the left-hand edge of this picture). The original slag-tip (much reduced and close to the ramp) survives as a grassy mound with a spiral path leading to the summit. The Llansamlet/Smith's Canal passes between a break in the ramp; further south the canal entered a tunnel, which is now blocked up.

(Swansea Museum)

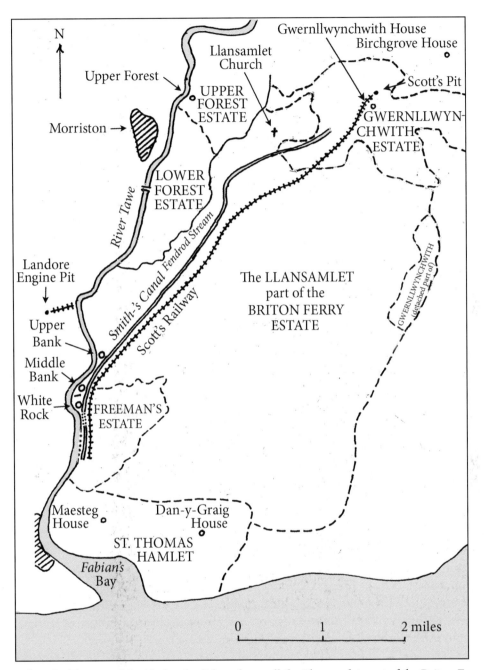

Upper Forest

Morriston →

Llansamlet
Church

Gwernllwynchwith House
Birchgrove House

Scott's Pit

UPPER
FOREST
ESTATE

GWERNLLWYN-
CHWITH
ESTATE

LOWER
FOREST
ESTATE

River Tawe

Smith's Canal

Fendrod Stream

Scott's Railway

Landore
Engine Pit
↓

GWERNLLWYNCHWITH
(detached part of)

The LLANSAMLET
part of the
BRITON FERRY
ESTATE

Upper
Bank

Middle
Bank

White
Rock

FREEMAN'S
ESTATE

Maesteg
House

Dan-y-Graig
House

ST. THOMAS
HAMLET

Fabian's
Bay

0   1   2 miles

*The East Side – the Townsend-Smith family did not lease all the Llansamlet part of the Briton Ferry estate,
only scattered parcels amounting to 260 acres. The Smiths also owned the freehold of a further 60 acres in
the same area. By Victorian times mining shafts had been sunk into the lower, often marshy ground where
both Smith's Canal and Scott's Railway operated. The Foxhole Quays (indicated by dots) are where both
the canal and the railway terminated. Also indicated by dots (two parallel rows) is a section of the canal
that passed beneath ground level and directly to the rear of White Rock's 'Great Workhouse'.*

White Rock Dock – ships laden with copper-ore entered this recess in the river bank, there to rest upon mud when the river level dropped with the outgoing tide. The curving river bank (top left) led to the coal wharves of the Townsend/Smith and Scott families.

White Rock was the third smelting works to be established in the L.S.V. Initially, it produced only refined copper ingots, which were sent to Bristol where they were converted into manufactured goods. The original workforce comprised of around 55 men, but the number increased when the works expanded to produce manufactured goods on site, including horseshoe-shaped manilas for the slave trade.

When Bussy Lord Mansel died in 1750, the Briton Ferry estate passed to his daughter, Barbara Louise, who later married Lord Vernon. That same year a wealthy London merchant by the name of Chauncey Townsend obtained a mineral lease on the Llansamlet part of the Briton Ferry estate. The lease gave Chauncey the right to mine coal as far north as roughly the modern A48 road. Beyond that lay Gwernllwynchwith, the estate of the late Charles Morgan. In the same year (1750) Chauncey obtained another mineral lease from Morgan's widow, Mary.

Using his vast wealth, Chauncey set about developing the Llansamlet Coalfield, and for that purpose he enlisted the services of George Kirkhouse, a Tyneside engineer. By 1756 he had constructed an intricate system of iron-shod wooden waggonways running from his many collieries, all of which joined with a main arterial line. The arterial waggonway ran from a colliery to the east of Llansamlet Church (a section of which is now occupied by Llwyncrwn Road) and continued down to his wharves at Foxhole, 'alongside which vessels were drawn by men and horses, barge fashion'. From these wharves the coal was shipped mainly to the West of England.

Chauncey also developed 5¼ miles of watercourses, the water used to power winding and pumping operations at his collieries (winding gear raised coal to the surface and pumps prevented mines from flooding). From c.1760 he began purchasing expensive steam engines to replace his waterwheels. His carefully planned mining and transport operations were in contrast to the independent enterprises on the opposite side of the river, where even Lockwood, Morris & Co. could not match the scale of Chauncey's undertakings. It has been estimated that, at the time of his death, Chauncey's output was more than 35,000 tons per annum.

In 1755 Chauncey built the Middle Bank Works, initially as a lead smelter, the lead-ore coming from his mines in West Wales. When he sold Middle Bank ten years later, the new owners converted it to a copper smelter. In 1757 Chauncey built the Upper Bank Works for both lead and zinc smelting, the ores again coming from his West Wales mines. When Upper Bank was sold by his son-in-law in 1777 the works were likewise adapted for copper smelting.

Last of the Upper Bank smelting halls – the hall probably housed two rows of furnaces. Note the blocked up ventilation apertures on the end wall. The hall owes its survival (2008) to its later use by Addis Ltd., producers of household plastics, brushes, etc., since 1964.

Chauncey's industrial empire included coalfields in the Llanelly area, which he developed from 1766 onwards. In 1762 he sank the Landore Engine Pit (later known as Calland's) on the west bank. By 1768 this pit had a steam-pumping engine on site, and a waggonway leading to the river (the steep section of Siloh Road now occupies part of its route). Abandoned in *c.*1780, the pit flooded, but was reopened in or soon after 1800. Fifty-eight years later a Cornish beam engine was installed at the pithead; thereafter it remained operational as a pumping installation until *c.*1926. Its closure led to the flooding of numerous pits on the west bank.

When Chauncey Townsend died in 1770 his business interests were divided between his five children, but management of the Llansamlet Coalfield passed to his son-in-law, John Smith, a London solicitor who held one-fifth interest by right of his marriage to Chauncey's daughter, Elizabeth. Whether Chauncey ever had a residence in Kilvey is unclear, but John Smith did – he bought the mansion of Gwernllwynchwith from the Morgan family in 1770. John is said to have invested upwards of

Gwernllwynchwith before its demolition in 1971 – constructed during the reign of Queen Anne (1702–14), this house was one of the first brick-built properties in Glamorgan (although there are those who would argue that the house was built by John Smith after he purchased the freehold in 1770). The property served as the seat of successive owners of the Gwernllwynchwith estate. It was bought by the coal master, John Smith, in 1770. Thereafter the house served as the Smith family's main residence until a grandson, Charles Henry, bought what became known as Derwen Fawr in c.1840. When exactly Charles Henry disposed of Gwernllwynchwith is difficult to determine, but in 1866 he moved to Tenby; six years later he sub-leased what remained of his Llansamlet Coalfield.

The Smith's Canal – at its lower/southern end the Llansamlet/Smith's Canal passed to the rear/landward side of the White Rock Copperworks. Viewed from the north after heavy rain, the section shown here is where the canal widens on the east side of what is now a much reduced and grassed over slag tip. In the distance the canal passes through a gap in what was once a ramp, one that carried an incline railway up the slopes of Kilvey Hill. The canal remained in use until 1854.

£54,000 in developing the Llansamlet Coalfield and, by the time of his death in 1797, output had reached a staggering 200,000 tons per annum. Much of his success was due to the construction of the Llansamlet (alias the Smith's) Canal in 1783–5. The canal replaced his father-in-law's arterial waggonway, but the shorter waggonways were retained as feeders between the collieries and the canal. From near his home of Gwernllwynchwith the canal led to the three Foxhole smelters (which it fed) and terminated at the shipping wharves further south. Few details have survived with regard to the working of this canal, but in 1811 a traveller wrote 'two men will haul a barge from Pwll Mawr Pit containing two weys of coal [ten tons] and empty it for 3s. At this laborious employ they will earn 4s. 6d. per diem'.

In the course of his 29 years as managing-partner, John purchased three one-fifths of the business from his in-laws, so that when he died he was able to pass on four-fifths of the business to his two sons, Charles and Henry. Little is known of Henry, but Charles was one of the few industrialists to acquire 'a radical knowledge of the Welsh language', which he learned after coming 'to reside in this country'. The brothers worked the Llansamlet Colliery until *c.*1812, at which point they surrendered their mineral lease on the Gwernllwynchwith estate. A few years later the lease was taken up by John Scott, a London attorney. John sank Scott's Pit in 1817. Two years later the pit began yielding coal, by which time John had also built an engine house (which still stands) for winding and pumping operations. He also laid a tramroad (Scott's Railway) to take coal from this pit to a shipping wharf at Foxhole. This was no ordinary tramroad. A steam locomotive – probably a George Stephenson's locomotive – ran on this tramroad, the earliest recorded locomotive to operate in the L.S.V. Unfortunately, the locomotive proved unreliable and had to be replaced by oxen. John Scott went bankrupt in 1828, having financially overstretched himself like so many other colliery owners.

Charles Henry, the son of Charles Smith, succeeded to the Llansamlet mineral leases in 1826. Two years later he bought back the Gwernllwynch-with lease, thereby reviving the Llansamlet Colliery, which by the mid-19th century was also known as the Foxhole Collieries. He also took over the abandoned Scott's Railway, which he used in addition to his grandfather's canal. An accident occurred in 1833 in which a 15-year-old boy fell upon the rails, suffering fatal injuries when 'the loco. Engine belonging to H. [Charles Henry] Smith' passed over his legs. Whether this was the same engine used by John Scott is unknown – it may have been as Charles Henry made use of anything second-hand as long as it saved him money.

Charles Henry was not noted for investment – perhaps because, by 1841, coal production had dropped to around 70,000 tons per annum, and the workforce reduced to 421 men. By then coal mining

Scott's Pit, Llansamlet – built in 1817–19 as an engine house (the engine pumped water from the pit), it also powered winding gear to raise coal to the surface. The pit, which is now sealed by a concrete cap, was worked until c.1842, then abandoned. The engine house was recommissioned in 1872 for draining purposes, and continued to fulfil that function for about 60 years.

on the East Side had moved northwards, to Birchgrove and Glais, which is why in 1845 Charles Henry leased Scott's Railway to those who were developing the coalfield further north. The railway was then utilized by the new owners as the southern part of their Swansea Vale Railway, although Charles Henry continued to run several engines on it.

Charles Henry was High Sheriff of Glamorgan in 1839, Mayor of Swansea in 1845, and has been described as 'a jovial, jocular' man 'who often descended his own pits to see what was going on below'; moreover, there is much in the records to suggest that Charles Henry was a thrifty, crafty character. However, one thing is certain – he was astute enough to sub-lease his colliery interests in 1872 to Evan Matthew Richards, and that, coupled with his retirement to Tenby six years earlier, effectively ended the family connection with the L.S.V.

The Grenfells of Kilvey

In *c*.1804 the Middle and Upper Bank Copperworks were taken over by the partnership of Williams & Grenfell. Owen Williams was the son of the Anglesey 'Copper King' Thomas Williams, whereas Pascoe Grenfell was a successful businessman of Cornish descent. When the partnership was dissolved *c*.1825, Pascoe formed a new company – Pascoe Grenfell & Sons – which retained control of Middle Bank. Pascoe died 13 years later, leaving his three sons to run what was very much a family concern. The family's principal seat was at Taplow on the Thames in Buckinghamshire, where they had copper rolling-mills. It must have been decided before Pascoe's death that the family should have a residence near their Middle Bank Works, and for that purpose a lease was acquired on the Maesteg estate, situated on the southern slopes of Kilvey Hill.

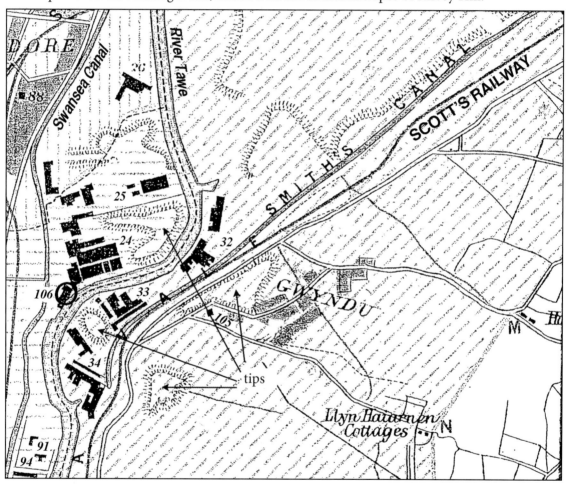

The Hafod, Morfa and East Side copperworks concentration in 1867.
Key: 24 Hafod Works; 25 Morfa Works; 32 Upper Bank Works; 33 Middle Bank Works;
34 White Rock Works; 91 Hafod Iron Foundry; 94 Hafod Phosphate Works;
105 Cnap Coch (a former mansion that provided worker accommodation);
106 site of the ruinous Hafod Works engine houses that can be seen today.

140

It was decided that Pascoe's second son, Pascoe St. Leger, should be the one to manage Middle Bank, and in *c.*1840 he built Maesteg House. Unlike other local industrialists, Pascoe St. Leger did not move to Sketty (as did the Morrises and the Smiths) so it would be appropriate to mention at this point that Maesteg House stood at the present-day junction of Grenfell Park Road and St. Leger Crescent. A lodge stood at the junction of Grenfell Park Road and Morris Lane, where there were stables, greenhouses and Maesteg Cottage. Another lodge stood to the south-east of St. Thomas's Church, at the junction of Kinley Street and Port Tennant Road. Maesteg House was demolished about 1920.

The Grenfells did not involve themselves in coal mining; the Smiths provided them with all the coal they needed. They were, however, involved in other business ventures, including shipping, mainly for business communications between Swansea, Liverpool and Deeside, although one clipper, the *Taplow*, was used as a family yacht during the summer months. About 1850 they acquired Upper Bank, which they converted to a spelter (zinc) works in 1868 – but rather than give a summary of their ventures and, indeed, their management of the Foxhole copperworks, it would be better to focus on one member of the family, Pascoe St. Leger, the man who resided at Maesteg House. In 1879 Pascoe St. Leger died, and the tribute paid to him by *The Cambrian* newspaper sums up the man and his achievements admirably. It included that:

> upon taking up his residence at Maesteg House, he set about ... repairing workmen's cottages and building new ones ... he maintained the most friendly feeling between himself and his workmen, and we believe there has never been such a thing as a strike or lockout at Foxhole. Besides, he paid the greatest attention to education, and the moral and religious culture of ... the East side ... He built All Saints Church, Kilvey, the Kilvey schools, which accommodate upwards of 1,000 children, together with the Music Hall ... For thirty years he taught a Bible class in the Sunday school ... He was chairman of the Harbour Trust (1850–59) ... served as Town Councillor, though he would never accept the civic chair [as Mayor]. He was Deputy Lieutenant for the County ... [and for many years thereafter] his voice was always heard in the Petty Sessions ... held at Swansea. The Swansea Savings Bank experienced the benefit of his careful direction, and the British and Foreign Bible Society, the London Missionary Society and other kindred associations received his warm and personal support; for although a Churchman, he was most tolerant and kindly in his religious views.

That Pascoe St. Leger was a philanthropist did not go unnoticed by his employees, for *The Cambrian* also recorded that

> at a meeting of all employees of Messrs. Pascoe Grenfell and Sons ... the following vote of condolence was unanimously adopted. That we in this meeting assembled, and representing the whole body of the officials, men and boys, working at Middle Bank, in the offices, mills and works, desire respectfully to express our deepest sympathy with the family of the late Pascoe St. Leger Grenfell, Esquire, our beloved master and friend ... for we shall sorely miss his kindly face and well known footstep, which so frequently encouraged us in our work, and made us thankful for a master who took such an unfailing interest in us – an interest not confined to our work, but extending to our spiritual and mental welfare, our homes and our children. We feel that we have lost our best friend. Signed by the agents and foremen.

The Foxhole copperworks continued as a family concern for a further 13 years, but all was not well. There were family squabbles and an unwillingness to adapt to changes in the copper industry. In 1892 Pascoe Grenfell & Sons went into voluntary liquidation. This was an unexpected announcement to everyone in the district, but more so to the firm's employees and their families. Nearly 600 men were expecting to be thrown out of work. Fortunately, both Middle and Upper Bank were taken over by Williams, Foster & Co., although the Grenfells continued to have a small stake in the establishment.

The best remembered of Pascoe St. Leger's offspring were his son, Francis, and his daughter, Elizabeth Mary, both of whom were held in high esteem. Born at Maesteg House in 1841, Francis, being a fourth son, settled for a career in the army. He served in many countries, but it was not until 1882 that his career took off. In that year he was present at the Battle of Tel-el-Kibur, which resulted in Egypt becoming subject to British rule. Three years later, Colonel Pascoe was appointed Commander in Charge of Egyptian forces, responsible for rebuilding the shattered Egyptian army. Earlier that same year, General Gordon had been killed at Khartoum in the Sudan, and by the end of the year Colonel Francis's new Egyptian army took part in the defeat of the rebellious Mahdi's forces.

It was while he served in Egypt that Francis sent to Swansea the mummified body of the priest, Tem Hor, along with several other artefacts and battle trophies, all of which are held by the Swansea Museum. Francis left Egypt in 1892. He returned to the country as a general five years later and took part in the reconquest of the Sudan. Thereafter he was appointed to several important posts, and the title of Lord Grenfell of Kilvey was bestowed upon him in 1902. The following year he became a field marshal. He died in 1925 as one of Swansea's most distinguished sons.

The women in the Maesteg household were no less remarkable. They were all practicing Christians and demonstrated compassion for those less fortunate than themselves. 'In the early years the whole of the East Side was spiritually parcelled out by the Grenfell family ... each of the [four] daughters being allotted a separate district as Bible readers and district visitors'.

The most self-sacrificing of the daughters was Elizabeth Mary (1836-94), usually referred to as Mary, who was no ordinary Anglican because she had a distinctly evangelical approach to the way she took her faith into the community. Mary never married. She had trained as a nurse, spoke several languages and was 'proficient on the organ, piano and harp'. It was, however, for her work in the community that Mary is remembered most. In Victorian times the East Side was a pretty tough area – full of copperworkers, railwaymen, dockers and navvies. Drunkenness prevailed; it was no place for a lady. Yet Mary was a regular 'visitor to the sick. For her no sickness or disease had any terror; she would wait for hours by a bedside, ministering comfort and consolation; moreover, she was frequently to be seen in a funeral procession of some humble working man or woman'.

St. Thomas had no church until Mary bought a house in Pinkney Street. Due to her efforts the house, and later a school, were superseded by a corrugated iron church in 1876. Ten years later her brother, Francis, laid the foundation stone of the present edifice – but Mary's intentions were not solely to erect a church for people to attend. She believed in taking her faith to the people, for not only did she build mission houses, she also formed several Bible classes for various groups of workmen, their wives and friends, among them the railwaymen and the police.

A strong supporter of the temperance movement, Mary established the *Golden Griffin coffee tavern* at her own expense. A few years later 'she erected a reading-room and library for railwaymen' right next door to her coffee tavern. Her wholehearted involvement in schooling is beyond the scope of this work. Suffice to say that the respect people had for Mary was such that, when she died in London in 1894, the result of undergoing 'a surgical operation of the most serious kind', and her body was brought home to Swansea by train, thousands waited at High Street Station to accompany the hearse to St. Thomas. For a week 'most of the shops in St. Thomas had shutters up, whilst a very large proportion of the dwelling houses had the blinds drawn ... There were signs of mourning on every hand ... Flags were hung half-mast ... and all day long the church bells' tolled. Mary Grenfell was a truly remarkable and self-sacrificing woman.

The Vivians (1) Expansion

The son of a Cornish vicar, John Vivian (1750-1826) had long been involved in copper mining when, in c.1800, he became managing-partner of the Penclawdd Copperworks. Eight years or so later he left Penclawdd to establish his own copperworks. The company that he set up became known as Vivian & Sons, and the site chosen for his works lay between the Swansea Canal and the River Tawe.

After building the Hafod Copperworks with its 24 furnaces in 1808-9, John supervised operations until, in 1812, he handed over the reins to his second son, John Henry. Having studied mineralogy and mining in Germany, John Henry had plans: once he had accumulated sufficient capital he would expand. Four years later he had money enough to marry and buy a house in Sketty. When exactly he began enlarging the Hafod Works is unclear, but by 1819 he had built steam-powered rolling-mills close to the river (near where the later riverside ruins stand today). Not content with that, he expanded further afield in 1822 by taking over the rolling-mills at both Upper and Lower Forest. That same year he began building a series of new smelting halls, with the result that by 1826 the riverside slag tip had grown to the extent that a steam-powered winding-engine had to be installed to haul waste waggons up to its summit.

John Henry Vivian – (1785-1855) born in Cornwall, the second son of John Vivian, he was appointed manager of the Penclawdd Copperworks in 1806; in c.1812 he took on the responsibilities of managing-partner of the Hafod Copperworks, while his elder brother pursued a career in the army. After settling at Sketty he became the founder of the Swansea branch of the family and the creator of a 250-acre estate around Singleton Abbey. He proved to be an enlightened employer, and was much involved in the development of Swansea Harbour. He served as a JP, was appointed Deputy Lieutenant of Glamorgan in 1820 and Sheriff of the county in 1827. Between 1832 and his death in 1855 he was borough MP for Swansea, Loughor, Neath, Aberavon and Kenfig.

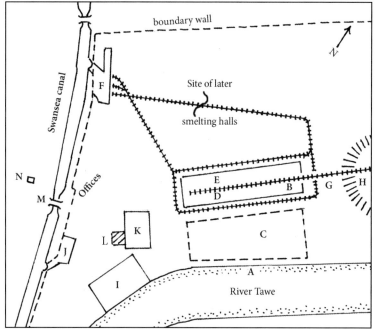

Hafod Copperworks – the earliest phase involved building (A) wharves and (B) a smelting hall running parallel to the wharves. Between these two constructions were yards (C) for stockpiling copper-ore. This simple layout ensured the greatest economy of working because ore-bearing ships could offload at the wharves. The ore was then stockpiled in the yards, from where it was wheel-barrowed into the smelting hall (B). Inside the hall – or Long House as it was known – were two rows of furnaces. The row nearest to the yards (D) comprised of nine calcining furnaces, their purpose to separate 'matte' from the huge quantities of waste material known as slag. The copper-rich 'matte' would then be transferred to the opposite side of the Long House, where 15 reverbatory furnaces (E) would subject it to lengthy and repetitive roastings. All coal arrived at the Hafod Works by barge; hence the canal dock (F). From barges the coal was then loaded into trams. A tramroad ran down either side of the Long House; thus coal could be offloaded from the trams to feed the furnaces day and night. The coal entered the Long House through giant ventilation arches in the side walls. Inside the Long House another tramway (G) ran down between the furnaces, its purpose to convey unwanted slag to the riverside slag-tip (H). Most of the later smelting halls (built to accommodate the ever-increasing number of furnaces) were sited to the north-west of the original Long House; each new smelting hall required its own network of tramroads to bring coal from the canal dock (F). In 1819 steam-powered rolling-mills (I) were built near the river. The 1819 rolling-mills had their own canal dock (J) for the delivery of coal, as well as its attendant steam-powered engine house. The later (1842) steam-powered rolling-mills (K) also had their attendant engine house (L), which partially survives, and can be seen clearly from the opposite side of the river. The canal bridge (M) served as the main entrance into the works. The canal bridge no longer exists, but the limekiln (N) still stands beside the recently-built road used by Park & Ride buses.

The works continued to grow to the extent that by 1833 he had increased the number of furnaces at his disposal to 65. It was due to the whitish smoke belching from these furnaces that local farmers got together and took the Vivians to court, intending to sue them for damages. The testimonies of the farmers were recorded in *The Cambrian* on 16 March 1833. One farmer testified that:

When I first knew that side of Llansamlet, the land was very good for corn, hay and pasture ... Cattle and horses grazed on it. It is barren now, and what grass is there, no cattle will eat it. The land is now ten times worse than ... 15 years ago (in 1818). The Hafod Works had been since doubled. Heard no complaint until Mr. Vivian's works were erected. The smoke has an effect through the bones – breaks the ribs of the cattle, and produces large knobs of their legs – some lying down could not stand. Many of the farms in Llansamlet are now untenanted because there is no grass ... There are now no trees there. They all died. Remembers oak, ash and sycamore there. They died in less than 20 years. They died standing and were cut down afterwards. The land is now barren from the Hafod up to the Wich-tree bridge, a distance of three miles. As you travel along the road, you get the smoke into your mouth and nostrils. The smoke is very unpleasant to the smell and taste. It has the effect of making people's breath short.

The Lower Swansea Valley in the 1860s – in Le Tour de Monde, *published in 1865, a French artist captures the smoke and filth of this man-made hell. With smoke that dense it is hardly surprising that Kilvey Hill became blighted. On the left, several sailing ships are unloading copper-ore at the Hafod Copperworks. Leftwards of the tall chimney, sulphuric acid chambers crown the top of a slag tip. On the right are the chimneys of the Middle and Upper Bank works. Near the bottom right-hand corner a river barge is moored. Barges such as this brought copper-ore from ships that were too big to sail far beyond the river mouth.* (Swansea Museum)

145

The Hafod Works – a drawing dated 1840-60. In the bottom left is a wall that now flanks a driveway on the east side of a social club car park. To the right is the Swansea Canal (its remains now hidden by trees), and further to the right is the low arch that permitted barges to enter the rolling-mills dock. The canal bridge, which once served as the main entrance into the works, is now gone, as are the offices that stood on the far side. Beyond the bridge (and to the left) is the incline tramway that once carried waste over both the main railway line and Neath Road to the enormous slag tip that stood on the site of today's Pentrehafod School (a surviving masonry pier that supported this incline still stands in the woods north of the car park). In the distance (right of centre) are the chimneys of both the Hafod and Morfa copperworks. Hardly anything in this drawing survives, but at the bottom end of the car park mentioned above are substantial remains of a limekiln; it stood just beyond the left-hand edge of this drawing.

Hafod Limekiln – built in the mid-19th century, this was one of 54 limekilns that are known to have stood near the Swansea Canal. The limestone came from Oystermouth, conveyed by the Mumbles Railway as far as the Strand, and from there by canal barge to the kiln. The Swansea canal also brought anthracite coal from the Upper Swansea Valley for use in the kiln. The lime was used for building rather than agri-cultural purposes.

Hafod Works bridge – a drawing of the 1920s. Note the canal barge carrying coal. In c.1900 the offices that, for almost a century, had stood to the right of this bridge, were relocated to a new building outside the works, one that in recent times has been converted for use as a social club.

Other testimonies were just as damning, but the defence stressed 'the commercial importance of the copper works' to Swansea. It was also pointed out 'that no proof had been adduced that the disease of the cattle ... had been caused by the copper-smoke. Such effects were as likely to have followed from bad land and worse culture'. In the final analysis there was too much at stake; the farmers were expendable and they lost their case. No one troubled to take the Vivians to court after that. And by 1844 John Henry had increased the number of furnaces at his disposal to 95, a figure that included rolling-mill furnaces to reheat copper sheets.

In 1838-9 John Henry took over the smelter at Tia-bach (which became known thereafter as the Margam Copperworks) and, in doing so, acquired a colliery that was connected with the works. His son, Henry Hussey, took mining a step further in 1847–9 by sinking the Morfa Pit in the same area. Morfa became the most productive colliery in Wales, and remained so until 1890, when an explosion – which claimed 87 lives – caused so much damage that the colliery never fully recovered its former output.

In 1841 John Henry acquired the disused Birmingham (Ynys) Copperworks and converted it to a zinc smelter. The following year he built steam-powered rolling-mills at the Hafod (close to the earlier mill of 1819) that enabled him to dispose of his rolling-mills at Upper Forest.

If 1842 was a busy year, it was also a bad one in that John Henry's elder brother, Richard, died. Although a partner, Richard had not taken an active part in the running of the business, preferring to pursue a career as a soldier and a politician. His death caused a crisis in that Richard's heirs wished to withdraw their father's interests in Vivian & Sons. That was not a good time for John Henry to pay out £70,000: the copper industry was in recession; the company was committed to new developments, including two large coalmines. Yet despite these difficulties John Henry managed to borrow £40,000 and pay off the loan in ten years. Then, in 1845, he handed over the running of Vivian & Sons to his eldest son, Henry Hussey, by which time the Hafod Works had become by far the largest copperworks in the L.S.V. – but by then a new competitor was challenging the Vivians' supremacy.

The Morfa Copperworks

In 1823 the Rose Copperworks had been taken over by the Cornish partnership Grenfell, Williams and Fox. Five years later the company built copper rolling-mills at Morfa (to the south of Morfa Stadium), the copper coming from the Rose Copperworks. The following year the company changed its name to Williams, Foster and Co. Then, in 1834-5, the new company established the Morfa Copperworks on land immediately to the north of the Hafod works, thereby preventing the Vivians from expanding in a northerly direction. The company also took over the Crown Copperworks, Neath, in c.1839, which they held until 1866. In 1840 they established a silver works, a chimney base of which survives to the south of the copper rolling-mills.

The Williamses were the dominant partners, but neither they nor their associates established local dynasties, even though the Morfa works expanded to the extent that it equalled and, at times, surpassed its southern rival. Several buildings that stood within the huge Morfa complex have survived, most of them in a ruinous condition. There is, for example, the huge rolling-mills, part of which may date from 1828. There are also the riverside wharves, the mid-19th century laboratory, the canteen (formerly a power house) with a clock turret on the roof, and a lifting bridge over the Tawe, dated 1910, which enabled a railway to take copper slag to waste tips on the east side of the river.

Laboratory ruins, Morfa – built in the mid-19th century, this was an 'assay office' where copper-ore was tested for its quality. An ornate building, it stood beside the main entrance into the works, entry into which entailed crossing a bridge over the Swansea Canal. This building and the two opposite can be seen from the Landore Park & Ride complex.

Morfa Rolling-mills – the largest copper rolling-mills in the world. The original building (erected in 1828) succumbed to fire in 1840. The succeeding mills may have incorporated much of the original walling. That the building still stands is due to the fact that it continued in use until 1980.
It is now used for storage by the Swansea Museum.

The Morfa Works canteen – once a power house. This mid to late 19th century building has the remains of a clock tower on its roof.

Tributaries, water power and the importance of Landore

Before moving on to consider the L.S.V. in the early part of the Victorian era, it would be as well to focus briefly on the importance of two tributaries, water power and why Landore became the most concentrated area of industrial activity in the valley. The two most important tributaries in the lower valley were both on the west bank. The lower of these tributaries was the Burlais Brook, which for centuries had served as the boundary of the Borough of Swansea. The brook has provided both water and water power for several installations – corn mills, the Cambrian Copperworks, the Cambrian Pottery and the Cwmfelin Tinplate Works to name but a few. The Cwm Burlais ravine was itself equally important in that it provided an easy gradient for a coal road to the Strand. Subsequently the ravine served as a through-route for the tramroads of both the Morrises and Messrs. Richard and Glasbrook.

A mile and half upriver the Nant Rhyd-y-Filais and its ravine served a similar purpose. Rising in the Penlan area, the Rhyd-y-Filais descended to a sharp bend in Cwm Level Road, then continued on its way through a V-shaped ravine before discharging near an equally sharp bend into the Tawe. In recent times the ravine was partially filled in, using slag from the Hafod tip. The infill was then levelled and grassed over to create the playing fields that are visible from Cwm Level Road.

There were numerous coal levels and pits in the Treboeth-Brynhyfryd area, and water from the Nant Rhyd-y-Filais and its tributaries was channelled into several leets so that waterwheels could power winding and pumping operations at deep pits. One of the longest leets serviced the Llangyfelach Copperworks (1717); it ran above the northern slope of the ravine, from near the sharp bend in Cwm Level Road to a point near St. Paul's Church, Landore, which is where the ravine opened out, not far from the Tawe. Leets and waterwheels continued in use at collieries and a variety of metallurgical works long after the first steam engine had been installed at a colliery in the Manselton area in c.1730. Leets from the Rhyd-y-Filais were still powering waterwheels in the Landore area in late Victorian times.

The sloping ground above and on either side of the Rhyd-y-Filais ravine provided an easy gradient for coal roads and waggonways, most of which terminated at shipping places at Landore, and later at loading places alongside the Swansea Canal. Coal roads and waggonways also took coal directly to the many and varied metal works that were sited on the low ground adjoining the Tawe.

Landore, then, was a focal point for coal supplies to shipping quays and industry. Add to that the Morfa flatland, which provided an idea site for a variety works, and it is easy to see why Landore became the most concentrated and diversified industrialized area in the L.S.V.

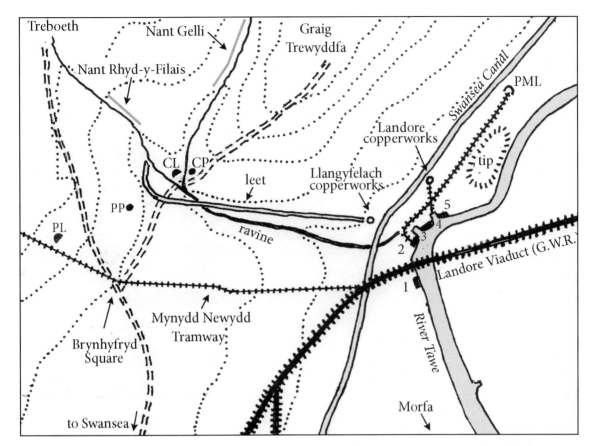

Landore – water from the Nant Rhyd-y-Filais and its many tributaries was siphoned off into numerous leets for powering winding and pumping operations at several collieries in the Brynhyfryd area, and also for powering numerous works at Landore; only the Llangyfelach Copperworks leet is shown here. No doubt the Rhyd-y-Filais valley provided a through-route for coal roads that have gone unrecorded. The sloping ground above the Rhyd-y-Filais ravine was certainly a through-route to convey coal by waggonway from collieries in the Brynhyfryd area (and occasionally from collieries further afield) to shipping places at Landore. Several of the riverside wharves and the two tidal docks were originally Lockwood, Morris constructions. In early Victorian times several tramroads terminated at shipping places on the Swansea Canal, the Mynydd Newydd (incline) tramroad being one of them.

Key

PL	Penyfilia Level	1	Llangyfelach Copperworks Wharf
PP	Pentre Pit	2	New Quay
CL	Cwm Level	3	Landore Colliery Dock
CP	Cwm Pit	4	Landore Copperworks Dock
PML	Plas-y-marl Level	5	Copper-ore Wharf for the Landore Copperworks

The Coal and Copper Industries in 1837

In 1837 – the year of Victoria's coronation – there were eight copper smelting works in operation.

Three were situated on the East Side:
> White Rock, established 1737, owned by J. Freeman & Co.
> Middle Bank, established 1755, owned by Pascoe Grenfell & Sons
> Upper Bank, established *c.*1757, taken over by Muntz Patent Metal Co. Ltd. *c.*1837

The other five were on the west bank
> Forest, established *c.*1746-48, owned by Benson, Logan & Co.
> Landore, established *c.*1793, owned by Henry Bath & R.J. Nevill
> Rose, established *c.*1780, owned by Williams, Foster & Co.
> Morfa, established 1834–5, owned by Williams, Foster & Co.
> Hafod, established 1808–9, owned by Vivian & Sons, who also held leases on the
> copper rolling-mills at Upper and Lower Forest.

Between them these eight copperworks, plus others situated between Llanelly and Tia-bach, produced more than half the world's copper requirements. By *c.*1850 the L.S.V. smelters alone were importing over 247,000 tons of copper-ore per annum (165,000 tons from Devon and Cornwall) and using 450,000 tons of coal per annum to produce some 22,000 tons of refined copper. A second glance at these figures will show that, due to developments in the smelting process, it now required less than two tons of coal to smelt one ton of copper-ore.

At roughly the same time (1853) Swansea was exporting over 500,000 tons of coal per annum. This incredible amount of coal (coupled with that used in smelting) all had to be mined by hand in dark, damp and dangerous conditions. The tools used at the sharp end of all this activity were the mandrill (a kind of pick) and the shovel. The Davy safety lamp (first used at Margam in 1816) was available for use, but because miners preferred the better light provided by candles, the lamp was used mainly to test for gas before work began. However, as fire-damp explosions became more frequent, so the Davy lamp became begrudgingly accepted. Wheelbarrows (run over planks) were still used, as evidenced in 1842 at an unidentified colliery in Llansamlet, but horse-drawn trams and tramroads were by far the most efficient way to move coal from the pithead (or from near the coal face in the case of levels) to canals, riverside quays and smelting works.

Light underground was provided by (a) a candle in an iron candle-holder, the spike of which could be pushed into a passage wall. Alternatively, colliers wore skull-caps having a leather band, into which the candle-holder (b) was thrust when the hands are employed in locomotion.
The Davy safety lamp (c) was initially used to detect firedamp, the presence of which was indicated by a change in the appearance of the flame.

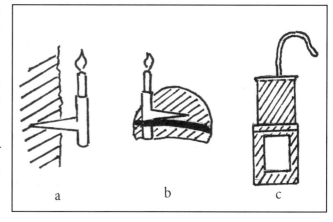

a · b · c

Child labour in coal mining

The stark reality of working underground is brought into focus by a government enquiry of 1841. Two sub-commissioners were appointed to conduct the enquiry in South Wales – Rhys William Jones and Robert Hugh Franks. Their findings (along with those of other sub-commissioners throughout the realm) were recorded in the *Report of the Royal Commission of Enquiry into the State of Children in Employment*, published in 1842. In the L.S.V. the sub-commissioners carried out detailed enquiries at Weeg Pit, Llangyfelach, owned by the Landore Colliery Co., an unidentified pit owned by the Llansamlet Colliery Co., and a general enquiry into the numbers employed by the Swansea Coal Co.

Female surface workers, Treorchy c.1880 – this may have been the dress of working girls in the L.S.V., but it was said in 1850 that the girls at Aberdare 'used to dress in fustian trousers with short skirts down to the knee, and these were made of a rough canvass material, with jackets something like a short coat put over the shoulders ... On their heads they wore flat straw bonnets or hats which were very like those worn by cockle women'.

Sub-commissioner Rhys Jones was pleased to find that no women were employed underground in any of the collieries mentioned above because it was not customary 'to subject females to such degrading labours as those imposed upon them in the mines of the more eastern districts'. There were, however, 23 women and three girls under the age of 13 employed as surface workers, most of them by the Swansea Coal Co. These females were not local girls, but migrant workers. Their job was to remove stones from coal that had arrived at the pithead. They worked 12-hour shifts, for which they were paid between 4d. and 1s. a day.

The Landore Colliery Co. and the Swansea Coal Co. had a total workforce of 805, of which 207 (almost 25%) were either women or young people under the age of 18 – and 76 of these were under the age of 13. Precisely how young the under 13s were is not stated, but 6 was the earliest age at which children were employed by the Llansamlet Colliery Co., in which case it would not have been unusual 'for fathers to carry their [young] children to the mines on their backs'.

The youngest males were air-door boys who sat in the dark for 12 hours at a time, 'opening and closing the ventilation doors' to allow horse-drawn trams to pass through. Their lot was a solitary one – except for the rats – listening for the sound of approaching trams. They were wet, they were cold and they breathed in the foul air of the mine. Officially they earned about 6d. a day, but their wages were paid to the father, or to whoever was responsible for them.

In the course of their enquiries, the sub-commissioners recorded the testimonies of children who worked underground. At Weeg Pit, William David, aged 12, declared:

> I have been working six months, keeping a door in the Six Feet Vein. The door ... is two miles from ... where the works are entered. I sometimes walk in and sometimes ride in the waggon. I go down at six o'clock and return in fully 12 hours. I work at night every other week. I have a light (as) there is not much fire damp (methane gas) where I am. I get 6d per day. I have not met with much hurt ... but one of the horses trod on my foot two months ago and I was home a week lame, but it did not hurt me much. There are four boys keeping doors in each turn (shift) in the same works where I am. I can't read, but I go to the Sunday Schools.

Air-door boy – in 1850 a visitor to a colliery in the Merthyr area noted: 'Drawn boldly on the smooth shale, in chalk, I saw the outline of a prancing horse. The accuracy, fidelity and spirit of the drawing were such that I stopped to examine it. I may state that the boys in the pits have in general a taste for drawing. The poor boy who has attended all day one of the doors, takes in his pocket – for the purpose of whiling away the tedium, a farthing's worth of happiness in the form of a piece of chalk. Swansea Valley air-door boys may also have occupied themselves in the same way, thereby alleviating the boredom of their 12-hour shifts in cold, dark and damp surroundings'.

In a slightly higher age bracket were the scooters and trammers, whose job it was to get coal from the coal face to the horse-ways. One of the seams at Weeg Pit was only 2 feet 10 inches thick. Consequently, in this vein only children could get coal through the narrow, low-roofed passageways that led from the coal face. That meant hauling as much as a quarter of a ton of coal in sledge-like carts called corves up to 80 metres from the coal face. A team of two boys would be attached to each corve. The youngest boy in each team – the scooter – dragged the corve by way of a harness and a chain; the older boy – the trammer – pushed from behind. It was agreed by all that the scooters and trammers worked harder than everyone else. There were 28 scooters and trammers at Weeg Pit. A 16-year-old trammer, David Evans, testified:

> I push the trams ... and have a little boy about seven or eight years old helping me [as a scooter] ... I was burned about a year ago and was home ill for three months. I was burned by the fire-damp ... but only my hands and face ... We work ... from six to six [six days a week] and at night

every other week ... I get 1s. 6d. per day and the little boy who is with me gets 7d. I pay him out, but the masters pay us both. The little boy's name is David. I don't know the other name, but his mother is called 'Mary Levi' and his father is dead. I have never been to school.

In some collieries, boys often worked alone, dragging smaller corves. This is borne out by an inquest, held in August 1855:

> at the Collier' Arms, Cwmbwrla ... on the body of Isaac Knight, a lad 12 years of age ... employed at the Gorse Colliery ... dragging small carts, containing about 1 cwt. of coal each, from the heading to the main level ... a distance of about 20 yards ... while the deceased was engaged in his usual occupation, a large stone, weighing about two tons and a half, fell from the roof ... upon him. He was extricated as soon as possible, but was found to be quite dead.

A scooter and trammer at work – the boy in front (the scooter) has a leather girdle about his waistline; attached to this is a chain, which, passing between his legs, is connected to a sledge known as a corve, which contained up to 5cwt. of coal. The boy at the rear (the trammer) was the older of the two. It fell to these boys to get coal from the face to a horse-way, where they loaded it into horse-drawn trams.

At Llansamlet a 16-year-old wheeler, David Davies, testified that he had

> been eight years at work; [I work] ... in the three-foot vein and wheels coal in a barrow from the workings to the main road, a distance of 80 yards. Each barrow contains about two hundred-weight of coal. We have to wheel down hill and throw the coal over into a tram ... I work 12 hours daily and it is the practice of the men to change every six months [to] the night shifts [not every second week as at Weeg Pit]. I have never been much hurt [and] never been off work more than two days from any hurt received. I have three brothers working below; one is seven ... and is an air-door keeper. None of us have been to day-school, but all of us are learning to read at the Sunday-school; we learn in Welsh. [Robert Franks added:] Reads Welsh very well; cannot write. I examined the brother, Isaiah Davies, who seems to have a great dislike of the darkness ... indeed it seemed to have made the child stupid.

The 14- to 17-year-old hauliers had it relatively easy. It was the haulier's task:

> to look after his horse, feed him in the day and [if he worked in a level] take [the horse] home at night: his occupation requires great agility in the narrow and low-roofed roads; sometimes he is required to stop his tram suddenly – in an instant he is [off the tram and] between the rail and the side of the level, and in almost total darkness slips a sprig between the spokes of his tram-wheel, and is back in his place with amazing dexterity; though it must be confessed ... he frequently gets crushed.
>
> As a class these youths have an appearance of greater health than the rest [probably from being more in the fresh air than the others] ... and on horseback, going to or returning from work, galloping and scrambling over the fields or roads, [they] bear the aspect of the most healthy and thoughtless of the collier-boys. [They earned 4s. (20 modern pence) a week.]

Pit cages, c.1840 – entry into a pit could entail descent by ladders, being lowered in a basket, or descending in a cage, powered by either a steam-engine or water balance. Early cages could be dangerous. In 1853, for example, an inquest was held at the Gwindy Inn, Bon-y-maen ... on the body of Henry Williams, aged eight years. Morgan Williams of Pentre, Llansamlet ... deposed: 'I am a trammer in the New Pit Colliery. The deceased was an assistant wheeler with his brother of the coal from the heading to the main way. On the 25th instant, about six o'clock in the morning, I was near the bottom of the pit when I heard something heavy fall down. I ran to the bottom of the pit and saw the body of the deceased on the ground. I raised him up, but he was insensible, and held him in my arms, and he died in about half an hour ... another collier, stated that himself, the deceased, and five other men and boys, were lowered [by cage] down the pit that morning ... They stopped at the upper vein. Some of them got out into the level of that vein; but the deceased got out the other side of the carriage by mistake and fell down about 14 fathoms [84 feet] to the bottom of the pit'. Verdict, 'Accidental death'.

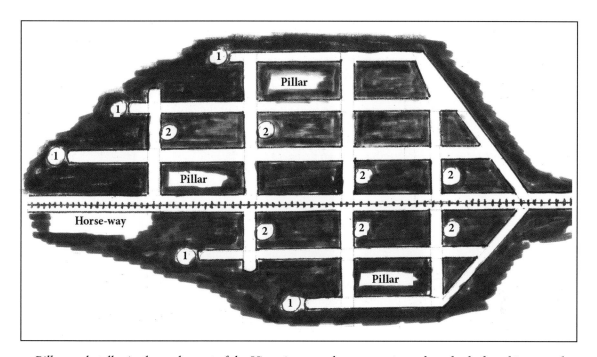

Pillar and stall – in the early part of the Victorian era, the most universal method of working a coal seam was known as 'pillar and stall', although this was not the only term used. In this idealized plan of an early phase of working a coal seam several stalls (1) run parallel to a horse-way, or waggonway; a stall would have been worked by two men. Cross-cuts (2) linked the stalls to the horse-way. The stalls and cross-cuts were sometimes referred to as 'streets'. Between the streets are the rectangular pillars of coal that were left to hold up the roof. When the men in the stalls reached a point where they could go no further, they turned back, reducing the size of the pillars, one by one, until it was no longer safe to do so. What coal remained in the reduced pillars was ultimately lost. Whether by level or via a pit, working a coal seam by this method could result in hundreds of pillars and numerous streets. It is amazing that men could find their way around these streets with only a candle or a lamp to light their way. Partitions and air doors were positioned at various points in the streets to direct fresh air to wherever men were working the coal face, rather than allow the air to dissipate into areas that had been abandoned, or were temporarily unworked. The air doors had to be kept closed at all times, except when a tram had to pass through without loosing momentum; hence the requirement for air-door boys.

At Llansamlet a 16-year-old driver (haulier), William Rosser, said:

> I have been below for seven years. I was two years at the air door before driving. I have occasionally got hurt, but never off more than two or three days. The length of road I drive is about 400 yards. I make 20 to 25 journeys a day ... we work pretty constantly. My wages last month were 28s. 7d. [about 35p a week] ... I think I went to school once, but I am just beginning to learn Welsh at Sunday-school. [Robert Franks added:] Just knows the Welsh letters. A very fair religious knowledge.

Once the coal face had advanced a considerable distance from the entrance to a level (or entry shaft in the case of a pit) one or more air-shafts would be sunk to improve ventilation. To increase the flow of air, fires were lit at the bottom of the air-shafts, the flames drawing air. At Weeg Pit, John Mordecai, aged 10, said:

> I go down with David Jenkins to mind a fire in an old part of the works, under the pit [air-shaft] at Cradley ... We have nothing to do but mind the fire. There are no men working within two miles of us. We have to walk about two miles ... under ground to reach the Cradley air pit. I go more for company for the old man than to work ... I get 6d. per day ... I have been to school a long time ... I can read a little.

Tram plates had to be laid to enable horse-drawn trams to operate underground. At Weeg Pit, John Phillips, aged 10, said:

> I lay down plates or rails on the roads. My work is called 'planking'. I was ... tramming before I went to my present work ... I broke my leg about five months ago and was at home three months. I was coming down with my tram to the horse road, and there was a waggon and horse coming along at the time. I slipped [and] the waggon went over my leg and broke it above the knee. It is well now, but I have not been tramming since. I don't know what wages I get, but I think 8d. per day. My mother has the wages. I was in school for four years, but I never learnt to read.

Rhys Jones was keen to find out why young children were working in mines. He discovered that they were not there on account of the employers. They were underground because the parents requested that it should be so. Rhys knew that parents were not indifferent to their children's welfare. Indeed, he had been told by a Swansea surgeon that 'Welsh people are kind and fondly attached to their children in a marked degree'. What motivated parents to send their sons down the mine was, of course, poverty.

Colliers' wages varied between districts. In West Glamorgan and Carmarthenshire their wages, according to Rhys Jones, were 'always rather inferior to those of the colliers ... in the Merthyr and Monmouthshire districts'. Rhys gave no figures for the L.S.V., but he did cite examples of what colliers in Carmarthenshire earned. Hugh Edwards, a collier (or colliery labourer) employed possibly in the Llanelly area, had a wife and six children. He earned 10s. a week and his sons brought home an additional 8s. a week. The family outgoings per week were:

	£	s.	d.
26lbs. of flour at 2 ½ d.	0	4	10 ½
19lbs. of barley flour at 1 ½ d.	0	2	4 ½
5lbs. of cheese at 5 d.	0	2	1
2lbs. of butter at 1s.	0	2	0
1 ½ lbs. of sugar at 8d.	0	1	0
1oz. of tea	0	0	6
2lbs. of salt	0	0	1
¾ lb. of soap	0	0	4 ½
starch and blue	0	0	1
tobacco	0	0	3 ½
rent including garden	0	1	9
Total per week	0	15	5

Hugh got 'coal from the works in addition to his wages', but without his sons earnings the family would have been in financial difficulty. So it is hardly surprising that a man in Hugh's position would send his sons down the mine. Any money that was due to the sons would have been paid to Hugh until such time as the sons married, or reached the age of 17.

Widows were even more dependent of the earnings of their offspring. One widow with seven children had a 10-year-old son, Thomas, working as a scooter at Weeg Pit, for which he was paid 4s. Two other sons also worked at Weeg, and the combined earnings of the three boys may have provided the widow with 12s. a week. Had the boys not worked, then the family would have entered the workhouse.

Officially everyone worked 12-hours shifts, but what was important was how much coal could be raised in the course of a shift. However, according to 'almost all the proprietors and agents [managers] and some of the foremen ... the regular hours of work were from eight to ten hours daily. The Children and Young [Persons], on the other hand, almost universally declare that they never work less than 12'. The children's statements were 'in general confirmed by' their elders, and in the opinion of Rhys Jones both men and boys 'very frequently work two or three hours overtime, which they are induced to do from some accidental circumstances interfering ... with the despatch of their labours' – meaning the amount of coal raised. Twelve-hour shifts persisted until 1872, when an Act of Parliament restricted boys under 16 to a 54-hour week.

Considering what was expected of them, it is hardly surprising that children, when interviewed, made references to their work being 'very hard or very fatiguing' and one lad declared, 'I am so very tired at times that I hardly care about eating'. Equally unsurprising are the many references to children falling asleep, despite the cold, constant drip of water and the rats. One boy stated that, 'When we rest a little we fall asleep', and another declared, 'When I fall asleep they shake me up'.

Several sub-commissioners in England commented on the 'extraordinary development of the muscular system' in children employed in coal mining; one went so far as to consider this development as 'a degree of deformity', saying 'That the muscles of the back and loins stood from the body and appeared almost like a rope passing under the skin'. The same man was also 'struck with the thin and gaunt appearance of the adults'. Other sub-commissioners commented on the 'stunted growth' of colliers in general. The one disfigurement that has been recoded locally was that some colliers were bow-legged due, it was said, to being 'continuously in crouching positions along low seams', although in some cases rickets due to a vitamin D deficiency cannot be ruled out.

As a result of the commissioners' findings, an Act was passed in 1842 prohibiting women and boys under ten from working underground. In some collieries the Act was not strictly adhered to because there were no inspectors to enforce it, but by the mid-1850s evasion is likely to have been rare. By the 1860s the attitude of a later generation towards child labour had changed.

A Collier's Lot

According to the report of 1842, colliers started their day with 'breakfast before they entered the works, and they take with them a small bag of bread and cheese [their almost invariable fare], which they eat at irregular intervals' and washed down with 'tea, sometimes cold and sometimes [warmed]. On their return from work they get their suppers, or perhaps what may be as correctly called their dinners [which consisted] of bacon and vegetables usually, for colliers rarely eat much fresh meat during the week. On the return from work it is usual for the workmen and children to be washed; in fact, in lodging-houses it is part of the bargain that the lodger shall be washed every night previous to retiring ... a point which ... is strenuously insisted on by the housekeeper'.

Night-shifts were common, the 12-hour shifts changing every six months at Llansamlet, and every Sunday evening at Weeg Pit on the west bank. One wonders – with so much time taken up by hard work – how colliers managed to find time to sleep, let alone drink or manage an allotment. Perhaps they catnapped below ground; they certainly had a reputation for missing shifts, the more so after pay day.

Colliers in the Swansea Valley were hired by the month, paid monthly, and may even have claimed a fortnightly draw. Their rates of pay would have varied between collieries – as they did between districts – but they may have been similar to those recorded at Llangennech in 1841 – between 14s. and 16s. a week, possibly more. Pay rates certainly fluctuated according to trade cycles, being cut during a depression such as the one that lasted from 1839 to 1843, which would have applied to the earnings of Hugh Edwards (mentioned above). Higher rates were paid in more prosperous times, as in 1848 when colliers in the Swansea area were earning up to £1 a week, and overmen as much as 10s. extra per month.

Carmarthenshire colliers were said to have got 'their coal from the works'; some grew their own potatoes and/or kept a pig worth between £4 and £4 10s., which they killed in November. Whether potatoes could be grown in the blighted parts of the L.S.V. is debatable, but the residents of Hafod certainly had pigsties at the bottom of their gardens. Coal was also provided by the L.S.V. coal masters.

A collier's dress would almost certainly have consisted of a dark blue flannel shirt without a collar, and long corduroy trousers to which thongs (yokes) were tied below the knees to prevent particles of coal working their way up to his knees while he knelt. He also wore a muffler (a strip of cloth around the neck) and kept his clay pipe in the buttonhole of his jacket. Otherwise his dress would have consisted of whatever else he could afford, or was handed down to him, including boots and a straw hat.

Colliers had to buy their own candles and gunpowder, which together could amount to 2s. per week. In some collieries the employers provided Davy lamps; in others the colliers bought their own. In any event they bought their own oil as well – a pint a week costing 6d. Colliers also had to provide their own tools – candle holders, shovels, mandrills and replacement helves.

Like other workers, a collier knew that his employer, or his employer's agent, had a range of disciplinary measures they could use against him. They could refuse to renew his monthly contract, they could fine him for all sorts of misdemeanours such as failing to close air-doors, for smoking underground, or for absenting himself from work without permission. They could also take him to court, for if he left his employment without giving a month's notice, or without the necessary 'discharge note', then he risked a heavy fine, or a month's imprisonment, although the sentence might be rescinded if he agreed to return to work.

If, on the other hand, a collier had a grievance against his employer, he had to tread carefully. If he took his employer to court, he was unlikely to get a fair hearing as local magistrates tended to be industrialists and were, therefore, not impartial, although, as time went by, more and more colliers sought redress in the courts for unpaid wages and for failing to issue discharge notes.

Women and children

Robert Franks maintained that, in Llansamlet parish, 'the health of the colliers is greatly to be attributed to the clean habits of the females, and their care in providing warm clothing for their children and husbands, a point on which the women of these parts are remarkably particular'. Robert also stated that 'the age at which they [girls] commence labour ... is not so early as that of boys, their usefulness in the house to assist the mother' being one reason for this. This latter comment was based on what Robert witnessed around Merthyr, where females worked underground. In the L.S.V., young women did not enter the mines, but they were employed in copperworks, tinplate works and the like.

'Intemperance', according to Franks 'seems rarely to be the vice of the women ... and however frequent and early the connection of the sexes may be, the cases of bastardy are comparatively trifling, it being usual ... for a youth to marry a girl when discovered to be pregnant by him. Many instances of improvidence occur, as may be expected from such early marriage – a mere child of 14 years of age becomes a wife, and her first important act is to open an account at the shop for goods, clothing, food, etc. This facility of procuring goods to the credit of her husband's labour induces extravagance'.

Giving evidence in the 1842 report, an Independent minister at Hirwaun thoroughly disapproved of the employment of women in industry on the ground that it was harmful 'to their morals and totally disqualifies them for domestic duties; it corrupts their minds, and makes them callous to religious impressions ... and from the continual contact with men of coarse habits, become as degraded as the most vulgar of the male population'.

With regard to children, Robert stated that, when a boy enters a mine 'the father or the employer [usually a relative] becomes the object of his imitation; he drinks, smokes and swears, the child follows his example, and children of seven years of age and even less will be found to enter in their expenses at the shop, their supply of tobacco; and the evidence will show that swearing, drinking and obscene language are vices too frequent amongst the young'. Robert later added that 'the working man after labour has no resort but the beer shop; his boy accompanies him'. No doubt this behaviour would have been apparent in the L.S.V., but to what extent is debatable as the influence of the chapel was strong.

The truck system

The report of 1842 states that:

> in many parts of Glamorganshire ... wages ... are very rarely paid in money, but a shop in the neighbourhood, not professedly in the hands of the proprietors of the works, advances goods to the workmen ... on account of the proprietors; the books of the shop and the books of the colliery are checked on the pay-day at the same office, and the balance, if any, is handed over to the men. It very often happens, however, that the men unfortunately have nothing to receive for months together. It is said by many that the necessities of life are dearer in these shops by 25 per cent. than in others perhaps five miles off.

There was nothing illegal about company-owned shops, or shops connected with works; nor were they necessarily a source of grievance. In remote areas company shops often provided a service that would otherwise have been non-existent. Sometimes a company established a shop to prevent local shopkeepers from charging high prices. In hard times company shops could often be a godsend, for in times of depression, or when a collier was off work due to sickness or accident, his family could survive on credit. These and other benefits were undeniable, and in some cases it was the workers who requested the establishment of a company shop – but what made these shops unpopular was when the company, instead of paying wages in money, introduced the truck system instead.

Truck, meaning barter, was made illegal in 1817 by an Act of Parliament which stipulated that wages should not be paid 'in goods, or by way of truck, or in any other manner than in money'. Unfortunately, there were no provisions for enforcing this Act; nor was it likely that colliers and other workers would take their employers to court. Consequently, not only was the Act virtually ignored, but by 1830 truck had become widespread.

By 1830 an anti-truck campaign was underway, the usual arguments being expounded. One argument was that payment by way of truck prevented heavy drinkers from squandering hard-earned money on ale, but the reality was that drinkers simply exchanged goods over the bar. The opposition, on the other hand, maintained that truck shops sold inferior goods at extortionate prices, which in turn was an indirect way of reducing wages. Truck also denied workers freedom of choice in how they spent their earnings; worse, it kept workers tied to their employers (hence the American verse, 'I owe my soul to the company store').

The campaign of 1830 led to new anti-truck legislation the following year. The report of 1842 makes it plain that this legislation was ignored in remote areas, but the L.S.V. colliers were not prepared to let their employers carry on regardless. What happened in the valley in June 1831 was reported in *The Cambrian*.

> On Monday last [6th June] a large body of workmen belonging to the Llansamlet Colliery, assembled at the Town Hall, Swansea, for the purpose of representing their grievance to the Magistrates against the Truck System ... Having respectfully stated their complaint, the Magistrates explained the powers vested in them to enforce the payment of the men's wages in money, and recommended its adoption. To this recommendation, the Agent of the Works immediately acquiesced, and the men then returned to their work. Their demeanour in the town was most orderly and peaceable. On the following day the men belonging to the Landore Colliery made a similar application; and their wishes were as readily complied with.

162

The Llansamlet Colliery Co. (owned by C.H. Smith) and the Landore Colliery Co. (owned by John Morris II) were among the largest coal producers in the Swansea Valley. Whether the example of these companies was followed by smaller concerns is not known, but in 1854 it was reported that in places where the truck system survived in a modified form, it was a grievance shared by women who, on calling at company shops on 'turn book day', 'stay perhaps from seven in the morning till six in the evening until they could be served'. Presumably the long delay was caused by the process of checking the shop's books against those of the works.

Strikes and unions

The main grievances of colliers were to do with pay cuts during depressions and with truck, and although miners were capable of unified action on a local level (as combinations), there was no miners' union in South Wales prior to 1831 – but that was destined to change when, in the middle of a depression, the Merthyr ironmaster, William Crawshay, announced his intention to reduce wages. The uprising that followed in early June that year has been summarized in Chapter One under **The Military**, and although order was restored, the colliers were far from beaten.

In March 1830 what became known as the Friendly Society of Coal-mining had been established in the North of England. The movement had spread southwards, its purpose to resist wage reductions. Branches of the society were established in and around Merthyr late in 1831. In October the miners went on strike, and despite harassment by the military, a food shortage and the employers dismissing more than 4,000 men, the strikers held out for five weeks. Then the strike collapsed and by the spring of 1832 the Friendly Society ceased to exist.

There are hints that the society may have taken root in the Swansea Valley where, in October 1831, the colliers are known to have been flexing their muscles, but there is no record of a strike. One reason for this may have been opposition from the Nonconformists. At Merthyr the Nonconformists had disapproved of intimidation by hard-liners to get men to join a combination that required members to take secret oaths. The Nonconformists may also have viewed the society's activities as undermining the chapel's role as a mediator between men and management, as it was not uncommon for educated and bilingual chapel deacons to meet management on behalf of monoglot Welsh workers with a grievance. The Nonconformists were becoming a force to be reckoned with in Wales, and no more so than in Swansea and its environs, which by 1860 was regarded as 'the Mecca of Nonconformity'. The influence of the chapel in the Swansea Valley may explain why, in October 1831, the colliers there did not strike.

There were two further attempts to form a union in South Wales in the early part of Victoria's reign – in 1844 and 1863 – both of which ended in failure following a strike. On a local level colliers continued to form temporary combinations, as in the early 1840s when the agent at Llansamlet Colliery told sub-commissioner Robert Franks, 'We had a strike last year, when the men stood out 13 weeks, and returned to the work with no further advance to themselves'.

Health hazards

Conditions underground were deplorable. The horse-ways were strewn with horse dung; the passageways were likewise strewn with human excrement – the stench must have been overpowering. Unsanitary conditions such as these, however, were as nothing when compared with the dangers that lurked underground.

Death as a result of roof falls or fire-damp (methane gas) explosions in which men were incinerated were ever-present dangers. In the dark, accidents were frequent, causing all sorts of injuries, the more serious ones resulting in amputations, or death. Employers were not indifferent to these tragedies. In the event of a collier being maimed, the employer might offer him light work. If a collier was killed, then the widow might have 'her house and coal found for her' until such time as her children could support her. One Swansea Valley coal producer maintained, in 1857, that in the event of a collier's death 'there is generally great sympathy felt for his family, and the proprietors of works find occupation for the children; they take an interest in them and get them brought up as colliers'.

The Llansamlet Colliery had its own 'medical fund for sickness and accidents to which all the workpeople contribute(d) 13d. per quarter'. This arrangement covered medical attention by the works surgeon, but colliers also made regular payments to friendly societies so that, in the event of death, their funeral expenses were paid; moreover, if they were off work though sickness or accident, then for a few weeks they would have something to cover their loss of earnings. Societies such as these were small, the members often meeting in public houses, but as lodges they were affiliated to much larger institutions such as the Oddfellows, the Foresters, or the indigenous order of The Ivorites, which, founded in 1836, had the dual aim of providing benefit and fostering Welsh culture and language, which it did by supporting the Eisteddfodau that were so popular in Victorian times. Women also enrolled in benefit societies such as The Lady Ivor Society.

There were, however, more insidious afflictions that could result from working underground – blood poisoning due to working in dirty clothes, rheumatism from labouring in cold, damp conditions, constant headaches from inhaling gas, pneumoconiosis and silicosis, both caused by inhaling dust, and blindness, the result of working in poor light. Respiratory diseases and rheumatism were undoubtedly the most common afflictions, but whatever the disability, if a collier could no longer work, he could not feed his family, nor pay his rent. And if he had neither offspring nor relatives to support him, then the workhouse became his new home.

With regard to accidents in other parts (at Aberdare, for example) Robert Franks stated that there was an 'unwillingness to communicate ... amongst those who ... are capable of affording the requisite information'. No records of accidents were kept 'either by the medical gentleman, who is invariably attached to each works or [by the coal masters]. In cases of fatal accidents ... many difficulties lie in the way of obtaining an impartial inquiry, for the jury in many instances [are] selected from the fellow workmen of the deceased ... who are unwilling to hear, even if they think it necessary to call, evidence which may possibly involve either their employer or anyone employed in the same work with themselves. [And no juries] could be found to return verdicts ... by which their employers would be injured' – which is hardly surprising as the colliers were hired by the month. Consequently, 'proprietors and culprits escape' responsibility. With regard to chronic diseases connected with mining, surgeons (doctors) attached to works were inclined to play down the ill effects of mining; some even maintained that employment underground was far from unhealthy. It is likely that these generalizations applied to the L.S.V. as well.

Early safety regulations

Reports on the shocking death toll in coalfields resulted in Parliament introducing the Coal Mines Act of 1850, which required coal producers to keep accurate plans of their collieries, and to notify the Home Secretary of all fatal accidents. Unfortunately, only four inspectors were appointed throughout the realm, South Wales being part of a south-western district. The inspectors had the right to enter any colliery and, after inspection, notify owners or their agents of anything that was 'dangerous and defective'. In the opinion of the inspector for the south-western district, some accidents were due to the ignorance of recently recruited newcomers to mining, but most were attributed 'to the neglect or recklessness of the proprietors or managers'. Armed with only advisory powers, the inspector worked tirelessly to enlighten both men and management as to what was required of them.

In *The South Wales Coal Industry 1841 – 1875* by Morris and Williams, the causes of death between 1851 and 1855 in the South Wales Coalfield are enumerated as:

300 by falls of roof and sides
173 by explosion
143 by accident in shafts
98 by miscellaneous causes, and
24 as a result of surface accidents.

The total for the 4 year period was 738

The situation improved following the introduction of the Mines Act of 1855, which required compliance to seven general rules to do with ventilation, the lining of unsafe shaft walls and the cages that took men hundreds of metres below ground. Failure to observe these rules rendered the men liable to a fine or imprisonment, and the owners to fines and a penalty of £1 for every day a defect remained un-rectified. Better still, South Wales had its own inspector. The Mines Regulation Act of 1860 increased the number of rules and raised the fines. These, and later Acts, did not make mining safe, nor the environment less hazardous to health, for no legislation could do that, but they were small steps in the right direction in that they curbed the reckless practices that had gone on for centuries.

How effective the regulations were can be gauged by what happened in 1860 at Copper Pit in the L.S.V. This pit was sited in the midst of the Forest Copperworks complex and was an old Lockwood, Morris & Co. pit, worked by Messrs Richard & Glasbrook from c.1854 onwards. *The Cambrian* reported on a 'colliery explosion' at Copper Pit, 'which took the life of a little boy named Joseph Howells, aged 13 years, and seriously injuring a man named William David'. Much of the evidence was provided by Thomas Lewis, 'overman and fireman' of the said pit. Like all firemen it was Thomas's responsibility to carry out inspections of the workings before the men began their shifts. His main concern was to ascertain whether there was fire-damp in the workings, and the way he did that was to observe the flame in his safety lamp. The appearance of a large 'cap' on the flame was a clear indication of the presence of fire-damp, in which case it would be unsafe for men to work until the gas had been dispersed.

Thomas Lewis (fireman) deposed:

on Saturday, the 7th April, he went down about three o'clock in the morning, and found [everything to be] all right, except in one part where there was some fire-damp ... About four the same morning, six men and about seven boys came to their work. One of the latter was the deceased, [Joseph Howells, a trammer]. William David, one of the men, went to work coal where the fire-damp was. He had a safety lamp with him. Deceased went to the same part of the colliery with other boys, to tram the coal to be worked by William David.

[Thomas Lewis] left the colliery, but returned about six o' clock, and went at once to the place where he had directed William David to work. There was some fire[-damp] there, but not much. He was about leaving David's stall ... when he saw deceased and another boy coming up with a tram. They had a naked lighted candle in front of the tram. He called to them to stop ... Almost immediately there was an explosion of gas ... The deceased and William David were hurt [burnt]. Witness threw himself down and escaped. Deceased was much burnt about the face and hands. He was taken to the engine house, and Mr Cook, surgeon, was sent for. Deceased was afterwards carried to his father's house at Pentreherne. [Young Joseph died 12 days later.]

The inquiry was ... adjourned in order that the Government Inspector might be appraised of the accident ... The jury re-assembled [on 24th April], and were assisted by ... the Government Inspector, who [had] made a minute and careful examination of the pit previous to the inquest being resumed. [When the overman/fireman was questioned by the Government Inspector, he maintained] there was a little gas in the place where the accident happened about two or three days before ... The day before the accident I told the manager there was a little gas in William David's stall – that there were six or seven yards there. He told me to get it out as soon as we could. We intended to get it out by making a hole through to the next heading.

[The fireman also stated that while William] David was working in the stall ... I noticed his safety lamp; it was between two and three yards from the face ... it was on the floor. There was a little 'cap' on it ... I found the lamp on the Monday following – it was not at all injured by the explosion ... The firing of gas must have been from the naked light of the deceased or another boy ... All the tammers had naked lights.

[The colliery manager claimed that] the whole of the underground working is upon me ... I did not know that William David worked in a heading ... with six or seven yards of gas in it. I do not recollect Thomas Lewis [fireman] telling me, on the day before the accident, that there was gas in David's stall ... We never found fire-damp in this colliery before.

The examination continued [with the fireman saying] after we had bored through to get the gas out, the gas would have to pass the boys who were tramming with naked lights ... I blew out every candle before the gas passed the boys.

[In response to this the Government Inspector raised the question] Do you think this a proper thing – it is certainly one of the most dangerous experiments I ever heard of. [He then] drew the attention of the witness to the first rule for the management of the colliery, which is to the following effect:- 'An adequate amount of ventilation shall be constantly produced at all collieries, to dilute and render harmless noxious gases to such an extent as ... the working places ... shall ... be fit for working'. [He] contended that this pit was not properly ventilated, and therefore the manager was liable ... This was certainly a most serious case, and it was lamentable to think that the men should have been allowed to go on working in a heading where it was known there was some six or seven yards of gas.

The coroner, in briefly summing up ... said it was for the jury to decided whether the manager ... was criminally liable. In his opinion it certainly did appear that great blame was to be attached both to [the manager and the fireman], but whether evidence amounted to so strong a case as to justify a verdict of manslaughter it was for the jury to decide. There was no doubt the life of the poor boy was sacrificed to a want of proper care, and the question for the jury to decide was – is any person or persons criminally responsible.

The room was cleared for the consultation of the jury, who in a few minutes returned a verdict of 'Died from a sudden explosion of gas ... and we are of opinion that considerable blame is attached to the manager and overman'.

The Cambrian stated: 'We understand that proceedings are to be taken against the manager ... for a breach of the rules'. The newspaper could have added that it was unusual for a jury to point a finger at management and fellow workers. It was a sign of changing times.

Child and female labour in copperworks

Sub-commissioner Rhys Jones was told by two foremen at the Hafod Copperworks that, 'We should not like to bring our daughters in the works'. Yet despite the foremen's personal opinions, there were 83 women and girls employed at Hafod, which was far more than at Morfa (which had 12), White Rock (which had 6) and Middle Bank (which had none).

Rarely were children under the age of 10 to be found in copperworks. At Hafod there were 41 boys under the age of 13; there were no girls in the same age bracket. In the young persons bracket there were 92 males and 38 females aged between 13 and 18. There were also 45 women aged 18 and above. Boys under 13 and girls under 18 were mostly employed in 'wheeling coal and ashes [in barrows] to and from the ... furnaces', Monday to Saturday, for which they were paid between 4s. and 5s. per week. John William, aged 13, and William Davis, aged 12, had been at Hafod for three years. They told Rhys Jones 'we are both wheeling coals and coke. We begin at six or seven in the morning and can sometimes wheel enough for the furnaces by dinner time, but sometimes we are at work until six o'clock. The work is very hard if we stick to it so as to finish by dinner time, but it is not very hard when we take time to it. We get 4s. [20p.] per week'.

Older children would appear to have been paid more, as was the case of Sarah John, aged 16, who said 'I have been working here for four years. I am wheeling coal and ashes. I wheel for one furnace. I begin about six o'clock in the morning and leave about two o'clock in the day. I get 5s. 5½d. [27p.] per week. My father is a labourer here ... I have a sister also working here. She is wheeling ore and gets 7s. 6d. [37½ p.] per week'.

Females who were 18 years old and above, wheeled copper-ore, as did Elizabeth Mathews, aged 24. Elizabeth said 'I have been working since I was 10 years old. I began wheeling coal and ashes, and have been labouring and sweeping the floors and passages ... I now work in the ore yard. I fill the barrow and wheel it to the carriage, which takes it [the barrow] up by the engine to the stage leading to the tops of the calcining furnaces. I wheel about 20 yards, and about 150 barrows in a day of 3 cwt each [about 22½ tons in total]. I get 9s. to 10s. per week. I work on Sundays ... until three or four o'clock in the afternoon ... I go to the Chapel sometimes ... but am often too tired to do so. I can sew and make my own clothes, except gowns. I can sew them but cannot cut them out'.

Elizabeth referred to a carriage, which raised the barrows to a stage above the calcining furnaces. Thomas Hopkins, aged 16, stated 'I have been working for seven or eight years ... I now wheel ore on the stage. The ore is raised from the ore yard by an engine to the stage, and I wheel it along the stage to the tops of the calcining furnaces. [At this point, Rhys Jones commented on the fact that Thomas had fallen] off the stage about four months ago and broke his leg. I get 10s. 4d. per week [Thomas continued]. My father is a labourer in the works. And my brother works a furnace. He is 21 years old and is married. He gets 21s. per week. My father gets only 9s. per week and he has two children at home not working'.

The calcining furnaces were the first stage in the smelting process. In these furnaces the copper-rich 'matte' was separated from unwanted slag. The slag had then to be taken to a gigantic tip. Elizabeth Williams, aged 20, described how this was achieved. 'I have been working for 11 years in these works. I began wheeling coal and ashes, and two years ago I went to fill slag into waggons. The slag is wheeled out of the works into a yard where it is broken and filled into waggons, which are pulled up by an engine to the top of the slag bank. I work with other girls in the yard, filling the slag into the waggons. I come at seven and work until about four or thereabouts, and have meal times, about half an hour for breakfast and about an hour for dinner. Filling slag is much harder work than wheeling coal and ashes. I get 9s. per week ... My father works here when he is not employed in stamping the clay and bricks. He is blind and lost his sight from a cold, which he took by getting wet in the river [which was probably polluted]. I have two sisters in the works. They are wheeling coal and ashes'.

Boys aged 13 to 16 also attended the calcining furnaces, working not 12-hour shifts, but 24- and sometimes 48-hour shifts, and did so on a fortnightly basis. The reason for the long shifts was 'because the expense of putting [the furnaces] out and relighting [them] would be enormous'. The furnaces were, therefore, fully operational day and night, six days a week. On Sundays the furnaces were reduced to 'deadfire', but had to be returned to full heat by five o'clock Monday morning.

John Richards, aged 15, and David Davis, aged 14, worked these long shifts. 'We work the calcining [furnaces] from six o'clock in the morning to six o'clock the next morning. We sleep during the night three or four spells of an hour each. There is a watchman to call us up'. These boys usually had 24 hours or more off after a shift. Every second weekend they worked what they called the 'long watch'. 'We work from Saturday morning to Monday morning [48 hours] and the next [weekend] we have that time free'. In total, the boys worked five 24-hour shifts and one 'long watch' each fortnight, for which they were paid 7s. 7d. [38p] per week.

John Barnett, aged 11, worked at White Rock as a 'mason's boy, assisting the masons ... to repair any flaw in the furnaces'. He earned 2s. 6d. a week.

When the Hafod surgeon stated that the children at the works were 'employed in light work', Rhys Jones must have known the man was playing down the physical demands that were made on both women and children. Rhys did not respond to the statement, he simply recorded what they said. What concerned Rhys was why children were employed in such backbreaking work? His enquiries led him to believe that they were not taken on at the instigation of the employers, but 'at the instigation, or rather [the] supplication, of the parents or friends'. However, unlike the collier, Hugh Edwards, the copper worker and his wife could not plead poverty. The copper worker's skills and his adaptability to various health hazards made him by far the best paid worker in the L.S.V. Rhys concluded that the parents wanted their children to work because 'the men are rather fond of drink and the women were generally bad managers, [adding that] colliers appear to save more money than the copper men, although they do not get as much'.

As to the children themselves, the agent of the Morfa Works stated that 'we have no system of ... punishment excepting small fines for misconduct. Corporal punishments were never inflicted ... We take means to check bad language, etc., from which we levy a small fine'.

It was customary for children to take meals to their fathers, brothers, etc., at both collieries and copperworks. This routine chore exposed children who did not work to danger. A clerk at White Rock maintained, in 1842, there was 'nothing in our works which can be said to be dangerous'. Yet twelve years later *The Cambrian* reported on an inquest held 'at the Joiner's Arms, Foxhole, on the body of Sarah Jenkins, aged nine years ... [in which] Charles Stephens deposed that ... the deceased ... had been brought up by Daniel Beddoe and his wife at Foxhole. She was in the habit of bringing meals to a workman named Henry Evans ... [at] White Rock Copper Works. About nine o'clock ... [at] night she brought Evans' supper as usual, and after the meal was finished the deceased was going back with the empty things ... I [Charles Stephens] heard a fall and some ware break. I and another man immediately lighted a candle and went out to ... observe a child's bonnet on the surface of a tapping pit [near a furnace] ... about twenty yards from where she left us, and we concluded the child had fallen in, and with a large pike we got the body ... up from ... about 8 feet of boiling water. The child was quite dead'.

A Copperman's lot

According to the report of 1842, the Hafod Works had 345 adult males on their books. Many of these men were labourers, earning up to 12s. a week. Exactly what they did is difficult to determine. They may have unloaded copper-ore from ships at the wharves, or coal from barges in the canal docks. The work of furnacemen, on the other hand, is fairly well documented. The furnaces were in operation day and night, six days a week. On Sunday they were reduced to 'dead fire', but had to be returned to full heat by 5 a.m. Monday morning. Rhys wrote:

I have seen the copper men [at work, each] skimming his furnace (a process of 15 to 20 minutes duration) standing within [a few] feet of an open door, exposed to the reflected heat of the large body of molten metal within, and the ... slag ... flowing in a stream of liquid fire ... I have seen him ... stretching his heavy iron rabble or skimmer into the furnace until the perspiration ran off his person like drops of rain, and the few clothes he wore dripping wet and it is not, the men say, until this profuse perspiration appears, or as they term it, they become 'wringing wet with sweat', that they can easily bear the smarting influence of the fire'.

During these operations the men usually carry a towel on their shoulders to wipe the perspiration from their faces, and as soon as the labour is over they not infrequently run to a jug of cold water and drink off a pint or two with impunity ... children and young persons are not employed in the process ... Indeed, it requires a long standing in the works, a hard apprenticeship, to become inured to the severe and exhausting labours of the ... furnace.

Rhys recorded that, 'from the nature of their work at the fires, [coppermen] wear out more clothes, particularly shoes [than colliers]. They mostly wear flannel shirts and wear out four [shirts] in the year when two [shirts] will serve the colliers'. With regard to their appearance, coppermen have been described as 'desiccated, wiry and thin' with a sallow countenance[1], which is hardly surprising; nor is it surprising that, depending on whether the furnace doors were open or shut, the furnace-men 'alternatively sweats and shivers'. They worked in an environment in which the air contained 'sulphurous acid, sulphuric acid, arsenic and arsenous acids, various gases and fluoric vapours with solid particles mechanically swept into the air beside the coal smoke'. Consequently 'pneumonia, pleurisy [and] bronchitis were noted as the prevailing diseases'. Accidents would have been frequent, many of them burns from hot surfaces or molten material.

> In 1843 *The Cambrian* reported: 'A furnace-man, named Griffith Henry, was scalded … severely at the Middle Bank Copperworks … He was engaged in taking the metal out of the pan – a square iron box suspended over the tapping pits – when, by the fastening of the pan giving way, he was precipitated with it into the pit full of boiling water. His fellow workmen ran instantly to his assistance, raised him out of the water, and carried him home, where he was promptly attended to by Mr. O.G. Williams, surgeon; but the injuries he had received were so great that he died, after suffering excruciating agonies, within twelve hours … He left a wife and three children utterly destitute'.

One hazard that few in a responsible position would admit to were the fumes that contained sulphuric acid. Local dignitaries and surgeons had, for decades, played down the harmful effects of such a toxic substance on the body. These worthies could not, of course, deny the effects that sulphuric acid had on vegetation – that stared them in the face each time they looked across the river at Kilvey Hill. It was towards Kilvey Hill that prevailing south-westerly winds carried billowing clouds of smoke, the acid in which had destroyed vegetation to the extent that the topsoil had been washed away, leaving the hillside scarred by gullies.

In 1815 Charles Collins, surgeon, admitted that 'the injury to vegetation here is very obvious … cattle are affected by swellings and abscesses in their feet, premature loss of teeth, and paralysis of the extremities; sheep in the same way, and horses, but in a less degree' – but when it came to workmen he said 'the skin of the workmen, also, becomes much darkened. They look sallow; but are healthy, strong, and have large families'. Some 26 years later, medical men were still playing down the harmful effects of copper smoke on the human body, as did the Hafod Works' surgeon when he declared that 'those dwelling close to the works are generally the most healthy'.

Those who took the trouble to observe what went on in smelting halls would have seen for themselves that 'the men suffer greatly; they cover the mouth and nostrils with a handkerchief, and occasionally rush to a distance to inhale a less impure air'. Such men had been 'inured to the … fire', but for newcomers the affects of fumes were far worse. In 1850 a pickler at the Morfa Works confessed that 'when I came here from the ironworks six years ago, I suffered much from my stomach. The sulphur affected me. I spat blood for some time, but I became used to it'. So why were men like the pickler prepared to stick it out?

The answer, of course, was money. According to an article in *The Cambrian* in 1843, ore-smelters earned 26s. per week, slagmen 30s., metal-smelters 30s. and roasters 31s. 6d. These rates may have been applicable to the Hafod workforce where the men were paid individually, but the rates would not necessarily have applied to other copperworks – certainly not to the Morfa where earnings were paid to gang leaders, then distributed among gang members, probably in a public house. Wage payment to workmen in a public house, which encouraged men to drink, was to be found among colliers as well as coppermen. The practice was made illegal in 1842, but two further Acts (in 1844 and 1852) were necessary for this kind of reform to become effective. That said, the weekly rates that appeared in *The Cambrian* were more than double what the collier, Hugh Edwards, earned the previous year. That, however, is not the complete picture.

In 1843 *The Cambrian* reported 'that copper men [in the L.S.V.] are entirely free from the system of Truck which has been so much complained of in other ... districts. They receive each week their wages in hard cash'. The coppermen at White Rock also had 'a sick fund to which members pay 3d. per week and receives, when sick or laid up, 5s. per week'.

The coppermen's wages, then, were high, but like the colliers, their rates of pay could be reduced during a depression. Wage reductions often led to strikes, as happened in the summer of 1843, when the copper masters agreed to cut wages, some by as much as 25%. What made the ensuing strike unusual was that the coppermen in the Swansea and Neath areas had no union, but they still formed a united front to oppose the cuts. The five-week strike, as recorded in *The Cambrian*, provides an insight into what went on when men withdrew their labour.

The strike of 1843

With the exception of those at the Forest Works, all the men at the Swansea and Neath copper-works stopped work on Friday 2 August. The following day they were joined by men from the Forest Works, and at 1 p.m. over 1,000 strikers assembled outside the Hafod Works. They then marched on Swansea where they were met by four men on horseback, the mayor and old J.H. Vivian among them. The mayor addressed the strikers, telling them that government directives forbad large numbers to enter a town in procession (at the time the Rebecca Riots had prompted a state of emergency). He then advised them to go home, at which point J.H. Vivian told the strikers that, 'if they would return to a field above the Hafod Works, he would willingly hear anything they had to say'.

Incredible though it may seem, the huge procession turned about and, 'proceeded by the mayor', Mr Vivian and two others, the men returned to the field 'where they formed a circle, allowing the gentlemen on horseback to occupy the centre'. Mr. Vivian addressed the men, thanking them for their orderly conduct. '"And now," he said, "if there is any man who has any grievance, let him come forward and state them."' After a moment one man stepped forward, saying '"We want our price, as we had it before."' Mr. Vivian tried to reason with them, pointing out the depressed state of the metal trades, and how the price of copper had fallen from 12d. a pound to 9d. He then asked them to compare their reduced wages with the reduced wages of other workmen in the kingdom.

'A long desultory conversation then ensued' until, finally, Mr. Vivian said, '"I am going into the works; if any man wishes to come down, let him come."' All the Hafod men followed Mr. Vivian into the works, where 'further conversation ensued', but no agreement could be reached because 'the men had bound themselves to act in union' with those of other works.

The strike continued. There were reports of 'intimidation ... to prevent those who might ... return to work from doing so', and also to force the few remaining at work to abandon it'. Some Hafod men were reported to have approached a Mr. W.P. Evans of Morriston (who may have been a chapel deacon) to express 'an apprehension that, in consequence of their [inability] to speak English sufficiently well they had not made out a proper statement of their grievances, and requested Mr. Evans to draw up a written detail of their complaints, which they intended presenting to Mr. Vivian. Mr. Evans complied with their request', but his involvement came to nought because, as a result of 'a meeting of men from all the other works, [the Hafod men] changed their minds'.

There were rumours that the strikers 'intend dividing among themselves the funds of their benefit clubs, and of drawing their deposits out of savings banks'; moreover, *The Cambrian* could not resist commenting on:

> one of the characteristics ... of the Welsh is, that they mix up all their actions with their devotions. As an illustration of this, we might mention the fact that the coppermen regularly hold prayer meetings at seven o'clock every morning, to implore the divine aid upon their exertions in maintaining the strike.

And while all this was going on, 'a considerable number of colliers were thrown out of work' because production had been halted.

Towards the end of the second week a few Hafod men returned to work, in consequence to which several hundred strikers gathered at the gates, demanding that the strike-breakers be sent out. The demand was ignored. That night 'the windows and doors of two houses near Landore, occupied by men working at Hafod, were broken'. The following day some hundreds assembled on the hillside above Middle Bank Copperworks 'in a menacing attitude', their intention being to intimidate those who had refused to come out on strike. A police presence at the works eventually led to the strikers dispersing 'without any violent act having taken place'.

As a well-paid body of men, 'entirely free from ... truck', the coppermen did not share the grievances of miners, nor the same hardships. So it is hardly surprising that they were not enrolled in any union; nor would they be for some time to come. Yet a week after the strike had started, *The Cambrian* had reported that there were, of late, 'designing demagogues ... among them'. A further week later *The Cambrian* reported that 'the ringleaders or spokesmen [in a dispute outside the Hafod gates] were all strangers and were not recognized'. Who these strangers were, or where they came from is not known, but their involvement was to no avail because, five weeks after the strike had started, the Hafod men returned to work 'at the reduced rate'. The Forest workers soon followed suit, as did others, until finally the Upper Bank men yielded to the inevitable. Six weeks after the commencement of the strike, *The Cambrian* newspaper announced 'that all the works were back in production'.

The situation around 1850

By 1848 the furnacemen at Hafod had regained their price, as outlined in *Cliffe's Book of South Wales*, which states that 'furnacemen [received] from 28s. to 32s.; and the men whose duty it was to ladle the liquid metal from the furnace into moulds were paid £2 and upwards. [The book also states that] Messrs Vivian then employed about 500 men, and about 500 women and girls'. Some of the women who were not wheeling ore may have been employed in the collection of urine for pickling copper sheets – if so, they are likely to have called on company-owned houses, where saving urine was part of the tenancy agreement. 'Children [of which there were 100 in 1847, none of them below the age of 13] were not employed during the night watches. The children earned 3s. 6d. to 6s. 6½d. a week'.

By 1850 a few further changes were apparent. The drinking habits of the Hafod furnacemen had been curbed, possibly because men who drank too much often failed to turn up for their shifts. The Vivians' answer to the problem had been to employ young girls to provide the furnacemen with water 'specially selected for its purity'. Another change was that the 24-hour shifts had been reduced to 12. Presumably there had been similar changes at Morfa where, in 1850, it was said that 'strikes are of very rare occurrences indeed. The son succeeds his father in the works [as he did at Hafod], and lives his time out, without apprehension of change or discomfort arising from adverse times'.

Numbers employed by the copper and coal masters

In 1849 George T. Clark stated that 'works for the production of copper gave direct employment to about 2,800 persons, [excluding those employed in the] numerous collieries, zinc and iron works, etc'. Today the figure of 2,800 copperworkers is considered too high by researchers, who used the census returns to obtain figures ranging from around 1,100 in 1841 to 1,300 in 1861, which includes ancillary workers such as clerks, labourers and masons. The report of 1842, however, provides the following figures:

	Males			Females	Total
	under 13	under 18	adults		
Hafod	41	92	345	83	561
Morfa	13	74	484	12	583
White Rock	20	34	196	6	256
Middle Bank	13	27	240	0	280
Totals	**87**	**227**	**1,265**	**101**	**1,680**

Three further works to those listed in the table above were producing copper in 1842 – Forest, Rose and Landore – which may have brought the total closer to 2,000. Two other works had also been converted for the production of a copper-zinc alloy (yellow metal) – Birmingham (in 1841) and Upper Bank (in c.1837); the latter had a workforce in 1842 of 105.

As to colliers; the sub-commissioner, Rhys Jones, recorded that 421 people were employed by the Llansamlet Colliery Co.; 357 by John Morris's Landore Colliery Co.; and a further 448 by the Swansea Coal Co. The total number employed by these three large colliery concerns was 1,226 – a figure that includes women and children. There were also a number of smaller concerns on both sides of the river. How many were employed by the smaller concerns is unknown, but it states, in the report of 1842, that the 'smelting works and coal works ... on the Swansea river, including Messrs. William's Crown [copper] Works at Neath [which employed 143 men and boys] affords employment for at least 3,400 persons'.

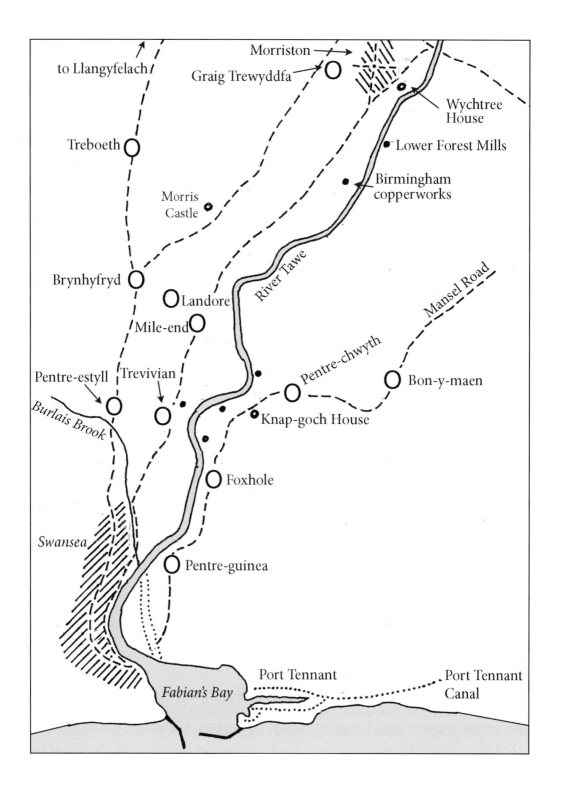

to Llangyfelach

Morriston

Graig Trewyddfa

Wychtree House

Treboeth

Lower Forest Mills

Birmingham copperworks

Morris Castle

River Tawe

Brynhyfryd

Mansel Road

Landore

Mile-end

Pentre-estyll

Trevivian

Pentre-chwyth

Bon-y-maen

Burlais Brook

Knap-goch House

Foxhole

Swansea

Pentre-guinea

Port Tennant

Port Tennant Canal

Fabian's Bay

174

The Industrial Villages

So where exactly did all these colliers, copper workers and their dependents live in the early years of Victoria's reign? The census of 1841 – the first to provide details of employment – gives some interesting figures on the subject. On the west bank, for example, 113 copper workers and 80 colliers lived in the northern part of Swansea, roughly the area between what is now King's Street on the south, and Greenhill on the north. Beyond these limits, collier cottages within garden plots lined the Llangyfelach Road. These dispersed roadside cottages extended all the way up to Tirdeunaw (above Treboeth). There were, however, some concentrations of roadside cottages around Pentre-estyll (at the top of the Cwm Burlais ravine where there were collieries to the north); Brynhyfryd (where there were several collieries in the immediate vicinity); and Treboeth (where there were more collieries on what was then Treboeth Common).

From Brynhyfryd Square another road (once the main road to Clydach) led over the summit of Graig Trewyddfa. This road was also lined with dispersed cottages within garden plots, but there was a minor concentration of such cottages along what is now Graig Road. The Graig Road concentration was an old settlement, dating back to the late 17th century. It originated as a mining settlement because the Swansea 5-foot coal seam outcropped on the sloping ground to the east, and this outcrop was riddled with a row of mining levels. This was a squatter settlement on the edge of a common, which may have been the origin of most collier cottages along the Llangyfelach Road. The 1841 census records 210 homes on Graig Trewyddfa – between Landore and Morriston – the resident population being 1,023, of which 140 were colliers and 93 were copper workers.

Closer to the river (and on both banks) there were several blocks of terraced houses in the vicinity of copperworks. The blocks were referred to as 'the Barracks' (as they were at Penclawdd). They were built by the copper masters, originally for the benefit of their key workers. These small communities might consist of ten terraced houses, or two rows of five terraced houses. In

Right: Cottage with an 18th century past – sited a little to the west of Pentre Pit, 535 Llangyfelach Road was still standing in the 1970s. Single-storeyed cottages similar to this one were common to rural areas all over West Wales, as well as the Tawe Valley. The front door gave access into the larger of two rooms, one that served as a kitchen-cum-living area with a chimney at the gable end. The smaller room at the other end of the building doubled as a bedroom and a parlour; there was no fireplace in this room. Above the smaller room was a croglofft – a sleeping area for children – which was accessed via a ladder. There were two small widows flanking the front door; there were no windows at the back.

Opposite: Settlement in the Lower Swansea Valley c.1849 - the dashes represent main roads and the circles indicate industrial villages. The solid black dots show the position of known copperworks' barracks. Note there are no docks at Swansea, although, by 1845, the Tawe had been diverted to what was known as the New Cut (indicated by parallel lines of small dots). When built, the North Dock was to occupy the original river bed (close to the Strand); it was not officially opened until 1852.

Wychtree House, Morriston – otherwise known as 'The Hostel'. Built by John Morris I, it stood beside the old road between Wychtree Bridge and the Forest Copperworks. It may have originally served as a barracks, despite its impressive appearance, as John was inclined to be ostentatious with regard to anything that he built. According to a list of ratepayers, dated 1864, the coal producer, John Glasbrook occupied this building as a tenant of the local landowner, William Martin. The two storeys seen here fronted the roadway, whereas the rear of the building (with two lower storeys built into sloping ground) faced the river. The upper storeys were demolished in 1964; the lower storeys in 1975.

Morris Castle – as seen from the high ground above Brynhyfryd Square. Despite its appearance, this was not a castle, but a 19th century block of flats for colliers. In 1876 it was described as a ruin. It became even more ruinous when, in 1990, a hurricane reduced its east wall and a tower to rubble.

1841 the two blocks of five terraced houses at the Lower Forest Copper Rolling-mills provided accommodation for 47 people, among them one collier, four coppermen, two blacksmiths, two hammermen, two rollermen and two bargemen – 13 workmen in all.

Colliers were rarely provided with accommodation by their employers, except perhaps head colliers or watchmen who required cottages near the entrance to levels and pits. As a coal master John Morris I was evidently an exception. In *c.*1773 he built for his colliers at the Treboeth Level a block of flats, one of the earliest in the U.K. The ruins of this block (later known as Morris Castle) appear on the skyline when viewed from the east and from Brynhyfryd Square. The fact that it was designed to look like a castle with its whitewashed walls topped by battlements, suggests that it was intended to display John's wealth and ingenuity. The block consisted of 24 apartments around an internal courtyard; there were also 24 garden plots lining the approach road from the north. The apartments were occupied until *c.*1850.

Morriston and Landore

Further north John Morris I had indulged in a more enduring creation. In 1779 he bought 'a farm for the purpose of inducing the artificers and labourers ... to build' homes for themselves. He then arranged for his architect, William Edwards, to plan the layout of a new township on the farmland, one that was to be called Morris Town (Morriston) and consist of 'well formed and spacious streets'. John did not build houses himself. His 'plan was to grant ground leases on plots of land, about a square rood each [about a ¼ acre] for three lives, or 50 years, at 7s. 6d. a year each plot. The lessees were to build [their houses] according to prescribed plans'. And each plot was sufficient for a house and 'for raising potatoes'.

By '1796 there were 141 houses inhabited by 619 persons' in Morriston. By 1819 John could claim that he had 'lived to see about 300 stone cottages with tiled roofs' in a township in which (three years earlier) the population was said to have been about 1,100. At the time of the 1841 census the number of houses had risen to 443, and the population to 2,187. The working population then stood at 557, half of whom (278 according to Stephen Hughes in *Copperopolis*) were undoubtedly employed in the local copperworks and rolling-mills. A further 73 (masons, smiths, carpenters and the like) may also have been employed in the copper industry, bringing the total to 351 (63%). There were also 50 colliers in the town, plus 20 men in jobs connected with the coal industry.

So John leased plots on which workers built their own homes 'in well formed and spacious streets'. The workers, of course, had to obtain the necessary building materials. In the L.S.V. the walls of most buildings (including smelting halls, chapels, schools, etc.) consisted primarily of Pennant Sandstone, which could be quarried on almost any hillside. Initially, the sandstone was undressed. Limestone mortar was available from limekilns that, from 1794–8 onwards, stood alongside the Swansea Canal. Bricks for chimneys and window dressing could be purchased from local brickworks; the raw material coming from red clay. Roof pantiles were also made from local red clay, and they continued in use until slates were shipped into Swansea in the late 19th century. Wood for rafters, doors and windows came from timber merchants; glass from suppliers at Swansea.

Where possible the would-be homeowner would have done whatever jobs he could, aided perhaps by neighbours with some experience in building walls, etc., but there were many tasks that had to be carried out by carpenters, masons and the like. And the census of 1841 makes it plain there was no shortage of tradesmen. Of course, the would-be homeowner had to find the money for both materials and for employing tradesmen, which was why the Quaker businessman, William Bevan of Morriston, set up Glamorgan's first savings bank at Morriston in 1816. William Bevan became the bank's first treasurer, and John Morris I its first president. The following year the hard-earned savings of depositors at Morriston (and elsewhere in the United Kingdom) were protected by an Act of Parliament, which forbade the bank's trustees profiting from their trusteeship. John Morris II went a step further in 1827 when he founded the Swansea Savings Bank, which two years later absorbed the Morriston bank to become the largest savings bank in Glamorgan.

There is evidence to show that some homeowners built two houses, using rent from the second house to pay off any loans. Larger house-building enterprises also took place. Towards the middle of the century, chapels became the focal point of building clubs in which members pooled their savings. Clubs of this sort were dissolved when all the planned houses had been erected and the loans repaid. Saving clubs flourished intermittently until *c.*1880 when the first permanent building societies came into existence.

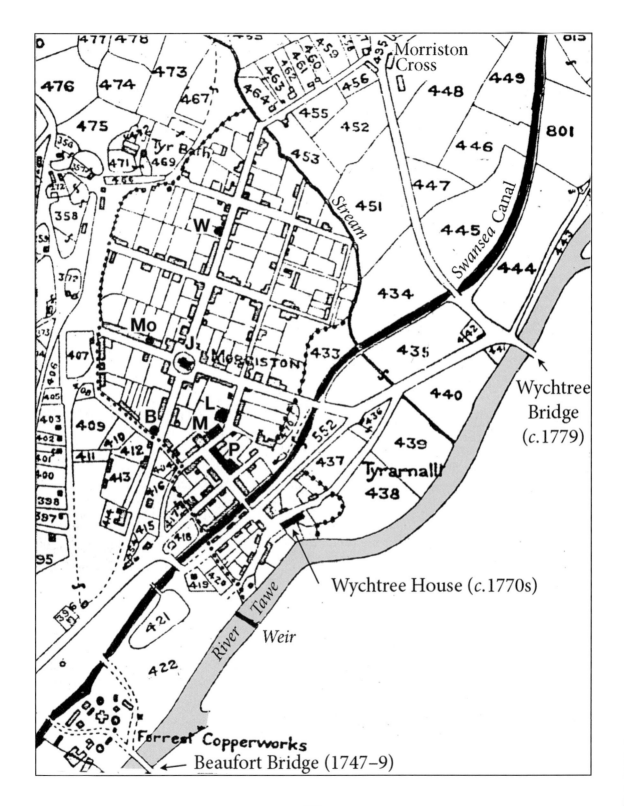

Morriston Cross

Stream

Swansea Canal

Wychtree Bridge (*c.*1779)

Tyr Bath

Tyrarnall

Wychtree House (*c.*1770s)

River Tawe

Weir

Forrest Copperworks

Beaufort Bridge (1747–9)

Opposite: *Morriston tithe map 1838 – two gridirons stand out. The smaller, south-easterly gridiron with its narrow streets may have been the earliest part of the township. Notice how the Swansea Canal (1794-8) cuts through this gridiron, the canal here being quite narrow. The larger gridiron, with St. John's Church (1789) as a focal point, came a little later. The top end of the main (Woodfield) street terminated at the boundary of John Morris's property (the boundary here being a stream). Beyond the boundary the main road continued on a different alignment (as it does today) before linking up (at Morriston Cross) with the road from Wychtree Bridge. In the latter part of Victoria's reign the spaces between the original houses were gradually built upon – possibly as a result of division of the plots among offspring – so that by late Victorian times the original houses were no longer detached, but absorbed into terraces. By then the guidelines on building to prescribed plans had long been ignored. The dotted line represents the boundary to J. Morris's property.*

(West Glamorgan Archive Service)

Key to plan:

L   *Libanus Chapel (1782)*
Mo *37 Morfydd Street (late 18th century)*
J   *St. John's Church (1789)*
W   *91a Woodfield Street (c.1800)*
P   *Philadelphia Chapel (1829)*
B   *Birmingham CWs School (1815)*
M   *Market Hall (1827)*

Right: *37 Morfydd Street – said to be of late 18th century build and, therefore, the oldest house in Morriston. The front door led into the larger of two ground-floor rooms (the kitchen), on the end wall of which was a central hearth. Between the hearth and the back wall was a spiral stone staircase, which led up to the first of three bedrooms. Family members originally had to pass through the first and middle bedrooms to reach a third bedroom that was furthest away from the staircase. There were no windows in the rear wall, only a back door. The living space was 634 square feet.*

Settlement at Landore began in earnest on farmland belonging to the Morrises in the early 1820s. Building was sporadic and to no particular plan, though the focal point appears to have been Siloh Road. The majority of buildings were cottages built by the workers themselves. There were also dispersed blocks of terraced houses. Some of these terraces were built by John Morris II, presumably for his employees at the Millbrook Iron Works. Other terraces were built by Messrs. Williams, Foster & Co. for their key workers at the Morfa Copperworks.

91a Woodfield Street – built c.1800 and, therefore, the second oldest house in Morriston. This property was similar to the house in Morfydd Street, except that it had an L–shaped staircase adjoining the kitchen hearth. At the rear of the property an extended roof provided space for two additional ground-floor rooms – possibly a back kitchen and a service/storage room. The two ground-floor front windows were undoubtedly enlarged when the premises was converted into a shop. The floor space, including the extension at the back, was 710 square feet.

Trevivian

The workforce at the Hafod Copperworks in 1812 (two years after its foundation) stood at around 80, a figure that included the agent (manager), two clerks, one refiner and one refiner's assistant. The previous year the refiner, William Howell, had entered into an agreement with John Henry Vivian. William agreed 'not to disclose (except to his own child or children) the Art and Mystery of Smelting or Refining of Copper as practised at the Hafod Works without the consent of John Henry Vivian or his partners'. In return, William would be paid 30s. a week; he was also promised 'two pounds of candles every week and one Wey (five tons) of coal every year, and ten guineas (£10 10s.) every year in lieu of a House and Garden'.

William Howell lived in Swansea (the town boundary at that time being the Burlais Brook) and it may be presumed that the greater part of the Hafod workforce also lived there. Throughout the following three decades, John Henry erected no workers' houses himself, except a barracks near the main gate and Aberdyberthi House for his agent. Then, in 1837, he authorized the building of Trevivian (Vivian Town), later to be known as the Hafod. Some historians maintain that Trevivian was built because the Vivians were philanthropists, whereas others argue that John Henry was only safeguarding his reputation and his business interests. In 1832, for example, he became an M.P. and may, therefore, have been concerned about his image. After the establishment of the Morfa Copperworks in 1835, he may also have been concerned that his new neighbour might poach his key workers.

Early Trevivian houses – this row at the upper end of Neath Road, Hafod, was part of the earliest development of worker dwellings at Vivian's Town. The row of houses immediately south of this junction are of the same date, as are most of the houses in Vivian Street. They were built in 1837–9 and consisted of two up, two down, with the rear bedroom under a 'catslide' roof extension.

Whatever his motives, John Henry arranged for 'some 50 houses' to be built at Trevivian in *c.*1837, and by 1849 'about 30 additional houses [were] in the course of being built'. These houses were a big improvement on what was available in Swansea The earlier ones had four rooms, two up, two down, with a total floor space of 519 square feet. The size of the rear/children's bedroom, however, was constrained by the slope of a catslide (a downward extension of the rear roof). The two earliest rows that align the top end of Neath Road had large gardens back and front, whereas later houses had only 'a long garden behind, in which, at a distance from the houses, was a privy and a pigstye'; what is more the windows in these houses were made to open. In 1849 the houses were rented out at 2s. a week, which was the rent charged for the smaller one up, one down houses in Swansea.

The 1841 census records that the first 48 houses built provided homes for 256 people, 67 of whom were employed. Between *c.*1851 and 1867 the Vivians built an additional 119 houses, each with two full-height bedrooms (these houses had no catslides). The floor space of these houses was 589.4 square feet. The Vivians continued building intermittently until 1914, the houses becoming progressively larger and the gardens smaller. Trevivian proved to be the best built, best planned township in the Swansea Valley, the total number of houses erected being 263.

Villages on the East Side

On the east side of the Tawe there was nothing resembling a grouping of dwellings until 1722, when the then Lord Mansel built 75 cottages for his colliers in the vicinity of Bon-y-maen. Like the Graig Trewyddfa grouping, the settlement is presumed to have consisted of scattered roadside cottages in garden plots, possibly along Mansel Road, or Cefn Road where the Swansea 5-foot coal seam outcrops on the northern side of Kilvey Hill. Each of the three copperworks on the East Side appear to have had their own barracks, apart from which, communal accommodation was provided by the Cnap-goch mansion on the slopes above the Middle Bank Copperworks. The last Lord Mansel had bought the Cnap-goch estate with the intention of establishing what later became known as the White Rock Copperworks. Initially, Cnap-goch House provided accommodation for the agent at White Rock, but in *c.*1771, when White Rock House was built for the agent, Cnap-goch and its outbuildings were used to accommodate 24 families of White Rock employees.

At Foxhole, further south, there were several rows of houses in existence by 1793. Twenty years later, the short rows had developed into two almost contiguous terraces on the east side of the main valley road. In the following two decades houses were also built on the higher ground above the road. Some of the houses had been built by the Grenfells for their Middle Bank employees; most had been erected by the workers themselves, on land leased from the Grenfells. The highest houses on the hillside, such as Freeman's Row, were built by Messrs. John Freeman and Copper Co., owners of the White Rock Copperworks. For the most part, the Foxhole of Victorian times no longer exists, the houses demolished and replaced by scenic woodland. However, the 1841 census records 50 copper workers and 11 colliers living in the 77 houses that once lined the east side of the valley road.

In 1803 the Upper and Middle Bank copperworks passed into the possession of the Owen Williams and Pascoe Grenfell partnership, and during the following decade they built a more orderly arrangement of dwellings at Pentre-chwyth. Forty dwellings of the two up, two down variety were built in a locality that, until *c.*1850, was known as Grenfell Town. The houses were arranged in three terraces staggered across the hillside. Each house had a rear garden; each provided around 555 square feet of floor space. Although altered in the late 19th century, these houses survive in terraces known as Grenfelltown, Taplow Terrace and Rifleman's Row.

Summary of the industrial villages

In 1849, George T. Clarke, the philanthropic manager of an ironworks at Dowlais, came to Swansea to conduct an enquiry into the sanitary conditions in both the town and the industrial villages of the L.S.V. In his report to the General Board of Health, George stated:

> according to the census [of 1841] the population grouped in the villages [and][2] Swansea proper equals about 19,000 inhabitants ... Of these villages Trevivian, Mile-end and Landore number about 1,500 persons. Morriston, containing about 2,000 persons, is ... connected with the rest by a range of straggling cottages. Opposite Swansea, a district with about 1,200 inhabitants has sprung up on the east bank of the Tawe.

According to George's calculations the combined population of the villages was roughly 4,700. It is therefore apparent that a large proportion of those who worked in the L.S.V. actually lived in Swansea proper, mainly in the northern working-class suburb between Waunwen and Kings Street.

Unsanitary places to live

Most of the dwellings in the L.S.V. were whitewashed, the roofs of thatch or pantiles, but the industrial villages were far from idyllic. In his report of 1849, George Clarke stated that:

> Morriston is a large village, laid out in regular lines upon the steep hill-side above the right bank of the Tawe ... separated from the river by the Swansea Canal. The streets and roads are ill made, and no care has been taken to keep them clean ... many of the houses are built too close against the hill-side, and are, in consequence, very damp, and have no back premises. They are almost all ill provided with privies, and the people draw water, often contaminated with sewage, from various springs and brooks within two to ten minutes walk, or from the canal.
>
> The position is ... so good that, although the houses do no lie very closely together, they are capable of being cheaply drained and supplied with water. The people are chiefly employed in the adjacent collieries and copperworks, and, although they have suffered under the temporary depression of trade, I found the interior of their houses particularly clean and neat, and they lamented that their landlords would not provide them with a tolerable drainage and with privies. In visiting these and the adjacent villages of Landore and Trevivian, I was accompanied by Mr. Evans, surgeon to those works, who pointed out that Morriston ... contains about 2,000 inhabitants, who are, for the most part, colliers and copper-men; they are, on the whole, a well-fed and well-clad population (a description which will apply to all other places mentioned in our report) ... Notwithstanding that the topographical position of Morriston is favourable to health, the place is scarcely ever without fever of some form or another ... which frequently breaks out epidemically, and often with great virulence and fatality.
>
> This unhealthy condition of the place is ... owing to its possessing ... no drainage whatever; no privy accommodation. The weir situated ... below Morriston is unquestionably another very fertile source of disease ... it receives nearly the whole of the animal and vegetable filth of the town, as well as ... foul water from the collieries; in the summer months it is stagnant (excepting now and then a freshet clears it), and at these times especially the foetid exhalations arising from the weir are highly offensive, and as the supply of water for drinking purposes in Morriston is insufficient, and at a distance, the bulk of the inhabitants drink their tea and beer brewed with this filthy water. ... In Morriston the sewage is left to find its own way along the open street-gutters, which at the time of my visit were in divers places clogged up with it.
>
> Landore, Mile-end and Trevivian are also straggling villages, more or less connected with each other ... Mr. Evans has drawn up the following statement, concerning these villages ... Landore and Mile End – A populous and scattered place, inhabited by the same class of people as Morriston ... There is always a great deal of illness in this neighbourhood, and we are seldom without cases of fever. Drainage in the same neglected condition as in Morriston. Within an area of half a square mile are upwards of 200 houses without privies. The few that may be found are confined almost exclusively to the shops and public-houses.

The report singled out

> **Squance Row** – A row of 13 houses; no drainage; a large hillock of filth behind each of them; two asses are kept close under one of the houses; the stench from this place is exceedingly offensive in warm weather. There is also a slaughter-house behind Phillip's-row, which is much complained of.
>
> **Club-houses** – There is a large stagnant pool immediately before these houses, caused by the South Wales Railway damming the water-course; this is also very offensive, and, during the last spring, summer and autumn, we had a very heavy crop of fevers in its immediate neighbourhood.

Trevivian is the nucleus of a town situated on a hill, a little more than a mile north of Swansea; it is the property of J.H. Vivian, Esq., M.P., and is inhabited by his workmen employed at the Hafod copperworks; it consists ... of some 50 houses ... [and] there are about 30 additional houses in the course of being built ... It is proper here to state, that the houses were not in the first place erected by Mr. Vivian. They were built about twelve years ago [1837]. Up to 1845 the sanitary condition of this place was very unsatisfactory; there was a bog behind the buildings; of drainage there was none. Fever of one type or another was almost always present, and frequently became epidemic. In 1843, cases of scarlatina were numerous and fatal. In 1845, the same epidemic again broke out, and with so much virulence and fatality as to throw the inhabitants into a state of the greatest consternation. On representation being made to H. Hussey Vivian, Esq., of this alarming state of things, accompanied by the expression of an opinion that the malignancy of the disease was in great measure consequent on there being no system of drainage ... that gentleman, on the instant, directed that a complete and effectual system of sewage should be laid down. This was successfully accomplished in a very short time.

The gratifying result of this prompt act of benevolent humanity has been, that since 1845, epidemics, though they have occasionally occurred, have been mild, infrequent and easily subdued, and the inhabitants generally have enjoyed a comparatively high degree of health. Where formerly almost daily medical attendance was invited and necessary, latterly it has frequently occurred that it has been neither requested nor required for a space of one or two months at a stretch.

George Clark also stated in his report that 'Trevivian has at present no regular supply of water' other than from 'the canal or a pump in the works'. He also noted that there was no water 'soft enough for washing nearer than the canal, "a good ten minutes' walk with a two-gallon water jar"'. At a later date H. Hussey Vivian went to considerable expense in sinking wells, but to no avail due to the local geology.

Across the Tawe, and upon its steep bank opposite to Swansea, are built the long and irregular villages of Fox-hole and Pentre-guinea. The houses are for the most part niched into the hill-side, and are old, damp and very dirty, and have no back premises. The water-springs used by the lower cottages are defiled by those living above them on the hill, and the roads and gutters, when I visited them, were in a filthy state. The copper smoke here affects the vegetation and the glass in the windows, so that it is not impossible that it may also affect the water.

George Clark mentioned one other village, one that owed its existence firstly to the construction of the Tennant Canal (1818-24) which brought coal from the Neath area to what was then Fabian's Bay at the mouth of the Tawe, and secondly to the existence of wharves where the canal terminated at Fabian's Bay. This village, named Port Tennant after the builder of the canal, George Tennant, was:

below Pentre-guinea, upon the sea shore, a short distance from the east pier, and about the mouth of Tennant's Canal ... [where there] are several new and well-built houses, all within the borough. None of the owners on this side of the river have taken advantage of the copious springs above them [on Kilvey Hill] to secure a proper supply of water; neither has any advantage been taken of a position so excellently suited for drainage.

Epidemics

So colliers and coppermen in the L.S.V. worked long and exhausting hours in hazardous conditions, then walked home through filthy streets, breathing in noxious fumes and 'the foetid exhalations arising from ... raw sewage'. There were unfenced tramroads and railways to cross, which, for the unwary, were as dangerous as modern roads. There was coal everywhere underfoot and, according to the report on education, there was 'not a blade of vegetation to be seen on the steep hills on either side of the river, which seem to have been greatly raised, if not in some places created by accumulations of slag. This, with the whitish smoke of the furnaces, and the penetrating taste of copper, makes the whole region as dreary and disagreeable as (one) can imagine any to be'.

The interior of a workman's house may have been 'clean and neat'; it may also have been 'old, damp and dirty'. Whatever the conditions, there was always the likelihood that some member of the family was recovering from an accident, or suffering from food poisoning, or the ill effects of what were later termed 'local diseases' such as convulsions, bronchitis and pneumonia. If the house was damp, some relative might be stricken with consumption (T.B.), or suffering from diseases such as croup, measles, diphtheria, whooping cough, typhus, diarrhoea, smallpox, or even the dreaded cholera, visitations of which occurred in 1849 and 1866.

The scarlatina (scarlet fever) that caused 'the greatest consternation' in Trevivian in 1843 and 1845 was probably the worst affliction. Caused by bacteria and highly contagious, scarlatina would make its appearance almost every year, and with varying intensity, but was most prevalent in the autumn. Its victims were mostly aged between 3 and 15. The onset was abrupt, with nausea, vomiting, sore throat, fever and the appearance of a rash of tiny red spots at the base of the neck, spreading over the whole body bar the face, which became flushed. After three days the rash faded and it could take six weeks for children to recover; that is, if they recovered. Possibly 25% of those afflicted died. In a bad year that could mean 2–300 deaths in Swansea and the L.S.V. As to those who recovered, they often suffered complications such as kidney infections. It was said in later years that scarlatina became epidemic because 'the crowded conditions of houses rendered isolation impossible', and because 'the humbler classes are rather attracted than deterred by the presence of ... disease in a neighbour's house'.

Mortality

It has been estimated 'that over 60% of the labourers and artisans of Swansea' (and presumably the more populous parts of the L.S.V. as well) 'who died between 1845 and 1849, died from some form of epidemic'[3]– cholera, typhoid, typhus, T.B., diphtheria, scarlet fever or smallpox. Infant mortality, of course, 'was high ... more than double that of' rural Gower.[4] It was so high that 'only 54% of the population reached the age of 15'.[5] The majority of those who died below the age of 15 – from 36 to 41% of the total deaths – died before the age of 5. With so many early deaths it is understandable that the 'mean age of death' among the labouring and artisan class was said to be 22 for men and 28 for women; for the gentry it was 39 for men and 46 for women.[6] Yet despite the appalling statistics the population increased dramatically due to the influx of migrant workers, one-third of whom (according to the census of 1841) had been born outside Glamorgan.[7]

Origins

In the report on education (1847) the Commissioner for South Wales stated that:

> my district exhibits the phenomenon of a peculiar language [Welsh] isolating the mass from the upper portion of society ... [also] this mass [is] engaged upon the most opposite occupations ... being on the one side, rude and primitive agriculturalists, living poorly and thinly scattered; on the other smelters and miners, wantoning in plenty and congregated in the densest accumulations. An incessant tide of immigration from the former ... to the latter ... [means that] the families, which are daily passing from the one [country] scene to the other [industrial], do not thereby change their relative position in society. A new field is opened to them, but not a wider [one].
>
> They are never masters; and if the rural portion of them does not grow in numbers [then] the other portion is daily increasing. [They are] still the same people. Whether in the country, or among the furnaces, the Welsh element is never found at the top ... In the country, the farmers are very small holders ... nowise distinguished from labourers. In the works, the Welsh workman never finds his way to the office. He never becomes either clerk or agent [manager]. He may become an overseer or sub-contractor, but this does not take him out of the labouring [class] and put him into the administering class ... his language keeps him under the hatches ... It is a language of old-fashioned agriculture, of theology, and of simple rustic life, while all the world about him is English. He jealously shrinks from holding any communion with classes either superior to, or different from, himself.

The commissioner's statements were, of course, generalizations that did not apply to middle-class Welshmen who were probably bilingual, and who were quite capable of holding responsible jobs in industry – several managers at the Hafod Copperworks were Welsh. The generalizations, however, were applicable to the peasants and industrial workers of South Wales. The generalizations also applied to workers in the L.S.V. where, in 1847, the overwhelming majority of people were either migrants from neighbouring parts of Carmarthenshire and Glamorganshire, or they were the descendants of such migrants. They were for the most part Welsh-speaking, many of them unable to speak more than a few words in English. Their presence in the valley kept the Welsh language and way of life alive long after it had declined in other parts of the Lordship of Gower and Kilvey.

In 1700 the L.S.V. had consisted of farms, fields and woodland with marshy ground adjacent to the River. There were, of course, mining levels with their attendant tips and coal roads to the river banks, but these early mining ventures would not necessarily have dominated the landscape – certainly not enough to prevent the poet, Richard Savage, from devoting 60 lines to his *Delightful Hafod, most serene abode*. His 'delightful' description may have applied to other districts in the valley as well.

By 1750 the early copperworks and the ore vessels leaving with return cargoes of coal had created a demand for labour, and the demand went on increasing, the more so in prosperous times. Almost as if to meet the demand the population of rural Wales had been increasing since Tudor times. For the offspring of farmers – particularly the more numerous smallholders – the outlook was not good. Only the eldest sons stood to inherit their fathers' property, and heirs often found themselves struggling to make a living, whereas the younger sons had to find their own way in the world, and that meant becoming a migrant worker, or joining the ranks of farm labourers.

One would expect that an ever-increasing rural population would find it difficult to find work, even casual work, which should have kept wages low – but that did not happen. The opportunity to migrate to England was there, and no doubt many took advantage of the opportunity, often on a seasonal basis, but many more South Walians migrated to the towns and to the coalfields in South Wales.

In the early part of the 19th century a large proportion of the immigrants in the L.S.V. came from Carmarthenshire where, in 1841, the commissioner Rhys Jones reported that the wages of three farm labourers were 10s., 11s. and 12s. a week, earnings that were on a par with the 10s. paid to the Carmarthenshire collier, Hugh Edwards, that same year. In such circumstances there was little incentive for farm labourers or landless sons to take up employment as colliers, but 13 years later, when the coal industry experienced a period of prosperity, the Vivians had to recruit men for their collieries from Penclawdd, Carmarthenshire and Pembrokeshire offering a wage of around £1 a week, whereas the farm labourer's wages had remained virtually unchanged.

When they arrived in the valley many migrants found shelter in the homes of relatives, or former neighbours from their place of origin. Even if there was no-one familiar to turn to, they would still find themselves amongst people who shared a common language and a common culture. They were likely to experience little difficulty in finding lodgings because householders were only too willing to take in lodgers to supplement the family income. Alternatively, they could rent a home in Swansea's northern suburb, between what is now Kings Street and Greenhill. In time they could build their own homes as squatters, by taking out a loan, or by joining a building club connected with a local chapel. Wherever they settled, migrants would soon experience a sense of belonging, the street, or a straggling row of houses taking the place of the communities from whence they came. So what did the well-to-do English industrialists make of them?

The People

In the report of 1847 persons of note were invited to comment on the districts they were most familiar with. On the East Side, Pascoe St. Leger Grenfell stated that the men were 'generally very respectful' towards their employers, 'staying a long time in the same employ', but they were, in his opinion, 'very ignorant and narrow-minded, with some cunning, and very little appreciation of the truth'; moreover, he considered them to be 'very limited in the extent to which English was understood. Many of the workmen', he said, 'speak none [no English] and those that do, scarcely understand anything beyond the common routine phrases applying to their own station'.

Commenting on how the Welsh managed their finances, Pascoe maintained they did so 'but little; they spend nearly all they get', though they were prudent enough to subscribe to sick-clubs'. As to whether their condition improved in good times, he stated, 'I think not ... as good wages do not make them more prudent or comfortable; for if wages increase, they either work less or drink more'. Sobriety in his opinion was 'at a low ebb, to judge from the immense number of public-houses and beer-shops, and the number of men who may be seen intoxicated'. However, on a more positive note he said 'the dissenting chapels are very well attended generally; great numbers attend funerals, and there is an outward reverence for religious ordinances'.

With regard to women he was somewhat less critical. 'The women,' he said, 'seem hard-working and industrious. I have never seen one intoxicated, nor, among the working-classes out of town, is there much outward evidence of immorality. I am told they are not good managers, dirty in their appearance, and careless of the appearance of their children, and generally very ignorant. I believe generally they are good wives'. As to parental responsibility he stated, 'in this they seem deficient; the children exceedingly dirty, playing all day in the road ... generally looking well fed and sufficiently clothed, the want of shoes and stockings being no sign of poverty'.

Pascoe's answer to the problems that prevailed amongst the Welsh working class was 'to give the rising generation a good knowledge of the English language, by which their views may be extended beyond the narrow circle of which their own language confines them'. His low opinion of the Welsh language was typical of prominent Englishmen; it was a view shared by many prominent Welshmen as well.

Women

Women also migrated to the L.S.V., some with their husbands, some following after them. Some women came on their own initiative; they came in search of employment because, despite the physically demanding work, dirt and danger, employment in a colliery or a copperworks was preferable to domestic service, and for good reason. In industry a woman could earn a wage (albeit an insultingly low one) and could do so in the company of like-minded females without being subservient to an insensitive householder; they also had more time off. The women who came on their own initiative were no doubt rough and ready, well able to hold their own in a physically demanding, male-dominated environment, which is hardly surprising. The Penclawdd cockle-women, the women who hauled limestone from quarries at Oxwich, and many more had been inured to hard work to survive.

Infanticide

For some migrant women a move to the L.S.V. could be traumatic, as evidenced in July 1852 when *The Cambrian* reported on 'a rumour ... that a mother had destroyed her newly-born infant at [Landore during the evening of Friday 2 July]. Information was speedily conveyed to Mr. C. Collins, the coroner, who had a jury summoned to inquire into the cause of death'. The following day an inquiry was held at the Landore Inn. It was stated that the 'mother of the babe was a very good-looking woman, of the name of Mary Davies, but well known in the neighbourhood by the name of Mary Aberystwith [which is presumably where she came from]'.

One witness, 'Mary Matthews, a very intelligent girl of 15 ... deposed that she knew Mary Davies, who was employed helping her wash [bedding, clothes, etc.] in John Matthews's house'. It was stated that Mary Davies had 'complained to the witness of pains, and went out to the garden; in about half-an-hour witness went out after her, [and found her] sitting on the seat of the privy'. The witness then asked Mary Davies 'if the pain had eased'. Mary, who 'looked pale ... said very little', but followed the witness 'towards the house'. The witness entered the house, and 'two or three minutes [later] she heard a child cry, and thought it was the child of Mrs. Jane Matthews (the lady of the house), who had been confined the Tuesday before'. On hearing two screams the witness 'went out to the privy and looked in' to see Mary Davies 'standing with her face towards the seat'. Then the witness ran off to summon help.

John Matthews, on being sworn in, stated that 'he was a copperman, residing at Mile-end; and between eight and nine o'clock on Friday evening, a girl named Matthews [obviously not his daughter] called me as I was lying down with my little boy, and said, "Oh, dear! Get up, and go down to Jane" [his wife], who told him what was the matter. He got up and ran for John Hopkins and Rees Rees [two neighbours], and they all three went into ... the privy, which was at the top of the garden. Witness had a candle with him, and looked down the hole of the privy. He saw the child there, lying on its left side. He saw the child move, but heard no cry. We tried to reach the body, but could not, till ... we got a crow bar, and removed the seat, and Hopkins succeeded in getting the body up; I saw him deliver it to his wife, Mrs. Hopkins. Witness then went to inform the police of Swansea ... After the body was found, Mary Davies was ... in the back kitchen. Mrs. Hopkins said to the prisoner, "What have you done?" She replied, "I was only sitting on the seat." That was everything [John Matthews] heard her say. He observed a little blood on the privy seat, and a little on the front side, but not until it was pointed out to him'.

Mrs. Sarah Rees, Trevivian, widow, stated that Mary 'Davies had lodged at her house about three weeks; she maintained herself ... as [a] charwoman; she had observed [Mary] was in the family way ... and told her ... [so, but Mary had] said she was not'. Mrs. Rees then said that Mary 'was brought back [to the house] by two women in the evening ... She was very ill ... and was put to bed ... Mary Davies, of her own accord, said "she went to John Matthews garden, being there working, and was taken very ill there, and the child fell down the privy, and that she could not move off the seat." ' Mrs. Rees also stated that Mary Davies 'was very poor ... she went out sometimes two or three days in a week, and got 6d. a-day'.

A surgeon deposed that 'he was perfectly satisfied the child breathed after it got into the [night] soil', but despite this statement 'the jury asked for an adjournment for a week, as they were by no means unanimous'. Six days later, when the inquest was resumed, the coroner 'addressed the jury, stating that he himself could not see the least evidence against the mother, [and] the jury, after a very short consultation, acquitted her of any intention of concealment of birth'. The coroner may have been sympathetic towards Mary Davies, but the police were not. When she appeared before the magistrates, the coroner 'said he wished to know what the charge now was against the prisoner? Superintendent Tate said he charged the prisoner with concealment, but the magistrates might, if they considered the evidence ... commit her for manslaughter or murder'. The magistrates, however, were of the opinion that the case 'had been fully investigated by the coroner's jury, and they acquitted her ... on the ground that her accouchment appeared to be somewhat premature'. Consequently, Mary Davies was discharged.

Wedding ceremonies

In was said in the 1842 report that 'cases of bastardy are comparatively trifling; it being usual ... for a youth to marry a girl when discovered to be pregnant by' him. Settlements such as this may have been frequent, but many more young women would have settled for an engagement before taking their vows. So what, then, can be said of wedding ceremonies?

In his history of Llansamlet (1908) W.S. Williams maintained that 'the last Saturday of the month was the special day for the weddings ... Yes, the day for weddings was normally pay-day, and that pay, you may be sure, was given to the young wife, every penny of it'. Arranging a wedding to coincide with a monthly pay-day was common practice among both agricultural and industrial workers. So what kind of wedding arrangements were common practice in the L.S.V.?

Prior to 1837 no marriage (except those uniting Jews or Quakers) was legally binding unless the ceremony had been conducted according to the rubric of the *English Book of Common Prayer*, that it took place in an Anglican Church, and that either banns had been called, or a licence had been obtained from a bishop or a surrogate clergyman. Yet despite these rulings, a large proportion of the working population is believed to have settled for any one of a number of common-law unions, which were mistakenly believed to be legal, and which were often trial unions in that they could be terminated within the first year.

In 1836 Parliament compiled new legislation, which was enacted the following year. The Dissenters' Marriage Act permitted Nonconformists and Catholics to marry in their respective places of worship, whereas the Marriage Act permitted couples to marry with the minimum of expense and without a religious ceremony. In the case of the latter, the bride had only to put on her best dress, turn up at a registry office and leave with a certificate – her marriage lines. As a result of the new legislation the number of common-law unions gradually decreased.

It is unfortunate that *The Cambrian* is silent about the festivities that accompanied working class weddings. A bidding wedding, for example, certainly took place in the upper valley in 1838, and a wedding of this sort at Llanrhidian is referred to in *The Cambrian* in 1870, but there is no hint of similar festivities in the L.S.V. That is not to say that festivities of this sort did not take place – it simply reflects the fact that working class weddings were not newsworthy events. Indeed, the bidding wedding that took place at Llanrhidian in 1870 only appeared in *The Cambrian* because one of the organizers had been charged for selling alcohol without a licence.

Drinking, of course, was an integral part of the festivities connected with both weddings and the creation of common-law unions. One interesting commentary relating to drink and a South Walian common-law union states that some women 'procure a man to wed them privately, which will not cost above two or three mugs of ale. Sometimes half a dozen couples will agree to a merry meeting and are thus wedded and bedded together. This they call the '"little wedding" and is frequently made use of among miners and others to make sure of a woman ... The little wedding does not bind them so effectively [as a church wedding], but after a month's trial they may part by consent ... and the girl is not worse looked upon among the miners than if she had been an unspotted virgin, so prevalent and arbitrary is the custom'.

Marriage

In law the age of consent was 12, and remained so until 1875 when it was raised to 13. A girl might, therefore, marry in her early teens, although in early Victorian times the average age of a bride was 23; for a groom it was 25. Prior to marriage a woman could inherit property. After marriage, any property she had – including any money she earned – became her husband's; he could do with it as he pleased – unless her parents had insisted on a marriage settlement to safeguard her interests. These points of law would have been important to those of means, but whether they were recognized by working class women is debateable. In the South Wales Coalfield (including the L.S.V.) it appears to have been general practice for colliers to hand over most, or all of their wages to the wife (after the truck shop had deducted what was owing to them). The wife, therefore, handled the finances.

Equally debateable is to what extent working class women would have acknowledged the concept of separate spheres. Men had always regarded themselves as head of their households, but according to the concept of separate spheres his role was to provide for his family and, if his rank in society permitted it, to take part in public life. His wife's role was confined to the home and to caring for their children. The concept also had a religious aspect in that the wife was expected to espouse the virtues of godliness, respectability, cleanliness and thriftiness.

The concept originated in the early 19th century among the middle classes in English towns and cities. By 1850 the concept is said to have taken root in Wales. The religious aspect was certainly promoted by middle-class Welsh Nonconformists after 1847, the year in which statements in *The Report on the State of Education in Wales* criticized the morals of working class Welsh women. Consequently, the virtues of godliness, etc., were taken up by working class chapel-goers. And so, with a Bible at hand and her house spotless, the archetypical Welsh *mam* was born.

Of course, a large proportion of the population had no religious convictions. So the virtue of godliness would have been irrelevant to them. Cleanliness would appear to have been general, but thriftiness was not one of the virtues of L.S.V. women, as several commentators make it plain they were 'bad managers'.

A bride could expect a lifetime of unremitting work and repeated pregnancies. Her most backbreaking tasks involved carrying water from the nearest well, stream or canal, then heating it so that husband, sons and lodgers could have a bath at the end of a shift; added to which, hot water was required for washing clothes and bedding by hand. As a wife she could be pregnant a dozen times or more, only to find that half the pregnancies might end in miscarriages or stillbirths, due to hard work and heavy lifting. If six children survived birth, then at least one of them would die during infancy. If her husband died, or was out of work, then she faced destitution.

So what, then, was a woman to do? *The Cambrian* voiced complaints of 'systematic begging, especially by children, from door to door daily', but there is nothing as shocking as the report on an inquest held in London in 1850. In November that year *The Times* reported on the death of a 38-year-old man whose body was little more than a skeleton, and whose wife was described as being 'the very personification of want', and her child as a 'skeleton infant'.[8] It is likely that L.S.V. residents were far too watchful of their neighbours to be unaware of an extreme case of destitution; nor are they likely to have been uncaring about a desperate family's plight. They were certainly aware of what went on around them in Morriston in 1893, for in that year *The Cambrian* reported on an incident in which about 70 women stoned the house of a man who refused to work and support his daughter.[10]

Funerals

When someone lay sick or injured it was common practice for neighbours to relieve distraught wives and mothers of the burden of constant attendance and ongoing chores. When someone died the body would be kept at home, and the windows of neighbouring dwellings would often have their blinds drawn as a mark of respect. A carpenter would call to take measurements for a coffin. Many more would call, expressing sympathy, but the most important callers were those whom N.L. Thomas described in *The Story of Swansea's Districts and Villages* as 'friends and neighbours [who] came of one accord to clean the cottage, answer the door to callers, accept flowers and make a list of donors. They fetched and carried for the bereaved and demonstrated their sympathy in a kind but practical manner'. These friends and neighbours also washed the body and attended the wake.

It is unfortunate that working class funerals were rarely newsworthy events, but what happened was not that different from what took place in living memory. If the deceased had had religious convictions, a short service might be held within the home. The coffin would then be brought out and, as everyone walked – miles if need be – the coffin might be carried on a bier.

This is evidenced by a reference in *The Cambrian*, dated 1846, to 'four men, residing in Vivian's Town', proceeding (on the day before a funeral) 'to Llansamlet Church for a bier, on which to convey the body of a young woman'. The relatives took their place behind the pall bearers and, with everyone else following in procession, proceeded either to the burial ground of a church or chapel, or, after 1856, to the municipal cemetery at Dan-y-graig. A service followed, after which the men would indulge in a drink.

Pascoe St. Leger Grenfell stated, in 1847, that 'great numbers attend funerals'. This was certainly the case when the deceased had been a member of a benefit society. In 1839, for example, *The Cambrian* reported on an Odd Fellows funeral that took place in Neath.

> At two o'clock [several lodges of the society] assembled ... at the Plume and Feathers, Water Street, [to accompany the body of] a young man, [a member] of the Owen Glyndwr Lodge, [one who] was universally respected by those who knew him ... The procession moved at three o'clock to the solemn tune of a mourning peal. [Numbering] about 350 [men, the Brethren walked two abreast. In the lead were members of the] White Hart Benefit Society, [followed by three lodges of Odd Fellows, the Brethren of which wore] sprigs of thyme, black silk scarfs and white gloves. [They were followed by] The Body, bourne by four Odd Fellows, who were intimate friends of [the] deceased, and twelve friends ... bearing pall. Then came the Relatives and crowds of persons ... about 3,500.
>
> When the procession reached Cadoxton it divided and let the corpse and relatives pass between, the rear of the procession filing off after them. The service was read by the Rev. D.H. Griffith ... the funeral address was delivered by N.G. Close, and when he concluded, the Brethren walked round the gave, each dropping in a sprig of thyme, in token of esteem for their departed brother. The procession again formed, conducting the relatives to their door, and letting them pass through'. [This was some funeral for a working man.]

Ethnic minorities

The Irish had been coming to Swansea and South Wales in ever-increasing numbers from *c.*1780 onwards. They obviously came by sea, though not necessarily to ports such as Swansea, as that would have placed ships' masters on the wrong side of the authorities. One of the earliest recorded disembarkations locally is to be found in *The Cambrian*, which reported in March 1851 that 'a master of a vessel landed a party of Irish at Mumbles this week, having brought them over ... for 2s. each'. These people were 'in a state of great destitution', due to the potato famine of 1845–9; that troubled the authorities because they could be a burden to the parish.

As migrant workers the Irish usually took up employment as unskilled labourers. Whether they took up this form of employment out of choice, or because they had been excluded from better-paid occupations is debateable. That they were easily identifiable by their accents – or even their Gaelic language – and the fact that they were overwhelmingly Catholic may have set them apart from the local Welsh, who were overwhelmingly Welsh-speaking and Nonconformists. In some parts of South Wales these differences – coupled with the belief that the Irish, by their willingness to accept low wages, were a threat to existing wage rates and job opportunities – sometimes led to violent clashes, as at Pontypool in 1834.

In 1826 a Swansea magistrate, Lewis Weston Dillwyn, noted in his diary: 'Drove to Swansea chiefly on Magisterial business to protect some Irishmen who have been employed in the Rose

Copperworks, and who the other men have violently driven off. Committed the two chief offenders ... to hard labour'. Two years later the same magistrate noted that all the Irishmen had been driven out of the local copperworks.

By the time of the 1841 census (the first to record occupations) Irishmen were once more in the employ of copper masters, but their number was small. The 1841 census for Swansea (where the majority of Irish immigrants lived in the Greenhill-Dyfatty area) records only eight coppermen and two miners with Irish surnames. The 1847 report on education confirms that there were 'few ... Irish' in the Hafod workforce. Those few must have travelled to work from the Greenhill-Dyfatty area because, according to the census for 1851, there was only one Irish-born resident in the parish of St. John – which is where the Hafod Works were situated – and that resident was a copperman.

At the time of the 1861 census there were no Irish-born residents in St. John's, but there were 21 at Mile End (Landore), 14 of whom were employed in the local copperworks. The largest Irish family was the Shehans, which comprised of Richard Shehan, a copperworks' labourer, his wife, Margaret, their six children and one grandchild. Richard's three eldest sons were also copperworks' labourers. Next door to the Shehans lived the Casey family, which comprised of Michael Casey, copperman, his wife, Catherine, and their two young children, both of whom had been born in the parish of Llangyfelach. Five Irish-born men bearing the surname Clancy were also to be found at three different dwellings in the same locality, four of whom were coppermen.

In the report of 1847 it states that there were 'few English' in the Hafod workforce and, presumably, in the L.S.V. as well. Some of the Englishmen would have been managers who lived near their works, but the majority of English workers came from the copper-ore counties of Cornwall and Devon. These migrant workers are likely to have come over on the copper-ore vessels, but unlike the Irish, they would not have encountered discrimination from the authorities. With regard to religion, the presence of a Wesleyan Methodist chapel in Wern Road, Landore (1860–1) is not only evidence of English-speaking residents in that locality, but it suggests that many of these residents were from Cornwall and Devon, as both counties were Wesleyan strongholds.

That said, the census returns from 1851 onwards record people's place of birth, be it a country such as Ireland, a city such as Bristol, or a county such as Cornwall. In the parish of St. John, for example, the 1851 census records that, out of a population of 1,215, the overwhelming majority of residents were born either in the parish itself, or in some other part of South Wales. The largest non-Welsh minority were from the West Country – 21 of whom were Cornish-born and another nine had been born in Devon. Ten years later there were 55 Cornish-born and 55 Devon-born residents in the parish, and their numbers went on increasing to the extent that a Cornish denomination known as the Bible Christians established a chapel on Neath Road, Trevivian, in 1873.

Few West Country residents were employed in coal mining and copper smelting – the 1851 census for the parish of St. John records only one miner, two coppermen and one lead and silver smelter. However, unlike the Irish who tended to congregate in the Greenhill-Dyfatty area of Swansea, the West Country migrants were dispersed throughout the parish. The Cornish-born residents in the 1851 and 1861 censuses bore names such as Sampson, Champion, Grenfell, Williams and even Morgans, whereas the Devon-born residents had names such as Gough, Larkin and Beer. Hancock appears to have been a name common to both counties.

In 1867 H. Hussey Vivian took control of the old Forest Copperworks. In January the following year it was reported that he had converted the Forest Works into a 'zinc or spelter works, and that he expected 30 German workmen [to arrive] with his (German) manager, Mr Daehne'. This is perhaps the only specific reference to the arrival of continental workers in the L.S.V., but there were others because the Germans had developed a process for smelting zinc that was far more efficient than the English process. The German (Silesian) process required a skilled workforce as furnace temperatures were critical. Skilled furnacemen were also required for the Belgian process, which was technically even more advanced than the Silesian.

Furnaces suitable to both continental processes had been installed at the old Birmingham Copperworks by 1848, but only furnaces connected with the English process were in operation there at that time. Three years later, the 1851 census for the Morriston area (which is where the Birmingham Spelterworks were situated) records the names of many British-born spelter smelters in the township, but no German or Belgian-born speltermen. Ten years later, the 1861 census reveals there were 71 speltermen residing in Morriston, the majority of them British-born. The same census also records the presence of 19 Belgian-born residents in the township, most of whom – 16 in all – lived in just one dwelling on Neath Road. The dwelling contained three families with seven children between them, and three male lodgers. All the lodgers and the three heads of households were spelter smelters; a seventh Belgian spelterman lived in another street. The other three Belgians – two of them speltermen – lived in the barracks of the former Lower Forest Rolling-mills.

It is likely that most, if not all the speltermen in the Morriston area were employed at the old Birmingham Copperworks (which the Vivians had converted to spelter production in 1841) as the only other spelter works on the west bank at that time was Dillwyn's Landore Silver & Spelter Works, where production was geared 'chiefly for the sake of silver'. On the East Side (in 1861) there were upwards of 20 speltermen, all of them British-born, and all of them living within walking distance of Dillwyn's Cambrian/Llansamlet (spelter) Works. It would appear, therefore, from the patchy evidence that is available, that Belgian speltermen and their dependents had already settled in the valley at least seven years before the arrival of the 30 German workmen in 1868. Although the number of continental workers in the valley was small at that date, thereafter the number increased significantly.

Some of the Belgian-born speltermen who, in 1861, resided at a house on Neath Road, Morriston, had surnames such as Benjamin, Goes and Gaillard. Benjamin is a surname that can be found more than a dozen times in today's telephone directory, as is Gillard, which could be a variant spelling of Gaillard, but it has to be said that a John Gillard was listed as a Swansea burgess 26 years earlier. Interestingly, Emile Gaillard (or Jaillard Domier) lived at the Neath Road address with his wife and two children in 1861. Ten years later he was a foreman spelterman, residing at the same address. He was described as married, but no other family members were recorded as living with him, just one Belgian-born lodger. Equally interesting is that the name Dahne also appears in today's telephone directory; it is a variant spelling of Daehne, the surname of the Vivians' German manager. The 1871 census records that 'Dahne' (the manager) lived in Church Street (now Morfydd Street) Morriston with his Morriston-born wife, Elizabeth Ann, their five children, a governess and two servants.

Collieries in 1854

Hunt's *Mineral Statistics of the United Kingdom* names nine coal producers operating in the L.S.V. in 1854. On the East Side, C.H. Smith owned the Llansamlet Colliery, and Messrs. Davey & Pegg were proprietors of Birchgrove Colliery. The west bank producers were Jones & Davies (Clase), D.H. Rees (Townhill), William Jones (Trewyddfa), Gregor & Co. (Weegfach) and Major C. Phillips (Millwood in Cwmbwrla). The biggest producers on the west bank were the Swansea Coal Co., owners of Cwm Level, Mynydd Newydd, Pentrefelen and Tyrcenol collieries; and Messrs. Richard & Glasbrook, owners of Weeg (fawr), Gorse and Landore collieries. Both these last-named companies are worthy of mention in some detail.

The Swansea Coal Co.

Dependency on John Morris II for coal was not an ideal situation as far as John Henry Vivian was concerned. Unfortunately, there was no hope of him mining his own coal, as all mineral leases relating to the west bank had long been in the hands of a number of coal producers. Perhaps what really bothered him was the fact that coal reserves on the west bank would not last forever. By 1837 the need to exploit reserves further afield was already apparent to the Penyvilia Vein Co., and for that company to extend its operations a huge investment of capital was required. That gave John Henry an opportunity to involve himself in coal mining. In collaboration with J.T. Foster of the Morfa Copperworks he bought a controlling interest in the Penyvilia Vein Co. Two years later he and Michael Williams (who had taken J.T. Foster's place as the representative of the Morfa concern) renamed their coal interests the Swansea Coal Co. Between 1840 and the early 1850s the company took over all the mineral leases that had been held by John Morris II.

The main aim of the Swansea Coal Co. was to 'work collieries for the supply of their own [copper] works'. By 1844 the company had two new collieries in operation. One of them, the Pentrefelen (or Penrhiwfelen) Colliery, was situated on the edge of Morriston golf course. From this colliery to the Swansea Canal the company laid a 1½-mile-long self-acting incline-plane, which consisted of two parallel tramlines laid close together, but separated at a point midway along their length to allow trams to pass in opposite directions. The trams on both lines were linked by a steel cable which, at the top of the incline, passed round a drum. Thus the weight of loaded trams descending to the canal, pulled empty trams to the top of the incline. Self-acting incline-planes had been in use in the L.S.V. since the mid-18th century, but what was remarkable about this one was its length – 1½ miles. At the bottom of the incline the coal was loaded onto canal barges, then taken south to feed the Forest and Rose Copperworks, whereas any surplus would have been taken to the harbour. The Pentrefelen Colliery and its incline proved to be a successful undertaking, and remained so until the colliery closed in 1893. However, the other new colliery opened at that time is better known and even more remarkable.

Mynydd Newydd Colliery and its Incline

Situated at Penplas (about ½ mile north of Caereithin traffic lights), the Mynydd Newydd Colliery proved to be the Swansea Coal Company's most productive undertaking. The pit was sunk in 1842–4, principally to provide coal for the Hafod Copperworks. At a depth of 348 feet the five-foot coal seam was exploited first. An accident in which a man fell to his death suggests that, initially, the men had to descend or ascend the 348 feet by way of ladders, a strenuous climb at

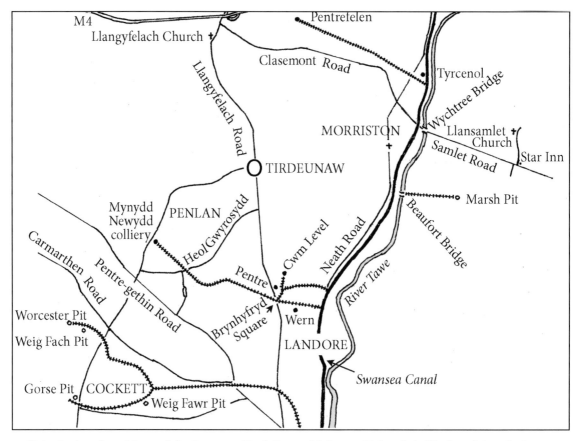

Principal undertakings of the Swansea Coal Co. and Messrs. Richard & Glasbrook in relation to modern roads; also the tramroads connected with these collieries. The former company produced coal mainly for the smelters; the latter for export.

the end of a 12-hour shift. Cages were soon installed, and by 1845 the six-feet seam was struck at a depth of 774 feet. By 1887 the three-foot seam was worked at 813 feet, and by 1914 the two-foot seam was productive at 930 feet.

During the early years there were several explosions in which men were killed or injured, although in each case the number of fatalities was small. These explosions were almost entirely due to men refusing to use safety lamps, preferring the better light provided by candles. In later years it was claimed that, in 1844, five men were burnt to death in an explosion, although there is no official record of this occurrence. Whatever the truth, it was said that this explosion led to a group of men approaching management with an unusual request:

> On Monday morning, the 18th August [1845], in the Mynydd Newydd Colliery ... a Prayer Meeting was held underground. About 100 people were present. Their agent, Mr. Daniel, was favourably inclined to the event and promised them every support. They intended to hold the meeting every Monday morning at 6 o'clock ... How fine to think of so many men starting the week's work with prayer ... It is said that not a swear-word was heard throughout the day.

The first Bible to be used at those early prayer meetings was purchased from a bookshop in High Street, Swansea; a boy, Stephen Hughes, being sent there to pick it up on a Saturday evening. The prayer meetings led to the construction of a chapel in the six-foot seam, and at a later date the five-foot seam had its own chapel as well (between 1908-10 this latter chapel had to be abandoned due to 'creeps' (see below) and a new chapel was built in another part of the seam). The two chapels were caverns fitted out with wooden benches and pulpits, the walls white-washed and, therefore, reflective of the candlelight that provided illumination. The Monday morning services lasted for an hour and were conducted by deacons. Prayers, readings from scriptures and the voices of men, singing in Welsh, must have echoed throughout the pitch-black passageways of the mine.

However, not everyone attended or approved of these prayer meetings. On one occasion there were complaints about how the services affected both output and the wages of those who did not attend. The complaints were understandable: the rules were 'that nothing was to be moved during the service. The horses were not even harnessed until the service was over'. The complaints were dismissed as those who attended the services had the full support of management, ultimately of the Vivians themselves. Underground chapels were rarely to be found in mines, but they were not rare in collieries owned by the Swansea Coal Co. Mynydd Newydd had two underground chapels. Tyrcenol (Tir-canol), Morriston, had one, and in 1871 it was recorded that, at Pentre, prayer meetings were held underground, but there is no reference to the existence of a chapel at this pit.

Explosions may have been uppermost in the minds of those who prayed at Mynydd Newydd, but many accidents at the colliery were due to roof falls, particularly in the five-foot seam. The ground immediately above this seam comprised of blue clift and this, coupled with the existence of 'pans', made roof falls inevitable. A pan, when it collapsed, left a hole the shape of an upturned pan; it could collapse without warning, bringing down debris and rocks on unwary colliers. The five-foot seam was also subject to 'creeps', which occurred when the soft shale underfoot heaved upwards. The colliers had then to cut away the swelling to allow traffic to move freely. There were, of course, numerous other ways in which men could suffer injury or death, but it has to be said that conditions at Mynydd Newydd were probably no worse than at any other colliery – if anything, they were probably better, as the Swansea Coal Co. had the resources to avoid cutting corners.

Boulders as well as pans were responsible for roof falls. On 23 November 1860 *The Cambrian* reported:

> A man named Dd. Roberts, who was employed [at] 'The Gorse' [colliery] lost his life whilst engaged in ... cutting coal ... by an immense stone, weighing upwards of three tons, falling on him, killing him instantaneously. The poor fellow was immediately taken from under the immense mass, most fearfully crushed, and was conveyed ... home. He unfortunately leaves a widow and four young children totally unprovided for.

To convey coal from Mynydd Newydd to the Swansea Canal the company laid a two-mile-long tramroad. The tramroad from the pit passed over fairly level ground for about a mile, so horses were used to pull the trams. From roughly what is now Llangorse Road, Penlan, a half-mile, self-acting incline-plane operated on the steep hillside to Brynhyfryd Square (much of its route survives as a footpath known as 'the Incline'). From the square the tramroad continued on down to join the Swansea Canal below Pwll Street. At an unknown date prior to 1877, the tramroad at the bottom of the incline was diverted to Pentre Pit, where a much older incline was used to convey Mynydd Newydd coal to the canal. In 1899 a W.W. Moore wrote of his experience when, as a passenger on his way to Mynydd Newydd, he was conveyed up the incline in an empty tram.

> Mynydd Newydd is ... situated on a barren hilltop ... My visit was on a tempestuous day, and as I took advantage of the facilities afforded by a surprising and novel means of locomotion, I met with what is conveniently termed 'an experience.' To save the trudge ... up the steep hillside above the grim suburb of Landore ... the visitor ensconces himself in one of a string of empty iron coal trains. This suddenly starts up the steep hillside with tremendous velocity, drawn by a steel cable from a winding-drum three-quarters of a mile above. About the middle of your wild flight skywards you pass a heavily-laden railway truck coming down on the other track. It is your motor, for it is by its weight that you are taken upwards in a series of startling jumps. The cable glides over the big iron pulleys fixed in the middle of the track, sometimes in the groove, sometimes out, grinding and roaring past obstructions, or giving the wheels sudden impulses, and the newcomer feels that his life is not worth a moment's purchase till he finds himself on terra firma at the winding-house above.
>
> Here, before a roaring fire, and in the midst of a group of waiting colliers who are going up to the pit's mouth, you await the departure of the next [horse-drawn tram] and being hauled aboard this, you cover the rest of the distance to the pit.

No collier village sprang up in the vicinity of Mynydd Newydd. From what W.W. Moore had to say it seems obvious that many of the colliers came from the Brynhyfryd-Landore area and travelled to work on the incline, but other sources make it plain they came from as far afield as Fforestfach and Morriston. As to how many worked at Mynydd Newydd, it was recorded in 1891 that 144 men were employed underground and a further 55 worked on the surface. The number is likely to have doubled during the boom years of the Edwardian era.

Unfenced tramroads were a danger to all, particularly young children, as evidenced by an entry in *The Cambrian*, which, in June 1853, recorded an inquest held

> at the Collier's Arms, Penyvilia ... on the body of Mary Griffiths, aged three years. From the statement of David John, a collier in the employ of the Swansea Coal Company, it was his duty to received the loaded coal waggons as they were sent down the incline from the Mynyddnewydd colliery. [He stated that on] Thursday afternoon ... I had four waggons at the foot of the incline, which I hooked on to the chains and gave the usual signal. I then went into the coal yard. On hearing the waggons move [a half hour later] I came out of the yard [and] saw the deceased under the last of the four waggon, which [had] passed over her. I picked the child up, it was not quite dead, but died within 10 minutes afterwards. The wheels [had] passed over the small of the back ... The jury returned a Verdict of Accidental death.

The Swansea Coal Co. (2) dissolved

During the early years of its existence the Swansea Coal Co. built up a huge mineral estate of some 3,000 acres. Within this estate there were numerous collieries, many of which had been worked by John Morris II. Once the new Pentrefelen and Mynydd Newydd collieries were producing, the company had no need to continue working all the old levels and pits, many of which were near exhaustion, though coal could still be gleaned from them by small producers. So the company sub-leased many of the old collieries to up-and-coming producers such as Messrs. Richard & Glasbrook. By 1854 – according to Hunt's *Mineral Statistics* – the company worked only Pentrefelen, Mynydd Newydd, Cwm Level (Landore) and Tyrcenol (Morriston) – in fact it also worked Pentre (Brynhyfryd) and Cathelid (Cwm Clydach)

In *c*.1863 the Swansea Coal Company was dissolved by mutual consent, its assets shared between the principal partners. William, Foster & Co., owners of the Morfa Copperworks, had Tyrcenol, whereas Vivian & Sons took possession of the other collieries, including Townsend's Engine Pit, alias Calland's, which prevented many pits in the area from flooding. By 1926 only Mynydd Newydd and Calland's were still functioning; everything else had either been sold or closed down. These last two installations the Vivians sold to a local syndicate. Unfortunately, the syndicate could not afford to keep the pumps at Calland's going. So they closed it down, and one by one the remaining pits in the area were flooded.

When water broke into the six-foot seam at Mynydd Newydd in 1929 there was a last minute scramble to get the horses out. The two men responsible for 'boxing' the horses were almost overwhelmed by the rapidly rising flood water. The five-foot seam continued to yield coal until 1933, by which time the owners were heavily in debt. The miners were persuaded to work without wages for several weeks in the hope that the situation might improve, but these were the Depression years. The end was, therefore, inevitable and 200 men were thrown out of work.

Tyrcenol

Tyrcenol, alias Tir Canol, was an old pit, sunk in the late 18th century. Located behind the present-day fire station on Sway Road, Morriston, it was therefore near the Swansea Canal. In *c*.1833 the colliery became idle and remained so until 1844, when the Swansea Coal Co. made use of it to work coal seams at a much greater depth. After the Swansea Coal Co. was dissolved *c*.1863, Tyrcenol became the property of Williams, Foster & Co. until 1870 when they sold it to Messrs. Richard & Glasbrook. The pit closed in 1875.

Messrs Richard & Glasbrook

The Swansea Coal Co. no sooner had its new collieries in operation than a new consortium began to make its presence known. This was Messrs. Richard & Glasbrook, the proprietors being Philip Richard (1813-76) and his brother-in-law, John Glasbrook (1816-87). Little can be said of Philip Richard other than his mining ventures. John Glasbrook, on the other hand, came from a Llangyfelach family of farming stock. In 1851 his father held some 230 acres to the north-west of Morriston, and was described as a farmer with six labourers in his employ. John was usually referred to as 'of Brynwillach', which was the name of the estate on which his father's holdings lay. During his ascendancy as a coal master, John became the owner or occupier of many residences, the most notable being Morfydd House, Morriston (though not the later build that stands today) and also owned

Russel House, Swansea, and Norton House, West Cross, where he died in 1887. John become a J.P. and was Mayor of Swansea in 1871-2. As a borough councillor he proved to be outspoken and controversial.

In the 1860s there were moves to set up a public library in Swansea. As a town councillor John Glasbrook was totally opposed to the idea on the grounds that 'people have too much knowledge already; it was much easier to manage them twenty years ago; the more education people get the more difficult they are to manage'. Then, in July 1868, a meeting was held in Swansea to ascertain whether the ratepayers were prepared to pay a penny rate for the establishment of a public library. The Morriston ratepayers were not happy about the imposition on the ground that a library would be of no benefit to them. John saw this as an opportunity to block the proposal. He arranged for the Morriston ratepayers to be taken to Swansea in three canal barges. It was even suggested that he had promised free beer if they voted against the proposals. The Morriston men did a fine job, disrupting proceedings with their heckling to the extent that the meeting was adjourned – for two years, as it turned out.

Messrs. Richard and Glasbrook first appear in the mid-1840s as a partnership that took over many of the older collieries in the Morriston and Landore areas, collieries that were near exhaustion, but which gave Richard & Glasbrook a foothold in the coal industry from which they were able to develop new collieries beyond the limits of the L.S.V.

One of their first new collieries was Marsh Pit, which, sited on the low ground on the East Side (directly opposite the Forest Copperworks) began yielding coal in c.1846. Another early venture was Gorse Pit, situated near today's Dylan Thomas School, Cockett. Gorse Pit began yielding coal in 1848. That same year the partners applied for permission to lay a tramroad down Cwm Burlais to the Strand. The line followed the same route as John Morris's earlier tramroad of 1790 (lifted in 1839). From roughly what is now Cwmbwrla roundabout a self-acting incline-plane was laid on the southern side of Carmarthen Road, all the way up to the Cwmdu Industrial Estate. Above the incline, a horse-drawn tramroad curved to the south to arrive at Gorse Colliery. This tramroad also served the Weig-fawr Pit (situated near Weig-fawr farm), which the partners also opened (or reopened) at about the same time. Coal from both the Gorse and Weig-fawr pits was destined mainly for export.

It was not unusual for partners to work independently in pursuit of other ventures. This would appear to have been the case in 1849, when Philip Richard drove a level into the slopes of Graig-y-bedw, some two miles up the Dulais Valley, near Pontardulais. The undertaking was small-scale until, in 1868, John Glasbrook opened another colliery nearby, at the same time laying a tramroad to link up with the main line to Swansea's South Dock. This later colliery proved to be very successful.

Another successful venture of the partners – the result of a three-year sinking operation – was the Forest New Pit, Morriston, which began yielding coal in 1860. Between 1863–6 John Glasbrook's brother, Thomas, sank the Worcester Pit (on the upper part of what later became the Fforestfach Trading Estate) and a branch tramroad from this pit ran eastwards to join, at Cwmdu, the incline mentioned above. In 1870 Thomas also worked Weig-fach Pit in the same area. This pit would have been the Weegfach owned by Gregor & Co. in 1854, which they sold two years later.

Philip Richard's death in 1876 may have brought the partnership to an end, but both families continued to be involved in coal mining, opening up some of the most successful collieries within the Lordship of Gower. Prior to his death, Philip Richard appears to have initiated mining operations at Dunvant and in Clyne Valley. His son and namesake, Philip Richard II, certainly took over mining operations in both these areas; he succeeded to the Worcester and Weig Fawr collieries as well. In 1870 John Glasbrook and his sons opened up Garn Goch No.1 Pit, but as this and the later No.2 and 3 pits lay outside the L.S.V. they will be dealt with in a subsequent publication.

The Copperworks in 1851

According to *The Swansea Guide, 1851,* 'the number of "calciners" and "furnaces," used for smelting copper, has been estimated at 550 in round numbers'. The number of copperworks remained the same, but the ownership of some had changed.
On the East Side:

> White Rock was still owned by John Freeman & Copper Co.
> Middle Bank by Pascoe Grenfell & Sons
> Upper Bank by Pascoe Grenfell & Sons, which they took over from
> Muntz Patent Metal Co. Ltd. in *c.*1850.

On the west bank:

> Hafod was still owned by Vivian & Sons
> Morfa was likewise still owned by Williams, Foster & Co. who also owned Rose (since 1828)
> Landore, which they took over in 1840
> Forest was owned by Messrs J.H. Vivian and Michael Williams (of Morfa), who acquired
> the works as a private venture in 1851.

Output at six of the above works was devoted to copper smelting, whereas Upper Bank appears to have been both a copperworks and a spelterworks (producing '*yellow metal*'). The Hafod Works were involved in the production of copper, silver and gold, whereas the old Birmingham Works (which the Vivians acquired in 1841) had been converted for the production of yellow metal. How all these companies fared in relation to one another is difficult to ascertain, but by 1851 the Vivians and the Williams, Foster concerns were each smelting around 27 to 28% of the copper-ore shipped into Swansea, whereas the Grenfells (owners of both Upper and Middle Bank from *c.*1850) and Freemans (White Rock) were each using around 15% of the imported ore.

The Vivians (2) diversification

Copper smelting may have been the prime concern of the Vivians, but they were also involved in other profit-making ventures. In the 1830s, for example, John Henry Vivian established a small fleet of fast sailing ships, the vessels running from the Hafod Works – where they appear to have had a shipping office – to destinations such as Liverpool (where they had another office), London and Rouen. The earliest vessels were smacks (such as the 40-ton *Sarah* and the 56-ton *Eliza*) and schooners (such as the 74-ton *Henry* and the 86-ton *Brothers*). In the 1850s and '60s they were employing steam ships such as the 379-ton *Morfa* and the *Augusta* for voyages to France, Spain, Cuba and Chile. It is likely that the Vivian fleet was primarily engaged in company business, and that costs were offset by extending the service to paying customers. It has been said that the Vivian vessels resembled private yachts, with their brasses highly polished and the officers dressed in smart uniforms.

Henry Hussey Vivian (1822-94) – born at Singleton Abbey, the eldest son of J.H. Vivian, he became a partner in Vivian & Sons in 1842 when he took up an appointment as manager of the firm's Liverpool office. Three years later he became managing-partner of the Hafod Works. Hussey proved to be an industrial giant, an enlightened employer and was probably the most compassionate member of the Vivian family. He had a keen interest in his Park le Breos estate, where he kept a model farm and had a reputation as a stock breeder. A staunch Liberal, he was elected M.P. for Truro (Cornwall) in 1852, M.P. for Glamorgan in 1857, and M.P. for Swansea and District in 1885. In 1889 he became the first Chairman of the newly formed Glamorgan County Council. He became a baronet in 1882, and eleven years later he was elevated to the peerage, taking the title of Lord Swansea. He died of heart failure at the age of 73.

Mention has already been made of John Henry's involvement in coal mining, and his involvement in the production of yellow metal will be considered in due course, but his eldest son, Henry Hussey, was to make diversification one of his prime objectives, for at a later stage in life he wrote, 'I had seen the success of our neighbours, the Williams, who were engaged in a variety of undertakings and I resolved if possible to emulate them'. In 1845, at the age of 24, Hussey took over the management of the Hafod Works. The following year he 'erected a silver mill [at the Hafod] there being a considerable quantity of silver found in the different foreign ores' that were shipped into Swansea at that time. In 1850 he involved himself in the production of gold. By 1854 the side of the business that was not directly involved in copper smelting amounted to half the firm's total profits.

When John Henry died in 1855 his four sons succeeded to the business as shareholders, but the eldest, Henry Hussey, retained overall control of the Hafod Works. Under Hussey's direction the company addressed the problem

Right: *The northern and southern complexes of the Hafod Works, 1879 – A marks the entrance to the northern/copperworks complex; B the entrance to the southern/diversified complex. C is the approximate position of the ruinous engine houses that can be seen today. D marks the site of the Sulphuric Acid Chambers (situated on top of the original riverside slag tip), E the incline railway that took slag to the later tip (now the site of Pentrehafod School), F the Phosphate Works, G the Hafod Isha Nickel and Cobalt Works, and H the Hafod Foundry. The Hafod Sawmills were sited below the bottom edge of the map.*

(West Glamorgan Archive Service)

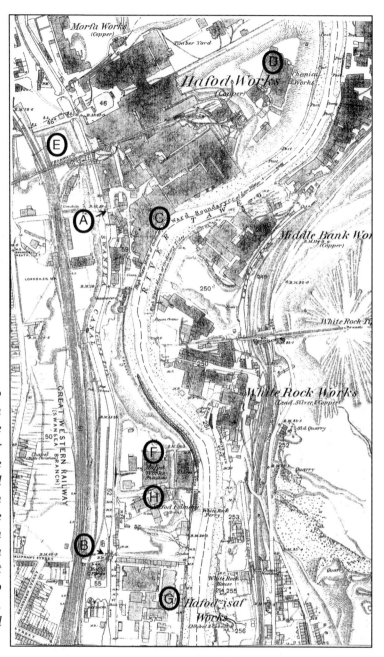

Opposite bottom: *One of two surviving engine houses – built in c.1860-3 to house a steam engine that provided the necessary power to operate the Hafod's riverside copper rolling-mills. Incorporated in its walls are the remains of an earlier engine house of 1842. The darker, upper brickwork with the ventilation apertures is of a later period (the 1890s) when it was necessary to raise the roof to accommodate an internal crane. The chimney stack is unconnected with the engine house.*

of smoke pollution. For years the Vivians had tried – unsuccessfully – to tackle the problem, and for years people had unsuccessfully taken them to court for loss or damage caused by smoke. Then, in *c.*1864 (when the old riverside slag-tip had long been superseded by a new tip on the site of the present-day Pentrehafod School) the problem was, in part, solved by 'the adoption of the Gersten-höfer [blast] furnaces', which gradually replaced the old calciners. Smoke from these new furnaces was directed into flues that took it up 'the old [riverside] slag banks, which had been levelled at the top [to form a] flat area on which had been erected immense wooden structures whose internal sides and tops' had been lined with lead. In these 20-foot high chambers the fumes of copper smoke were converted into sulphuric acid. Consequently, not only had the L.S.V. been relieved of the worst effects of toxic smoke, but the fumes had been converted into a profitable by-product. In time Gerstenhöfer (blast) furnaces and lead-lined chambers were installed at other copperworks.

By the 1860s the Vivians were making use of a narrow strip of land to the south of their over-crowded copper-smelting and rolling-mill complex. The entrance to this new southern complex was to the east of Maliphant Street, beyond the railway lines, and like the northern complex it was accessed by a bridge over the Swansea Canal. The first new works to be established here in 1864 was the Hafod Phosphate Works, which produced chemical fertilizers and pesticides from phosphate rock that was unloaded at nearby wharves. Three other major works were established in this area before 1869. The first was the huge Hafod Isha Nickel & Cobalt Works, which refined ores shipped from Canada, where the Vivians had acquired mines. The second was the Hafod (Iron) Foundry; the third the Hafod Sawmills. By 1867 the Vivians also owned the Morriston Brickworks, which was situated between Wychtree Bridge and the Swansea Canal.

Control of the Market

In the 18th century the sale of Cornish copper-ore had taken place in Cornwall at auctions known as ticketing. From 1804 onwards ticketing also took place at Swansea, the ore for sale here being mainly foreign and Irish. By the time of Victoria's coronation the Swansea auctions were held in the Assembly Rooms, Cambrian Place, and the proceedings were formal almost to the point of being a ritual. Potential buyers were invited to a dinner over which the sellers' agents presided. The high point of the proceedings occurred when the sealed bids were opened and the name of the winning bidder announced. The amount of ore sold at ticketing peaked at over 650,000 tons in 1855; thereafter the amount declined as ticketing gave way to private transactions.

On two separate occasions the Swansea smelters formed a cartel to control the price of both copper-ore and refined copper the world over. In 1824–29 and again in 1844–67 they formed a Copper Trade Association in which the members did not bid against one another, but bought the ore, then auctioned it among themselves. That kept the price of ore low, but the Swansea smelters' world domination came under threat, in part, because more and more copper-producing countries were partially smelting their ores prior to export.

A Welsh colony in Australia

In 1842 copper-ore was discovered at Burra Burra in South Australia. The first cargo of Burra Burra ore arrived at Swansea in the brig *Amelia* on 27 June 1846, after a passage of 150 days. Burra Burra ore was copper-rich, far more so than Cornish ore, but a problem lay in the fact that the Burra Burra mines were some 50 miles from the nearest harbour. Transporting the ore by bullock-drawn carts through wild and inhospitable terrain was, therefore, both time consuming and costly. In a bid to cut transportation costs it was decided that, on the return/inland journey, the carts would be laden with coal from South Wales. The coal was to be used to partially smelt some of the ore near the mines, thereby ridding it of unwanted slag. The resulting copper-rich matte – or regulus as it was known – would therefore be a far less wasteful load for a cart, and a much more profitable cargo for a ship. So how was a smelting hall of calcining furnaces set up in the middle of nowhere?

The answer, in part, can be found in an article in the May 1990 edition of *The S. Wales Industrial Archaeology Society Bulletin*. In this brief but informative article the author describes how, in 1848, the Swansea barque *Richardson* sailed with locally recruited furnacemen and a cargo of fire-bricks, fire-clay, furnace doors, silica sand, shovels, wheelbarrows and other items too numerous to mention, to arrive in Australia in October that year. The furnacemen and those with them established a settlement called Llwchwr (Loughor). Today, Llwchwr is a district within the town of Burra, and the street names that survive bear testimony to where the furnacemen came from – Llanelly Street, Aberavon Street, Morriston Street, Penglawdd (Penclawdd) Street and Landore Street being the most suggestive.

Llwchwr, however, was not the fist colony of Welsh furnacemen to be established far from home. Similar, though not so well documented settlements must have been established in Chile on the west coast of South America. The partially smelted Chilean ore – or regulus – led to the establishment of a new kind of copperworks at Swansea, one that differed from the established smelters firstly because it was not sited in the L.S.V., but on the coast at Port Tennant, and secondly in that it did not smelt imported ore, but simply refined imported regulus.

The Port Tennant Copperworks

In *c.*1820 Charles Lambert, a mining engineer from Alsace in France, sailed to Chile to take up employment with a copper mining concern. Four years later he had his own mine. Chilean ore was rich in copper – far richer than Cornish ore – and the bulk of it was shipped to Swansea in vessels that, on the outward journey, were usually laden with coal. Charles Lambert must have seen there were advantages to be gained in using the coal to partially smelt his ore, the advantages being that as a cargo his semi-refined ore – or regulus – would be a more profitable cargo, and also it was less likely to shift in a ship's hold. In *c.*1840 he came to Swansea and established a business relationship with one Henry Bath, proprietor of the shipping firm Messrs. Henry Bath & Sons.

By 1842 Charles had established his own smelters in Chile, which would have entailed furnacemen from the Swansea area migrating to Chile, where their expertise in the art and mystery of calcining would have been indispensable. At a later date, Welsh furnacemen from the Swansea area were migrating to both Australia and the U.S.A. where their skills were put to similar use.

In *c.*1852 Charles Lambert leased a 12-acre site at Port Tennant, on which he established the Port Tennant Copperworks, otherwise known as Lambert's. Under the name of Charles Lambert & Co. he refined the regulus that Henry Bath & Sons shipped from Chile. Lambert's works prospered: in 1888 the company was described as 'copper smelters and rollers, sulphate of copper [sulphuric acid] manufacturers, electro depositors, copper, silver and gold smelters and refiners, and colliery owners'. The Lambert mines are believed to have been in the Dany-y-graig area, but the company was probably dependant to some extent on collieries situated on the east side of Kilvey Hill and on coal brought from Neath via the Tennant Canal.

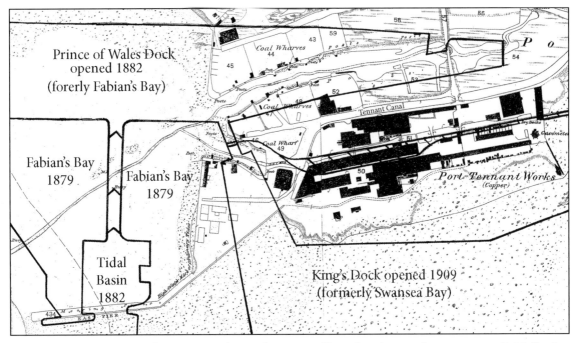

Port Tennant Copperworks in 1879 – the works were well sited with regard to transport. Initially the works stood alongside the Tennant Canal (from Neath) and close to shipping places on the east side of Fabian's Bay. Its situation improved with the arrival of the railway (c.1863) and the construction of the Prince of Wales Dock (1882). The row of houses extending eastwards to the gasometer was known as Lambert's Row; it was where many of the company's employees lived. The works were demolished in c.1904 when, with the planned construction of the King's Dock, the land was required for railway sidings. The dark lines represent the Prince of Wales Dock (opened in 1882) and the railway sidings (hatched) to the Kings Dock (opened in 1909) that called for the closure of Lambert's Copperworks.

(West Glamorgan Archive Service)

The little copperworks

The late 1850s and '60s saw the establishment of four small smelting works, three of them built initially for extracting arsenic from copper-ore. An early attempt at extracting arsenic from copper slag had been made at the Nantrhydyfilais Works, Landore, in 1814, but the venture failed and the works closed within two years. No further attempt was made to produce arsenic until Charles Lambert established the Port Tennant Works in *c.*1852. Some six years later, Nicholas Jennings started extracting arsenic at his Dan-y-graig Works (situated alongside the Tennant Canal, roughly a quarter-of-a-mile east of Lambert's). For reasons unknown, Nicholas Jennings moved his operations to Llansamlet in 1866, and the Dan-y-graig Works continued as an arsenic-cum-copper smelting complex until 1895; thereafter it was an arsenic only works until its closure in *c.*1912.

Nicholas Jennings, meanwhile, appears to have been proprietor of the Llansamlet Works for about a year, after which two successive owners concentrated on copper smelting until the works closed in 1905. On the opposite side of the Tawe, the Landore Arsenic & Copper Co. set up shop in the recently abandoned Calland's Pottery near the river. In 1869 this 'little' works was advertised in *The Cambrian*:

TO BE SOLD OR LET

A small copper and arsenic works, situated at Landore ... containing six smelting and roasting
furnaces, three calciners, a refining furnace, with copper that is in the bottoms
(of the furnaces). Also several hundred feet of arsenic detecting chambers, with a chimney
100 feet high. It lies between the canal and the River Tawe, where vessels can discharge
cargoes, and close to the Great Western Railway ... It might easily be converted
into a Tin Plate or Galvanised Sheet Iron Works, and many other purposes.
For terms and to view the premises, apply to Mr. JOHN GLASBROOK, Morriston.

The site later became known as the Little Landore Copperworks, by which time production
was geared solely to copper smelting. The Black Vale Works, Cwmbwrla, differed from the above
works in that production – when it began in 1852 – was geared to smelting copper and tin. The Black
Vale Works were situated near the Burlais Brook (in the angle formed by the old Gorse Road and
Carmarthen Road, about a quarter of a mile from Cwmbwrla roundabout), and closed in 1913.

Communications

Several turnpike roads either passed through, or skirted the L.S.V., all of which, save one, converged
on Swansea. It can, therefore, be said that Swansea was ringed by tollgates, but even those who did
not wish to enter the town still had to pay tolls because they could not avoid using turnpike roads
to get from one locality to another. Such was the frustration over tolls that by the summer of 1843
Rebecca and her Daughters were active within the Lordship of Gower and Kilvey.

Rebecca's attack on the Pound-ffald gate in Peninsula Gower has already been considered.
Almost three week after that attack *The Cambrian* reported that on Thursday 3 August the Tycoch
tollgate in Llansamlet parish was destroyed. Where exactly Tycoch tollgate stood is difficult to
determine. It was said to be 'about half a mile distance from Swansea' Borough, at a place where
two roads met, 'one leading to Foxhole and the other to Danygraig', which would place it in the
hamlet of St. Thomas. The local magistrates were amazed that such an attack should have taken
place so close to Swansea, because, 'in spite of the number of policemen, both rural and borough,
... in the town – in spite of the number of the military, including companies of the 73rd and 75th
Regiments, together with between forty and fifty Light Dragoons, the Tycoch gate ... was levelled to
the ground unobserved, excepting by the toll-receiver', Margaret Arnold, 'who ... recognized one ...
of the thirty or forty rioters'. Margaret had been able to recognize the man, 'a collier named David
Lewis', because he had 'committed a most cowardly and disgraceful assault upon her'. Having been
sworn in, Margaret stated that she was a single woman, and collected tolls at Tycoch tollgate:

> When in bed about three o'clock this morning, I was disturbed by a noise outside ... Several
> heavy blows were given [to] the door ... and the shutters, the latter of which together with
> the windows had been smashed. When I ... opened the door, a man came from the turnpike
> towards me. He had an iron bar in his hand, with which he gave me a severe blow on the arm.

I had held up my arm for the purpose of avoiding ... the blow on any other part. The prisoner, David Lewis, is the man who struck me ... and [I] ran into the house. He struck the door repeatedly ... until it was broken to pieces. I again went to the door, and observed the prisoner break down the toll-board which was fastened to the wall. There were about thirty or more men scattered ... about the house ... I screamed out 'murder' as loud as I could, upon which they all fled in various directions. They appeared to be working-men, colliers, etc., and were not disguised. One of the party rode a dark-coloured horse which appeared to be a cart-horse. In leaving he rode on before them. The gate appeared to have been cut down with saws [and then] placed on the limekiln ... I well knew the prisoner ... He had passed through the gate on the preceding afternoon with a cart. He rose his hand in passing, which intimated that he had no money ... but would pay again. I have frequently trusted him before, and he has always paid me.

A Mr. Melvin entered the courtroom and 'said he appeared on behalf of the prisoner, and asked permission to cross-examine the ... witness'. Margaret's response to the cross-examination was that 'it was rather dark, but light enough for her to see his features ... She knew him well. He is rather lame'. Mr. Melvin then 'offered to produce witnesses who could prove that the prisoner was in bed from nine o'clock on the ... night until five ... that morning'.

The magistrates did not wish to consider an alibi, but committed David Lewis 'for trial at the next Assizes on a charge of felony'; nor would they accept bail. David was committed to the House of Correction (the site now occupied by County Hall). A week later a Mr. Price made an application for bail on behalf of David, and did so on the ground that 'it was then August, and probably the assizes would not take place until the latter end of February, being seven months' imprisonment, which ... was a severe punishment even on the supposition that the man was guilty, but would be very hard, indeed, if he were innocent ... A brother and mother were dependent upon the prisoner and ... Mr. Price had certificates of good character from four of the prisoner's employers'. The Magistrates declined acceding to the application. David spent eight months in the House of Correction. It has been said that, on 13 March 1844, he was 'discharged by proclamation', but a trawl through *The Cambrian* has failed to confirm this. It is possible that his discharge was due to the non-appearance of the only witness, Margaret Arnold. If so, David must have breathed a sigh of relief, for had he been found guilty his sentence would have been transportation to Tasmania.

Besides turnpike roads there were numerous tracks criss-crossing the valley on both sides of the river, tracks which, if they were important enough, were maintained by the parish in which they lay. No tolls were payable for using these tracks; nor is there any evidence to suggest that tolls were payable for using the Beaufort Bridge below Morriston, which was undoubtedly used by locals. Apart from travelling on foot, horseback or in horse-drawn vehicles, canal barges may also have been used for conveying people as well as bulk commodities, as was the case in 1868 when Morriston ratepayers travelled to Swansea in three barges.

The Swansea Vale Railway

Tramroads such as the one connected with Mynydd Newydd Colliery were used by colliers to get to work. It was, therefore, only a matter of time before horses were superseded by locomotives, and the trams by passenger carriages – at least that is how the Swansea Vale Railway came into existence. The railway originated in 1817–9 when John Scott built what became known as Scott's Railway,

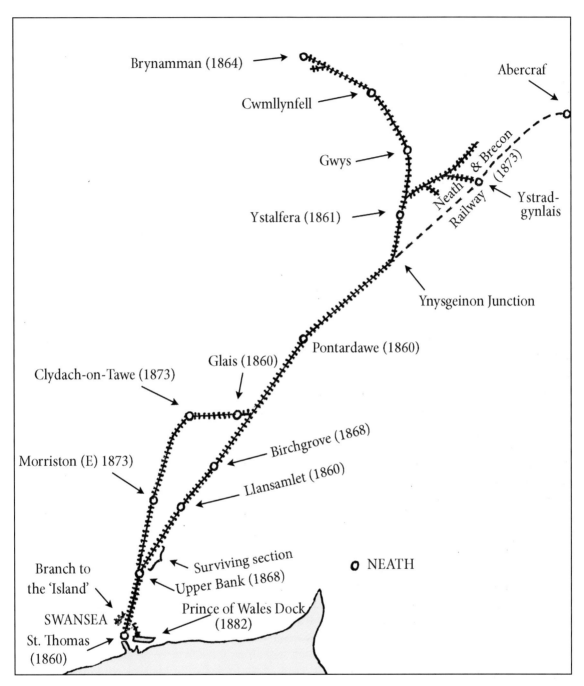

The Swansea Vale Railway (S.V.R.) – formed in 1845 by a group of local industrialists, the S.V.R. was as much a local innovation as the Mumbles Railway. It is regrettable that virtually nothing of the SVR survives, although sections of its route up the Swansea Valley can still be explored by keen walkers.

which from its inception was designed to take locomotives. Although the first engine proved more trouble than its worth, and the owner had to make use of oxen instead, by 1833 the second owner of the line, Charles Henry Smith, had at least one locomotive operating on it, which he used to convey coal from his Llansamlet collieries to three copperworks and to wharves at Foxhole.

Aware that his Llansamlet coal reserves were depleted, Charles Henry combined with others in a venture that was intended to open up collieries around Glais and transport Graigola coal to the riverside wharves at Foxhole. To this end Charles Henry and his associates (Pascoe St. Leger Grenfell and Henry Bath amongst them) formed a joint stock company in 1845, which they called the Swansea Vale Railway (referred to as the S.V.R. below). Starling Benson, chairman of this new company, issued a statement to the effect that 'the railway is formed ... in connection with Mr. Smith's road [Scott's Railway, which he leased to the new company] and the line [is] now in the course of execution and relaying', meaning Scott's Railway was in the process of being relayed and extended towards Glais. It is not known exactly when the line was extended beyond Scott's Pit, but the extension was certainly in existence by August 1849, as evidenced by an article in *The Cambrian*, which referred to coal from the Birchgrove area being conveyed to Foxhole by the S.V.R.

In 1853 the S.V.R. bought its first two second-hand locomotives and in 1855 acquired its third second-hand engine. By an Act of Parliament that same year, the company obtained authorization to lay a branch line across the Tawe to the North Dock (opened in 1852) for shipping coal. The same Act also gave permission to carry passengers and, to this end, the company bought its first new engine in 1858. The following year a Board of Trade inspector noted that not only did the S.V.R. have locomotives on the line, but Charles Henry also had at least three engines of his own on the same single-track line, all of them conveying coal from his collieries.

A passenger service between St. Thomas and Pontardawe began in February 1860, the journey taking half an hour to complete, and the line was 'supplied with telegraph from end to end'. St. Thomas Station stood on an embankment between the Tawe and the houses that still stand on the lower part of Thomas Street. There were several stations *en route*, initially at Llansamlet and Glais; later at Upper Bank and Birchgrove. In 1861 an extension opened between Pontardawe and Ystalyfera; this was followed by the opening of another single-track extension from Ystalyfera to Brynamman in 1864. So successful were the S.V.R.'s undertakings that a spokesman said, in 1867, 'The company was not a large one, nor the line a very long one, but it managed to bring down over something like a million tons of coal'.

Between 1871 and 1873 the S.V.R. laid a loop line from Upper Bank to Morriston, Clydach and round to Glais where it joined the existing line to Pontardawe. Morriston Station stood on the east bank of the Tawe, a little to the south of Wychtree Bridge. The line then crossed the river a little to the north of the said bridge, and continued on to Clydach-on-Tawe, after which it re-crossed the river to connect with Glais. The S.V.R. was a success in all its undertakings, yet in 1874 the company leased its network to the Midland Railway, which had already taken over the neighbouring Neath & Brecon Railway. Two years later the S.V.R. sold everything to the bigger company, and soon passenger trains were travelling from Birmingham via Brecon to St. Thomas Station.

The progress of the Midland Railway around Swansea's expanding East Side docks is beyond the scope of this work. Suffice to say the company continued to hold its own until 1950. Closures followed until almost everything connected with the line was swept away apart from one small section that survived. Tucked away at the top, eastern end of the Swansea Enterprise Zone this 1½ mile section runs between what was once Six Pit Junction (near Second City) and the Upper Bank Works (near the disused ski slope). For many years a local preservation society kept an impressive array of railway stock on this surviving section of the line. Unfortunately, the stock was badly vandalized in recent years and the preservation society could no longer display its treasures of the past.

Before moving on, a brief mention should be made of the South Wales (later the Great Western) Railway line that cut across the L.S.V. from Neath to Landore, where it forked, one line continuing west, the other turning south for Swansea's High Street Station. The line across the valley, including the magnificent Landore Viaduct, was built c.1847–50. This particular line will be dealt with in a later volume on Swansea.

Messrs. Davey & Pegg and their Birchgrove Colliery

As happened at Dunvant – when plans were prepared for a railway line to pass through the Dunvant Gap – the extension of the S.V.R. to Glais led to the creation of new collieries in an area that had been considered to be remote from Swansea Harbour. In the mid-1840s the London coal and coke merchants, Messrs. Davey & Pegg, acquired a 200-acre mineral lease near Birchgrove. The partners were attracted to the area because the coal seams provided a smokeless fuel which was ideal for household use and for fuelling the iron steamships that were built in ever increasing numbers. Their first colliery, the Birchgrove Pit, began yielding coal in 1848; it was connected to the S.V.R by a half-mile long self-acting incline-plane.

In 1852 William Pegg took up residence at Birchgrove House. Between 1852 and 1856 he purchased some 780 acres freehold, which increased the size of his mineral estate. Unlike his neighbour, C.H. Smith, William Pegg took an interest in both the welfare of his employees and in farming the land. He chose not to reside in Sketty – as did the Morrises, Vivians and Smiths – but settled where his interests lay; by 1861 he had enlarged Drumma House and taken up residence there. The following year his newly sunk Sisters Pit began yielding coal, but four years later William was in trouble and obliged to put his Birchgrove Colliery up for sale, but no buyer could be found. He died in 1869 to be succeeded by his son, William Duncan Pegg, who finally sold the Birchgrove Coalfield in 1874 and the family returned to London.

Spelter

Another metallurgical industry to be established in the L.S.V. was that of zinc which, when alloyed with copper, produced brass. In the 18th century, small quantities of brass were produced at both the Forest and White Rock copperworks, though where the zinc came from is unclear. Zinc-ore was certainly smelted at Upper Bank, but production there lasted for only 20 years (1757–77). No further attempt was made to smelt zinc in the valley until, in 1836, Evan John established the Llansamlet Works, which initially consisted of five furnaces. The works were sited alongside the Smith's Canal, which was still in use, 'free of tolls with wharfage at Foxhole' for unloading ore imported mainly from the Continent. Barges brought both coal and ore to the works, whereas the canal itself provided the necessary water supply; the marshland to the west became a dumping ground for slag.

In simple terms, what went on at Evan John's Llansamlet Works was that crushed zinc-ore was calcined in furnaces that were similar to those used by the copper smelters. The resultant zinc oxide was then mixed with coal dust and heated in sealed containers until such time as the zinc oxide 'distils in the form of vapour' and, when it condenses, 'is then poured into ... moulds, forming, when cold ... ingots of crude zinc, commonly referred to as spelter'. The process by which all this was achieved was known as the 'English process' (developed in 1740). It was a costly process in that it required 25 tons of coal to produce one ton of spelter.

Undercapitalised, Evan John was in difficulty by 1839 and his Llansamlet Works closed the following year. In the meantime, new developments had taken place that were to make spelter an important element in the local economy. The first of these new developments occurred in 1832, when a Birmingham industrialist, George Muntz, patented a form of brass known as 'yellow metal'. The ideal composition of this new alloy was 60% copper and 40% zinc. When rolled into sheets, yellow metal became a cheap and effective substitute for sheathing the hulls of wooden ships.

In partnership with the Grenfells, George Muntz produced yellow metal sheaves at Upper Bank between 1837 and 1842. This would not have pleased the Swansea smelters who, with their more expensive copper sheaves, were unable to compete. No doubt legal advice was sought and, after litigation, the Vivians were allowed to manufacture yellow metal under licence in 1841.

That same year (1841) Vivian & Sons took over the disused Birmingham (Ynys) Copper-works and converted it into a spelter works for the purpose of producing yellow metal. Initially, they used the English process for smelting, but other more efficient processes were at hand. The Silesian (German) process, which was more economical with regard to fuel, required only 12 tons of coal to produce one ton of spelter. The later Belgian process, on the other hand, required only six tons of coal to produce one ton of spelter. The problem with these continental processes was that they required a skilled workforce as temperatures were critical. The Vivians were probably the first to install continental furnaces for it was said by a Dr. Percy that 'In 1848 I saw English, Silesian and Belgian zinc furnaces in the [Birmingham] works then carried on by the late Mr. Vivian; but only the first were in operation'. Why the continental furnaces were not in operation is not stated, but it may have been due to a failure to recruit foreign workers.

In 1851, J.H. Vivian and Michael Williams of the Morfa Works entered into a partnership and bought the Forest Copperworks from the Bank of England. Forest continued as a copper smelting complex until, in 1867 (and for reasons that are unclear), ownership passed to Vivian & Sons, at which point Forest was converted for the production of spelter. H. Hussey Vivian certainly succeeded in recruiting skilled continental labour on this occasion because it was said, in January 1868, that 'he expected 30 German workmen to arrive with his manager, Mr. Daehne'.

That same year (1868) the Grenfells converted their Upper Bank Works to the Belgian process. The result of this conversation and those mentioned above was that three 18th-century copper-works – Birmingham, Forest and Upper Bank – had been adapted for the production of yellow metal sheaves. It has been calculated that, in 1869, the Vivians' spelter works (including Margam presumably, as that had also been converted for the purpose) sheathed 123 vessels, and between them Williams (Morfa) and the Grenfells (Upper Bank) sheaved 169 ships.[9] The production of sheaves, however, was by then beginning to decline as the total tonnage of iron ships launched exceeded that of wooden.

It is likely that other spelter producers brought in foreign labour, if only to get the new processes up and running, but in later years it was said that 'the English [meaning British-born presumably] did not care for the work', and for several reasons. The work was exhausting, particu-larly in hot weather, whilst in the calcining furnaces the ore had to be constantly rabbled (stirred

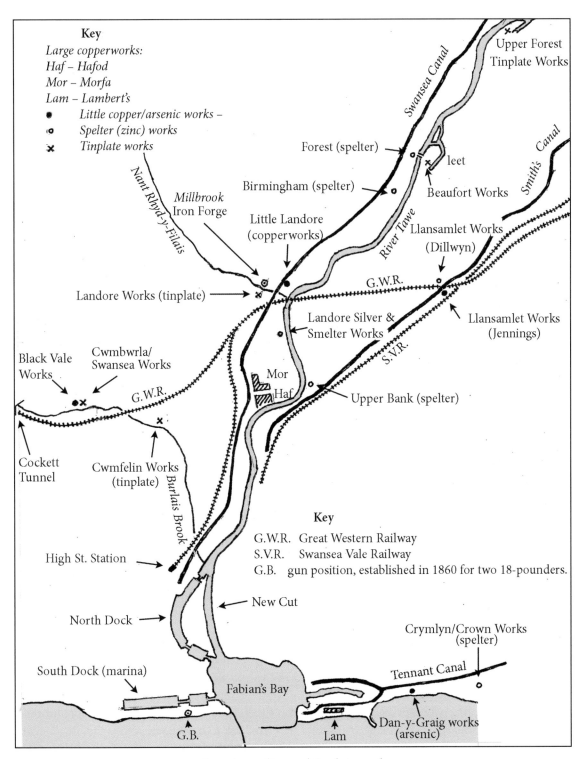

Key

Large copperworks:
Haf – Hafod
Mor – Morfa
Lam – Lambert's

● *Little copper/arsenic works –*
◖ *Spelter (zinc) works*
✕ *Tinplate works*

Upper Forest
Tinplate Works

Swansea Canal

Smith's Canal

Forest (spelter)

leet

Birmingham (spelter)

Beaufort Works

Nant Rhyd-y-Filais

Millbrook
Iron Forge

Little Landore
(copperworks)

River Tawe

Llansamlet Works
(Dillwyn)

G.W.R.

Landore Works (tinplate)

Landore Silver &
Smelter Works

Llansamlet Works
(Jennings)

Black Vale
Works

Cwmbwrla/
Swansea Works

S.V.R.

Mor
Haf

Upper Bank (spelter)

G.W.R.

Cockett
Tunnel

Cwmfelin Works
(tinplate)

Burlais Brook

Key

G.W.R.   Great Western Railway
S.V.R.   Swansea Vale Railway
G.B.   gun position, established in 1860 for two 18-pounders.

High St. Station

New Cut

North Dock

Crymlyn/Crown Works
(spelter)

South Dock (marina)

Tennant Canal

Fabian's Bay

G.B.

Lam

Dan-y-Graig works
(arsenic)

Arsenic, spelter and tinplate works

213

or raked) through ports, and while the ports were open the furnacemen were exposed not only to incredibly high temperatures, but also to noxious fumes of sulphur dioxide which could rot their teeth. Equally frowned upon were the 24-hour shifts that (unlike the Sunday 'dead fire' that prevailed in the copperworks) required workers to function at full capacity even on Sundays. Shifts such as these were unacceptable to those with religious convictions. As to the dense clouds of white vapour that belched from the works, they were a familiar sight, as were the green flames that arose from the furnaces. The vapour exacerbated the pollution problem in L.S.V.

A second new development relating to spelter occurred in 1837, when W.H. Crauford patented a process whereby iron (and later steel) products such as buckets and corrugated sheets could be galvanized (coated with a thin layer of liquid zinc) to protect them against rust. During the latter part of Victoria's reign the galvanizing industry was to have a tremendous impact on the local economy, the reason being that there were many treeless places in the world – in the U.S.A., Australia, South Africa and South America – where corrugated iron sheets could be used for building barns, mining camps and even churches.

Among the early spelter works unconnected with the copper smelters were two concerns that succumbed to setbacks. Messrs. Hermann Berger & William Williams, spelter manufacturers at Morriston (of whom little is known) dissolved their partnership by mutual consent in 1858. On the Crymlyn Burrows at Port Tennant, Messrs. Shackleford, Ford & Co. erected a spelter works in 1866. The following year their new works suffered fire damage. The business was uninsured and the company had to auction its remaining assets. That same year (1867) the Swansea Zinc Co. took over the works, but two years later the company was declared bankrupt. The works were then purchased by Messrs J. Richardson & Co. (alias the Crown Zinc Co.) and survived until 1883, when they were taken over by the English Crown Spelter Co. Ltd. The Crymlyn/Crown Works were situated to the east of Lambert's Copperworks, alongside the Tennant Canal from which it drew water, and by which it received its supplies of coal and zinc-ore. The works survived until 1930.

Among the more successful early zinc smelters was Lewis Llewelyn Dillwyn, M.P. for Swansea and District. In 1850 Lewis disposed of his interests in the Cambrian Pottery. Three years later he established the Landore Silver & Spelter Works (on the site of the later Siemans Steel Works). He then acquired the disused Llansamlet Works in c.1858, which Evan John had abandoned some 18 years earlier. By 1860 the furnaces at the Llansamlet Works, which were sited to the west of Cwm (near Bon-y-maen), had been converted to the Silesian (German) process. At a later, unrecorded date the works were again converted, this time to the Belgian process. The Llansamlet Works became one of Swansea's best known spelter concerns, due to its connection with Lewis's daughter, Amy Dillwyn; it survived until 1926. The Landore Works, on the other hand, Lewis converted to become the Siemans Steel Works in 1867 or soon after.

The spelter industry – or at least that part of it that was not in the hands of the copper masters – may have got off to a painful start, but those works that survived beyond 1867, plus the three new ones established beside the Smith's Canal between 1873 and 1887, all contributed enormously to the local economy, the more so after c.1870 when the copper industry went into decline. The production of spelter and the galvanizing of corrugated iron sheets did not make Swansea the Spelteropolis of the world, but the six spelters that existed in 1912 are said to have been responsible for around 90% of the total production in Britain.

Iron

With regard to the L.S.V., the nearest iron-ore deposits of any significance were to be found to the north of Ystalyfera, although the most productive ironworks were situated in and around Merthyr Tydfil. The ore in the Upper Swansea Valley was 'scoured' from outcrops and taken to furnaces such as those at Ynyscedwyn, founded about 1712, if not earlier. After smelting, molten metal was tapped into moulds to form blocks of cast (pig) iron. Cast iron was too brittle for many uses and so had to be processed at forges to remove impurities, the end product being wrought (bar) iron. There were several forges alongside the Tawe and its tributaries. Among the earliest were those sited at Ynys-pen-llwch (Clydach) and at Upper Forest (on the east bank above Morriston). At both these locations water was diverted from the river through leets to power waterwheels, which in turn operated bellows and heavy rolling machinery.

Probably the first and certainly the best-known iron works in the L.S.V. was the one established in what is now the Millbrook Industrial Estate, Landore. Between about 1793 and 1807 a small part of this industrial estate had been the site of the Landore Copperworks Stamping and Rolling-mills, which used water from the Nant Rhyd-y-Filais to power its machinery. The mills were probably taken over by the Nantrhydyvilas Air Furnace Co. in 1814 and the furnaces and machinery adapted for use as an iron forge. The forge had several charcoal-fuelled furnaces and, strange though it may seem, the owners, William Bevan & Sons, attempted to extract iron and copper from copper slag. The venture was not a resounding success and, from c.1817 onwards, the works continued to function as a forge and a foundry known as the Landore Forge. The foundry section produced cast-iron tramlines, railings, etc., and brass products such as bells, whereas the forge produced tools – everything from shovels to machinery required by the coal, copper and tinplate masters.

William Bevan of Morriston went bankrupt during the depression of 1830, and the works were taken over by John Morris II and his associates to become the Millbrook Iron Forge, by which time the works were making use of steam engines to power at least some of its machinery. The works expanded to become a five-acre, integrated complex with furnaces for the production of iron and steel bars, engineering facilities for making agricultural machinery and steam-engines, as well as pickling and tinning machines for the tinplate trade. It had a smith's shop, a pattern shop, a boiler-makers' yard, a turning and boring mill, and an internal railway. One of its most ambitious projects was the construction of the first iron bridge over the New Cut, Swansea, which it completed in 1851. The works – one of the few that continued to smelt iron up to the eve of the First World War – closed in 1966 and part of the site now lies beneath the Cwm Level playing fields.

There were other forges and foundries established in the L.S.V. The more productive forges were built in connection with a growing number of tinplate works, and will be referred to below.

Tin

Cornish copper-ore contained a small percentage of tin, and copper alloyed with tin produced bronze, or bell-metal as it was otherwise known. In *Copperopolis* Stephen Hughes refers to entries in the Llangyfelach Copperworks accounts that suggest small quantities of bronze accumulated in furnace bottoms. The bronze was apparently 'either used to cast bronze goods at the works, or sold to bell-founders'.

The Forest and White Rock copperworks also profited from such accumulations. However, on their own neither iron nor tin made a big impression on the local economy, but when combined these metals were to create an industry that was to employ more men than the copper masters ever did. This industry was to make Swansea and its surrounding region a metallurgical centre of world importance for the second time.

Tinplate

Tinplate – or tinned-plate to be more accurate – is the end product of 'iron or steel bars rolled into sheets and coated with a wash of tin'[11] to prevent corrosion. Prior to Victoria's coronation, tinplate had been used primarily in the production of roofs and walls for buildings, and also in the manufacture of pots, pans, kettles and sealed containers for commodities such as tea, coffee and confectionary. However, in 1809 a French chef came up with the idea of preserving food in tins. Initially, it was the military and the navy that recognized the advantages of tinned food, but by the time of Victoria's coronation the U.S.A. was importing large quantities of tinplate, the purpose of which was to provide building materials, household utensils and tinned food for the settlers who were moving westwards.

The tinplate industry was very labour intensive, meaning a large workforce was required to process the raw materials through a lengthy sequence of operations. In some works, wrought/bar iron was purchased from elsewhere ready for processing in the mills. Other works preferred to purchase cast/pig iron and convert it into wrought/bar iron themselves. With regard to the latter option, the first stage took place in a forge. This was where cast/pig iron was subjected to the intense heat of furnaces to remove impurities and convert it into wrought/bar iron. The bars were then taken to a building that housed several mills, each mill being a unit of production. In simplified terms each mill had its own furnace, a pair of water- or steam-powered rolls and shearing equipment.

In the mills the wrought/bar iron had to be reheated in the mill furnaces, after which they were passed between water- or steam-powered rollers several times until they were flattened into sheets. The sheet were 'reheated, doubled over and rolled, doubled over and rolled again and again'. The sheets were then sheared, separated and 'pickled' – that is, cleaned with sulphuric acid (or some other substance) to remove the film of iron oxide (scale) that had accumulated during rolling.

After passing through several additional stages of reheating and re-rolling, the sheets were transferred to the tinning house. Tinning involved passing the sheets through vessels (pots) of molten tin, and then dipping them into baths of molten palm oil (to allow surplus tin to drain off). The tinned-plates were then polished and examined for faults. It was important that faulty plates (wasters) were put to one side – a company with a reputation for faulty plates could loose orders. Finally the faultless plates (primes) were packed into boxes and stored, ready for dispatch.

The term 'tinman' (or tinplate worker) covered many different job descriptions, ranging from furnaceman, rollerman, behinder, shearer, washerman and annealer to name but a few. Many of these tinmen were regarded as skilled workers. Such were the skills of tinmen that they were reluctant to pass on what they had mastered to anyone other than close relatives. Indeed, at the close of Victoria's reign an American commentator described Welsh immigrant tin-workers as 'intensely clannish', adding that 'they cherished their trade secrets so mysteriously that for years the making of tinplate was considered to be something of a black art'.

Yet despite their skills, a tinman's pay was not considered good, certainly not as good as a copperman's. The reason for the disparity is that the tinplate industry was highly competitive; it was also one in which profits were low compared with copper smelting. Unfortunately there are no pay rates for tinmen until 1874, when *The Cambrian* reported that rollermen earned £2 a week, doublers £1 15s., furnacemen £1 10s., behinders 15s. and grease boys 13s.. These figures, however, are deceptive. Tinmen were paid according to a contract system whereby key millmen entered into a contract with their employers to provide an agreed amount of tinplate. At the end of each month the key millmen were paid, and they in turn distributed pay to the men who were members of their team.

Tinmen worked 12-hour shifts – either by day or by night – six days a week. They were paid monthly in arrears and often took fortnightly subs. Their stature was described in 1842 as 'frequently stunted'. They wore flannel shirts, either blue or grey, and were noted for their leather aprons. In many respects their lot was similar to that of coppermen, except that their pay was not as good, and their employment was subject to the fluctuations of a boom and bust industry. When trade was good, tinmasters not only increased the number of mills at their disposal, but enterprising local businessmen were inclined to form new partnerships and establish new works. This sort of expansion invariably led to over-production, followed by falling prices and recessions in which large numbers of tinmen were thrown out of work.

The conditions in which tinmen worked were hot, dusty and dangerous. Cuts were frequent as the edges of rolled sheets were razor-sharp. Care had to be taken when handling them; a watchful eye was needed when they came, skimming across the floor. T.B. and other respiratory disorders were common complaints as were rheumatism, cancer and diseases of the nervous and urinary systems.

As to the women and children who were employed in tinplate works, their part in the process did not begin until after the plates had been rolled and sheared to size. Women were employed in the pickling, packing and cold roll sections, whereas children had the task of polishing the finished tinplates with dusters. Females were not only susceptible to the same complaints as men, but they were also prone to a blood disorder known as 'green sickness'.

There were several reasons why the tinplate industry became established in the L.S.V. Iron was available from the furnaces and forges in the Upper Valley, although the bulk of it came from the Merthyr area. Tin-ore, on the other hand, could be shipped from Cornwall and, to a lesser extent, from Malaya and Australia. Another factor was the availability of cheap coal for furnaces and for heating tin and palm oil. The harbour and the canal were likewise important considerations. Finally there was an abundance of water, both from the Tawe and its tributaries, and from the canal. Initially, water was required to provide power, and there were several existing water-powered iron forges and copper rolling-mills that could be adapted for the production of iron sheets; tinning houses could be added to these buildings.

The first tinplate works in South Wales had been established at Pontypool in 1682; the first in the Lordship of Gower was at Ynys-pen-llwch (Clydach) where, in c.1747, a tinning house was added to an existing forge. However, it was not until 1845 that the first tinplate works was established in the L.S.V. This particular works is a classic example of how enterprising men made use of an existing industrial site.

When the Vivians surrendered their lease on the Upper Forest water-powered site in 1845 (which they had used as copper rolling-mills) the property was immediately taken over by Messrs. Hallam & Madge and was then known as the Upper Forest Works. Initially, the works consisted of only one water-driven mill, but there were soon five tin mills on site, each with rolling machinery to convert bar iron into thin metal sheets, and also furnaces for reheating the sheets when necessary. There were also eight coke-fuelled furnaces for converting cast/pig iron (from furnaces further inland) into wrought/bar iron, as well as other furnaces and machinery. At the end of the production line the tinned sheets were packed into boxes ready for export. A box of 20 inch by 14 inch sheets usually contained 112 such sheets, and by 1853 the five mills at Upper Forest were producing 10,000 boxes of tinplate each month.[12]

Compared with a copperworks, a tinplate works did not require a large investment to get things up and running, particularly when it involved converting existing mills for the purpose. It has been estimated that, at the beginning of Victoria's reign, the average cost of establishing one tinplate mill stood at around £3,500, and although the figure doubled over the next 30 years, it nevertheless proved to be an investment that local men could afford when they entered into partnerships. The tinplate industry was, therefore, noted for the number of local men who combined to raise the necessary capital, whereas the copper industry had owed its existence to the large investments of well-to-do partnerships from England.

The tinplate industry was also one in which local men of humble origin could rise to become men of wealth and influence. A classic example of this is the Clydach-born John Jones Jenkins. At the age of 14, John took up a lowly position at the Upper Forest (tinplate) Works in 1850. At the age of 23 he was appointed 'outside manager'; as such he acquired books and established a library for his workforce. In 1859 he became the manager of, and a major shareholder in, what later became known as the Beaufort (tinplate) Works near Morriston. In 1869 he built the Yspitty (tinplate) Works at Loughor; that same year he became mayor of Swansea. He was knighted in 1882 and created Lord Glantawe in 1906. For many years he lived at Bath Villa, Morriston, before moving to the Grange at West Cross.

The second tinplate works to be established in the L.S.V. was the Landore Works; it was created by a partnership in 1851 that included John Morris II. The Landore Works differed from Upper Forest firstly in that it used bar iron from its charcoal-fuelled furnaces (which provided a better quality iron) and secondly 'the mills were apparently the first in the trade to be driven by steam power'. The site of the works was between the Millbrook Iron Forge (on the north and west) and Neath Road (on the east). By 1876 there were seven mills in operation here.

The demand for tinplate increased during the late 1850s, in part because of the Crimean War (1853–6) and this led to the establishment of three more tinplate works in the L.S.V. The first of these – the Cwmfelin Works – was established in 1858 by David Davies & Sons; it was built on land that had been occupied by the Millwood Colliery. For water the works relied on the Burlais Brook and a reservoir that had been connected with the colliery. How may tin mills the works had in 1858 is unknown – it had three 16 years later. What was unusual about Cwmfelin was that the men held prayer meetings before work began on Monday mornings. What Cwmfelin is remembered for most is 'an appalling catastrophe [in which] the lives of five young men were sacrificed and four other men were severely injured'.

The catastrophe occurred on 4 April 1866 when 'a young man named Philip Thomas ... was engaged cutting tin-plates'. The cutting machine was 'somewhat out of order'. So Philip 'incautiously placed his head between the sheers', which 'closed, inflicting a fearful wound – in fact almost talking off the top part of the head ... The accident becoming known throughout the works, the men congregated from all parts around' Philip, which 'was fortunate, for had the men been ... in their accustomed places', many more of them would probably have died.

> A terrific explosion was heard in another part of the building, and in an instant ... walls ... were blown down, roofs shattered, beams snapped, and heavy stones and pieces of machinery were flying about in all directions ... A large tubular boiler 40 feet long ... had exploded ... five men and boys were found in the immediate locality of the exploded boiler, writhing in agony, having received such fearful scalds and wounds ... One poor fellow [had been] blown a distance. [The others] were buried beneath debris and were extricated with all possible speed, and conveyed to their homes [where they died, two of them only] 11 years of age.

When *The Cambrian* reported on this catastrophe four other men were said to have been severely injured, and the sheerer, Philip Thomas, 'still survives ... but lies in such a critical state that but faint hopes are entertained of his recovery'. As to the works, such was the damage that 'about 300 men, women, and girls were deprived of their means of sustenance'. Fortunately the machinery was comparatively unscathed and there were 'hopes that operations [would be] resumed in ... a few weeks'.

Near Morriston the Vivians had leased the water-powered Lower Forest Copper Rolling-mills in *c.*1822. When exactly they surrendered the lease is unknown, but in 1859 John Jones Jenkins (mentioned above) and his associates took over the lease. That same year John ordered a steam-powered engine from Neath Abbey Ironworks, which he used to augment the existing water-powered facilities. By 1860 two tinplate mills were operating within the main building, each mill producing quantities of sheet metal. The sheets were then transferred to a tinning house that had been added to the main building. From 1872 onwards these works were known as the Beaufort Works, so named because in that year the works became the property of the Beaufort Tinplate Co.

Built in 1863, the Cwmbwrla (later the Swansea) Works was the last of five tinplate works to be established in the L.S.V. during the early part of Victoria's reign. Sited near Cwmbwrla Roundabout (in the angle formed by the old Gorse Road and Carmarthen Road), these works used water from the adjacent Burlais Brook and coal from the nearby Cwmbwrla Colliery (on the south side of the old Gorse Road). How many mills the works had initially is unknown; it had four in 1876.

In the mid-1860s the tinplate trade was badly affected by the American Civil War (1861–5), but by 1867 the market had recovered. The L.S.V. still had only five tinplate works at that time, with no more than 20 mills between them. Calculating how many men, women and children were employed in these works is difficult. Bearing in mind that the industry was labour intensive with operatives working day and night, it would not be unreasonable to assume that the number would not fall far short of the number employed in the local copperworks. All things considered, the L.S.V. tinplate industry as it stood in 1867 did not make Swansea the Tinopolis of the world – but the situation was about to change.

During the next 12 years the number of tinplate works in the L.S.V. doubled, added to which there were a several technological developments during this period, but the most important development of all was the opening of the Prince of Wales Dock in 1882. Prior to that date most Welsh tinplate was sent to Liverpool, from where it was shipped to foreign ports – to America in particular. The opening of the new dock did away with the cost of shipment to Liverpool, with the result that Swansea became the largest tinplate port in the world.

Other Metallurgical Industries

Lead was used mainly for roofing, plumbing and in the manufacture of paint; moreover, lead-ore contained a small percentage of silver, a valuable by-product for the smelter. The ore was mined at several locations in the British Isles, the nearest deposits to Swansea being in Flintshire, northern Cardiganshire, north Devon and Cornwall; small quantities were also present in the Vale of Neath and the top end of the Swansea Valley. However, unlike copper smelting, which required huge quantities of coal, lead-ore could be smelted near its source, using far less coal. Swansea, therefore, never became a major lead port.

The Llangyfelach Copperworks (1717–49) had not been simply a copperworks, but an integrated copper, lead and silver smelting complex. Indeed, the Llangyfelach Works had more lead smelting furnaces than it had for smelting copper-ore. Following the closure of the Llangyfelach Works in 1749, lead smelting took place at both Middle Bank (1755–64) and Upper Bank Works (1757–82). In the early part of Victoria's reign the Morfa Works began producing silver in 1840, and the base of a 200-foot chimney connected with this works is immediately to the south of the surviving Morfa Copper Rolling-mills. The Hafod Works also became involved in the production of silver in 1846. Finally, Lewis Llewelyn Dillwyn produced silver at his Landore Silver & Spelter Works between 1853 and 1867. Lead and/or silver production at all these works, however, was relatively small when compared with what went on at White Rock after 1870, especially after *c*.1874 when the works became yet another Vivian acquisition.

The Vivians' business empire was undoubtedly the most integrated of all the L.S.V. concerns. In the early part of Victoria's reign the Vivians alone produced gold (from 1850), nickel and cobalt (from 1855) and were also involved in the manufacture of brass products.

Restored quarry tram – trams similar to this one (photographed at Taly-y-bont, near Brecon) may have carried Pennant Sandstone from Cnap Llwyd Quarry (on Graig Trewyddfa) to Neath Road, Plasmarl. The quarry was in use for 50 years 1826–76) and a tramroad – possibly a self-acting incline-plane – may have operated on a raised embankment that ran all the way down the steep, eastern slope of Graig Trewyddfa.[12]

Miscellaneous Industries

Coal and metal were not the only industries to take root in the L.S.V. The coal seams contained low refractory fire-clay, which could be used to produce firebricks and furnace linings. Several clay/pug mills are known to have existed in connection with copperworks. High-refractory bricks – those able to withstand extremely high temperatures – were originally imported from the Midlands until, with the construction of the Swansea Canal, silica-bricks were made and transported from Dinas at the head of the Vale of Neath. Silica sand was also conveyed to the L.S.V., making it possible for the larger smelters to produce their own firebricks; moreover, both silica sand and bricks were shipped to distant lands, so much so that the Russian word for silica is Dinas.

Houses, smelting halls, chapels and a host of other buildings were built, using the local Pennant Sandstone. There were quarries everywhere; besides quarrymen, there were an incalculable number of tradesmen engaged in the various aspects of building. Most of the quarries were on land leased by industrialists and the stone used to satisfy their needs. Quarries may also have been leased by quarrymen for the purpose of supplying stone to whoever needed it. However, apart from this random and ill-recorded quarrying activity, all other industries – such as pottery and chemical – were comparatively small and are beyond the scope of this work.

Landowners on the west bank

Much has been said about leading industrialists, but little about who were the principal landowners in the L.S.V. On the west bank the dukes of Beaufort were lords of the 900-acre fee of Trewyddfa. On this estate the dukes leased the land and they granted mineral leases that gave industrialists such as Robert Morris the right to work the several coal seams beneath the surface. From the land the dukes received rent; from the mineral leases they claimed royalties on coal raised.

From 1746 (when Lockwood, Morris & Co. took out the first of several mineral leases on the Duke's Trewyddfa estate) until 1800 (when the partnership was dissolved) the majority of collieries in this area were the creation of the Lockwood, Morris concern. In the early part of Victoria's reign the principal holder of mineral leases in Trewyddfa was the Swansea Coal Co., which, between 1837 and the early 1850s, took over the leases in the possession of the Penyvilia Vein Co. and John Morris II. In 1863 these leases passed to Vivian & Sons, although by then a number of old workings had been sub-leased to up-and-coming coal producers such as Messrs. Richard & Glasbrook.

To the north of Trewyddfa lay the manor of Clase, which extended from the Tawe as far west as Penllergaer. This 3,000-acre estate was held by the bishops of St. David's. The manorial court still functioned here as late as 1902, its main venues being the Penllergaer Arms and the Plough and Harrow, Llangyfelach. There was coal under this estate, although it was not worked in earnest until after c.1840.

South-west of Trewyddfa lay the Pentre estate, consisting of more than 500 acres, stretching from Brynhyfryd to a point west of Blaen-y-maes. At the time of Victoria's coronation the Pentre estate was held by Calvert Richard Jones II, who also held properties in and around Swansea. In 1797 Lockwood, Morris & Co. took out mineral leases on the 5-foot, 6-foot and 3-foot coal seams on the Pentre estate. After 1800 these leases passed to Lockwood & Co., the Penyvilia Vein Co., John Morris II, the Swansea Coal Co. and finally, in 1863, to Vivian & Sons.

It should be pointed out that there were many landowners who held much – if not most – of their land on leases from either the duke or the bishop, or from men such as Calvert Richard Jones. The Morrises, for example, had been big landowners in Llangyfelach parish during the late 18th century, much of their property held on leases, but by 1838 (when the tithe survey for Llangyfelach was carried out) their estate had shrunk to just over 400 acres in the hamlet of Clase Lower, although they still held leases on over 1,000 acres in the parish of St. Mary. Another big landowning family of former times were the Popkins of Forest Hall. In 1798 the Popkins were forced to sell off much of their estate, and the biggest buyer was Charles Calland. Charles acquired some 500 acres on the East Side and another 260 acres on the west bank. He then took up residence at Forest Hall. When he died in 1836 he was succeeded by his son, John Forbes Calland.

Further south lay the parish of St. John. That part of the parish to the west of Llangyfelach Road coincided with the 225-acre manor of East Millwood, within which the manorial court still functioned until at least 1828. In the 18th century the manor had been worked for coal by the Prices of Penllergaer, their most productive colliery being the Pentre(gethin) Level in Manselton. At the time of the tithe survey of 1844 the manor was held by Major C. Phillips, proprietor of Millwood Colliery, which he sold in 1848. Between Llangyfelach Road and the Tawe lay the Hafod district. The Vivians owned 79 acres here, most of it containing scattered cottages. The Earl of Jersey owned 117 acres along the banks of the Tawe, ten acres of which were occupied by part of the Morfa Works, and 21 acres by the Hafod Works. Most of what remained of the earl's 117 acres was later leased to the Vivians for the development of Trevivian and their southern works complex.

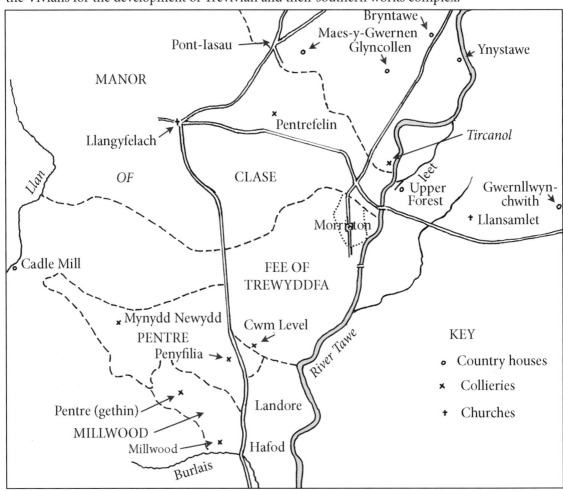

Land ownership on the west bank – for landownership on the East Side
see the map on page 235.

Some industrialists made use of existing country houses and farms to provide homes for themselves (as did Robert Morris when he bought Tredegar farm in 1739), or for their agents and key workers (as did the proprietors of White Rock when they utilized the mansion of Cnap-goch on the slopes of Kilvey Hill). Then, in the early 1770s, John Morris I built Clasemont, by far the most impressive mansion that ever stood in the L.S.V. After John's death in 1819 the house was abandoned; by 1826 it had been more or less demolished. Nothing remains of the house, nor the extensive parkland that surrounded it – except a small piece of land that is now Morriston Park.

Some industrialists were attracted to Sketty (as were the Vivians). Others chose to make use of country mansions in the L.S.V. (as did the Smiths when they acquired Gwernllwynchwith). One area that proved attractive to those involved in industry lay to the north and north-west of Morriston. The area was good agricultural land, so much so that several gentry houses had been established there prior to the coming of industry. By the time of Victoria's coronation these old houses had become the residences of those with a stake in industry.

Ynystawe Hall, for example, along with its 130-acre parkland had been in the possession of Edward Martin since the early 19th century. Edward was an engineer/surveyor from Cumberland

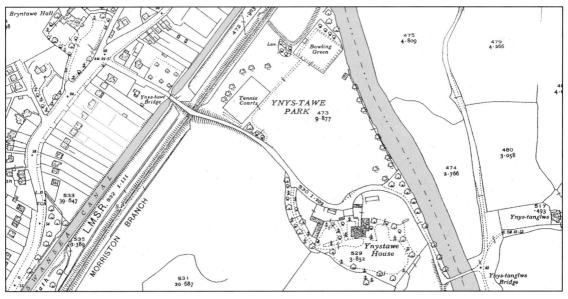

Ynystawe Hall 1937 – there had been an imposing country residence at Ynystawe in Medieval times, one that had belonging to the influential Hopkin/Popkin family. The hall that existed in Victorian times could be dated to two periods – the rear to the late 18th century, and the front (which was castellated and had an octagonal tower protruding through the roof) to c.1850.
The census for 1841 records that Martha Martin lived here with her sons, Thomas and William, and her daughters, Ann and Jane. All were described as of independent means, as were two other residents, Martha and Suzanah Davies. There were also four resident servants. Ten years later only William Martin, a stable boy and a servant were in residences. In the 20th century the hall was converted into flats and demolished in c.1960. The parkland is now known as Ynystawe Park; it can be accessed via Park Road. Near the top left-hand corner of the map is Bryntawe Hall, a neighbouring country house demolished in 1974.

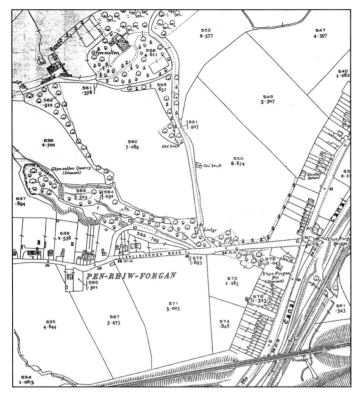

Glyncollen House 1937 – in Victorian times this 14-roomed house could be dated to two periods – the rear to 1773, and the front (with a veranda) to the early 19th century. In 1838 the house was owned by Joseph Martin who in 1841 conveyed it to his younger brother, William. Glyncollen – meaning Valley of the Hazel Trees – was demolished in c.1972 to make way for the M4 Motorway, which cut the adjoining 65-acre estate in two. Ynysforgan Roundabout now occupies the area just beyond the right-hand edge of this map. The lodge house near Llanlleianwen Road is all that survives today. Note the Swansea Canal near the lower right-hand edge of the map. The canal is gone, but the railway viaduct still passes over the old road between Morriston to Clydach.

who, for many years, had resided in Morriston (Martin Street may have been named after him). Acclaimed as 'the greatest authority on coal and coal mining in South Wales',[14] he also surveyed and advised on the construction of canals, roads, Swansea Harbour and Oystermouth Tramroad. A part owner of collieries in the Upper Swansea Valley, he also acted as agent for the sale of properties ranging from collieries to shops. When he died in 1818 his wife, Martha, continued to live at Ynystawe until her death in 1844 at the age of 78.

Martha gave birth to at least four boys, three of whom were still alive in 1838. The most prominent son was Joseph (d.1850), a barrister-at-law who married the daughter of the Morriston industrialist, William Bevan. Joseph made his mark as a speculator, buying and selling mineral leases. Several leases he sold to the Swansea Coal Co. (of which he was a director) and to Messrs. Davey & Pegg, which resulted in the creation of the Birchgrove Colliery.

The tithe assessment of 1838 records that Martha and her three sons held between them over 1,100 acres throughout the length and breadth of Llangyfelach parish. Her son, Joseph, owned four properties in the vicinity of Ynystawe, which amounted to almost 200 acres. He also owned two country houses in the same area – Glyncollen and Maes-y-Gwernen (on the site of Morriston Hospital).

In Morriston there were many fine houses, as a number of industrialists, businessmen and works managers either lived or had second homes there. The most notable house was Bath Villa, home of the tinplate magnate, John Jones Jenkins until at least 1864. Situated above Slate Street and, therefore, just outside John Morris's planned township, the house is depicted on the 1877

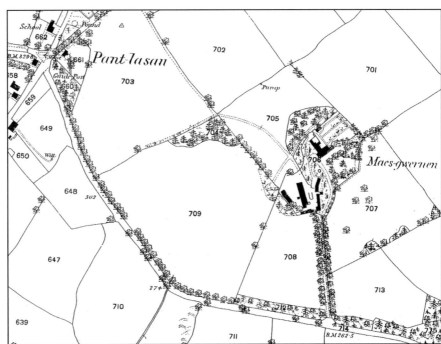

Maes-y-Gwernen Hall 1877 – the 65-acre estate connected with this house is now occupied by Morriston Hospital. In Victorian times it was owned by the Martin family and leased to others.

O.S. map as one in which the grounds are surrounded by trees (as were most country houses). By 1873 John had moved to the Grange, West Cross, but his parents continued to live at Bath Villa, apparently sharing it with one E.F. Daniel. Both parents died at the villa, the father in 1883 and the mother in 1902, after which the property (which included cottages in Bath Road) was put up for sale. What happened to the house after 1902 is difficult to determine. Modern housing now occupies the site.

Landowners on the East Side

On the East Side the Lordship of Kilvey belonged to the Dukes of Beaufort who, as manorial lords, claimed all minerals beneath the surface, for which they received royalties 'for every wey of coal shipped ... over the bar' at the entrance to Swansea Harbour. As landowners the dukes owned several parcels, the largest being the 229-acre Lower Forest estate.

The tithe survey that was carried out within the parish of Llansamlet took place in 1844, six years after the one in Llangyfelach parish. At the time of the Llansamlet survey the largest land-owner on the East Side was the Earl of Jersey, who owned around 3,000 acres in Llansamlet parish as part of his Briton Ferry estate. In the early 18th century the estate had been owned and worked for coal by the Mansels of Margam and Penrice. In 1750 a large part of the estate in Llansamlet was leased to Chauncey Townsend, whose successors, the Smiths, successfully developed it as part of their Llansamlet Colliery undertaking. In 1844 C.H. Smith held on lease some 400 acres in scattered parcels; he also owned 60 acres freehold in the same parish.

Immediately to the north lay the 570-acre estate of Gwernllwynchwith, owned by Mrs. Lucy (née Morgan) Bowen who, sometime after 1844, appears to have sold it to the Gregorys of

Styvechale Hall near Coventry. The estate had been leased to the Townsend-Smith family in 1750, and they continued to hold it (except for the period *c.*1812-28) until 1872 as part of their Llansamlet Coalfield.

In 1844, Lucy Bowen jointly owned with two other women a further 300 acres, presumably to the north of Gwernllwynchwith. At the same time Joseph Martin owned 260 acres in the Birchgrove area, which he soon increased to around 500. In *c.*1846 he sold 200 acres to Messrs. Davey & Pegg for their Birchgrove Colliery undertaking. In 1852 William Pegg enlarged the estate by purchasing some 780 acres, which he worked for coal and developed for agricultural purposes.

In the far north of the parish John Lucas of Stouthall owned the 390-acre Garth and Glais estates. Other big landowners were Callands with almost 500 acres, including the 223-acre Upper Forest estate. Messrs. Pascoe Grenfell & Sons held 270 acres, and Messrs. John Freeman & Co. held a little over 200 acres.

Within Llansamlet parish were four houses of note, one of which, Gwernllwynchwith, was the residence of C.H. Smith. To the north stood Birchgrove House, which from *c.*1750 onwards had been home to the Morgan family, who appear to have moved to this house after they had leased

Drumma Isaf – this is the only country house (albeit in a ruinous state) to survive in the L.S.V.
The central part dates back to at least the 18th century. By 1861 the London coal merchant,
William Pegg, had enlarged the house and taken up residence here. The house was sold
in 1875 by William's son and successor, after which the family returned to London.
At a later date the house served as flats for colliers.

their Gwernllwynchwith estate (and probably their former residence) to Chauncey Townsend. Lucy (née Morgan) Bowen was still in residence at Birchgrove in 1841, but 11 years later the house became home to William Pegg, proprietor of the Birchgrove Colliery, until he moved to Drumma Isaf further north.

The last house in Llansamlet to be considered is Upper Forest on the banks of the Tawe, once the residence of a branch of the Popkin family. Built in the late 17th century and subsequently enlarged, this L-shaped, two-storeyed house stood near the Tawe. Sometime after 1845, William Hallem, proprietor of the Upper Forest (tinplate) Works, moved into Upper Forest, and probably remained in residence there until the works closed temporarily in 1869. Upper Forest eventually became buried under a slag tip and no longer exists.

Near the Tawe estuary lay the hamlet of St. Thomas, within which were two houses of note. Mention has already been made of Maesteg House, built by the Grenfells in *c.*1840, and surrounded by eight acres of parkland. The census for 1851 records that Pascoe St. Leger Grenfell lived there with his wife and three daughters. Also in residence was a governess, nine servants (including a butler and a footman), two gardeners and a lodge keeper. Less than a mile to the east was a much older house, that of Dan-y-Graig. There had been a country residence at this location in the 17th century. Little is known of the house that existed in the 19th century, but in 1844 both the house and its 160-acre estate (which belonged to the Earl of Jersey) were leased to Nathaniel Cameron, a landowner and industrialist who had been mayor of Swansea in 1835–7. The house is marked on a map of 1867 as disused.

Parishes

Peninsula Gower, East Gower and the Lordship of Kilvey constituted the Deanery of Gower, which was part of the Diocese of St. David's. The parishes within the Deanery that extended into the L.S.V. were as follows: to the north of Swansea Borough lay the parish of St. John, which corresponds with the Hafod, Cwmbwrla and Manselton districts. Further north lay the huge ecclesiastical parish of Llangyfelach, which was subdivided into several civil parishes known as hamlets or parcels. One of these parcels, that of Clase Lower, lay between the Tawe and the old Llangyfelach Road (the boundary actually deviated from this road more than once); its most southerly district was Landore. The hamlet of Penderry Lower lay almost entirely to the west of Llangyfelach Road, so only a small part of it bordered on the L.S.V.

On the East Side the situation was somewhat complicated. Near the Tawe estuary the hamlet of St. Thomas was part of the parish of St. Mary. To the north and east lay Llansamlet, which did not become an ecclesiastical parish in its own right until *c.*1840 (prior to that date it had been part of the ecclesiastical parish of Llangyfelach). For administrative purposes (Poor Law, etc.) most of Llansamlet was divided into two civil parishes – Llansamlet Higher and Llansamlet Lower (the eastern boundary of the latter was the Glan-y-wern Canal). The area of Llansamlet to the east of the Crymlyn stream was incorporated into the neighbouring civil parish of Coedffranc. The same stream (or at least its approximate course) is how the eastern boundary of the City and County of Swansea (see plan on next page).

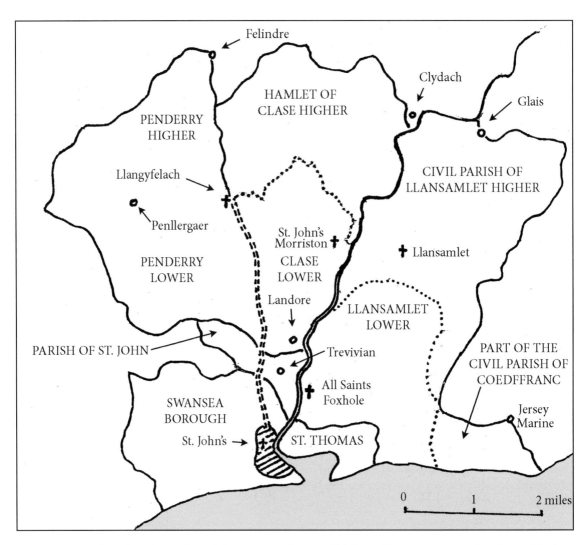

Ecclesiastical and civil parishes of the L.S.V. – the parallel dotted lines represent the Llangyfelach Road, which (except for minor deviations) served as the boundary between the hamlets of Penderry Lower and Clase Lower, both of which were civil parishes within the huge ecclesiastical parish of Llangyfelach. To the south the tiny parish of St. John comprised of what are now the Hafod, Cwmbwrla and Manselton districts. East of the Tawe the parish of Llansamlet was for the most part divided into two civil parishes – Llansamlet Higher and Llansamlet Lower – but the 'toe' of the parish (i.e. the land extending towards Jersey Marine) was incorporated within the neighbouring civil parish of Coedffranc. Near the Tawe estuary the hamlet of St. Thomas and Swansea Borough, together with the area to the west of the borough formed part of the ecclesiastical parish of St. Mary.

Anglican Churches

The *Religious Census* of 1851 lists four churches in the L.S.V. The oldest of these, Llangyfelach, originated as a monastic foundation in the Dark Ages. When Llangyfelach became a parish church it served a parish so large that it dwarfed even Llanrhidian. St. Samlet's Llansamlet was also an old foundation; it was certainly in existence in the Middle Ages. St. Samlet's had been a chapel of ease to Llangyfelach until 1840, when it became a parish church in its own right.

Closer to Swansea, the parish of St. John had no church within its bounds. The parish church of St. John (a 12th century dedication; now St. Matthew's) stood in High Street in the neighbouring parish of St. Mary. Clearly, with an ever-increasing population in the valley there was a need for additional Anglican places of worship. Yet the Church did not respond to the need, nor to the fact that the population was being won over to the Nonconformist causes. No doubt the local Anglican clergymen could see what was happening, but it was the resident copper-masters who provided the additional churches.

St. John's Morriston – built by John Morris I in 1789, the original 'island' church was intended to occupy a focal point in the township. The church seen here is an entire rebuild of 1859–62, although it was never finished according to plan.

All Saints, Foxhole – built as a chapel of ease by Pascoe St. Leger Grenfell in 1842–5; it was enlarged by him 14 years later. All Saints became the parish church of Llansamlet Lower in 1881.

The island church of St. John, Morriston (though not the rebuild that can be seen today) was built in 1789 by John Morris I in response to an appeal by local clergymen. Some 54 years later, Pascoe St. Leger Grenfell built All Saints Foxhole (1842-3), again after an appeal by a local clergyman. A few years earlier, John Henry Vivian had planned to build a church at Trevivian, but due to a dispute with the Bishop of St David's the project was shelved for almost 40 years. It has been said that the copper-masters' motives for building churches had been self-interest in that their generosity created a more quiescent workforce, which may well have been true, but there can be no denying the religious convictions of the men mentioned above.

The copper-masters' involvement in church building, however, did nothing to increase the size of Anglican congregations; that was something only the Church could do, and in that it failed dismally. On Census Day 1851, the morning congregation at Llangyfelach stood at 150 plus 40 scholars, which is amazingly small considering that the church could accommodate 700 people. At the morning services at Llansamlet and All Saints Foxhole there were 220 and 126 empty seats respectively. At St. John's Morriston the evening congregation stood at 74 worshippers plus 17 scholars, whereas the building had seating for a congregation of 108. There were two services at St. John's and at Llansamlet, one in English and one in Welsh, whereas at All Saints Foxhole both serv- ices were in English. From the above data it can be said that the four Anglican churches were never full and that the services were for mainly English-speaking congregations.

The Nonconformists, on the other hand, catered for mainly Welsh-speaking congregations, and in most places of worship not only was the seating capacity given, but standing room was given as well. In most chapels there was sufficient seating on Census Day to accommodate the largest assemblages, which usually meant the evening service assemblies. The two exceptions were Canaan Llansamlet and Libanus Morriston. The congregations at both these chapels exceeded the seating capacity. In the decades that followed, the Nonconformist congregations grew to the extent that chapels had to be rebuilt to cater for the increasing numbers; some chapels had to be rebuilt more than once.

The Anglicans may have had hopes of increasing the size of their congregations when, in 1858–9, they enlarged All Saints Foxhole, and rebuilt St. John's Morriston in 1859–62. Their hopes – if hopes there had been – were dashed by the Nonconformist revival of 1859, which resulted in huge numbers swelling the Nonconformist congregations. However, while the Nonconformists were benefiting from the revival, the Grenfells were evangelising in St. Thomas; they were, moreover, evangelising in a manner that Nonconformists would have been familiar with, and they were doing it on behalf of the Established Church. It started when Mary Grenfell bought one, then two houses in Pinkney Street. These premises were used as an Anglican meeting-house until, in 1862, the new infant school at St. Thomas became available for use. Further development did not take place until the latter half of Victoria's reign when a corrugated iron church was built, and later replaced by the stone church that can be seen today.

The Nonconformist chapels

The Established Church had a hierarchy of bishops, etc., whereas the Nonconformists did not; nor did they worship according to the Anglican Book of Common Prayer. Nonconformist chapels and meeting-houses were usually barn-like structures in which the pulpit occupied pride of place. The Religious Census of 1851 lists 20 buildings used for worship by the Nonconformists in the L.S.V. Fourteen of these buildings were situated on the west bank, seven of them in Morriston.

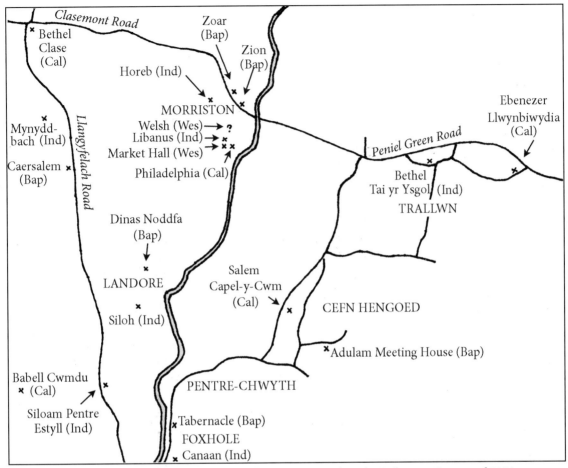

Nonconformist places of worship – those mentioned in the Religious Census of 1851.
They are marked (Ind) for Independent, (Cal) for Calvinistic Methodist, (Bap) for Baptist
and (Wes) for Wesleyan Methodist.

The services at 18 places of worship were in Welsh; only two congregations, both of them small, attended services in English.

Seven of the buildings referred to in the census were used by the Independents, by far the largest denomination in the valley. There was no noteworthy dogma within this gathered church to distinguish it from other denominations; what was noteworthy about this denomination was that it did not have a strong centralized authority, but formed a loose union in which every congregation was 'independent' in the sense that it had been established by its members, who elected their own deacons, called their own ministers and developed their own programme. Their strength lay in their ability to establish branches, which usually became independent of the mother church from which they sprang.

The Independents (in England they were known as Congregationalists) had a long history, being active in the Mynydd-bach area soon after the English Civil War of 1642–6. They erected their first purpose-built chapel at Mynydd-bach in 1762. Their cause prospered to the extent that the census of 1851 recorded 'upwards of 12 [daughter] churches have been established as branches of this place'.

231

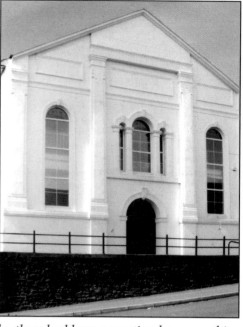

Above: *Mynydd-bach, an Independent chapel – an earlier chapel (built in 1762) was referred to in the census of 1851. The chapel seen here is a rebuild by Thomas Thomas in 1866–7, along with some 20th century modifications.*

Above right: *Libanus Morriston, an Independent chapel – there had been a meeting-house on this site in Market Street as far back as 1782. The chapel seen here is the result of a rebuild carried out by Thomas Thomas in 1857–8, before he perfected his distinctive style of chapel architecture.*

One of the earliest branches was established in *c.*1682, the members meeting at Ty-coch, a cottage at the northwestern end of the Graig Trewyddfa squatter settlement above Morriston. The actual location of Ty-coch cottage is interesting. It was one of several cottages that stood near the entrance to the old Clyndu Level – not the canal level, but one whereby the coal was 'taken out ... by [a] horse tramway'. Bath Villa (home of John Jones Jenkins, the tinplate magnate) also stood near the entrance to the old Clyndu Level. Today the Ty-coch cottage site is occupied by three terraced houses known as Ty-coch Villas.

In 1782, three years after the foundation of Morriston, the Ty-coch assembly leased from John Morris I a plot of land for 1,000 years at 1s. per annum. On this plot they built a barn-like meeting-house called Libanus. The congregation at Libanus grew to the extent that, 14 years later, the building had to be extended. The congregation continued to grow with the result that the chapel was completely rebuilt in 1831. On Census Day 1851, the evening congregation at Libanus stood at 621, and 341 scholars attended Sunday school in the afternoon. Libanus, however, was not the only Independent chapel in Morriston. In 1842–4 Horeb Chapel was built in what became Horeb Road. On Census Day 1851, Horeb had an evening congregation of 300, and 138 scholars attended Sunday school in the afternoon.

Further south the Independents at Mynydd-bach had established a branch chapel known as (old) Siloh Landore. In the early 1820s the Siloh congregation had met in a works office in the Nant Rhyd-y-Filais ravine. In *c.*1824 they built a day school (Y Coleg) in what is now Siloh Road, and for a while they held their Sunday evening services there. What is interesting about Y Coleg is the

Old Siloh Landore – built in 1829 by the Independents, this chapel still stands at the bottom of Siloh Road. It was enlarged in 1840 and 1862, and finally superseded by Siloh Newydd (higher up the same road) in 1878. For a while this old chapel served as a Sunday school. Then in 1884 it became a place of worship for the English-speaking element of the Siloh congregation.

way it was built. During daylight hours the women gathered stones, either from the Rhyd-y-Filais stream, or from abandoned buildings in the ravine. Then the men, after they had finished their shifts, dressed the stones and built Y Coleg, probably under the supervision of a local builder, who may also have been a member of the congregation. The cost of the building was £90, a remarkably small figure when compared with the £560 spent in 1829 on building (old) Siloh next to Y Coleg.

There is no record of an Anglican congregation participating in the building of either a church or a school, whereas the Nonconformists were prepared to work within their capabilities, as was the case at Foxhole. Between 1806 and *c.*1840 the Independents at Foxhole had worshipped in the local copperworks school. In 1839 they leased a plot of land on the hillside. After finishing their shifts the men then dug a shelf in the hillside on which to build Canaan, which was probably erected by tradesmen. A similar cost-cutting exercise by an Independent congregation was carried out at Bethel in the village of Tai yr Ysgol, Llansamlet (between Penial Green Road and Trallwn). The Independents in this locality had erected Bethel in 1818. When they demolished the chapel in 1849, to make room for a larger one, the men obtained permission to take stone from a nearby quarry, the quarrying and transportation of the stone being carried out after the men had finished their shifts.

The Independent congregations at the six chapels mentioned above, plus Siloam Pentre Estyll (1839), were all relatively large, varying on Census Day from 250 worshippers at Mynyddbach to over 600 at Libanus Morriston. One reason for the Independents' success was their ability to set up new house groups from which a branch congregation could grow. An example of how they infiltrated a district is to be found in the report on education of 1847. As a result of enquiries in the Trevivian-Landore area an assistant commissioner wrote: 'A great improvement was said to have taken place in the manners of the district; this was attributed to the Sunday schools; they were introduced about twenty-seven years ago; at that time the population was left without spiritual care'. That would have been in *c.*1820 when the Independents established a house group in a works office at Landore (Trevivian did not exist until after 1837); they established the Sunday school known as Y Coleg in *c.*1824. The assistant commissioner went on to say, 'I took down ... the following statement from a sort of clerk or overseer ... "At that time [1820] an Independent

Salem Capel-y-Cwm – this old chapel in Cwm Chapel Road (near Bon-y-maen) was built in 1823 by the Calvinistic Methodists who worked as best they could to save the expense. The roof was raised for a gallery nine years later. The building was superseded by a new Salem in c.1867, which was built by the chapel architect John Humphrey on an adjoining piece of land. A small part of new Salem can be seen silhouetted against the skyline.

minister came to look after us – if he had been Baptist, Churchman, or any one else to have drawn in the net, he would have had us all". The Independents built the original Siloh Landore in 1829. They also built Siloam Pentre Estyll ten years later, thereby ensuring that Trevivian became an Independent stronghold.

The second largest denomination in the L.S.V. were the Calvinistic Methodists, or Welsh Methodists as they were otherwise known. The Calvinistic Methodists were often singled out for their belief in predestination, meaning that salvation was only available to those whom God had ordained. Unlike the Independents, they were subject to a strong centralized authority in the form of a presbytery – a body of elders, the majority of whom were laymen.

Originating in the 18th century as a reform movement within the Anglican Church, the Calvinistic Methodists owed their existence in the L.S.V. to the fiery preaching of Howell Harris, who addressed mass gatherings in Welsh. Howell's preaching led to the establishment of house groups in which members sought to enhance their spiritual growth. The Church's unwillingness to reform resulted in schism, with the Calvinistic Methodists becoming a new Nonconformist denomination in 1811, but long before that date they were building their own meeting-houses. The first of these meeting-houses was Salem Capel-y-Cwm (near Bon-y-maen) Llansamlet, established in 1782. On Census Day 1851 the evening service at *Salem* stood at 643 worshippers, and 305 scholars attended the morning Sunday school.

It has been said that the second Calvinistic Methodist cause in the valley originated as a breakaway group from the Independents at Libanus. This has been contested on the grounds that members of different denominations were not averse to worshipping together when there was only one meeting-house in the locality. This would appear to have been the case at Ty-coch and at Libanus, where Calvinistic Methodists worshipped alongside Independents. However, in 1795–8 the Calvinistic Methodists began holding their own meetings in two converted cottages on the site of the later Market Hall. By 1802 they had moved to a purpose-built meeting-house in a nearby street, which they called Philadelphia. In 1829 the meeting-house was replaced by the chapel that can be seen today. The 1851 census records an evening congregation of 610, and 506 scholars had attended the afternoon Sunday schools.

In all, the Calvinistic Methodists had five chapels in 1851. Apart from the two mentioned above, they had Bethel Clase (1809) in the village of Llangyfelach, Ebenezer Llwynbiwydia (Lon-las), Llansamlet (1834) and Babell Cwmdu (1845), which, although in St. Mary's parish, served a growing industrial community in the Cwmbwrla area. On Census Day 1851, the Calvinistic Methodist congregations ranged from 115 at Ebenezer Llansamlet to 643 at Salem in the same parish.

Philadelphia, a Calvinistic Methodist chapel – built in 1829 and, therefore, the oldest surviving place of worship in Morriston. What is unusual about its design is that the main entrance is on a side wall (and not on the gable end). Its future is uncertain.

The Baptists – like the Independents – were part of a loose ecclesiastical organization. What set them apart from other denominations was not so much their insistence of total immersion, but that baptism had to be accompanied by a genuine profession of faith. Infant baptism was unacceptable on the ground that an infant had no understanding of what baptism meant.

Although the Baptists had a long history in Swansea, their chapel-building activity in the L.S.V. appears to have been late and initially unsuccessful. In 1809 they tried to establish themselves in Morriston, but their cause failed. Their second attempt to establish themselves was at Landore, where they built Dinas Noddfa in 1823 (not the later rebuild that can be seen today). On Census Day 1851, Dinas Noddfa had an afternoon congregation of 150, and 85 scholars attended the morning Sunday school. Other places of worship were established in the years that followed – Tabernacle Foxhole (1829), Caersalem Newydd Treboeth (1839), Seion (Zion) Morriston (1847)

Vestry, Caersalem Newydd Treboeth – the building on the north side of Caersalem was once the original Baptist chapel, built in c.1845. It became a vestry when the larger, more ornate Caersalem Newydd was built beside it in 1873.

and Adulam Meeting House (Cefn Hengoed) Llansamlet (1848). At all these places the services were in Welsh. Then in 1850 the Baptists founded Zoar Morriston and the services there were in

Morriston Market, Market Street – built by John Morris II in 1827, the front elevation was once flanked by two towers with battlements. Access to the market was through the arches on the ground floor. A large room on the first floor was used at various times as a dame school, a charity school and a Wesleyan chapel.

English. In total the Baptists had six places of worship in 1851, the congregations on Census Day ranging from 49 at Tabernacle Foxhole to 265 at Caersalem Treboeth.

The last denomination to be considered is the Wesleyan Methodists (who, incidentally, did not hold to the doctrine of predestination, but believed that salvation was available to all). In *c.*1800 a small group of Wesleyans established themselves on the site of the later Market Hall (possibly in the converted cottages that had been used by the Calvinistic Methodists in the late 1790s). In 1851 they were holding services in the large room above the Market Hall. On Census Day their evening congregation stood at 40, and 30 scholars attended the afternoon Sunday school. The services were in English, which is what one would expect in a Wesleyan place of worship. Yet strange though it may seem, Morriston had a Welsh-language Wesleyan Methodist group as well, its congregation on Census Day numbering only 15. It is not known where this group met, as the census stated only that they came together in a building 'not used exclusively as a place of worship'.

The religious census of 1851 makes it plain that Morriston was a centre of Nonconformist activity, the Independents having two places of worship, the Baptists two, the Wesleyans two and the Calvinistic Methodists one. It should not be difficult to image the streets of Morriston thronging with chapel-goers on a Sunday evening, either going to, or leaving their places of worship – 600 from Libanus, 600 from Philadelphia and 500 from five other venues, 1,700 in all, and that at a time when the population of Morriston and its surrounding area stood at around 3,400. The 90 or so Anglicans leaving St. John's (in the centre of the main thoroughfare) at roughly the same time must have felt outnumbered and overwhelmed.

Welsh Nonconformity

In the report on education in Wales of 1847 the commissioner for South Wales had stated that the Welsh workman, whether a peasant or an industrial worker, was isolated, in part by his language 'while all the world about him is English, [and in part because he] shrinks from holding communion with classes either superior to, or different from himself, [and also because] his worship, like his life, has grown different from the [Anglican] classes over him ... He has raised the buildings [chapels] and maintains the ministry of his worship over the whole face of his country'.

That Nonconformity should be so strong in Wales, a country in which the overwhelming majority were either peasants or industrial workers, was an anomaly in the U.K. Nonconformity appealed mainly to the middle classes – to farmers, shopkeepers, colliery managers, etc. – and at one time to lesser gentry as well, but by the time of Victoria's coronation a large proportion of the Welsh working class had swelled the ranks of the Nonconformist denominations, and the number went on increasing to the extent that Welsh Nonconformity became the religion of the lower classes. Towards the end of Victoria's reign the situation gradually changed as more and more industrial workers put their faith in politics and trade unionism, leaving Welsh Nonconformity to revert to its middle-class origin.

The commissioner (referred to above) stated that the reason why Nonconformity had become established 'over the whole face of [the country was due to Sunday schools]. These schools, [he maintained], have been almost the sole, they are still the main and most congenial, centres of education. Through their agency the younger portion of the adult labouring classes in Wales can generally read, or are in the course of learning to read, the Scriptures in their mother tongue'. The link between Welsh Nonconformity and the Welsh language was therefore strong, so strong that when the language went into decline, so too did Welsh Nonconformity.

The commissioner described how Sunday schools were established.

> A congregation meets in its chapel. It elects those whom it considers to be its most worthy members, intellectually and religiously, to act as 'teachers' to the rest, and one or more to 'superintend' the whole. Bible classes, Testament classes, and classes of such as cannot yet read, are formed. They meet once, generally from 2 to 4 p.m., sometimes in the morning also, on each Sunday. The Superintendent, or one of the teachers, begins the school by prayer; they then sing; then follows the class instruction, the Bible and Testament classes reading and discussing the Scriptures, the others learning to read.

There is little to be gained in listing the local Sunday schools. Far more enlightening is an understanding of the term 'adherents', and for that it is necessary to state that most congregations had their minister as well as a number of deacons; that is, spiritually sound men who had not been ordained, but whose purpose was to oversee the running of the ministry, and to deputize for the minister when necessary. Only a small percentage of the congregation were actually chapel members. The rest were called 'hearers or adherents'. They were the product of Sunday schools, people who had learnt to read in such places and were, therefore, familiar with the Scriptures. They might turn up at a Sunday evening service with their dependents to sing and hear what the minister had to say; moreover, whenever there was a revival it was from the ranks of adherents that new chapel members came.

The Great Revival of 1858-60

In his *Revival Comes To Wales* (1986) Eifion Evans describes this religious awakening as follows:

> Prayer was undoubtedly one of the leading characteristics of the revival in Wales ... The powerful influences of the revival were first felt, and continued to be felt, generally, in the prayer meetings. A strong – sometimes overwhelming – influence would pervade the meeting while someone prayed, or during the singing of a hymn ... This movement would be felt by all present, manifesting itself in different ways; bringing some to an overpowering sense of guilt and conviction of sin, and creating in others an irresistible desire to rejoice in and praise the God of their salvation.

When it came to Wales in 1858 the Great Revival was not a new phenomenon. As far back as *c*.1735 the country had experienced religious awakenings at regular intervals, so regular that Wales was regarded as 'the land of revivals'. Some of these 'visitations of the Holy Spirit' were local affairs. Others were regional; a few came close to being national. Eighteenth century revivals were invariably connected with the Methodists – both Wesleyan and Calvinistic – but from the early 19th century onwards the Independents and the Baptists also drew in large numbers of converts.

Revivals originated and flourished in mainly rural areas, their effects sometimes spreading into industrialized South Wales. This was certainly the case in 1828 when an awaking began in Carmarthenshire, then spread to industrialized areas where, at Morriston, the Calvinistic/Welsh Methodist congregation grew to the extent that Philadelphia had to be built the following year. This particular revival began at a prayer meeting, but they could also be the product of powerful preaching and even external issues such as fear. The cholera epidemic of 1849 caused many in industrial South Wales to consider eternity. Congregations in Swansea and the L.S.V. benefited enormously from this awakening, despite predictions that a 'relapse would follow this sudden increase' in converts once the epidemic had passed, but the revival continued into the following year.

There were no further awakenings – apart from purely local ones – for almost 20 years. The situation was viewed by some chapel leaders as a state of stagnation; the chapels were, therefore, in need of a spiritual awakening. Congregations prayed for another revival, and they went on praying. Then, in the closing months of 1857, word came of an awakening that was sweeping through America. It had begun at a prayer meeting in New York on 25 September that year.

The first signs of a 'visitation of the Holy Spirit' in Wales occurred in April 1858. At Llan-fairfechan there were 'strong impression' felt at a Methodist prayer meeting. What happened there spread to other villages and towns along the North Wales coastline. An awakening at Llangybi spread throughout northern Cardiganshire. In May 'some tens of people [were converted] in and around Swansea, [after which there were] powerful outpourings' at widely scattered locations throughout the country. At this stage the revival was not a national one, but in 1859 the movement spread from northern Cardiganshire like ripples in a pond to all parts of Wales, and beyond to Welsh communities in the Midlands. The revival peaked in January 1860; thereafter it gradually declined until the end of the year.

The revival was most active in industrial South Wales during the summer of 1859. Yet *The Cambrian* had virtually nothing to report on its effects in Swansea and the L.S.V. It could be argued that the 'visitations of the Holy Spirit' took place in chapels and meeting halls and were, therefore, not witnessed by outsiders. Indeed, some outsiders regarded the revival as man-made, an hysteria in which 'many persons of disreputable conduct [who] seem to be for the present changed ... will return to their former habits'. Even W.S. Williams in his *History of Methodists in West Glamorgan* had little to say beyond the fact that many were converted. What is evident, however, is the chapel building boom of the 1860s led, in the following decade, to the erection of chapels that were on a par with cathedrals.

The Welsh chapel-building boom

The need for bigger places of worship led to the simple, barn-like chapels being replaced by large, eye-catching structures, the elaborate frontages reflecting industrial wealth and the growing self-confidence of Nonconformists. In the latter part of Victoria's reign, some of these new-style chapels were to become cathedrals in their own right. They were to be found all over Wales and in Welsh communities in England, but their place of origin was, for the most part, the L.S.V. because it was home to three of the finest chapel architects in Wales.

The first of these architects was Thomas Thomas (1817-88), alias Thomas Glandwr (of Landore). Born at Llandeilo, the son of a chapel deacon, Thomas trained as a carpenter before his ordination as an Independent minister at the age of 30. In 1848 he was appointed minister of Siloh Landore; that same year he designed and supervised the building of his first chapel at Clydach. His innovative and easily recognized designs, coupled with his ever increasing reputation led to him becoming the builder, or re-builder, of no less that 119 chapels, to say nothing of schools and a college. In the L.S.V. alone he was responsible for building three schools and for rebuilding the Independent chapels of Bethel Llansamlet (1851), Libanus Morriston (1858), Canaan Foxhole (1864), Siloam Pentre Estyll (1864) and the Baptist chapel of Dinas Noddfa, Landore (1853). He was also responsible for building a chapel at Dan-y-graig (1860) near Lambert's Copperworks. This last chapel represented the establishment of an Independent cause in a relatively new community.

Simplified example of Thomas Thomas's work – the façade (the wall facing the street) is dominated by a giant recess arch, which breaks into a pediment (the triangular area at the top of the façade, marked A). Below the pediment the façade is divided into three sections (or bays) by four pilasters (decorative pillars). In the central section is a door (B), a triple, round-headed window (C) and a name plaque (D). In each of the flanking sections is a tall, round-headed window (E).

Right: *Philadelphia, Trevivian – this Welsh Baptist chapel on Neath Road, Hafod, was built in 1866-7 by the chapel architect John Humphrey. The chapel has many features that were copied from Thomas Thomas's work, but the oculus (circular opening at the top of the front elevation) was a feature that was common to John Humphrey's work.*

Thomas continued to design and supervise the building of chapels until 1885. However, in 1875 he suddenly resigned as minister of Siloh and moved to the Mumbles, where he continued his work, which included rebuilding Capel-y-Crwys, Three Crosses in 1877. Many copied his designs, particularly builders who had worked under his supervision, thereby adding to the number of chapels that serve as a reminder of how much his designs were admired.

Another prominent chapel-builder was John Humphrey, son of a Morriston collier and an Independent deacon. John trained as a carpenter and joiner, and worked with Thomas Thomas. At the age of 26 he was commissioned to build a school at Foxhole (1845) although there is evidence to suggest that this may not have been the first school he built. He was 47 when he began designing and supervising the building of chapels in his own right. He built Philadelphia, Trevivian for the Welsh Baptists, he rebuilt Mynydd-bach, Treboeth for the Independents and Salem, Llansamlet for the Calvinistic Methodists, all three of them in 1866-7, and all of them copies of Thomas Thomas's work. His own contribution to these chapels was the oculus (a circular opening near the apex of the front elevation), which was to become the hallmark of his later work. From 1870 onwards John developed his own distinctive style of chapel design. In all he built 54 imposing structures, ten of them in the L.S.V. His greatest achievements were Tabernacle, Morriston (1873) and Terrace Road School (1888). His later work and the work of other Swansea Valley chapel-builders will be dealt with in a later volume.

Nonconformist successes and failings

One of the prime concerns of Nonconformist leaders was to achieve legal equality with the Established Church. In 1836 they attained the right to solemnize marriages in chapel. In 1852 they were permitted to officiate at funerals in public burial grounds. In 1868 they witnessed the abolition of Church rates, and in 1871 they gained admission to Oxford and Cambridge universities. They were certainly in favour of the abolition of slavery, but improving the lot of Welsh peasants and industrial workers was not on their agenda. They gave no support to the Chartist movement; nor did they champion the grievances of the working man. It was a failing to their cost in that, during the latter part of Victoria's reign, more and more men took their grievances to the unions, then looked to the politicians for support.

Drink and fighting

One could be forgiven for questioning why there were so many chapel-goers in the L.S.V. and elsewhere, while on the other hand 'drunkenness was the prevailing sin' of many. The answer, of course, is 'that the sheep and the goats' lived together as neighbours. As to the number of public houses in a given neighbourhood, it was stated in 1847 that 'there were 15 or 16 public-houses between Pentre-[ch]with and the ferry [near Sainsbury's], about a mile and a half [in distance]. Drunkenness was the prevailing sin of the district. Wages were good, and there was little suffering except by the people's own fault'.

Cwmfelin Works c.1900-20 – although outside the period covered by this chapter, the photograph shows that drink was as much a problem then as in the early part of Victoria's reign. The women are said to have been congregating outside the works on pay-day, presumably to prevent their husbands spending hard-earned money in public houses. Note that the dress of most of the women is dowdy, consisting of long skirts and shawls, but one woman at least is wearing a colourful Welsh 'costume' even at this late date.

Public houses were not the only drinking venues. A cwrw-bach – meaning 'little beer' – was the illicit brewing and selling of beer, usually in someone's home. There were many who disapproved of the practice, and none more so than an anonymous innkeeper, who complained, in a letter to *The Cambrian* in 1853, about:

> the Cwrw-bach, or tea parties, that were held weekly and numerously in this town to the manifest injury of the licenced dealer, and to the social and moral injury to its juvenile inhabitants; for it is notorious that more young people, particularly females, are led to theft and prostitution by these tea parties, than by all other causes put together. It is not unfrequent for as many as six or eight of these parties to be held weekly in Swansea; commencing on Saturday night, and kept up day and night until Tuesday morning – selling all sorts of exciseable liquors, with music and dancing, card playing, etc., etc.

The innkeeper had started his letter with a reference to the action taken by Llanelly magistrates. He closed with an attack on Swansea magistrates 'who take no steps to put a stop to so glaring an evil. They surely possess the same power and means as the Llanelly magistrates. Let a poor publican only serve one glass of ale after certain hours, and he is immediately pounced upon'.

> Another popular custom at that time was to drink 'fetching' on the nearby fields. The meaning of the term is this: a number of men, mostly youngsters, would agree on Saturday night to buy a quantity of beer, enough under normal circumstances, to make them all drunk. Then on Sunday they would adjourn beyond the reach of the authorities, and there they remain drinking until the beer supply ran out. More often than not, these expeditions ended in bitter quarrels, sometimes in fights; frequently there was also a lot of skylarking whilst drinking.[15]

The above paragraph has been translated from a passage in John Williams's *Abertawe A'R Cylch 1860-1915*. John wrote about his recollections of Waunwen, where he grew up, and the neighbouring district of Cwmbwrla during the 1860s. What he had to say about fighting would have been evident in any of the industrial villages, as Swansea and District was a tough place. The men worked in a physically demanding environment. The women were likewise hardy, ready to vehemently defend their family honour. Add heavy drinking to the equation and outbursts of verbal and physical violence were inevitable. John Williams maintained that many 'would not have their usual period of sleep on a Saturday night [because] crowds of drunks went past their door and caused all kinds of mischief on the road between eleven and three or four on Sunday morning. [He could] remember whole families who excelled all others in the shameful bothers ... people whom it would be a danger to one's life to approach at the time, so vicious were their actions'.[14]

Every locality would have had its hard men, those who established their position in both work and their locality with their fists, but aggression could descend to another level – pugilism. According to John, arranged bouts 'occasionally took place on a Sunday morning, for then the pugilists chose to fight – stripped to the waist – until one or the other could fight no more. Pugilism was highly rated in this country between 1858 and 1866 ... and the habit of fighting was nowhere more glorified than in the Swansea District'. This was certainly the case in Waunwen where he knew 'several families who were actually pleased to see their own children winning renown ... as fighters. [He] knew one mother ... who was one of the leading enthusiasts in fighting affairs and a regular spectator of these bouts. [He] knew, also, several young men ... who went to their graves ... because their fine bodies had been disabled by fighting'.[14]

In the early part of Victoria's reign even Nonconformist preachers were not averse to a pint of beer, but the tolerant attitude towards alcohol was to change as the temperance movement gathered momentum, until eventually temperance and Nonconformity became inextricably linked. The movement began in Wales in 1832 – two years after the Beer House Act that led to the establishment of thousands of new beer-shops. It began with people pledging to abstain from alcohol, for which they received certificates. As the movement gathered momentum, it not only led to the closure of many beer-shops, but it forced Welsh brewers, both large and small, to produce weaker brews.

Between 1828 and 1853 licensees were not permitted to 'suffer any drinking ... during the hours of divine service'. The Lord's Day Act of 1848 prohibited public houses from opening before 1 p.m. on Sunday. Six years later another Act restricted Sunday opening hours to between 1 and 2.30 p.m. and to between 6 and 10 p.m. Until then the temperance campaigners had been on a winning streak, but two years later the government was forced to increase the Sunday opening hours to between 1 and 3p.m. and to between 5 and 11 p.m. It is likely that the restrictions of 1848 and 1854 led to an increase in illegal drinking fraternities such as fetching and cwrw-bach, which in other parts of the U.K. were known as shebeens.

Leisure

In the report on education (1847) there is a statement to the effect that 'the only intellectual resource of the adult population is the chapel, whether used for preaching or a Sunday-school; such as do not frequent the chapel pass their leisure time in the beer-house'. The statement, however, is not entirely true. Reading-rooms and other facilities were provided by some employers. In c.1858, for example, Messrs. Hallam & Madge, established reading and music classes at their Upper Forest Tinplate Works. Two years earlier William Hallam had 'arranged the first of his workman's day excursions. The employees accompanied by their family and friends, numbering about 700, paid a summer day's trip to Carmarthen where the "good conduct" of the men promised similar events in the future'.[16]

Such leisure pursuits were for those who wished to learn, or get away from their grim surroundings, but the hard-working valley people were capable of so much more. Poetry, prose and eisteddfodau had all been part of medieval Welsh culture. These pursuits, however, were not available to the labouring classes until after c.1850, by which time the eisteddfodau had taken on a new image and the development of railways made it possible for the masses to travel cheaply. As a result of these changes, colliers, furnacemen and farm hands with a flare for poetry, or who were able to write, saw the eisteddfodau as an opportunity to express themselves, allied to which was the added incentive of prize money. Young men aged between 19 and 26, who did well in contests, could find themselves sent to a Nonconformist academy to be educated with a view to becoming preachers. It was an opportunity to escape the hazards of the pit, the furnaces and the muddy fields in foul weather. Those who did not wish to be preachers moved on to become officials in friendly societies and trade unions.

When the eisteddfodau were revived in the late 18th century they were held in public houses and regarded as strictly for intellectuals, the supporters of whom were there for the revelry. The image changed when the proceedings became more colourful with the creation of bardic ceremonies and also when choral singing was added to existing contests in poetry, prose and performances of the harp. Choral singing had also been part of Medieval Welsh culture, as evidenced by a 12th century cleric. In the 19th century, it provided entertainment for the respectable, and eventually caught the attention of the Nonconformists. All sorts of choirs were formed – male, ladies, school, etc. – and they became very competitive; moreover, the choirs encouraged others to take an interest in music and, from 1855 onwards, music lovers were able to learn the tonic sol-fa method of reading music, which according to *The Cambrian* was introduced into Swansea by the arrival 'of Mr. Alfred Brown of ... London, who was specially invited to conduct a series of musical lessons ... the object [of which was] to improve more particularly congregational singing ... [the] sol-fa class ... the first [to be] established in Wales ... already numbers more than 800 members ... [and] the meetings [were] held alternatively in the different chapels ... on average about three times a night'.

Although the classes were held in Swansea, they undoubtedly attracted large numbers from the L.S.V. The classes coincided with the growing popularity of eisteddfodau, some of which were purely local affairs, while others attracted competitors from afar, drawing crowds and even local dignitaries, irrespective of whether they spoke Welsh. The first eisteddfod in the Lordship of Gower was held at Swansea in 1829. This was followed in 1840 by a 'Druidic Eisteddfod', one in which the Druid Society of Swansea took part in a procession to the Town Hall in Somerset Place. The first recorded eisteddfod in the L.S.V. was held at Morriston on 26 September 1854. This was not a Druidic Eisteddfod, but one organized by 'the various Ivorite Societies of Morriston', the dual aims of which were to provide benefit in times of need and to foster the Welsh language. The newspaper referred to a 'formidable assemblage of Bards, Essayists, Minstrels, etc., and 250 compositions [poetical and prose] were sent in for the occasion ... [due to] the favourable state of the weather, the event attracted an immense concourse of persons from Swansea, Neath, Aberavon, Merthyr and other Welsh districts, the number present being fully 3,000'.

Undoubtedly there were many workmen present, but *The Cambrian* was concerned only with naming the captains of industry who provided the prize money. William Hallem of the Upper Forest Tinplate Works; William Pegg, proprietor of the Birchgrove Colliery; George Byng Morris, son of John Morris II; and John Henry Vivian, MP for Swansea and District, were among those mentioned.

> The proceedings of the day were initiated by the assembling of the several Ivorite Lodges of Morriston, [the members of which set off] in procession, headed by a band, to meet the ... Mayor of Swansea. On his Worship's arrival, the Rev. M.R. Morgan, vicar of Llansamlet and Chairman of the Committee, presented him [the Mayor] with ... a very flattering address. [After the Mayor had responded to the welcome], the band struck up the 'March of the Men of Harlech', and proceeded by the Royal Standard, ... the cavalcade passed through the village and entered the [Eisteddfod Hall].

Speeches followed, the Morriston Choir then sang, and there were several recitals. Then the competition got under way. There were prizes of up to £12 12s. 'for the best poem, in English or Welsh'. There were prizes for the best elegies, the best singers, whether as solos or duets, and 'the best female performance of the Harp'. There were no choral competitions – the domination of the choirs at these events was yet to come. An Anglican presence was noticeable, but the Nonconformists appear to have had little or no involvement. The day when the chapel both promoted and dominated these events was likewise yet to come.

The next eisteddfod in the L.S.V. was a local one held at Llansamlet in 1861. This eisteddfod was devoted to choral singing, although the choirs were all small, their size ranging from three to 12 singers. Larger choirs did exist because, three years later, *The Cambrian* published an article entitled 'The Eisteddfod Chorus of 400'. This enlarged choir came into existence as a result of merging the 200 strong Swansea Valley Choir with other choirs in the West Glamorgan area.

Back in the 1850s there had been talk of a National Eisteddfod. In 1860 the newly-formed National Eisteddfod Council merged with the Gorsedd (the druids, etc.) to organize an eisteddfod at Denbigh, which was to establish a format that has continued to the present day. Three years later Swansea had two eisteddfodau in the same year – one in July and one in September, the latter being a National Eisteddfod in which the Morriston and the Swansea Valley choirs both competed.

Works Schools

The Report on the State of Education in Wales (1847) recorded the presence of a National school (formerly a Church school) in the village of Llangyfelach, the principal subscriber to which was the landowner, J.D. Llewelyn of Penllergaer. Llangyfelach was situated in a mainly rural setting. It is, therefore, unsurprising that the Village School was supported by a local landowner. In the L.S.V. the role of the gentry had been taken up by industrialists, who established a different kind of school – the Works school.

The first Works school in the valley was established in 1806 at Foxhole (on the opposite side of the road to All Saints Anglican Church), part of which became the Gwyn Mission in recent times. The site was provided by Freeman's, proprietors of White Rock. The cost of building what became known as Kilvey School was met by the Grenfells, owners of Middle and Upper Bank. In 1839 a new infant school (now a private house) was built a little to the north of All Saints and, as with the earlier school, the site was provided by Freeman's and the building costs borne by the Grenfells. A few years later the older building was adapted for use as a boys juvenile school, which accommodated 36 boys, five of them monitors. The master, a former mason, disabled 41 years previously, was 75 years old; he had taught at this school since its establishment in 1806. 'The master complained that the [older boys] could not come early in the morning because they had to take their parents' breakfast to the works; and that they were removed at a very early age from school [presumably to take up work]'.

There were 200 children at the new infant school, including the older girls, who sewed 'with the mistress in the afternoons; and members of Mr. Grenfell's family attended twice a week to teach them writing'. The master of this school was assisted by a sewing mistress (possibly his wife) and 14 monitors. According to the 1847 report, both schools were 'supported by stoppages [of 1d. per week] upon the wages of the men employed' at the three East Side copperworks. English-language books were used at both establishments, but 'Welsh was spoken in explanation of English books'. The masters at both schools were given a salary, a house and free coal. According to Stephen Hughes in *Copperopolis*, both schools were enlarged in 1850 to accommodate children from the new suburb of St. Thomas, the parents of whom had to pay school pence. This situation persisted until 1862, when Mr. Grenfell built a new school at St. Thomas. Then in 1865 a new girls school was built at Foxhole by the local chapel architect, John Humphrey. This last school (which no longer exists) was sited on the hillside above All Saints.

Pentre-chwyth Infant School – now St. Peter's Anglican church. This was originally built as a school by the Grenfells in 1854, the purpose of which was to spare young children the long walk to the schools at Foxhole.

In 1815 the Birmingham Copperworks School was established in Martin Street, Morriston. Rebuilt 30 years later, it was renamed the Lancastrian School after Joseph Lancaster, the man who came up with the idea of using older chldren as monitors. In 1848 it was revealed that this infant school 'was partly supported by the proprietors of the different copperworks and collieries in the neighbourhood, for the instruction at a moderate charge of the children of the persons employed by them'.

Other Schools

To list all the early Victorian schools in the L.S.V. is beyond the scope of this work. Suffice to say there were National, British and Nonconformist schools, and there were many private schools, six of them in the Morriston area. Private schools were small: Miss Rouse's, Landore, for example, was 'a dame school frequented by the [12] children of a few small shopkeepers'.

Only one more school need be mentioned in this section, if only to make the point that copper masters were not the only ones to establish Works schools. In 1842 a blacksmith entered into an arrangement with C.H. Smith, proprietor of the Llansamlet Colliery, to reopen an earlier school. A stoppage of 1d. in the pound was deducted from the wages of Mr. Smith's colliers to maintain the school, added to which, 'schoolpence [was taken from] the children whose parents were not subject to the stoppage'. Despite the fact that this was a Church school under the control of a clergyman, the master was an Independent. This might seem an odd arrangement, but Anglican industrialists recognized that the majority of their workmen were Nonconformists and would, therefore, install usually non-sectarian teachers in their schools. In 1847 this Works school had 85 children on its books, six of them monitors. Later that year the children were transferred to a new National school a little to the east of Llansamlet Church.

The Hafod Copperworks Schools

Like the Grenfells, the Vivians were responsible for the establishment of several schools in and around Swansea, but their three Hafod schools were unquestionably the most successful in the L.S.V. The man responsible for what was initially an infant school was John Henry Vivian, managing-partner of the Hafod Copperworks. The infants, as well as the later boys and girls schools, were partially 'maintained by each man being stopped one penny per week, for which he had the privilege of sending all his children (however many) to school'.

According to the report on education, an assistant commissioner visited the first Hafod School in February 1847 to discover that the school had 'opened only the day before, even though the carpenters were still at work'. Evidently J.H. Vivian had his mind set on the school appearing in the report. The schoolroom had 'a floor sloping upwards from the dais, on which stands the master's desk. The parallel desks are divided down the centre by a partition, so that when the children are in the desks ... the boys and girls are separated'.

The master, a 19-year-old former joiner, had trained 'at the Borough Road for six months in 1846'. He was to receive a salary of £85 a year, a house rent free, and free coal and candles. As to the pupils, 'there were 119 present' – 54 girls and 65 boys – and to control 'so large a number [the master] stood on one of the desks [and made] signals ... for the purpose of [getting the children to do] something in obedience. It was singular to observe how readily the master's collected manner won their obedience'. However, as the school was only in its second day, the 20 'monitors ... were ignorant of their duties'. Fortunately, most of the children had been attending a day School previously. Some of them may have attended a day school in a neighbouring locality such as Landore; others are likely to have been attending a temporary school established in Trevivian in 1846, its location unknown. Most of the children present were also attending a Sunday School in which lessons were mainly in Welsh.

The Hafod School used English books only. The intended curriculum was to 'include reading, writing, arithmetic, grammar, geography and history'. Religious instruction was to be limited

The Hafod Works Schools – the western wing seen here was once the infant school, built in 1848. The Infant Mistress's House (now a private residence) still stands to the left of this wing. The schools closed in 1905, being superseded by a new school (burnt down in 1992) that overlooked the Cwm Burlais ravine. After 1905 the Hafod schools served as a parish hall, a clothing factory and is now a community centre.

to 'reading the Scriptures', as the school was a British school and, therefore, non-sectarian. Evidently the Vivians, who were Anglicans, acknowledged that their workforce was overwhelmingly Nonconformist.

By 1848 two new schools – a boys and an infants – had been added to the original school (which became the girls school). Three houses were also added to the complex – a Master's House, a Mistress's House and an Infant Mistress's House (all three houses are now private residences). That same year J.H. Vivian employed a Mrs. Finlay of London, a lady imbued with the latest principles of teaching. Twenty-one years later the three schools were described by a British inspector of schools as 'excellent and efficient ... and at the head of the list of the best ... in Wales'. By 1865 the Hafod schools had over 500 pupils on their books. The success of these, and other schools sited between Sketty and Skewen, was due in part to the Vivian women, in particular Sarah, wife of John Henry, who devoted much of her time to visiting these schools on a regular basis.

The Reform Act of 1832

Prior to 1832 the L.S.V. lay outside the Borough of Swansea and, for voting purposes, was part of the county constituency, but that changed in 1832 when the Reform Act incorporated the more populous parts of the valley into the new Parliamentary Borough of Swansea.

Prior to 1832, the Town and Franchise of Swansea had consisted of a built-up area of around 230 acres, part of a much a much larger area of 1,918 acres, the bounds of which were the sea, the Tawe, the Burlais Brook and the Brynmill Stream. The Town and Franchise of Swansea was an ancient borough, and within its bounds only a minority of privileged adult males – the burgesses – were entitled to vote in parliamentary elections. Swansea, however, was one of eight ancient boroughs

in Glamorganshire that were represented in Parliament by a single M.P., the eight boroughs comprising Cardiff (the county seat) and its contributory boroughs of Llantrisant, Bridgend, Kenfig, Aberavon, Neath, Swansea and Loughor. The only people entitled to vote in parliamentary borough elections were the burgesses in each of the eight ancient boroughs. In Swansea, the burgesses numbered around just 100 adult males.

Left: *John Henry Vivian (1785–1855) – the first man elected to represent Swansea and District. Like the two county representatives (C.R.M. Talbot and Lewis Weston Dillwyn) John Henry was a member of the Whig wing of what later became known as the Liberal Party. His political views appear in his jottings: 'I am not for violent changes or for promising visionary schemes'. However, being an industrialist, he did vote for the repeal of the Corn Laws in 1846. John Henry was not a good speaker in the House of Commons, but he has been described as an assiduous worker on committees.[16] He held his seat for 22 years until his death in February 1855.*

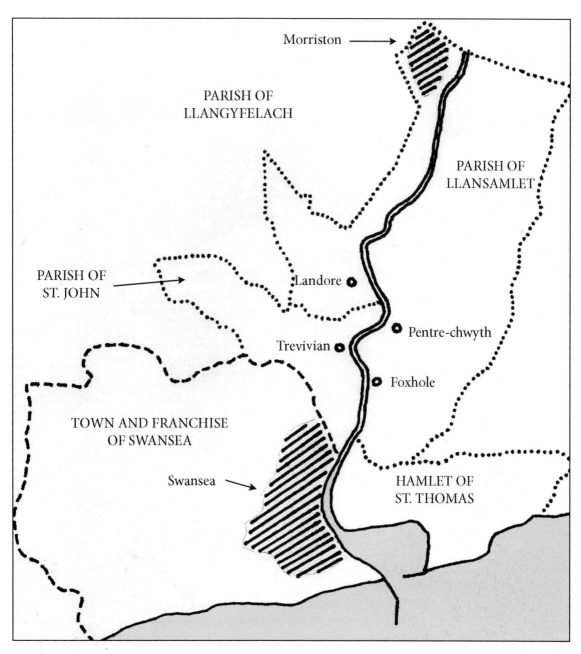

The Reform Act of 1832 led to the creation of the Parliamentary Borough of Swansea; this included not only the Town and Franchise of Swansea, but also the most populous and industrialized parts of the L.S.V. This gave many ratepayers in the L.S.V. the right to vote in parliamentary elections, which they did alongside the ratepayers who resided in the old Town and Franchise. Three years later the bounds of the Parliamentary Borough became the bounds of the newly-created Municipal Borough of Swansea, which meant that the same ratepayers could also vote in local council elections. The 24 winning candidates in these elections became members of the Municipal Borough Council.

The Reform Act of 1832 enlarged the franchise by extending the vote to all male householders within the boroughs who were Poor Law rated at £10 or more per annum. The burgesses of the day retained their right to vote, but that right was not passed on to new burgesses unless they also were rated at £10 or more a year. The Act also increased the number of borough M.P.s from one to three; Cardiff, along with its contributory boroughs of Llantrisant and Bridgend was represented by one M.P.; whilst Merthyr Tydfil – which had not been an ancient borough, but was nevertheless the most populous urban area in the county – became a new constituency. Further west, Swansea and its contributory boroughs of Kenfig, Aberavon, Neath and Loughor also became a new constituency, that of Swansea and District. With regard to Swansea itself, the voting area was extended beyond the age-old borough limits to include about 100 eligible ratepayers in the neighbouring parish of St. John, the hamlet of St. Thomas, and part of the parishes of both Llansamlet and Llangyfelach. This extended voting area included all the industrial villages in the L.S.V. and, as a result of this expansion, Swansea's electorate rose in 1832 from 110 burgesses to an estimated 1,000 ratepayers.[17]

POPULATION

There are no population statistics relating to the number of people who were absorbed into the newly-created Parliamentary Borough of Swansea in 1832. However, using statistics taken from the 1831 census it is possible to obtain a rough estimation.

The parish of St. John	690
Part of the hamlet of Clase	about 3,000
Part of the hamlet of Llansamlet	about 1,500
The hamlet of St. Thomas	438
	about 5,628
Town & Franchise of Swansea	13,256
Parliamentary Borough total	about 18,884

The Poor Law Amendment Act of 1834

As with Peninsula Gower, administration in the L.S.V. was, prior to 1834, in the hands of several civil parish councils, each of which was responsible for the administration of Poor Law, the maintenance of parish roads and the appointment of parish constables. After 1834 the parish councils continued to collect the poor rate, but the poor became the responsibility of Poor Law unions. The west bank of the Tawe, plus the hamlet of St. Thomas, were part of the Swansea Union. The two civil parishes of Llansamlet Higher and Llansamlet Lower, on the other hand, became part of the Neath Union, and remained so until 1875 when they became part of the Swansea Union.

The Municipal Corporation Act of 1835

For centuries the Borough of Swansea had existed for the benefit of the burgesses, and there were 104 of them in 1831 out of a population of 13,256. At that time almost all the burgesses had acquired their privileged status according to strict hereditary rules. These privileges included the right to vote in parliamentary elections, the right to levy tolls relating mainly to the harbour and the market, and the right to impose the tolls on anyone but themselves. The revenue taken in tolls was not used for the benefit of the town, rather the bulk of it was pocketed by the chief burgess – the Portreeve – an action justified by the lame excuse that it covered his expenses. The Portreeve was elected yearly, the election being little more than a formality, as the burgesses had become accustomed to taking it in turn to hold the office of portreeve – and for good reason. In 1833 the Portreeve for the year pocketed around £750 to cover his so-called expenses.

Naturally the non-burgesses who resided in the town resented the collection of tolls for personal use, and did so to the extent that the government appointed commissioners to enquire into the administration of not only Swansea, but a total of 246 boroughs throughout the realm. In Swansea the commissioners not only found fault with the burgesses, but they discovered that 'the Corporation [meaning the burgesses collectively] has for a long period been wholly under the control of the Lord of the Borough exercised through his Steward', the Steward being the man who had the final say in borough administration.

The commissioners' report led to the implementation of the Municipal Corporation Act of 1835. The Act created the Municipal Borough of Swansea, the bounds of which were exactly the same as the Parliamentary Borough, which (as stated above) comprised of the Town and Franchise, the parish of St. John, the hamlet of St. Thomas, and part of the parishes of both Llansamlet and Llangyfelach. Thus the size of the borough almost tripled to 5,400 acres.

The Reform Act also abolished the old system of administration and replaced it with a system whereby the new Municipal Borough of Swansea was to be administered by 24 elected councillors. The people who elected the councillors were the ratepayers, those who had been given the vote in Parliamentary elections three years previously. The burgesses of the day still had the right to vote, but that right was not passed on to new burgesses unless they also qualified as eligible ratepayers. The Act of 1835 may have done away with the privileges of the burgesses, but the town was now in the hands of a much larger group of well-to-do ratepayers; the majority of the population still had no vote.

The revenue from the Corporation Estate (from tolls, etc.) was used by the newly-elected council to finance its activities. The revenue was considered adequate to the extent that no council rate was levied on Swansea residents for almost 40 years. For several decades, however, little of that revenue was used to provide a better quality of life in suburbs such as Morriston. For the people living in the suburbs that were now part of the Municipal Borough virtually nothing changed. These districts continued to be administered by parish councils, each of which still had its own 'distinct parish officers, including five or six surveyors of roads' who in 1849 were described as 'practically irresponsible'. An example of how slow the Municipal Borough Council was in taking responsibility for the L.S.V. can be gauged by just one aspect of council services.

Policing

One year after its creation in 1835 the Municipal Borough of Swansea established a police force, consisting of one inspector and six constables. The force was responsible for policing within the limits of the built-up area of the town. The council did not consider itself responsible for policing industrial villages such as Morriston and Landore, even though the villages were part of the newly created Municipal Borough. Consequently, the outlying villages continued to rely on the totally inadequate parish constables for policing.

Then in 1842 the council came under pressure from magistrates who insisted that it faced up to its responsibilities in the outlying villages. It has been said that an early police house was established at Morriston sometime after 1844, as the Police Act of 1856 resulted in the establishment of police houses with cells at Landore and Greenhill, and cells were added to an existing police house in Morriston.[18] The 1851 census, however, refers only to a P.C. Francis Edwards of Lampeter occupying a police house at Pwllyroir (now Pwll Street) in Landore; it does not give the name of any police officer based in Morriston.

The census for 1861 names P.C. John Brown as the one based at Landore, and refers to a P.C. William Lloyd of Pembroke as one who resided with his wife and two children at a property on Neath Road, Morriston. On the East Side, a P.C. David Lewis of Llandeilo lived at a property on Port Tennant Road with his wife and five children. The same census also records the names of four railway policemen, all of them residing near the railway lines between Foxhole and Lon Las. There are no details relating how the borough constables conducted themselves, but what is certain is that these men did not have it easy.

There is no evidence to suggest that the L.S.V. was considered to be 'a seat of iniquity, [as was] the Twrch Valley' beyond Ystalyfera. It certainly had nothing comparable to Merthyr's China Town, where the 'worthless and lawless ... tended to ... form gangs for mutual protection' and for raiding the surrounding areas (the reigning gangster bore the title of Emperor; hence the

Left: *Borough constable 1867 – in the 1830s and '40s the borough police uniform had been similar to the one worn by county constables. The early uniform was intended to create an image in the eyes of the working class of a gentleman about town, or even the 'boss'; hence the stove-pipe hat. In the mid-1850s the swallow-tailed coat was replaced by a three-quarter length frock coat. In the early 1860s the stove-pipe hat gave way to French army cheese-cutters – a reflection of the fact that the French army at that time was considered to be the most efficient in Europe. The cutlass was dispensed with during this time of change, but the decorative truncheon – although concealed in a trouser pocket – continued to serve the dual purpose of a weapon and the equivalent of a warrant card.*

name China Town). Nevertheless, constables stationed in Morriston, Landore and Port Tennant had to be big, strong and determined to deal with drunken colliers and furnacemen, especially on Saturday nights after the workmen had been paid. When workmen tumbled out of pubs in the dark, arguing and expressing themselves in the foulest language, they could soon fall to fighting among themselves with fists, boots, stones and knives. A lone constable appearing on the scene, intent on restoring peace, could find the workmen ganging up on him, sometimes subjecting him to a barrage of stones. Even when it came to arresting a wanted man, the man was likely to put up a fight, aided perhaps by friends and family. In any event the constable was unlikely to receive assistance from bystanders. He stood alone and had to earn respect the hard way.

Whilst patrolling the streets in all sorts of weather, as well as roadways beside riverside works, the lonely village constables acted pretty much on their own initiative. Their only contact with fellow police officers came as a result of escorting offenders to the magistrates' court at Swansea, or the occasional visit by either the superintendent or an inspector who travelled up from the borough on horseback. The village constables would have come to know their beats well, checking alley-ways, communicating with shopkeepers and ensuring that licensees did not keep disorderly houses, nor sell alcohol outside lawful hours. Dealing with drunks and vagrants, intervening in domestic strife and in bitter quarrels between vociferous neighbours over children, noise and the disposal of ash and excrement are likely to have been regular occurrences. Executing warrants and arresting lawbreakers may also have been frequent occurrences, and although serious criminal acts are likely to have been rare, dealing with petty offences would have kept the village constables busy. Petty theft would have involved clothes and bedding, but in place of agricultural produce (as in Peninsula Gower) the theft of wood, metal and coal would have been common, the latter being rife in winter and during a depression.

In 1844 *The Cambrian* reported:

John Griffith, aged 32, of the parish of Llangyfelach, was charged with having ... stolen a quantity of coal, of the value of sixpence, the property of Messrs Jenkins and Brown. – Verdict: Guilty, with a recommendation to mercy. – Sentence. One month's imprisonment with hard labour.

On the same page *The Cambrian* reported on a prisoner who, in a drunken state, had stolen a mare. When confronted by his pursuer, the prisoner had turned on him and, with a knife, 'inflicted several wounds on witness's hand – beat and kicked him severely'. The prisoner 'was sentenced to transportation beyond the seas for a term of ten years'.

The 1871 census refers to a police station at Port Tennant that was occupied by one constable and his family; another constable and his family occupied a house in Delhi Street, St. Thomas. Whether the Port Tennant station was purpose-built is not stated, but Morriston was to have its own purpose-built station in 1877, and Landore had one the following year. By that time the level of policing in the borough was much greater than it had been. The increased expenditure resulted from the council levying, from 1872 onwards, a borough rate to supplement revenue from the Corporation estate. Morriston, however, had two police stations by 1877 because, according to the O.S. map for that year, the county police had a station opposite Seion Chapel in what is now Clase Road.

Rifle Volunteers

When, in 1859, C.R.M. Talbot called for rifle volunteers for local defence, three industrialists responded by raising what became known as the 4th, 5th and 6th Corps of Glamorgan Rifle Volunteers. There was nothing unusual about this response. In 1803 Thomas Lockwood of Lockwood, Morris & Co. recruited over 200 men for the Forest Rifle Corps, while on the East Side someone raised the Kilvey Infantry Volunteers. These apparent acts of patriotism undoubtedly prevented key workers from being balloted into the militia, which would have made them liable to lengthy periods of service. Key workers who enrolled in volunteer units were exempt from the ballot provided they undertook a limited amount of training.

In 1859 Pascoe St. Leger Grenfell of the Upper and Middle Bank Copperworks raised the 6th Volunteer Rifle Corps. The men were provided with French army-style uniforms (as were volunteers in other units) and armed with long Enfield rifles. It is likely that the men were not all Pascoe's employees; many would have been the employees of other industrialists who were anxious that their key workers would not be balloted. In 1864 *The Cambrian* reported that the strength of 6th Corps was 150 men, 30 of whom were marksmen. The unit was several times mentioned in *The Cambrian* up until 1871, after which it appears to have been disbanded.

The Vivians were responsible for raising the 4th Corps, the officers and sergeants of which were initially family members and works managers. No doubt other proprietors and their employees volunteered their services, as the corps eventually consisted of six companies and was, therefore, of battalion strength with H. Hussey Vivian holding the rank of Lieutenant Colonel. The volunteers drilled on the open spaces on the west side of Trevivian, but on occasion they engaged in fairly extensive manoeuvres. In 1869, for example, the 5th and 6th companies caught the 10 o'clock train for Oystermouth, then marched towards Caswell. At 10.45 the remaining four companies caught a second train for Oystermouth. As the latter contingent advanced over the fields towards Caswell, the 5th and 6th companies (acting as the enemy) resorted to skirmishing. Then, when the two sides met, 'a rattling volley [was directed] into the advancing four companies'. The exchanges continued from cover in the Caswell Valley. Then all six companies paraded on the beach where they were inspected by a general, who was well pleased with what he saw 'even though the equipment was five years old'. The men were given food and drink before returning home. *The Cambrian* continued to make reference to the 4th Corps until 1878, after which the Corps is mentioned no more.

The 3rd Corps was raised by another L.S.V. industrialist, Lewis Llewelyn Dillwyn, who in 1859 was one of the proprietors of both the Landore Silver & Spelter Works and the Llansamlet (spelter) Works. The 3rd Corps certainly enrolled men from other industrial enterprises, and for several years they drilled in the Cwmbwrla (tinplate) Works. After absorbing the 5th Corps (raised by Lewis's elder brother, John Dillwyn Llewelyn of Penllergaer) the 3rd Corps outlived all other volunteer units raised in the Lordship of Gower and Kilvey.

Later industrial villages

Expansion in industry – in coal mining, in the production of copper, spelter, tinplate and a host of comparatively minor industries – led to an expansion of the industrial villages mentioned in G.T. Clark's report of 1849. The population of Morriston, for example, grew in part due to building in the gaps between existing houses, and in part as a result of expansion into Pentreporth. Further

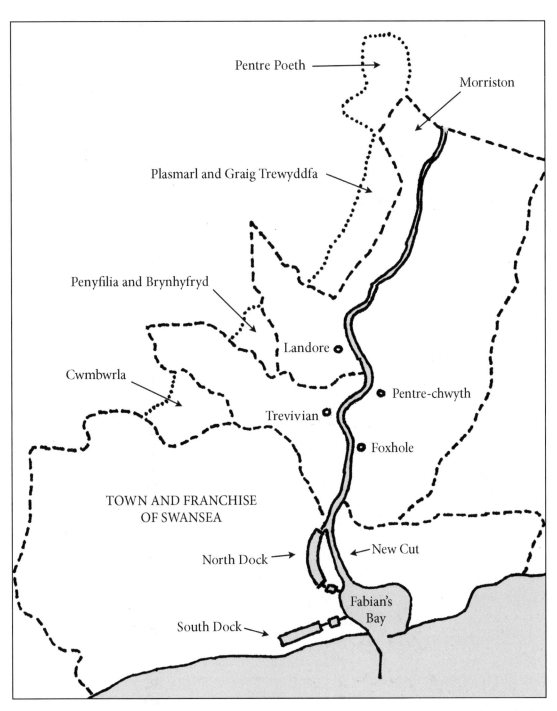

The Municipal Borough of Swansea – in 1867 the borough boundaries were extended to included several outlying areas in which the population had increased considerably. These extensions added an estimated 2,800 residents to the borough's existing population.

south the straggling roadside settlements of Graig Trewyddfa and Plasmarl, as well as the area around Penyfilia, Brynhyfryd and Eaton Town (Eaton Road) were all becoming populous Welsh-speaking communities, so much so as to warrant incorporation into the Municipal Borough of Swansea in 1867.

Population growth took place in areas where new industries had sprung up in the vicinity of copperworks and the Swansea Canal. The growth was also to be found in areas that were unconnected with copper smelting or the canal. Between 1850 and 1867, for example, Cwmbwrla became an industrialized village as a result of the growing number of works that were established close to the Burlais Brook, the most important of which were the Black Vale (1852 – copper and tin) the Cwmfelin Works (1858 – tinplate) and the Cwmbwrla Works (1863 – tinplate), as well as an iron foundry (1840) and several collieries in and around the same area. The majority of Cwmbwrla's early houses lined Carmarthen Road, usually as terraces, from Yscubor Fach Street, over the Cwmbwrla bridge (now the site of the Cwmbwrla roundabout) and up to what is now Cave Street and Vicarage Lane. There were similar terraces along the lower end of Gorse Road, Middle Road, Pentregethin Road and Caebricks Road. Cwmbwrla at that time was a community of mainly tinmen and colliers.

By 1867 the wedge-shaped area between the old Gorse Road and Pentregethin Road had become sufficiently populous to be incorporated within the bounds of the expanding Swansea Municipal Borough. By 1870 there were three chapels in Cwmbwrla, serving a predominantly Welsh-speaking population – Babell, Calvinistic Methodist, built in 1845 and replaced by an entire rebuild in 1869–70 (it stood alongside Carmarthen Road, about a quarter of a mile to the west of

Left: *Believe it or not this building near Cwmbwrla roundabout was a once a Baptist chapel called Libanus; it was built in 1870. In 1906 the building was superseded by a new Libanus, which today stands boarded up next to this one. In later times the old Libanus was converted into a warehouse.*

Opposite: *Morriston 1877 – far more houses appear on this O.S. map than on the tithe map of 40 years earlier, especially in the earlier gridiron around Market Street. Some of the street names have changed – for example, Edward Street and Church Street are now Morfydd Street. Near the upper left-hand edge is Bath Villa, home of the tinplate magnate, John Jones Jenkins. Immediately below the villa are three cottages, one of which is Ty-coch, once an early Nonconformist meeting-house. Below the cottages is the entrance to Clyndu Level Colliery (closed c.1841). The tramroad from this colliery ran down Duke Street (now Clyndu Street) to the canal.*

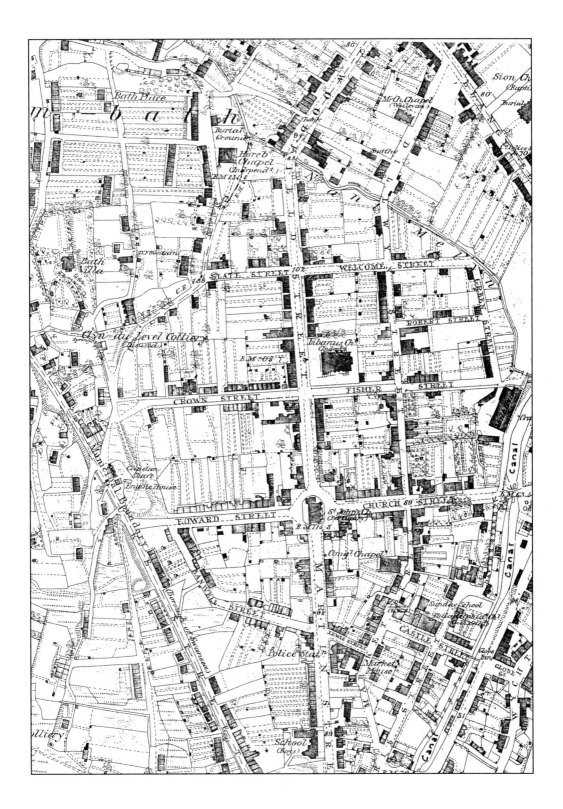

Cwmbwrla bridge); Capel-y-Gat, Independent, built 1862–3 near where Gorse Avenue joins Carmarthen Road; and Libanus, Baptist, built 1870, close to what is now Cwmbwrla roundabout.

On the opposite side of the Tawe the planned and populous township of St. Thomas came into existence in the late 1850s and early 1860s. At the time of the 1861 census, Inkerman, Delhi and Miers streets, as well as Fabians Row/Road, were already populous streets. Other streets were to appear in the years that followed, all of them conforming to a plan. Some of the street names – Inkerman, Sebastopol and Balaclava – commemorate actions fought in the Crimean War of 1853–56, whereas Delhi Street relates to the Indian Mutiny of 1857. St. Thomas had its own school in 1862, and a corrugated iron church in 1876, both of which owed their existence to the Grenfells

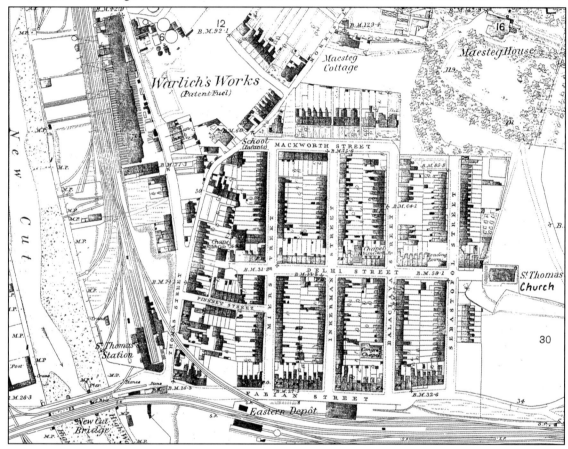

St. Thomas 1879 – today the street pattern is somewhat different. Delhi Street, for example, can be accessed from the west, after passing over the upper bridge that now spans the New Cut. At the eastern end of Delhi Street stands St. Thomas's Church. This was the corrugated iron building of 1876, later to be replaced by the existing stone church a little to the south-east. Pinkney Street (which is where Mary Grenfell established an Anglican meeting-house) no longer exists. Gone too are the houses that were removed to make way for Fabian's Way. Note the position of St. Thomas Station (bottom left) and Maesteg House (top right) home of the Grenfells; also the infant school built by Pascoe St. Leger Grenfell in 1862.

of Maesteg House. The close proximity of Maesteg House to this new township was reason for the Grenfells to take an interest in the educational and spiritual needs of the community.

Further east, there were several dispersed rows of terraced houses. Lamberts Row, which came into existence in the 1850s, was to remain almost a separate community. Other terraces such as Port Tennant Road, Dan-y-graig Terrace and Mile End Road were, from the late 1870s onwards, to become absorbed into the expanding villages of Dan-y-graig and Port Tennant.

Population statistics

It is difficult to give population statistics for the L.S.V. because the area has no fixed boundary; moreover, from *c.*1840 onwards, much of the coal that reached riverside works, the Swansea Canal and the harbour came from beyond the crests of enclosing hills. The most easily obtained figures are those for the Municipal Borough created in 1835 – less those for the Town & Franchise of Swansea.

	Municipal Borough	(minus)	Town Franchise	(equals)	L.S.V. suburbs
1841	24,604		16,720		7,884
1851	31,461		21,533		9,928
1861	41,606		27,161		14,445
1871	51,702		33,481		18,221

The figures are from Gamwell's *Guide* of *c.*1880. They do not give the population of all the L.S.V., only those areas within the municipal borough.

Epilogue

As with Peninsula Gower, there would appear, at first hand, to be little in the L.S.V. to serve as reminders of the early Victorian period (1837–67). The Welsh language no longer prevails, being replaced by English, although the accent is predominantly Welsh. Gone too is a way of life that was hard and exacting, a lifestyle whereby work and either the chapel or the beer house predominated, an existence in which danger and grief were everyday occurrences.

Neither collieries nor coal tips survive, but a number of modern roads – Clyndu Street (Morriston), and Cefn Road (Bon-y-maen) to name but two – were originally coal roads that pre-date the Victorian era. As byways these well-trodden tracks continued in use until, eventually, they were flanked by workers' houses. The route taken by several waggonways and tramroads have also survived in much the same way – Llwyncrwn Road (Llansamlet), Cwm Road (Hafod), Penyfilia Road (Manselton), Eaton Road (Manselton), Dinas Street (Landore), and the Clyndu – Pentrem-alwod route (Morriston) being the most obvious. These roads – along with faint tracks on the open slopes of Graig Trewyddfa, to say nothing of the 'Incline' above Brynhyfryd Square – may not seem much when one considers the millions of tons of coal that passed over them, but one can conjure up dusty, coal-blackened tramlines, along which driverless trams rumbled in the wake of a moving cable – beware the unwary child that crouched near the tracks!

Both the Swansea and Llansamlet (Smith's) canals are gone, though the line of the first can still be followed as a dual carriageway all the way up from Mile End to Morriston. A bridge that once spanned the Swansea Canal can be seen at the lower end of Morfydd Street (Morriston) and, on the East Side, a small section of the Llansamlet Canal survives where it passed to the rear of the White Rock Copperworks. It is easy to conjure up scenes of coal-laden barges towed by horses, but difficult to imagine ships sailing in the shallow waters of the Tawe above the Landore Viaduct – but, of course, the Tawe is no longer effected by tidal waters because of the barrage. Below the viaduct the river appears to have depth, and where the old wharves can be seen clearly it is not difficult to imagine ships, their sails furled, moored and men unloading ore with the aid of primitive cranes.

White Rock, Hafod, Landore and Morriston were once copper smelting areas; they are now focal points for the surviving remains of copperworks. The White Rock site, for example, is now an industrial archaeology park. On the surface the site is dominated by a much reduced and grassed over slag tip, near which are the remains of Smith's Canal, and also a ramp on which an incline tramroad conveyed waste to a secondary slag tip on the slopes of Kilvey Hill. The ruinous walls of buildings are hidden in the dense undergrowth to the south, but what is open to view is the dock, the only one of more than a dozen riverside docks to survive.

Across the river from White Rock are the remains of two engine houses and a chimney stack. The engine houses were connected with the Hafod Copper Rolling-mills that were sited near this stretch of the river. Hidden in the woods beyond is a depression, or trench, that was once part of the Swansea Canal. Beyond the trench are the remains of the Hafod Limekiln (it stands beside the service road used by Park & Ride buses). A short distance from the kiln is a Park & Ride barrier. It marks the site of the once famous Hafod Works canal bridge; it fronted the main entrance into the works. South of the kiln is a car park, at the higher end of which is a large, white building. The building is now a social club, but it was originally built in the late 19th century as the Hafod Works offices. Both the offices and the locomotive sheds further south (and hidden by trees) were Vivian property.

The Landore Park & Ride car park is dominated on the west by the huge Morfa Rolling-mills. The building now houses many exhibits belonging to the Swansea Museum. It is open to the public on Wednesdays between 10 a.m. and 4 p.m. There is much here for those with an interests in ships, old motor vehicles, motor bikes, and there is much more besides. Parking is free within the museum compound.

Near the entrance to the Park & Ride car park are the ruinous remains of the Morfa Works canteen (the wooden structure on the roof was once a clock tower). On the higher ground above the canteen are the remains of the Morfa laboratory. Only one other feature connected with the Morfa Works need be mentioned here. Directly north of the car park is an old railway bridge, one that allowed locomotives to take waste from the works to slag tips on the East Side. Dated 1910, the bridge was designed so that the centre section could be raised to permit ships to sail upriver. A short distance downriver there stands, on the far bank, a smelting hall connected with the Upper Bank Copperworks. The hall is easily recognized by its blocked-up ventilation apertures on the wall facing the river.

North of the smelting hall is a 1½ mile section of the Swansea Vale Railway line, which terminates at what was once Six Pit Junction (near Second City). Originally, the line continued on up to Scott's Pit, which still stands beside a minor road from Birchgrove. Further west, below

260

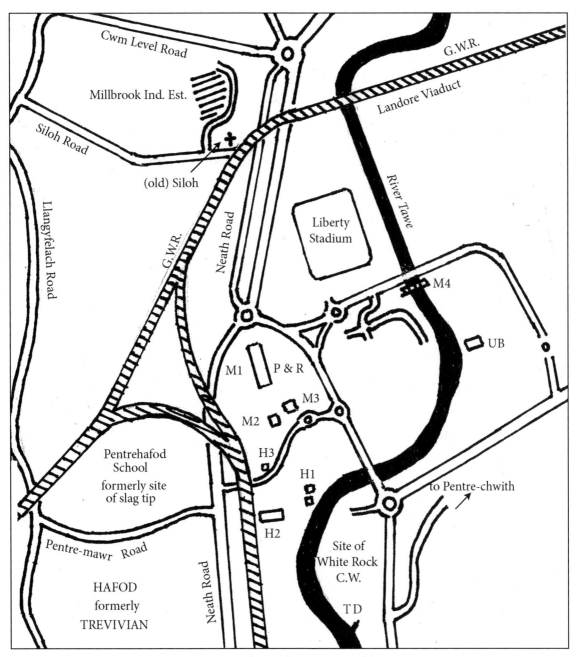

Surviving industrial sites in Landore

M1	*Morfa rolling-mills*	H1	*Hafod steam-engine houses*
M2	*Morfa laboratory*	H2	*Hafod works offices*
M3	*Morfa canteen*	H3	*Hafod limekiln*
M4	*railway bridge 1910*	TD	*White Rock tidal dock*
UB	*Upper Bank smelting hall*	P & R	*park & ride car park*

Morriston, is the Beaufort Bridge, built in *c.*1968 to replace the earlier one. This is a good reference point to see where exactly the Forest Copperworks once stood. Upriver one can see the old weir that diverted water to a leet, which in turn provided water power for the Lower Forest Copper Rolling-mills. Nothing of the rolling-mills remain, but on the east side of the bridge are the remains of an annealing house (built 1874) connected with the Beaufort Tinplate Works of 1860.

One may question why, when there was so much industrial activity in the L.S.V., that so few industrial buildings have survived. The question becomes even more intriguing when one considers that, when a works or colliery closed, many of the buildings would often be adapted for other purposes either by the new owners, or because the existing owners wished to engage in a new venture. This was certainly the case for the Forest Copperworks: built in 1748–52 by the Morrises, and converted into a spelter works by the Vivians in 1867–8, it continued to function until 1926.

The adaptation of old buildings for other uses was an ongoing process until after the First World War when, with the demise of heavy industry, owners of works simply walked away, leaving buildings to decay. Clearance began in earnest in the 1960s. Some buildings survived in fragmentary form simply because they were earmarked for preservation, the Morfa Works canteen being one of them. The only buildings to survive intact were those that continued to serve a purpose. Survivals in this latter category include the Morfa Rolling-mills, an Upper Bank smelting hall, the Hafod Works offices of the late 19th century and a few building within the Millbrook Industrial Estate, Landore.

Finally, there is the former G.W.R. line, the only relic of the early Victorian period to remain functional. The Landore Viaduct, built in 1847-50 and altered on two later occasions, also continues to serve its intended purpose, which was to carry the line across the Tawe and over the low ground on both banks.

The sheer scale of industrialization in the L.S.V. was, to a large measure, due to the sweat and toil of the working population. It is, therefore, fitting that what has survived most are workers' houses, communal buildings and, to a lesser extent, the industrial villages. This is certainly true for the Victorian era as whole, but less so for the early part of Victoria's reign. Morriston, for example – or at least that part of it that lies within the original township – still has the same street pattern

Morfydd House, Morriston – Morriston's history would not be complete without a brief mention of this particular building. There were two houses so named. The one shown here appears on the 1899 O.S. map. A different set of buildings occupy the same site on the O.S. map of 1877, though whether these buildings were the earlier Morfydd House is difficult to determine. The coal producer, John Glasbrook, is recorded as living at the earlier house in 1867 and 1873. The present-day Morfydd House has been used in recent times for many purposes. It now stands empty and abandoned.

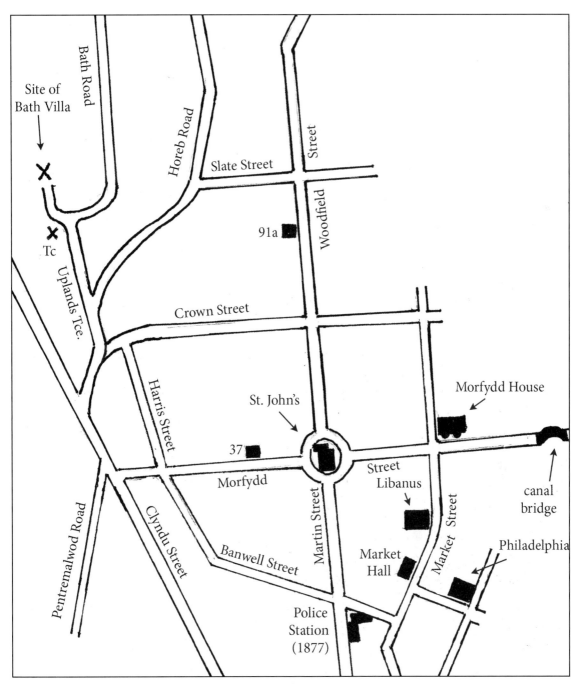

Historic sites in Morriston - the X marked Tc indicated where Ty-coch cottage once stood. A little to the south of the cottage site is the site of the Clyndu Level Colliery, which closed in 1841.

that it had at the time of the tithe survey of 1838. Two small houses are dated to around 1800, and several more in the older gridiron are likely to have existed in the early part of Victoria's reign. The canal bridge at the lower end of Morfydd street is also old (dating from 1794-8) as is the Market Hall (built 1827). Places of worship have also survived. Philadelphia Chapel, for example, was built in 1829, whereas St. John's (island) Church and the old Libanus in Market Street were rebuilt between 1858 and 1862.

What was once Trevivian (the Hafod) can be regarded as a truly early Victorian township. Pretty much all of the houses between Neath Road (on the east), Aberdyberthi Street (on the west) and Pentre Mawr Road (on the north) were built between 1837 and 1867. The three schools (built 1846–8) and the three adjoining teachers' houses are also of the same period, as is Philadelphia Chapel on Neath Road, which was built in 1866–7. The Hafod Schools are unique in that few schools built prior to 1867 have survived in fragmentary form, let alone pretty much as they were originally constructed. Interestingly, the streets in Trevivian are named after members of the Vivian family, or works managers; also there were no public houses in this township, other than those on Neath Road.

On the East Side – as on the west – there are many dwellings and communal buildings that were erected during the Victorian era as a whole, but few were actually in use during the early part of the period. The biggest concentration of workers' dwellings is in St. Thomas. This was a planned township, one in which the pre-1877 dwellings are to be found in the area that has Thomas Street on the west, Balaclava Street on the east, Mackworth Terrace on the north and Fabians Way on the south. Further north, and on a much smaller scale, are the three terraces that were once known as Grenfell Town – Rifleman's Row, Taplow Terrace and Grenfell Town. The 40 houses in this planned settlement of 1803–13 have all survived, although the roofs appear to have been raised in the late 19th century.

The early Victorian dwellings of other East Side settlements have not survived, but the road layout connecting these settlements remain virtually unchanged. As to places of worship, Salem Capel-y-Cwm is unique in that the older pre-1867 building survives as a ruin, while its successor stands close by on an adjoining site. All Saints Foxhole survives, but all other places of worship were built, or rebuilt, after 1867, including the parish church of Llansamlet.

One could labour the point that what has survived from the early Victorian period does not amount to much – certainly nothing impressive, nothing that could be described as a tourist attraction. There are, of course, some spectacular views from the high ground overlooking the valley and the estuary; there are also the gaunt remains of Morris Castle to serve as a reminder of a captain of industry who sought to impress and did not wish to be forgotten, but an older generation will have memories of indescribable dereliction in which abandoned buildings became roofless before walls crumbled and were finally cleared away. The one thing that remains intact is the literature that records the industrial development that made Swansea world renowned, the same literature that is a reminder of the hardship, grief and endurance of a hard-working industrious population, as well as the humanity of those who strove to improve the lot of the labouring class. All that remains in focus because the story of the L.S.V. has now been told.

Endnotes

Chapter One – Peninsular Gower

1. M.E. Chamberlain, *Gower 26*.
2. Other sources provide a different account with regard to this sale, but what is stated here has been taken from *RCAHM in Wales, Glamorgan Inventory Part IV, the Greater Houses*.
3   Margaret Walker, *Gower 56*.
4. B. Dean *Slums: Living Conditions in 19th Century Swansea, Part One*.
5. *Huw Huws neu y Llanfurwr Cymreig*.
6. Mr. and Mrs. S.C. Hall *The Book of South Wales 1861*.
7. W.N. Jenkins, *Gower 28*.
8. For more information on the Merthyr Rising and the Swansea and Fairwood Yeoman Cavalry see *Major Penrice's Dilemma* in *Gower 23* by David Rees, and Bryn Owen's *History of the Welsh Militia and Volunteer Corps 1757-1908, Volume 3, Glamorgan*.
9. For more information on the Mumbles Battery see *Guns Across the Severn* by A. Saunders, and *George Grant Francis of Swansea* by Sandra Thomas.

Chapter Two – The Lower Swansea Valley (L.S.V.) 1836–67

1. W.R. Lambert *Some impression of Swansea and its Copper Works in 1850* in *Glamorgan Historian Vol. V*.
2.   G.T. Clarke's 'Summary' has been slightly altered (with the use of brackets) as his statement 'the population grouped in the villages around Swansea proper equals about 19,000 inhabitants' is questionable. Even today it is difficult to establish exactly what the population in the villages around Swansea had been in early Victorian times; it is unlikely to have been as high as 19,000 in 1849.
3. W.R. Lambert in *Glam. Hist. Vol. V*, page 208.
4. The report of G.T. Clark, 1849.
5. W.R. Lambert in *Glam. Hist. Vol V*.
6. The report of Sir Henry de la Beche, 1845.
7. *Ibid*.
8. *The Times* 20 November 1850
9. J.V. Jones *Crime in 19th century Wales*.
10.   R. Toomey *Vivian & Sons 1809-1924*.
11.   N.L. Thomas *The Story of Swansea's Districts & Villages*.
12.   *Ibid*.
13.   Stephen Hughes *Copperopolis*.
14.   J. Childs *The Parish of Llangyfelach 1750 - 1850*.
15.   translation in N.L. Thomas's *The Story of Swansea Districts & Villages*.
16.   N.L. Thomas *The Story of Swansea's Districts & Villages*.
17.   *Oxford Dictionary of National Biography, Vol 56*.
17.   W. Glam Archive Service – document in folder SL 2/1 – 2/4.
18.   Walter W. Hunt *To Guard My People*.

Further Reading

Childs, J. – *The Parish of Llangyfelach 1750 –1850.*

Clark, G.T. – *Report to the General Board of Health, on a Preliminary Inquiry ... 1849).*

Cooper, R.N. – *Higher & Lower* (Llanrhidian).

Davies, Brian E. – *Mumbles and Gower Pubs.*

Dean, Bob – *Slums: Living Conditions in 19th Century Swansea.*

Etheridge, Ken – *Welsh Costume in the 18th and 19th centuries.*

Evans, Gareth – *Dunvant – portrait of a community.*

Evans, Eifion – *Revival Comes to Wales.*

Grant, Raymond – *The Parliamentary History of Glamorgan 1542–1976.*

Griffiths, R.A. – *The City of Swansea: Challenges & Change.*

Griffiths, R.A. – *Clyne Castle, Swansea, a history of the building and its owners.*

Hall, Mr. & Mrs. S.C. – *The Book of South Wales* (1861), *the Wye and the Coast.*

Hughes, J. Vivian – *CRM Talbot: the Wealthiest Commoner.*

Hughes, Stephen – *Copperopolis.*

Hughes, Stephen & Reynolds, Paul – *A Guide to the Industrial Archaeology of the Swansea Region.*

Jenkins, P. – *Twenty by Fourteen: A History of the S. Wales Tinplate Industry 1700–1961.*

John A.H. and Williams G. – *Glamorgan County History, Vol. 5,*
        Industrial Glamorgan from 1700 to 1970.

Jones, David J.V. – *Crime in 19th Century Wales.*

Jones, I.G. and Williams, David – *The Religious Census of 1851, Vol.1.*

Lambert, W. Rhys – *Some Impressions of Swansea and its Copperworks in 1850*
        in Glamorgan Historian Vol. 5.

Lewis, J – *The Swansea Guide 1851.*

Lloyd, Thomas – *The Lost Houses of Wales.*

Lucas, Robert – *A Gower Family.*

Morris & Williams – *The South Wales Coal Industry 1841–75.*

Orrin, G.R. – *Church Building & Restoration in Victorian Glamorgan.*

Owen, Bryn – *History of the Welsh Militia & Volunteer Corps 1757–1908, Vol. 3 Glamorgan, Part 2.*

Roberts, G – *The Municipal Development of the Borough of Swansea.*

Saunders, A. – *Guns Across the Severn.*

Smith, Carl – *Gower Coast Shipwrecks.*

Stradling, T.E. – *The Parish of Llansamlet, Lon-Las Llwynbrwydrau.*

Thomas N.L. – *The Story of Swansea's Districts & Villages* (several volumes).

Toomey R.R. – *Vivian & Sons 1809–1924.*

Williams, Glanmor (Ed) – *Glamorgan County History, Vol 5, Industrial.*

Williams, Glanmor (Ed) – *Swansea: An Illustrated History.*

Williams, Revd. W.Samlet – *History of the Methodists in West Glamorgan.*

Reports from Commissions of Proposed Divisions of Counties and Boundaries of Boroughs,
   1832 and 1834 (W. Glam Archive Service).
Report of the Commission on Municipal Corporations in England & Wales, 1835.
Reports of the Commssioners of Inquiry into the State of Education in Wales, 1847 (N7.1).
*Report of the Royal Commission on the Church of England and Other Religious Bodies in
   Wales and Monmouthshire,* 1911.

Gower – The Journal of the Gower Society – there are many interesting articles on Swansea &
   Gower, too numerous to list. More than 50 volumes are available to browse through
   at the Swansea Central Library.
Minerva – Transactions of the RISW – is another journal with a mine of information on
   Swansea & Gower.
L.S.V. factsheets Swansea Museum Service – these more than anything else provide a
   wealth of easily-read information on L.S.V. industry and industrialists.
South-West Wales Industrial Archaeology Society Newsletters – these are also a valuable source of
   information on industry and industrialists.
RCAHM in Wales, Glamorgan Inventory, IV, Domestic Architecture, Part 1 The Greater Houses

Internet

Cambrian Search Index – www.swansea.gov.uk/libraries – this is an extremely valuable source of
   information regarding newsworthy events in the 19th & early 20th centuries.

Report of the Royal Commission of Enquiry into the State of Children in Employment 1842 –
   www.cmhrc.co.uk/site/literature/royalcommissionreports/index.html

South Wales Police Museum – www.southwalespolicemuseum.org.uk – then go to 'visit the archives'.
   This will provide a wealth of information on the Glamorgan County Constabulary.

Index

BY THE SAME AUTHOR

The People of Gower
ISBN 0 9546544 0 4
136 pp. Illustrated. Card cover
Draisey Publishing 2003. £5.00

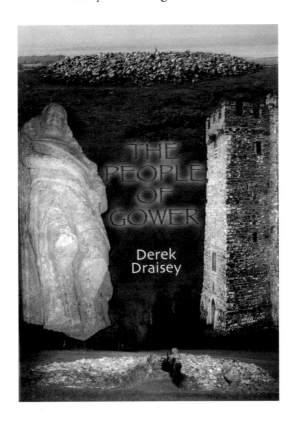

This book tells the story of man's presence in the Gower Peninsula and its upland extension between the Tawe and Loughor rivers. What happened in this unique area, where man's past achievements in earth and stone abound, is a reflection, albeit on a smaller scale, of the rise and fall of successive cultures that existed in Wales and, indeed, mainland Britain from Stone Age times to c.1400.

The people who spearheaded these intrusive, often invasive cultures settled, initially, in relatively small numbers in the coastal lowlands where they coexisted with, and eventually imposed much of their cultural identities on the indigenous inhabi-tants, leaving the natives in the upland areas to carry on in their time-honoured ways for centuries until they, too, became absorbed into the intrusive cultures.

BY THE SAME AUTHOR

Women in Welsh History

ISBN 0 9546544 1 2
205 pp. Illustrated. Card cover
Draisey Publishing 2004. £5

Most of what has been recorded of the past reflects the perceptions of men. Consequently, women have been marginalized. This book is, therefore, an attempt to give the women of Wales a rightful place in their country's history, from Celtic times to the present day.

The names and achievements of many outstanding women are to be found within these pages – and more: this is the story of women throughout the ages, both rich and poor, of courtship, marriage, childbearing, abortion, crime, employment, dress and a host of other issues that were, and continue to be, relevant to the women of Wales.

BY THE SAME AUTHOR

Gower Rogues

ISBN 0 9546544 3 9

248 pp. Illustrated. Card cover

Draisey Publishing 2006. £6.50

From the 12th century onwards the Lordship of Gower was more often the property of Anglo-Norman and English lords. At times it was held by kings of England, occasionally by Welsh princes, and for eleven years by Oliver Cromwell. Many of these men were rogues. The infamous King John requires no introduction, but his crony William de Breos, who succeeded him as Lord of Gower, became notorious for his greed and his murderous attacks on Welshmen. A later Welsh lord, Rhys Grug, engaged in ethnic cleansing.

Few of these lords resided at Swansea Castle, which for centuries served as the administrative centre of the lordship. The administrative and judicial affairs of Gower were in the hands of stewards, many of whom abused their positions to enrich themselves or enforce their will. One of the worst offenders was Sir George Herbert, who had no qualms about judicial murder. A more questionable rogue was Colonel Philip Jones who made hay while the sun shone, and who became one of the most powerful men in the realm. Gabriel Powell, on the other hand, was one steward who simply wanted all his own way.

BY THE SAME AUTHOR

The Last Lord of Gower
A Prophecy Unfolds
ISBN 0 9546544 2 0
203 pp. Maps & plans. Card cover
Draisey Publishing 2005. £5.00

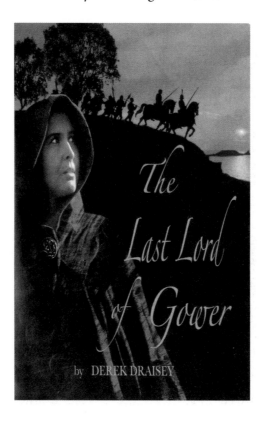

Set in 12th century Gower, the heart of this sinewy tale is based on the camaraderie shared by two foster brothers in their struggle to remain free from foreign rule. Running parallel to scenes of bloody conflict is an eternal triangle; when the foster brothers were youths it was Maredudd who first won Gwenllian's affection; at her father's insistence she married Rhydderch with whom she finds a different, more mature relationship – but the embers of her love for Maredudd still smoulder.

The invasion of Gower is led by two Norman-French knights; the resolute William de Londres and the brutal theomaniac, Henry de Viles, each seeking to outdo the other in terrorizing the native population into submission – but they have, first, to contend with Rhydderch's uncle, Rhys, Lord of Gower, and while he takes steps to offer battle, the foster brothers confound the invaders in several well-placed ambushes.

BY THE SAME AUTHOR

The Last Lord of Gower
Part Two, A Thorn in Flesh
ISBN 0 9546544 4 3
290 pp. Maps & plans. Card cover
Draisey Publishing 2007. £6.50

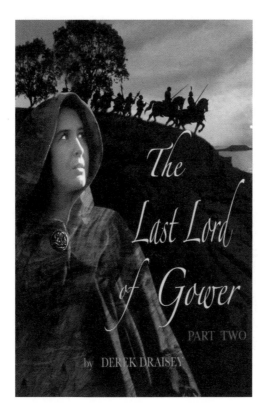

Ten years of relative peace have passed since Henry de Beaumont's invasion of Gower; now it is 1116, another year with a cursed six as its last number. For Rhydderch the trouble starts when a disinherited prince marches on Gower to attack the castle at Abertawe, thereby presenting him with the dilemma of whether or not to rebel. Rhydderch is not involved in the attack himself, but members of his household are, reason for his arch-enemies – the madman Henry de Viles and the resolute William de Londres – to insist that action be taken against him. His position is exacerbated by the soothsayer's prophecy that someone close to him will die, and by the fact that someone is informing on his covert activities to forge unity among fellow Countrymen far and wide.

BY THE SAME AUTHOR

The Rebecca Riots within ten miles of Swansea

ISBN 978 0 9546544 6 7
64 pp. Illustrated. Card cover
Draisey Publishing 2010. £5.00

It has been estimated that the Rebecca Rioters were responsible for around 250 incidents, mainly attacks on toll-gates, toll-bars and toll-houses. The incidents dealt with in this work are those that took place in the Swansea area; that is, within the old medieval lordship of Gower and Kilvey which extended northwards almost to Brynaman.

The accounts of what happened are largely taken from the locally-based newspaper, *The Cambrian*, between July 1843 and April 1844. The paper's reports are not only enthralling, they are amazing for their attention to detail; *The Cambrian* had a way of bringing what happened and the characters involved to life. Eye-witness accounts, the testimony of an informer and those of the law enforcement officers involved in a 15-minute shootout, create a lively and intense picture of events. Undoubtedly the most awe-inspiring reading of all is the desperate resistance to arrest that police officers encountered at Cwmcillau-fach farm, near Felindre. Eventually some 40 soldiers were deemed necessary to take the Morgan family into custody.

As to the name Rebecca — it as taken from Genesis 24, verse 60:

> And they blessed Rebecca and said to her,
> let thy seed possess the gate of those
> which hate them.